HIS SOUL GOES
MARCHING ON

Responses to
John Brown
and the
Harpers Ferry
Raid

HIS SOUL GOES MARCHING ON

*Responses to John Brown
and the
Harpers Ferry Raid*

Edited by Paul Finkelman

University Press of Virginia

Charlottesville and London

THE UNIVERSITY PRESS OF VIRGINIA
Copyright © 1995 by the Rectors and Visitors
of the University of Virginia

First published 1995

aloging-in-Publication Data

ɔnses to John Brown and the Harpers

elman.

ɔth). — ISBN 0–8139–1537–6 (paper)

;—History—John Brown's Raid, 1859.

359. I. Finkelman, Paul, 1949– .

973.6'8—dc20   94-20480
                                                    CIP

Printed in the United States of America

Frontispiece: John Brown, from a photograph by Martin M. Lawrence of New York, printed in *The Life, Trial, and Execution of Capt. John Brown* ...(New York, 1859)

For Abigail,
who came along just as I started working on this book
and has been living up to her name ever since.

John Brown's body lies a-mouldrin' in the grave,

John Brown's body lies a-mouldrin' in the grave,

John Brown's body lies a-mouldrin' in the grave,

But his soul goes marching on.

—Civil War song

Contents

Acknowledgments

Aₛ ɪɴ ᴀɴʏ ᴄᴏᴏᴘᴇʀᴀᴛɪᴠᴇ ᴠᴇɴᴛᴜʀᴇ, I owe a debt of thanks to my fellow contributors, some of whom have stuck with this project since its inception in 1988. I also thank Catherine Clinton, James B. Stewart, and Ronald Walters for their comments. In addition to writing their own contributions, Seymour Drescher, Charles Joyner, Bob McGlone, Peter Wallenstein, and Bert Wyatt-Brown helped shape this book in a variety of ways. William W. Freehling provided all of us with a superb reading of the manuscript. Karen Chaimson, Susan Huffman, Jacqui McNulty, Rob Osberg, and Jean Tanaka helped check citations and prepare the index. John McGuigan encouraged me to bring the project to the University Press of Virginia. After he left the press, Dick Holway and Boyd Zenner helped turn the project into a book. Pamela MacFarland Holway was a first-class copy editor whose work went above and beyond the call of duty.

Abbreviations Used in the Notes

BOOKS

Abels, *Man on Fire*   Jules Abels, *Man on Fire: John Brown and the Cause of Liberty* (New York, 1971)

Basler, ed., *Works of Lincoln*   Roy P. Basler, ed., *The Collected Works of Abraham Lincoln,* 9 vols. (New Brunswick, N.J., 1953–55)

Boyer, *Legend*   Richard O. Boyer, *The Legend of John Brown: A Biography and History* (New York, 1972)

Du Bois, *John Brown*   W. E. B. Du Bois, *John Brown* (Philadelphia, 1909; new ed., New York, 1962)

John Brown Year   American Anti-Slavery Society, *The Anti-Slavery History of the John Brown Year; Being the Twenty-Seventh Annual Report of the American Anti-Slavery Society* (1861; repr. New York, 1969)

Nevins, *Emergence*   Allan Nevins, *The Emergence of Lincoln,* 2 vols. (New York, 1950)

Oates, *Purge*   Stephen B. Oates, *To Purge This Land with Blood: A Biography of John Brown* (New York, 1970)

Potter, *Impending*   David M. Potter, *The Impending Crisis, 1848–1861,* completed and edited by Don E. Fehrenbacher (New York, 1976)

Potter, "Paradox"   David M. Potter, "John Brown and the Paradox of Leadership among American Negroes," in David M. Potter, *The South and the Sectional Conflict* (Baton Rouge, 1968), pp. 201–18.

Quarles, *Allies*   Benjamin Quarles, *Allies for Freedom: Blacks and John Brown* (New York, 1974)

Quarles, ed., *Blacks*   Benjamin Quarles, ed., *Blacks on John Brown* (Urbana, Ill., 1972)

Redpath, *Public Life*   James Redpath, *The Public Life of Capt. John Brown with an Auto-Biography of His Childhood and Youth* (Boston, 1860)

Redpath, *Echoes*   James Redpath, *Echoes of Harper's Ferry* (1860; repr. New York, 1969)

Ripley, ed., *Abolitionist*	C. Peter Ripley, ed., *The Black Abolitionist Papers,* 5 vols. (Chapel Hill, 1985–92)
Rossbach, *Conspirators*	Jeffrey Rossbach, *Ambivalent Conspirators: John Brown, the Secret Six, and a Theory of Slave Violence* (Philadelphia, 1982)
Ruchames, ed., *Reader*	Louis Ruchames, ed., *A John Brown Reader* (London and New York, 1959)
Ruchames, ed., *Revolutionary*	Louis Ruchames, ed., *John Brown: The Making of a Revolutionary* (New York, 1969)
Sanborn, ed., *Life*	Franklin B. Sanborn, ed., *The Life and Letters of John Brown, Liberator of Kansas, and Martyr of Virginia* (1885; repr. New York, 1969)
Simpson, *Wise*	Craig M. Simpson, *A Good Southerner: The Life of Henry A. Wise of Virginia* (Chapel Hill, 1985)
Villard, *Biography*	Oswald Garrison Villard, *John Brown, 1800–1859: A Biography Fifty Years After* (1920; repr. New York, 1943)
Woodward, "Private War"	C. Vann Woodward, "John Brown's Private War," in C. Vann Woodward, *The Burden of Southern History,* rev. ed. (Baton Rouge, 1985), pp. 41–68.
Wyatt-Brown, "Antinomian"	Bertram Wyatt-Brown, "John Brown's Antinomian War," in Bertram Wyatt-Brown, *Yankee Saints and Southern Sinners* (Baton Rouge, 1985), pp. 97–127.

JOURNALS

AHR	*American Historical Review*
CWH	*Civil War History*
JAH	*Journal of American History*
JSH	*Journal of Southern History*

MANUSCRIPTS

Child, *Correspondence*	*The Collected Correspondence of Lydia Maria Child, 1817–1880* (microfiche series), edited by Patricia Holland and Milton Meltzer (Millwood, N.Y., 1979)

Part I
An Introduction to John Brown

PREFACE

PAUL FINKELMAN

John Brown and His Raid

On October 16, 1859, John Brown and eighteen followers seized the federal arsenal at Harpers Ferry, Virginia. Brown's plans were audacious, grandiose, even fantastic: he hoped to start an insurrection that would attract slaves to his guerrilla force. His raid lasted about a day and a half. On October 18, United States troops under the command of Brevet Colonel Robert E. Lee captured Brown in the engine house on the armory grounds. By this time most of the raiders were either dead or wounded.

Ten days later, in Charlestown, Virginia (now Charles Town, West Virginia), Brown was put on trial for treason, murder, and conspiring with slaves to rebel. He was convicted on November 2 and sentenced to death. Before his sentencing, Brown told the court that his actions against slavery were consistent with God's commandments. "I believe," he said in a speech that electrified many Northerners who later read it, "that to have interfered as I have done in behalf of His despised poor, is no wrong, but right. Now, if it is deemed necessary that I should forfeit my life for the furtherance of the ends of justice, and mingle my blood with the blood of millions in this slave country whose rights are disregarded by wicked, cruel, and unjust enactments, I say let it be done."[1] In the month between his sentencing on November 2 and his execution on December 2, Brown wrote brilliant letters that helped to create, in the minds of some Northerners, his image as a Christ-like martyr, who gave his life so that the slaves might be free.

This book explores how various segments of American and European society responded to John Brown's raid and its aftermath. For abolitionists and antislavery activists, black and white, Brown emerged as a hero, a martyr, and, ultimately, a harbinger of the end of slavery. Most Northern whites, especially those not committed to abolition, were aghast at the violence of his action. Yet there was also widespread support for him in the region. Northerners variously came to see Brown as an antislavery saint, a brave but foolish extremist, a lunatic, and a threat to the Union. Massachusetts Governor John A. Andrew summed up the feeling of many Northerners when he refused to endorse Brown's tactics or the wisdom of the raid, but declared that "John Brown himself is right."[2] But most Republican politicians worried that they would be tarred by his extremism and lose the next election. Democrats and Constitutional Unionists, by contrast, feared that Brown's raid would polarize the nation, put the Republicans in power, and chase the South out of the Union.

For white Southerners, Brown was the worst possible nightmare, a fearless, committed abolitionist, armed, accompanied by blacks, and willing to die to end slavery. Indeed, in the minds of Southerners, Brown posed a far greater threat than their own slaves to their section and their peculiar institution. Even though they feared slave rebellions, Southerners had convinced themselves that most slaves were content with their status and that, in any event, blacks were incapable of anything worse than sporadic violence. But Brown raised the ominous possibility of armed black slaves, led by whites who would encourage them to destroy Southern white society.

Numerous biographers have explored Brown's route to the gallows at Charlestown. His body was hardly in its grave when James Redpath, working with the cooperation of Brown's widow Mary and some key abolitionist leaders, published an "authorized" biography, *The Public Life of Capt. John Brown* (1860). In 1910 Oswald Garrison Villard, the grandson of the abolitionist William Lloyd Garrison, published the first scholarly biography of Brown, *John Brown, 1800–1859: A Biography Fifty Years Later.* Although by this time a journalist, Villard had previously taught history at Harvard and thus brought rigorous scholarly standards to his book. In the modern era three studies of Brown stand out: Jules Abels, *Man on Fire: John Brown and the Cause of Liberty* (1971); Richard O. Boyer, *The Legend of John Brown: A Biography and History* (1972); and Stephen B. Oates, *To Purge This Land with Blood: A Biography of John Brown* (1970). Other fine books—especially Benjamin Quarles, *Allies for Freedom: Blacks and John Brown* (1974), and Jeffrey Rossbach, *Ambivalent Conspirators: John Brown, the Secret Six, and a Theory of Slave Violence* (1982)—have focused on Brown's supporters. We thus know a great deal about Brown, his raid on Harpers Ferry, and those with whom he associated. We know less, however, about the meaning of that raid and the nation's response to it. This book explores these issues.

Before we turn to the various responses to Brown's raid, it is necessary briefly to sketch out Brown's life and career. Born in 1800 into a family of deeply religious Connecticut congregationalists who were Puritan in their heritage and overtly antislavery in their views, Brown learned antislavery from his father, a lifelong opponent of bondage and an early supporter of the new abolitionism that emerged in the 1830s. Brown was raised in the Western Reserve district of Ohio, where his father was involved in trying to make Western Reserve College into an antislavery stronghold. When that failed, the elder Brown supported the creation of Oberlin College as a racially integrated coeducational institution of higher learning with an anti-slavery bent.

Despite his father's association with colleges, Brown had little formal education. For his first fifty years, Brown was a businessman, a sheep farmer, and a tradesman—all without success. A failure at almost everything he tried, he was often in debt, and at times he was only a few steps ahead of his creditors, who on occasion sued him for large sums of money. At the age of forty-two he was officially declared bankrupt.

During this period, however, Brown emerged as an unyielding opponent of slavery. He participated in the underground railroad and in 1851 helped found the League of Gileadites, an organization of whites, free blacks, and runaway slaves dedicated to protecting fugitive slaves from slave catchers. He moved often, living in Ohio, Massachusetts, New York, and Pennsylvania. In the 1840s Brown was in contact with such antislavery leaders as Gerrit Smith and Frederick Douglass. Yet as late as 1855 Brown remained a marginal figure in the antislavery movement and in all other ways historically insignificant.

In 1855 Brown moved to Kansas with some of his adult sons, settling along the Osawatomie River. In December he helped defend Lawrence, the center of antislavery settlers, from an armed attack by proslavery forces. On May 21, 1856 though, when Brown was elsewhere, proslavery men sacked and burned the free-soil town. Three days later Brown and his band of free-state guerrillas killed five Southern settlers along the Pottawatomie River, although most of these men, who were unarmed, had not been involved in any attacks on free-soil settlers. After killing them, Brown's soldiers decapitated some of them with swords. Later that summer a proslavery minister, working as a scout for the United States Army, murdered Brown's unarmed son Frederick, shooting him in the heart at close range.

Throughout the rest of 1856 Brown and his remaining sons fought in Kansas and Missouri. By the end of 1856 Brown was one of the most renowned (and either hated or adored) figures in "bleeding Kansas," and in the East he became known as "Osawatomie Brown" or "Old Osawatomie." For some New England abolitionists he was approaching the status of a cult figure. Taciturn, blunt, gruff—and armed—Brown had become a symbol of the emerging holy crusade against slavery. Those back East knew he fought against slavery, but few were aware of the exact nature of his role in the gory events at Pottawatomie. Within two weeks after the incident the play *Ossawattomie Brown* appeared on Broadway. The play accused Brown's enemies of the massacre at Pottawatomie and suggested that the real killers had blamed Brown in order to discredit him. Moreover, ever since the massacre James Redpath, an English journalist who later wrote Brown's biography, had been assuring readers that Brown was not responsible for the murders. Thus, when Brown went on a fund-raising trip to Massachusetts and Connecticut in 1857, no one saw him as a killer. At the time he denied any role in the Pottawatomie murders, and his abolitionist supporters in the East gladly accepted his disavowal at face value. Brown's eastern contacts thought their donations would go to support the war against slavery in Kansas. Actually, Brown was already planning a raid on Harpers Ferry.

As early as 1854 Brown had been thinking, and talking, about an organized war against slavery in Virginia. His focus, from the beginning, seems to have been on Harpers Ferry, the site of a federal arsenal and armory. By 1857 his plans were beginning to take shape. In March 1857 he hired a Connecticut forgemaster to make a thousand pikes, allegedly for use in Kansas, but actually to be given to slaves who he believed would flock to his guerrilla army once he invaded the South. In January and February 1858 he spent a month at the home of Frederick Douglass, planning his raid and writing a provisional constitution for the revolutionary state. Douglass was sympathetic to Brown's goals but believed the plan was suicidal: "You're walking into a perfect steel-trap and you will never get out alive," he told Brown.[3] Nevertheless, Douglass introduced Brown to Shields Green, a fugitive slave from South Carolina who joined Brown—and who was eventually hanged, after the raid, by the Virginia authorities.

In the early spring of 1858 Brown began raising large amounts of money for his raid, writing potential backers that he was planning some "[underground] Rail Road business on a *somewhat extended* scale."[4] However, in person he made it clear that he intended to do more than merely help large numbers of slaves to escape. On February 22, 1858, Brown revealed his general plans—and his provisional constitution—to Gerrit Smith and Franklin Sanborn. Brown also contacted black leaders—the Reverend Jermain Loguen in Syracuse and Dr. J. N. Gloucester in New York City—to help recruit free blacks. In March 1858 Brown met in Boston with the Reverend Thomas Wentworth Higginson, Theodore Parker, George Stearns, Samuel Gridley Howe, and Franklin Sanborn. These five, along with Gerrit Smith, made up the "Secret Six," Brown's primary financial backers. In June 1858, traveling as "Shubel Morgan," Brown headed west, raising more money and recruiting more raiders in Cleveland. While Brown continued on to Kansas, John E. Cook, one of his raiders, moved to Harpers Ferry, where he found work and learned what he could about the community, the armory, and the lay of the land. He also fathered a child and married a local woman.

In December 1858 Brown once again made headlines for his exploits in the West. He invaded Missouri, where he killed a slaveowner, liberated eleven slaves, and brilliantly evaded law enforcement officers as he led the freed blacks to Canada. There Brown met a black printer, Osborne Perry

Anderson, who would later take part in the Harpers Ferry raid. Although a wanted man with a price of $250 on his head, Brown returned to the United States, traveling and speaking in Ohio, New York, Massachusetts, and Connecticut. He had tea at the home of the antislavery Congressman Joshua Giddings in Ohio and met in Massachusetts with Senator Henry Wilson, the industrialist Amos Lawrence, and John A. Andrew, who would soon become governor of the state. Brown also contacted the "Secret Six" who were financing him.

In June 1859 Brown visited his home in North Elba, New York, for the last time, where he said good-bye to his wife and daughters. Brown probably knew that he was unlikely to see his family again, something he stoically accepted as a cost of his crusade against slavery. He was less accepting of his son Salmon, however, who decided he would not join his father on an apparently suicidal mission into Virginia.

Brown and his sons Oliver and Owen arrived in Harpers Ferry on July 3, 1859, and Brown rented a farm in Maryland, about seven miles from Harpers Ferry. He expected large numbers of men to enlist in his "army," but by September only eighteen had arrived, including another of Brown's sons, Watson. In mid-October two blacks from Oberlin, Ohio—John Copeland and Lewis Leary—arrived, as did Francis Jackson Meriam, the nephew of Francis Jackson, the publisher of the nation's most famous antislavery newspaper, *The Liberator.*

On Sunday, October 16, Brown and his men began their raid. They made a strange assortment: veterans of the struggles in Kansas, fugitive slaves, free blacks, transcendental idealists, Oberlin college men, and youthful abolitionists on their first foray into the world. The youngest was eighteen. The oldest, Dangerfield Newby, was a forty-four-year-old fugitive slave from Virginia who hoped to rescue his wife from bondage. But most of the raiders were in their twenties, half the age of their leader, the fifty-nine-year-old Brown. Brown left three of his recruits—Barclay Coppoc, Francis Jackson Meriam, and his son Owen—to guard their supplies and arms at the farmhouse in Maryland. The remaining eighteen raiders, thirteen whites and five blacks, marched with John Brown to Harpers Ferry.

Brown's small army arrived in Harpers Ferry at night and quickly secured the federal armory and arsenal and later Hall's Rifle Works, which manufactured weapons for the national government. With the telegraph wires cut, Brown might have easily seized the weapons in the town, liberated slaves in the neighborhood, and then taken to the hills. Inexplicably, though, he remained in the armory, waiting for slaves to flock to his standard. They never came. Instead, townsmen and farmers surrounded the armory. These civilians were probably not strong enough to dislodge Brown, but they kept him pinned down. Although Brown tried to negotiate with the civilians, his emissaries, including his son Watson, were shot while under a white flag. By the morning of October 17 eight of Brown's men were dead or captured, and that same day militia from Virginia and Maryland arrived. President James Buchanan had dispatched U.S. marines and soldiers to Harpers Ferry, with Brevet Colonel Robert E. Lee in command. Directly under Lee was another Virginian, Lieutenant J. E. B. Stuart. On the morning of October 18, marines stormed the engine house of the armory, capturing Brown and a few of his raiders and killing the rest. By the end of the raid, of the twenty-two who had been involved in the plot, ten of Brown's men, including his sons Watson and Oliver, were dead or mortally wounded; five, including Brown, had been captured.[5] Seven escaped, but two were later captured in Pennsylvania and returned to Virginia for trial and execution. The other five—Brown's son Owen, Francis Jackson Meriam, Barclay Coppoc, Charles Plummer Tidd, and Osborne Perry Anderson—successfully made their way to safe havens in Canada and remote parts of the North. All but Owen Brown later served in the Union Army.

Brown's capture on October 18 set the stage for his trial and execution. Severely wounded, Brown had to be carried into court on the 25th for a preliminary hearing and on the 27th for his trial. The judge would not even delay the proceedings a day to allow Brown's lawyer to arrive. The trial was speedy. On November 2 Brown was convicted and sentenced to death. He was executed on December 2, and on December 8 he was buried at the family farm in North Elba, near Lake Placid. Many Northerners interpreted the hasty actions of the Virginia authorities in trying and executing Brown as another example of Southern injustice. The apparent lack of due process in his trial thus contributed to the Northern perception that Brown was a martyr. Most Southerners, however, saw Virginia's actions as a properly swift response to the unspeakable acts of a dangerous man whose goal was to destroy their entire society.

By the time of his execution, the entire nation was fixated on this bearded man, who spoke and looked like a biblical prophet and whose deeds thrilled—whether with fear or admiration or both—an entire generation. Indicative of this fixation is a shared aspect in the otherwise divergent responses of Wendell Phillips and Edmund Ruffin—the great abolitionist orator and the fire-eating Virginia secessionist. In the year following the raid each of them prominently carried and displayed a "John Brown pike" that Brown had ordered from the Connecticut foundry. For Phillips the pike symbolized the glory, and for Ruffin the horror, of a servile insurrection led by a resurrected Puritan willing to die to overthrow slavery. The following essays illuminate the range of responses across the nation and in Europe to Brown's raid on Harpers Ferry, his imprisonment and trial, and his execution.

Notes

1. Quoted in Oates, *Purge,* p. 327.
2. [Thomas Drew], *The John Brown Invasion, an Authentic History of the Harper's Ferry Tragedy* (Boston, 1860), p. 97. See also Villard, *Biography,* pp. 559–60.
3. Quoted in Abels, *Man on Fire,* p. 260.
4. Quoted in Oates, *Purge,* p. 227.
5. For a new interpretation of the capture of Brown and his attempt to surrender, see Robert E. McGlone, "Forgotten Surrender: John Brown's Raid and the Cult of Martial Virtues," *CWH* 40 (Sept. 1994): 185–201.

1

BERTRAM WYATT-BROWN

"A Volcano Beneath a Mountain of Snow": John Brown and the Problem of Interpretation

Not the raid of midnight terror,
  But the thought which underlies;
Not the outlaw's pride of daring,
  But the Christian sacrifice.

John Greenleaf Whittier[1]

No SESQUICENTENNIAL CELEBRATION, no upsurge of scholarly interest in the causes of the Civil War, prompts the publication of *His Soul Goes Marching On: Responses to John Brown and the Harpers Ferry Raid*. Instead, every generation of historians must wrestle with the meaning of this event and John Brown's relationship to the coming of the Civil War. Combining the highest of ideals with ruthless deeds, Brown's behavior has always aroused a confused mixture of admiration and condemnation. Currently these moral issues are no clearer than they ever were. Ambivalence arises from the conflict that readers feel between sympathy for Brown's liberating cause and their resistance to the legacy of hard-hearted destructiveness that he left behind in Kansas and proposed for Virginia in 1859. As Brown planned, the assault at Harpers Ferry on October 16 was a dramatically symbolic act that proved to have far-reaching political and moral results. The intention was to seize federal weapons, strike at the plantation system, and arouse slaves to fight for freedom. Yet, had Brown's dreams been realized, the most likely outcome would have been an escalation of cruel reprisals between Brown's slave insurgents and their masters—along with the civil war that did occur. As William A. Phillips, a friend of Brown in Kansas reported, "With him men were nothing, principles everything."[2] Phillips's remark reflects a sentiment both inspiring and disturbing.

In retrospect the historian can perceive Brown's raid at Harpers Ferry as the political and moral equivalent to contemporary guerrilla and terrorist campaigns, ventured by radicals whose convictions burn with an ardor

similar to Brown's. Yet such zealotry and indifference to the life of innocents strikes us as inhuman, not to mention personally threatening. The
almost daily explosions of car bombs and the chatter of assassins' guns
somewhere in the world remind us that ordinary expectations of political
stability cannot be taken for granted today any more than they could in
mid-nineteenth century America. Abraham Lincoln captured the ambiguity surrounding Brown's attitude when he pronounced him "an enthusi-
ast" who fancied himself "commissioned by Heaven" to avenge an oppressed people. Although Lincoln did not discountenance Brown's aim, he
noted that fratricidal war would be its tragic consequence.[3] The violence
with which Brown pursued his course in Kansas suggests that he would
have welcomed a similar state of affairs in Virginia—an insurrection or even
threat of insurgency that white Southerners regarded as savage and frightening.

International anarchists later called this strategy an *attentat.* Terrorism is
designed to challenge the power of the state by arousing the victimized
masses to justifiable indignation and rebellion. In theory, the strike against
oppression also degrades the honor of the institutions against which the
enterprise is directed. America had not experienced a subversive mission of
this kind before John Brown's conspiracy against slavery. Of course, as ben-
eficiaries of that war against slavery, Americans of every race must honor
Brown for his immense contribution to the eventual outcome. Nevertheless, he remains an enigma, a figure of both majesty and folly.

Although Brown's action carries meanings both heartening and horrify-
ing, other aspects of his life—and indeed his afterlife in the American
mind—can be more easily delineated. The essays in this book concern the
repercussions of Brown's raid, including the execution of the conspirators
who were captured. Historians have seldom treated this subject in so systematic and interpretive a way. The studies in this volume help to reveal the
significance of Southern white reaction, but they also show how Brown
managed to represent Northern courage and love of liberty, thus fashioning
himself to suit the prevailing passions of more than one position on the
political spectrum.

Brown had already gained notoriety during the Kansas skirmishes between slaveholding Missourians and Northern free-soil settlers. Yet he burst
upon the public stage in late 1859 as either a monster or a "warrior-saint,"
according to the sectional and political disposition of the observer.[4] Some
even regarded Brown as a sectional Judas Iscariot, the betrayer of long-
standing political and moral compromises. Moderates on both sides of the
great division hoped to diminish his stature, whether as either Satan's en-
voy or God's archangel. His actions, moreover, profoundly subverted the

fledgling sense of national unity that the states of a baronial Union were beginning to forge. But if we are to understand the full impact of the events at Harpers Ferry, questions about Brown himself—his background and the nature of his personality—must be treated first, lest he be casually dismissed, and therefore historically diminished, as mentally disordered.

The issue of insanity first arose while Brown was awaiting trial in the Charlestown jail. Ever since historians have reintroduced the matter and have offered different interpretations of his temperament, opinions that reflect contemporary fashions in social and individual psychology. After World War II, for instance, Allan Nevins in *The Emergence of Lincoln* (1950) offered a definition of Brown's purported mental troubles as "ambitious paranoia," a condition that involved "systematized delusions"—terms then in popular academic use to help explain the Red-baiting of that era. In the late 1950s C. Vann Woodward, exploring John Brown's inner war against himself, linked his madness to genetic factors and argued that these mind-shaping elements led not only to Brown's own paranoia but, through his actions, to a sectional suspiciousness that bordered on the irrational. Writing in the same period of bourgeois plenty and expectation of order, David Potter proposed that Brown's repeated displays of incompetence in business and other matters led him to seek compensation in ludicrously extravagant ventures.[5]

Contrary opinions arose during the civil rights era of the 1960s and early 1970s. Brown's dedication to emancipation, not his mental state, became the chief historical concern. Proclaiming that the ends justified the means, Louis Ruchames and others voiced this new theme with fervor. In his 1970 biography, Stephen Oates insisted on Brown's legal sanity while approving his moral integrity.[6] In the current era, one of the contributors to this volume, Robert McGlone, has elsewhere claimed that Brown's "bipolar disorder" led to his dynamism as an agitator in a moral cause.[7] This approach is well worth exploring and expanding upon, although it by no means fully explains the unique response Brown devised to counter internal pain or his remarkable bravery in the face of utter failure. His alienation from conventional society and from ordinary modes of thought encouraged him to take extreme measures in instructing his fellow Northerners about the enormity of slavery's crime. Mental depression, along with an unusual combination of religious and racial convictions, provided the stimulus for the startling events at Harpers Ferry. When the raid failed to begin an era of internecine warfare in the slave states, as Brown had anticipated, he found a surprising opportunity for ennobling self-sacrifice. His gloom of mind, religious fatalism, and active fantasy life prepared him for this new and widely appealing role—at least among some Northerners—as if he had been so anointed by a merciful God who had designed his mission all along.

*   *   *   *   *

"I felt for a number of years, in earlier life, a steady, strong desire to die," John Brown wrote in 1858 to a young and newly acquired antislavery friend in Massachusetts. The older abolitionist had expected, he confessed, "to 'endure hardness.' "[8] At the time, Brown was enjoying a happy period in his otherwise hard existence. He had recently found new supporters and was energetically embarking on his final enterprise. But his remarks suggested that depression and suicidal inclinations remained in his mind. He could not put a sense of hopelessness behind him even when he was vigorously plotting the overthrow of slavery. A chronic inclination to depression may explain the emotional source not only of Brown's peculiarities but also of his ultimate triumph as an agitator.

Deep psychosis prevents the depressive from functioning with any degree of rationality or inspiration. When less troubled, however, the depressive can reach great heights of originality and wisdom. A combination of voices and moods may provide the soil for a rich harvest of imaginative expression. That was John Brown's dramatic achievement. The abolitionist leader drew upon the anxieties, resentments, and inclination toward impossible dreams that he felt himself and that other leaders of the crisis on both sides of the Potomac harbored as well. He externalized and brought into active play what he, as both devil and hero, and they experienced within. This role required a genius of a peculiar kind. The historian cannot easily imagine that any other sort of personality could have outperformed Brown in stimulating the fruitful complexity of reactions that he generated on the national scene.

Depression is most often associated with troubled artistic and intellectual geniuses—philosophers, scientists, artists, writers, and musicians from Michelangelo to Gustav Mahler or Virginia Woolf.[9] Yet several key figures—politicians, reformers, even generals—in the sectional crisis were sorely tried by a sense of dejection and frustration, most notably Lincoln. Although Lincoln's most agonized period—his early years in Springfield, Illinois, in the 1830s and 1840s—had long since passed, the president's episodes of melancholy persisted until his assassination, which his own depression seemingly foretold in a dream ten days earlier.[10] The malady also completely, though temporarily, disabled General William T. Sherman early in the war.[11] Edmund Ruffin, the Virginia secessionist who donned a militia uniform to watch Brown mount the gallows on December 10, 1859, had several times contemplated killing himself in the 1850s. In the midst of the war he had helped to initiate, the rabid secessionist would write, "Every day of my life is a continuation of the same unvarying affliction of *ennui*— wearysomeness of everything, including life itself. There is for me no alleviation, no remedy, until death relieve me." In 1865 Ruffin placed a gun in his mouth and fired it, to free himself from his personal agony and the humiliation of Confederate defeat.[12] Similarly, Jefferson Davis, the Democratic senator from Mississippi and later president of the Confederacy, endured both the physical and mental debilities of melancholy. His disorder helped to account for his outbursts of inappropriate temper and his periods of almost paralytic indecisiveness. In 1859 and 1860 he often dueled verbally in the Senate with members of both sections, engaging in reckless exchanges that were thought attributable to his ill health and discouragement.[13] Alexander H. Stephens of Georgia, the Confederacy's bachelor vice president, was also sorely afflicted with melancholy. Like Davis, Stephens was chronically ill from several physical maladies, but loneliness, despair, and uncontrollable temper were scourges that he found equally dismaying.[14]

On the other side of the political divide, the ailment troubled some abolitionists. Particularly in the years of young adulthood, David Lee Child, Sydney Howard Gay, Theodore Weld, John Greenleaf Whittier (whose poem about Brown is quoted above), Henry C. Wright (one of Brown's earliest champions in the East), Joshua R. Giddings of the Western Reserve (Brown's sometime congressman), and Charles Torrey and Elijah P. Lovejoy (both remembered as martyrs for emancipation) were among those who experienced bouts of "the hypochondria" or the "blues."[15] The wealthy Gerrit Smith of upper New York State was a leading member of the "Secret Six" who provided financial support for Brown's adventure in Virginia. Like Brown himself, Smith came from a family genetically prone to severe mental depression.[16] According to the *New York Evening Post,* Peter Smith, Gerrit's wealthy father, had been "subject to fits of profound despondency, during which he was under the impression that he would die a beggar." Gerrit Smith's two brothers, one an alcoholic and the other a lifelong but harmless psychotic, were both subject to the disorder that afflicted their father.[17] When Brown's captured papers publicly exposed the names of the "Secret Six," Smith suffered a nervous breakdown. He entered the Utica Insane Asylum, not, as some historians speculate, to escape the law but because his mental problems were all too sadly real.[18] These reflections suggest that melancholic passions intensified the emotional climate in which political action took place.

Nearly every one of these Civil War figures had lost one parent or both at an early stage of life.[19] The death of a parent or parent surrogate, or, equally significant, the emotional if not physical withdrawal by a figure upon whom a child depends, can leave the young person with a sense of being unloved and with an anger over the apparent desertion, emotions that must be buried deep in order to avoid further disappointment. Depressive

parents, being themselves ill-tempered and withdrawn, are likely to produce depressive children. So it was in the case of Abraham Lincoln. He lost
his mother at nine, and his father apparently had difficulty showing affection toward his son; Lincoln hardly ever spoke of his father with any sign of
affection, even in his adult years.[20] Jefferson Davis had a similarly strained
relationship with Samuel, a father who, his son later recalled, "sought to
repress the expression of [love] whenever practicable." The death of cold-
hearted Samuel Davis left his seventeen-year-old son Jefferson, who had
long resented his father's lovelessness, confused and guilt-ridden. Alexander Stephens, at fourteen, watched in horror as his father, ill with pneu-
monia, died in a delirium. "The light of my life went out. Despair! Despair!
Despair!" he recalled.[21] Edmund Ruffin lost his mother at age five, his father
at sixteen; Thomas Cocke, the guardian who reared him to adulthood,
committed suicide with a gun. Ruffin, who was the first to reach the corpse,
later used that weapon for his own death.[22] Gerrit Smith always felt that his
father failed to love him: as a teenager at Hamilton College, he once wrote
his mother that he considered Peter Smith no more than his "nominal"
father.[23]

John Brown's early history conforms to the backgrounds of these and
many others whose difficulties with the mourning process guided them
toward a melancholy disposition. "Squire" Owen Brown, a tanner in Hudson, Ohio, was a taciturn father. An orthodox Calvinist, he moved his family from Connecticut to Ohio's frontier Summit County early in the nineteenth century and raised his son to follow his trade and his religion. In
1858, using the third person in his narrative, John Brown wrote to young
Henry Stearns a long letter about his earliest memories. In it, Brown recounted that "when John was in his Sixth year a poor *Indian boy* gave him a
Yellow Marble the first he had ever seen." When he lost it some time later,
Brown declared that *"it took years to heal the wound &; I think* he cried at
times about it." Other pets and playthings also vanished or died. As he later
reminisced, these losses introduced him to "the school of *adversity:* which
my young friend was a most necessary part of his early training."[24]

Although inadequate substitutions, these toys were replacements for the
human loss that Brown had experienced. His most serious deprivation,
however, came in 1808 when his mother died in childbirth—a baby daughter dying as well—when Brown was eight years old. Grief and anger over the
loss of his mother drove Brown still further into himself.[25] Brown learned to
lie, *"a very bad & foolish* habbit" in order to "screen himself from blame; or
from punishment," he confessed to young Stearns.[26] Yet lying, if bad and
foolish, was also a form of fantasy life, a counterworld, into which artists
and writers of similarly lonely disposition learn to mold imaginative
forms.[27] Indeed, from the age of ten Brown acquired considerable taste for

reading, which, he later declared, "formed the principle [*sic*] part of his education." Reading in adolescence often serves to comfort the lonely child and provide a safe haven of imaginative wonders. But young John Brown's study was confined to histories and Bible stories.[28]

Religion, not letters, would be the center of his interior life. His melancholy and its accompanying sense of both sinful unworthiness and, paradoxically, moral superiority, would find expression in his religious preoccupations rather than in the creation of fictional voices, even though "the whispering of the wind on the prairie [of Kansas] was full of voices to him," as Brown's friend William Phillips later reminisced, adding that "the stars as they shone in the firmament of God seemed to inspire him."[29] A second outcome of his mourning might have been a poor school record, although for many depressives hard studying can be a welcome escape from the external world. Although letters and ciphering frustrated the motherless boy, he felt at home in the aggressive play of the school yard, delighting in such antics. He loved throwing snowballs at "seedy wool hats," fighting, and giving orders to playmates in a boisterous spirit, presumably as a way to distract himself. But he was more reclusive than his memory of himself as a swaggering bully suggests. As young as age twelve, he was thrilled to be "sent off through the wilderness alone to very considerable distances."[30]

A blow no less painful than the hardship of losing his mother, Ruth Mills Brown, was the appearance of her replacement at his father's side. Within eleven months of his first wife's death, Owen Brown married Sally Root, a twenty-year-old, when the widower was almost forty. John Brown's reaction was distinctly unfriendly. He said himself that he *"never addopted her in feeling;* but continued to pine after his own Mother for years. This opperated very unfavourably uppon him; as he was both naturally fond of females; & withall extremely diffident; & deprived him of a suitable connecting link between the different sexes; the want of which might under some circumstances, have proved his ruin."[31]

The death of either parent when a child is forming primary attachments may be emotionally covered up in subsequent years. During adulthood, however, the deaths of other loved ones—wives, children, a surviving parent—can then reinforce the foreboding and gloom that makes clear decisions and normal living seem impossible, even though the first losses continue to lie below the threshold of consciousness.[32] It was Brown's fate, as he said to himself many times, to be harried by death. Yet, according to a member of the Perkins family, whose head, Simon, was once Brown's business partner, Brown revealed a peculiar callousness when he and Dianthe Lusk, his first wife, lost a baby. Anna Perkins remembered that he refused to call a doctor during the infant's illness and did not wish a minister to come to pray after the child died. Instead, Brown "simply put the little body in a rough wooden box" and buried it in the yard. But his decisions were not so heartless as Perkins's remarks might seem to imply. They were instead outgrowths of his sense of God's just punishment to which he should be resigned.[33]

Nonetheless, Brown by no means lived in a state of cold mental distraction all his life. He had a warm heart for his family members, a solicitousness about those for whom he was responsible, and a relentless sense of moral purpose. When ministering to his ailing youngsters or coaxing a dying ewe lamb back to health, he was medically skillful and sensitive in his nursing. Brown's son Salmon remarked that at times "the suffering of others," especially of those dear to him, "brought out the woman in him, for he was ever the nurse in sickness, watchful, tireless, tender, allowing no one to lift the burden of the night watch from him." He could be equally tenderhearted when moved to pity over the misery of a slave and could weep like a lost child in his silent way over the cause of those in bonds. His sense of being outside the safe conformities of conventional life made him understand the plight of the black race, whose members also earned few earthly rewards and were denied social advantages.[34]

Tenderness, however, was a commodity that often sank beneath the weight of Brown's sense of desperation. As if fearful that his own fantasy life was sinful, he leapt on the children whenever he discovered them fibbing, showing no compassion, even to his daughters. Ruth Brown Thompson remembered that he "used to whip me quite often for telling lies," and "he had such a way of saying 'tut, tut!' if he saw the first sign of a lie in us, that he often frightened us children."[35] John Brown was determined that his young ones should not develop the same tendency to fantasize that he thought had made him a lying sinner. Thus, when he punished them, he chastised himself as well, something to which his son Jason offered graphic testimony. At age four he told his mother that he had found a baby raccoon in the corn crib. Under her persistent questioning, though, he admitted that he did not know whether he had imagined the sight or whether the coon was real—a normal enough mental phenomenon for one at his stage of development. She called her husband, who at once fashioned a switch. Offering no explanation, Brown pulled down the boy's pants and, in Jason's words, "took both my hands in his and held me up in the air and thrashed me. How I danced! How it cut!" Tears welled up in the father's eyes "while he did it, and mother was crying. That was the kind of hard heart he had. He would tell us to do a thing once, without any threat. Next time, came the 'limber persuader,'" as the Browns called the all too familiar instrument.[36]

During these years, the state of Dianthe's mental health was fragile, adding to the burdens of her struggling husband. Some members of the family and neighbors in Hudson put the blame on Brown himself, claiming that he had destroyed her spirit with his dictatorial ways. One neighbor, Ransom Sanford, proposed that although Brown never beat her, he was known to be very unkind. George Abraham Griswold and Benjamin Kent Waite, two other neighbors, however, argued that he had been very considerate of her feelings. "Dianthe had times of being deranged," recalled eighty-nine-year-old Mrs. Danley Hobart in 1908; when her "cloak would fall off" on the way home from church, John Brown used to retrieve it and tenderly put it around her shoulders.[37]

Often enough those subject to melancholia marry partners with a similar tendency, and so it would seem to have been in this instance. There were signs of emotional disorder in the Lusk family; two of Dianthe's sisters were afflicted. Although according to Mrs. Hobart, Dianthe was peaceable most of the time, Annie Adams, one of Brown's daughters, reported that in one of her fits her mother threw John Brown, Jr., then newly born, into the hearth. The father quickly retrieved the baby, and only the clothes were slightly burned.[38]

Then at the age of thirty-one, Dianthe, along with another newborn son, died of puerperal fever. John Brown suffered a nervous breakdown or an emotionally paralytic state—"a dead calm"—in which he felt the loss "but verry little" and could "think or write about her . . . with as little emotion as of the most common subject." Milton Lusk, Dianthe's brother, later recalled that Brown's conversation, manners, and behavior had become peculiar enough for people to question his sanity.[39] Perhaps the saddest aspect of his mental condition was that he had no idea that beneath the deadness he described, he really cared deeply. A lifetime of hiding from his deepest feelings made him think that his affection for his wife was not as "warm & tender" as that of other men, similarly aggrieved. Other episodes in his life also indicated his disposition toward severe depression. But in this case the loss of someone about whom he cared so much may have been compounded by disturbing memories of his mother's death. Knowing no other course, he turned to his faith, remarking to his father, Owen, with traditional but still angry words, "We are again smarting under the rod of our Heavenly Father."[40]

After three months of unrelieved gloom, however, the widower returned to work and soon married again. According to Ina Emery, who was one of Brown's Ohio neighbors, his second bride, Mary Ann Day, was "a curiously crude woman who clung to the few religious ideas to which she had been educated with all the strength of a crude mind." In contrast, Richard Henry Dana, Jr., a young reformer who met the family in Springfield, Massachusetts, thought her a woman of dignity, who "looked superior to the poor place they lived in." Now, at the age of thirty-three, Brown decided to prove his capacity for making money to his new wife. Yet in business, as in health, he was bedeviled by problems, mostly of his own making, for, along with the lows of his depression, Brown suffered at times from a manic ferocity that gave him no rest.[41]

The times encouraged financial overspeculation throughout the country, but when the inevitable crash came in 1837, Brown was emotionally unprepared to change course. He refused advice to act with prudence, as if his dreams of wealth and respectability could become real through simple faith alone. Neighbors later remembered that he was not altogether straightforward in his dealings. He lacked, the Reverend Andrew Wilson complained, "any proper manly sense of responsibility."[42]

As two historians have noted, by 1852 he "had suffered fifteen business failures in four different states."[43] With a total of twenty offspring, at any one time Brown had to provide for at least twelve at home, a worry that surely did not increase his efficiency. From 1851 to 1854 he was almost "imprisoned," as one historian phrases it, in lawsuits, courtroom appearances, consultations with lawyers, and other complications. Most of his troubles arose from his incompetence as a wool speculator for Perkins & Brown, his Ohio partnership with the wealthy Simon Perkins. A fellow wool merchant named Aaron Erickson reported later that Brown had "almost childlike ignorance of the great enterprise in which he was embarking." Brown boasted of following a "theory" of his own devising that, claimed observers, defied all "the known laws of trade." When he had wasted thousands of dollars on purchases of wool that he could not profitably resell, he would become "greatly depressed in spirits," and yet with much heat he pledged his honor on the "infallible accuracy" of his calculations and expectations.[44]

Brown also exhibited the same obsessional behavior with regard to abolitionism. Given his Yankee location, however, his views on this subject were more conventional than they were regarding the wool trade. The Western Reserve, the district from which he came, was probably the most intensely antislavery section of the country. The settlers, largely Calvinists and Federalists from New England, used their convictions about the evils of slavery partly as a device to distinguish themselves politically and culturally from the proslavery and democratic Virginians and Marylanders who populated the lower part of Ohio. In 1837 Brown was incensed by the assassination of Elijah P. Lovejoy, the antislavery editor, during a fierce proslavery riot in Alton, Illinois. The Ohio tanner subsequently resolved to devote his life "to increasing hostility toward slavery."[45] In 1851 at Springfield, Massachusetts, he formed a band of black fighters. Calling them the United States League of Gileadites, he admonished his recruits to remember "Lovejoy and Torrey," as well as the Old Testament counsel: "Whosoever is fearful or afraid, let him return and part early from Mount Gilead."[46] The league helped fugitives escape to nearby Canada, and Brown had hopes of forming the band of local blacks into a first-class guerrilla force. Yet, with his finances ebbing away, he had to return to North Elba, New York, where he had left his family.

Since 1849 he, Mary Ann, and their sons and daughters had been operating a farm rented from Gerrit Smith. The antislavery philanthropist had placed black tenants, many from New York City, on part of a tract consisting of 120,000 acres in the Adirondacks. Burdened with debts and lawsuits, Brown had welcomed the chance to live near "these poor despised Africans," as he called them. He showed his respect for his neighbors by cordial visits and by his courteous use of the titles "Mr." and "Mrs.," a gesture that few other whites practiced in that day. But he approached the topic of slavery with a ferocity that contemporaries found objectionable and threatening. Once, for example, S. N. Goodall, a neighbor, conversing with Brown on a train from Springfield, commented that Kentucky would perhaps have freed its slaves but for the interference of ultra-abolitionists. As Goodall recalled, Brown at once "sprang to his feet with clenched fists and eyes rolling like an insane man (as he most assuredly was) [and] remarked that the South would become free within one year were it not that there were too many such scoundrels as myself to rivet the chains of slavery."[47] Brown's explosive rudeness that so startled his interlocutor may have signified a desperate compulsiveness; more charitably, it was an example of his bold and just indignation. Such is the enigma that John Brown's war with conventional conduct often presented.

Before the Civil War, religion conveyed the language of the inner mind; Brown always immersed his deepest feelings in the waters of faith. Yet the nature of his religion differed from evangelical orthodoxy in its equal emphasis upon the Old along with the New Testament—a religion of punishment, violence, and rigid adherence to petty rules. His fixated handling of his son John Brown, Jr., well illustrated the character of his single-mindedness. In 1831, the son later explained, Brown presented the ten-year-old with a document that listed his alleged misdeeds. His son's accumulation of debts was probably more detailed and precise as a moral ledger than Brown's own business accounts: "For disobeying mother . . . 8 lashes; unfaithfulness at work . . . 3 lashes; telling a lie . . . 8 lashes" and so on. As John Brown, Jr., remarked, the piece of paper revealed so awesome a "footing up of *debits*" that he could not have survived the beating his father was planning. Weeping in his vexation, Brown suddenly stopped the thrashing, removed his own shirt, and seated himself on the block. The father then commanded his son to lash him with the "blue-beech switch." Hesitant to strike with full force, the son heard Brown order him to lay on "harder! . . . harder, harder!" until, as John, Jr., concluded the story, "he *received the balance of the account.*" The son disclosed that years passed before he understood his father's purpose as a "practical illustration of the Doctrine of the Atonement." By that term he meant the spilling of innocent blood for the salvation of the guilty.[48] Psychologically, however, Brown's severity was meant not only to punish himself for sins he could not articulate but to lead his son into the same sense of unworthiness that religious faith and upright deed were supposed to relieve. Not many Christians in that era so thoroughly combined religion, violence, and despair. It is hardly a wonder that Oliver Cromwell was John Brown's hero.[49]

In 1855 his sons by Dianthe Lusk—John, Jr., Jason, Owen, and Frederick—urged Brown to move with them to the plains of Kansas to fight the proslavery Border Ruffians.[50] For years Brown had favored an aggressive policy against slavery. Here was an opportunity to carry it out. He had even studied the subject, writing notes to himself: "Guerilla warfare see Life of Lord Wellington Page 71 to Page 75 (Mina)" and "Deep and narrow defiles where 300 men would suffice to check an *army*" in the Swiss Alps.[51] Although his health was poor and he was emotionally drained, he relished the notion of war to the last drop of blood—perhaps not surprisingly, since, for the depressive, the idea of war and death in battle can have special meaning. The warrior tradition often involves an attempt to escape dejection as well as the ordinariness of human existence.

The decisive moment came with the passage of the Kansas-Nebraska Act, which repealed the old Missouri Compromise prohibiting slavery in that region. The installation of an intimidating, corrupt, proslavery territorial government followed, and free-state settlers were at once forced to challenge its legitimacy. Brown joined his sons in Kansas and began operations to avenge the atrocities and coercions of the Southern immigrants. Hearing the news that the enemy had murdered several free-soil settlers and bent on reprisal, he and the others voted to counterattack.

Indeed, Brown and a group of antislavery settlers worked themselves into a frenzy against the proslavery neighbors in the Pottawatomie country. The idea of retribution by a midnight attack upon their settlements seemed a matter of justice and necessity—to terrorize the opposition into impotence. As preparations were being made, someone whispered that caution should be the watchword, to which Brown sternly replied, "Caution, caution, sir. I am eternally tired of hearing that word caution. It is nothing but the word of cowardice."[52] In carrying out the mission, he found that his religious and racial convictions permitted him license to seek the destruction of the great whore, slavery, and all her Southern champions. On May 24, 1856, Brown, joined by his strapping sons Owen, Frederick, Salmon, and Oliver, and a pair of free-soil supporters, visited several cabins.

They seized five proslavery settlers, walked them a distance in the dark, and then hacked them to death with sharpened cutlasses that Brown had brought with him from Akron, Ohio. The gruesome state of the bodies showed how angry and determined the killers were.

Shortly afterwards, Jason Brown, a son whose nonviolent scruples held him back from homicide, dared to confront his father, defining murder in cold blood as "an uncalled for, wicked act." Brown, however, stiffly replied, "God is my judge"; self-defense demanded it.[53] Later, Jason reflected, "I wish Father had been well, & his mind entirely clear" during the whole episode of planning and executing these acts of retribution. John Brown claimed not to have killed any of the victims himself, but he admitted approving the action. The historian Stephen Oates, however, narrates that Brown was fully involved in the commission of the murders and returned home from the expedition "transfixed." Thereafter Brown referred to himself more than once as "an instrument in the hands of God to free the slaves," a military as much as a religious assertion.[54] The enigma remains. The incident might be seen simply as the result of passions aroused in a time of anarchy. But disposing of human beings as if they were cattle for market might also signify a moral and psychological insensibility regardless of the merits of the cause.

* * * * *

Given Brown's peculiarities and stubborn solitariness, it is hard to imagine how he garnered the support he did from men who belonged to a richer stratum of society. Part of his success in that leap across class lines can be attributed to the relative success of his Kansas activities. No longer mired down in the tedium of everyday business transactions that he could not fully grasp, his career as a frontier warrior gave him a new confidence. His seething indignation over the injustice of slavery lent meaning to a hidden anger. For the upcoming mission, about which he told his supporters only as much as was needed to stir imaginations, he raised large sums among the wealthy abolitionists of Massachusetts. For Brown, this task was easier than buying and selling wool in a volatile market.

Yet his success in winning new friends remains something of a puzzle. The intellectuals who rallied to his cause scarcely resembled the rash and romantic young men of both races who soon were to pledge their fate to Brown's direction at Harpers Ferry. Middle-aged men such as Ralph Waldo Emerson, Henry Thoreau, and Ellery Channing, along with townspeople of Concord, heard him speak of how "it was better that a whole generation of men, women and children pass away by violent death" rather than that a violation of the Holy Gospel or the Declaration of Independence be further tolerated. His admirers thrilled to his stories of mayhem and bloodshed in the Border War of Kansas. Even in a hotbed of transcendentalism such as Concord, the American taste for violence was evident. But his hosts, Channing and Emerson, who entertained the gaunt Ohio tanner at dinners, and their guests heard only what they wished to hear. Brown was speaking the language of terror—arson, the slaughter of civilians, old and young, whereas they thought in terms of midnight rides, Minute Men, and Bunker Hill—scarcely the same level of action, with its possibility for the escalation of violence.[55]

Despite, or perhaps because of, their differences, a symbiotic relationship thus developed between the inner circle of committeemen—the abolitionist "Secret Six"—and the Kansas guerrilla fighter. Though hobbled by business failure, Brown subscribed to all the Victorian values that his prosperous and even distinguished supporters had used to gain their wealth and position.[56] By far the most prominent figure was Theodore Parker, whose scholarly writings and pulpit eloquence lent to the unpopular cause of abolitionism a new degree of respectability. He supplied an intellectual depth that a polemicist like William Lloyd Garrison could not have achieved. At the time of John Brown's raid, though, Parker, long a victim of consumption, was in Rome, where he died in 1860.[57]

The well-born Thomas Wentworth Higginson, a Harvard graduate and protégé of Theodore Parker, was also attracted to the charismatic Brown. Higginson was a major figure in the antislavery movement and a popular preacher, although he was ostracized by his fellow Unitarians for his radical religious and racial views.[58] Samuel Gridley Howe, the third among the "Secret Six," boasted no less an aristocratic lineage than Higginson's. A Harvard-trained reformer with strenuous convictions, Howe had fought for Greek independence in the 1820s, in which cause he underwent a lengthy imprisonment. The Bostonian also headed the renowned Perkins Institution, where the blind and deaf were taught. Following the raid, however, Howe fled to Canada when he was named in the newspapers as a coconspirator—probably because he feared a repetition of his earlier prison experience.[59]

As a prospering manufacturer of linseed oil, used in shipping, George Luther Stearns had a hardheaded business approach to matters. Stearns exemplified the virtues of steady work and shrewdness better than the others. Yet Brown inspired trust in men with common sense and entrepreneurial skill as easily as he did in intellectual circles. Gerrit Smith, another in the circle, has already been mentioned. The committeemen were all solid men of cultivation, philanthropy, and civic impulse. (Higginson, among the most loyal and boldest of Brown's "Secret Six," was later instrumental in the founding of the Boston Symphony Orchestra.)[60] These were times of increasing sectional violence not only among hardhanded settlers in Kansas but also in unexpected quarters back East. Bostonians much resented South Carolina Congressman Preston Brooks's blows against Charles Sumner and were eager to applaud measures that would teach the haughty, honor-conscious Southerners a lesson in Northern retribution. In May 1856 Brooks had mercilessly struck the antislavery leader, even after Sumner had fallen to the floor of the Senate Chamber of the national Capitol. American history thus teaches us that the appeal of romanticized violence may extend to the highest intellectual, political, and social levels.

Although Brown was once thought to have mesmerized a naive set of dreamers, Jeffery Rossbach argues convincingly that the abolitionist combined an undoubted charismatic appeal with an attitude of rough valor. As sedate and civilized Bostonians for the most part, his admirers could only hope to aspire to such heights of manliness. As Theodore Parker observed, "Young lads say, 'I wish that heaven would make me such a man.'" Rossbach concludes that "Brown's system (their *own* system) was the model which had to be presented to slaves." The black man's nature, white allies believed, would be glorified by participation in a bloody uprising.[61]

If Brown inspired white support in unexpected quarters, he also overcame the mistrust of blacks, too often victims of white betrayal. He enlisted Osborne Perry Anderson, Dangerfield Newby, Lewis Sheridan Leary, Shields Green, and John Anthony Copeland, Jr.,—all African Americans, some of whom were fugitive slaves. Yet their recruitment did not signify black unanimity about the prospects for a successful raid, however noble the gesture. In the summer of 1859 Frederick Douglass (who, like Howe, later fled to Canada) and Shields Green visited Brown when the insurrectionists were gathering at a site in Pennsylvania. Douglass was deeply moved by Brown's passion but, expecting only a plan to run off slaves, decided that an attempted seizure of the arsenal was foolhardy. Green, a fugitive slave, was no less a realist than his companion and had little faith that the plan would succeed. To Douglass's surprise, however, he declared, perhaps with a sense of resignation, "I b'leve I'll go wid de ole man."[62]

Having inspired and assembled his forces, Brown expected to bring a guerrilla war to the slaveholders' doorsteps. Yet the way that he conducted himself during the expedition against the arsenal at Harpers Ferry presented the active and demonic facet of this depressive's condition. Historians, even those most sympathetic with Brown's achievement, have long argued over his puzzling decisions and omissions, especially the failure to strike with dispatch and leave with the armaments before being surrounded. His study of guerrilla warfare should have made that a key tactical principle. In the same period, 1859 and 1860, Garibaldi and his Red Shirts succeeded in guerrilla warfare and in almost monopolizing the European headlines, as Seymour Drescher observes later in this volume. In contrast, John Brown and his brave if reckless followers failed.

As preparation for the raid, the abolitionist first set up headquarters at a farm near Chambersburg, Pennsylvania. In mid-July 1859, they moved nearer to the arsenal, posting themselves at the farm of Dr. Booth Kennedy, which Brown had rented. The farmhouse was located seven miles from Harpers Ferry, on the Maryland side of the border. Luck more than sound policy kept the plan secret from prying neighbors. Some of his score or so of men were loquacious and naive in what they disclosed to Maryland neighbors and what they wrote in letters home. With about eighty free-state supporters thus aware of the conspiracy, hints were bound to reach the authorities. In late August Secretary of War John Floyd received a message, addressed from Cincinnati (but originating in Scott County, Iowa), that laid out the whole scheme. Written by an Iowa abolitionist who sought to save John Brown and his friends from what he regarded as a foolish and self-destructive plan, the letter mentioned that "the armory in Maryland" would be attacked, a mistake of location that led the vacationing cabinet officer to doubt the authenticity of the communication. A subsequent letter with a similar import went astray.[63]

The conspirators' second error was to leave a mass of incriminating documents at the Kennedy farm, which would compromise so many of John Brown's disciples and financial sponsors. In all fairness to Brown, the men left in charge of the farm fled following the raid, presumably with no time to destroy evidence of the conspiracy. Some forethought on Brown's part, however, might have led to the safe burial or destruction of such important materials before the group left on the expedition to Harpers Ferry. In addition, publication of the captured documents did much to terrorize the slaveholding population. The papers suggested to the authorities that Brown had larger aims and more hidden allies in the South than his limited admissions after his capture suggested.

Moreover, Brown carried no provisions on the expedition, as if God would rain manna from the skies as He had done for the Israelites in the wilderness. "The Commander-in-Chief of the Provisional Army of the North," as Brown pompously dubbed himself, thus made the suffering of his men worse, reducing them while at Harpers Ferry to hunger. The scholar David Potter contends that "he sometimes behaved in a very confused way," faulting him for alternating "between brief periods of decisive action and long intervals when it is hard to tell what he was doing."[64] C. Vann Woodward has summarized the history of the Harpers Ferry debacle succinctly: Brown "cut himself off from his base of supplies, failed to keep open his only avenues of retreat, dispersed his small force, and bottled the bulk of them up in a trap where defeat was inevitable."[65] John Brown, Jr., just back from recruiting in Cleveland, Ohio, was left in the dark about when the assault would begin and therefore failed to forward supplies and additional men.[66]

Years later, Salmon Brown said that he thought that the old man was doomed to fail: "I did not want to go to Harpers Ferry very much. I said to the boys before they left: 'You know father. You know he will *dally* till he is trapped!'" Even the sympathetic Oswald Garrison Villard referred in his biography of John Brown to the "curious indecision" that he exhibited throughout the whole operation. Villard concluded that "he had in mind no well-defined purpose." When first interrogated, Brown himself admitted that he could offer no good explanation for being "too tardy after commencing the open attack." But Brown, not known for his truthfulness and candor, later claimed that humanitarian considerations about his civilian hostages had deterred him, as if he were protecting them from an enemy outside the engine house.[67] Salmon Brown remarked that his father "had a peculiarity of insisting on order" and mastering his environment. One sure way to vex him was to "egg strangers on to offer to help" him pack for a trip, a courtesy that thoroughly "stirred him up." Salmon knew that "Father . . . would insist on getting everything arranged just to suit him before he would consent to make a move."[68]

Brown's managerial inadequacies were even more serious than his son Salmon admitted. How could the guerrilla captain, after only a few hours' detention, permit a passing B & O train to proceed on its way to Baltimore and thus spread the news of the strange events at Harpers Ferry? Like the melancholic Jefferson Davis during a Confederate presidency soon to begin, Brown had spells when he could not make decisions: unacknowledged self-doubt paralyzed him.[69] John Henry Kagi, one of the shrewdest members of the group, tried to get his commander to evacuate the town with the munitions as soon as possible. Brown, however, restlessly moved about his command post at the engine house, sometimes in full command of his senses and at others in an apparent daze.[70]

Not only did Brown fatally procrastinate but he completely failed to understand why the slaves would not rise. Perhaps he never expected them to do so and offered that plan only because it had appeal. He was given to fantasies—his "lying"—and they appeared at the Kennedy farm in the form of maps of the Southern states with mysterious markings, coded messages, and a schoolboyish constitution prepared for the proposed freed people's government that he dreamed of establishing in the midst of the slavocracy.[71] Living too much in the imagination, Brown, as one might expect, had trouble making his fancies come true.

All these blunders might simply be attributable to Brown's confused reaction to the failure of insurrectionary slaves to materialize. Warfare is always messy, and the unforeseen often determines victory or defeat. But suppose another motive was at work: a mysterious desire not to succeed in the ordinary sense but to sow sectional discord by making the whole enterprise, and himself in particular, a human sacrifice to the cause of freedom. Viewed in these terms, the outward failure of the raid becomes an inner triumph in the cause of Christ and bleeding humanity. Such a motive of self-sacrifice, even if Brown repressed it from his conscious awareness, would help to explain why he did not insist that John Brown, Jr., his eldest son, should join the guerrilla band, why he tarried so long in town, and why he placed the river between himself and his base of supplies, a tactic that would have made it difficult to carry off the arms, head for the hills, and begin hit-and-run operations against plantations, the supposed object of the plan. By failing to carry the war against slavery much beyond the engine house (the capture of George Washington's great-grandnephew excepted), Brown also assured that no genuine slave insurrection could have broken out, even if slaves had long been waiting for a signal. The limiting of terrorist options later made possible his acceptability as a "martyr" in the North. After all, in that section, popular opinion would have reacted strongly against assaults on white women and children and civilians, as had occurred during the Nat Turner revolt. As it was, once in captivity, Brown would regret that his men had killed a free black trainman during the raid. The grizzled leader would also boast of his humanitarian regard for the civilian hostages he held in the engine house.[72]

Finally, surrounded on all sides and with no escape possible, Brown passively let matters run their inevitable course. When a detachment of marines, sent up from Washington under Colonel Robert E. Lee, stormed the engine house at seven in the morning of October 18, Brown quietly and resolutely refused to surrender, thus recklessly jeopardizing the lives of his men. The fate of the black participants was particularly grim. Shields Green and John Copeland, an Oberlin collegian, were captured, tried, and executed, and their cadavers delivered to the Winchester Medical College for the instruction of the students. Lewis Leary, Copeland's uncle, was mortally wounded during the raid; Dangerfield Newby was felled while guarding the bridge over the Potomac. Among the black members of the force, only Osborne Anderson escaped, but in 1872 he died a pauper in Washington from tuberculosis and lack of care.[73] Brown had the good fortune to survive, though sorely wounded. He had lost two sons, Oliver and Watson, and eight other raiders had been killed. Only five were captured alive; of the seven who were able to flee, two were soon apprehended and later tried and executed.

Despite this record of tragic blunders, Brown apparently had become increasingly self-possessed once it was clear that no escape was possible. Colonel Lewis W. Washington, the most prominent of Brown's hostages, reported afterwards, "With one son dead by his side, and another shot through, he felt the pulse of his dying son with one hand and held his rifle with the other, and commanded his men with the utmost composure." In captivity, he remained cool and dignified in the immediate hours and days of his recovery from his wounds.[74] One could attribute his coolness to extraordinary presence of mind or interpret it as a serene resignation to the self-induced death that he long wished for—or both.

* * * * *

If Brown's composure under fire at the engine house and his later serenity as he faced the prospect of the gallows testified to his religious strength of character, it also bespeaks his melancholy satisfaction in ending a life of inner rage and darkest mood. He had contemplated his own death for many years, and the issue was now settled. Without having to encounter the moral dilemma of self-destruction, long considered an offense against God's will, Brown could face the terminus of his life with devout tranquility. Thus he entered the most creative period of his antislavery career, fulfilling the role of martyr with almost artistic perfection. He fashioned himself into an emblem that represented an atonement to his wrathful God and a living example of black freedom. Offering himself on the altar of slavery would obliterate the failures of the past and an inner wretchedness that he understood to be a deserved visitation of divine punishment. When asked by his captors who had sent him, he replied, "It was my own prompting and that of my Maker, or that of the devil, whichever you please to ascribe it to."[75] The sentiment was almost jocular, but one wonders if Brown himself did not feel that he was inspired by both supernatural elements—an amalgamation of the Manichean division that seemed to have empowered him to create the tumult he wished for. In a letter to his wife Mary Ann, he declared not long afterward, "I have been *whiped* as the saying *is;* but am sure I can recover all the lost capital occasioned by that disaster; by only hanging a few moments by the neck; & I feel quite determined to make the utmost possible out of a defeat."[76]

In his last days before his execution on the gallows, December 2, 1859, it seems that Brown genuinely did achieve a more tender vision of Christ the Redeemer. He became kinder to his fellow men than he had ever been when he was a free man. Like a suicide who has resolved past confusions by preparing for the final act, Brown set his affairs in order with resignation: he looked forward to the coming, Christ-inspired event with "all joy," he said. Indeed, from the time of the ancient Greek tragedies, a warrior's self-willed death has signified escape from the humiliations of defeat and public mockery. By this means, Brown could also achieve human resurrection in the form of heroic legend making, the ingenious translation of his own magical thinking into popular myth. As a result, the constraints of convention were loosened, and Brown could shape his past to suit present needs.[77] He told the court in his last speech that he had no intention of arming slaves or inciting rebellion. The benign quality of his last hours stood in sharp contrast to the compulsiveness and rage that long bedeviled him. Now that the prospect of death was appeased, the anger he had felt for years subsided. To the Reverend Heman Humphrey, who had expressed his sorrow over Brown's *"infatuation & madness,"* he wrote that God had miraculously preserved him from one danger or another. (Perhaps he had in mind his astonishing escape from the federal marshals in Kansas after the murders at Pottawatomie.) "I am, to say the least," Brown continued blandly, "quite cheerful," particularly in the knowledge of divine favor.[78] In Brown's state of emotional as well as spiritual composure, all could be passively entrusted to God's hands.

Brown's self-possession as he faced death was perhaps the most significant manifestation of the melancholy state of mind with which he had so long contended. Precision about the extent of Brown's illness is scarcely possible at this point. His occasional thoughts of suicide, periodic indecisiveness, sense of unworthiness, and fantasies of glory all suggest, however, that his peculiarity lay in this realm of mental disorder.[79]

Historians have often dismissed the insanity in the Brown family's annals. Yet the affidavits from Brown's neighbors regarding the question of mental health, particularly on his mother's side, indicate that there was a genetic predisposition to some form of "affective disorder." Oswald Garrison Villard summarized the record in these words:

> Brown's grandmother on the maternal side, after lingering six years in hopeless insanity, had died insane . . . his grandmother's children, Brown's uncles and aunts, two sons and two daughters were intermittently insane, while a third daughter had died hopelessly lunatic . . . Brown's only sister, her daughter and one of his brothers [Salmon Brown, editor of the New Orleans *Bee*] were at intervals deranged; and . . . of six first cousins, two were occasionally mad, two had been discharged from the state lunatic asylum after repeated commitments, while two more were at the time in close restraint, one of these being a hopeless case.[80]

In addition, Brown's sons John Brown, Jr., and Frederick Brown (assassinated in Kansas) suffered from serious mental disorders, and late in life Salmon Brown committed suicide. It is worth noting that a Freudian stance is not necessary for the pursuit of this line of reasoning: the malady of depression itself is not entirely psychological but has neurological dimensions that have only lately come to light through genealogical and genetic investigations.[81]

Despite their political overtones, the affidavits, which emanated chiefly from Ohio and were presented to Governor Wise in an effort to mitigate Brown's crimes, are documents that help to authenticate Brown's emotional instability. They are not, however, very specific about the nature of his disorder. All refer to Brown either as insane or as a monomaniac, referring to his obsessional rigidities. Yet such vagueness of terminology, as Robert McGlone observes later in this study, was typical of the day. In the mid-nineteenth century, alienists described patients suffering from melancholia or any other mental aberration as simply being "insane." John P. Gray, the most noteworthy physician in this field, had rejected the idea of moral weakness as a factor in mental disturbance, proposing instead that physical afflictions and hereditary determinants were the essential causes. The testimony of irrationality that Brown's relatives and neighbors in Ohio offered to Governor Wise, however, demonstrates that he was a victim of self-delusions and a despair of which he was not always conscious. As Robert McGlone asserts, "Brown was not 'psychotic,' but his moods affected his judgment and may have been symptomatic of the affective disorder that haunted his son Frederick."[82]

*   *   *   *   *

By and large the essays that follow take up the story of the raid after John Brown's capture. The ambivalent character of the abolitionist's role, however, helps to explain the continuing divergence of opinion about him that these studies exemplify. The newspapers and other contemporary sources, upon which the essays are based, dutifully aired the different voices that Brown used to project an image of himself—whether as saint, as Whig patriot upholding the true meaning of the American Revolution, as an avenging instrument of an Old Testament God, or as a terrorist leader of black insurgency. Among the several groups and communities treated in the following pages are the white and black abolitionists, the originators of the popular agitation against slavery from the 1830s onward. For them the choice of which of the many John Browns to pick was very clear. All of them had their uses in different contexts, but clearly John Brown, the Christian martyr, had the widest appeal. The effort to make an icon of his remains— even against the wishes of Mary Ann Brown, his widow—is thoroughly explored in Paul Finkelman's revealing account. She had her own opinions about the venture into Virginia but held her tongue, exhibiting a remarkable kind of erect and stoic dignity.

As for the reaction to the raid in abolitionist circles, Thomas Wentworth Higginson, one of the "Secret Six," summed it up exactly in a letter to his mother. "Of course," he wrote, "I *think* enough about Brown, though I don't feel sure that his acquittal or rescue would do half as much good as his being executed."[83] With more perceptiveness, William Phillips, Brown's Kansas friend, recognized the depth of his passion and the peculiarity of his outward tranquility and inward mordancy: "I had seen him in his camp, had seen him in the field, and he was always an enigma, a strange compound of enthusiasm and cold, a volcano beneath a mountain of snow." Capturing his complexity and his odd swings of mood, Phillips defined Brown on another occasion as "a strange, resolute, repulsive, iron-willed old man" who stood "like a solitary rock in a more mobile society, a fiery nature, and a cold temper, and a cool head." So equipped with manly appeal—and with a dynamism arising from his complex temperament—Brown had long exploited the guilt of the armchair revolutionaries in their comfortable Boston clubs and snug Concord houses, and they all knew it. It was now their turn to use these gifts to benefit the antislavery crusade. Wendell Phillips, the great antislavery orator, urged his friend Ralph Waldo Emerson, a favorite on the Lyceum circuit, to speak out at Brown memorial meetings that he was attending: "You know what a vein and stratum of the public you can tap far out of the range of our bore."[84]

Phillips, Garrison, and most other abolitionists had once strenuously opposed violent means to end slavery. Partly through Brown's influence and partly through a growing frustration with polemics and meetings that produced no results, however, Brown's antislavery allies gradually embraced the abstraction of violent policies.[85] Brown would doubtless have appreciated the almost obscene exploitations of his situation that Paul Finkelman recounts. The publicizing of his deeds and death surrounded the moral import of his actions with still further ambiguity, confusion, and sharp excitement. All these factors enhanced the great cause in various parts of the North, including the already well-persuaded Northern black community. As Daniel Littlefield points out in this collection, the Reverend Henry Highland Garnet, long an advocate of militant resistance and revolt, found himself more critical of Brown than even he might have expected. He pledged that were he to lead an insurgency, he "would spare even a man-stealer, if he stood not in the bondman's path to freedom." At a meeting in Boston, William Lloyd Garrison, editor of *The Liberator*, portrayed Brown as a peaceful missionary. In the veteran abolitionist's opinion, "Old Osawatomie" never proposed to harm anyone. Yet, contradicting himself, Garrison also portrayed the Kansas fighter as a fierce patriot like the Boston "Indians" who dumped tea in the harbor to begin the bloody fight for freedom. Garnet and other African-American leaders, however, questioned the wisdom of trying to seize the federal arsenal, not out of fear but out of a sense of realism.

As several essays explain, Southern whites at first reacted in terror to the news of Brown's raid but then felt considerable relief at the minimal re-

sponse he aroused among the slaves and white nonslaveholders. Some
weeks later, though, their complacency evaporated with the discovery of
Northern sympathy for the conspiracy, particularly after Brown's execution. Peter Wallenstein brilliantly shows just how ominous was the martyr's
success in heightening sectional tensions. Northern resentments tough-
ened Southern political demands. When the abolitionist Theodore Parker
thundered that "the South is our *foe*—far more dangerous, meaner, and
more dishonorable" than the country's natural enemy, the English, he
spoke not for his fellow reformers alone.[86] In Brown's death, a growing
number of Northerners saw that warning fulfilled.

Veneration, or at least sympathy, for Brown in turn affronted white
Southerners who believed that they could not tolerate a loss of sectional
self-respect. For secessionists like Edmund Ruffin, Brown's raid was a welcome tocsin "to stir the sluggish blood of the South" into a proper sense of
its insulted honor. Still worse, as Wallenstein further illuminates, white
Southerners perceived two additional perils: the union of slaves and white
nonslaveholders in a common cause and the section's own lack of a unified
response to all these threats, both at home and from abroad. These perils
were very much on the mind of Governor Wise when he dealt with the
issue of Brown's insanity, as Robert McGlone's suggestive essay elucidates.
As the historian observes, nearly everyone found a personal use for their
special evaluation of Brown's mental stability. McGlone shows beyond
doubt that Governor Wise refused to accept the notion of Brown's lunacy
and "monomania" on the subject of slavery. For him to do so, the governor
would have had to belittle "Virginia's honor," a stain he had no intention
of inflicting. With Brown acting so amicably and calmly, the governor had
no reason to think him a lunatic or incompetent fool; he seemed a rational
man, even admirable in his fortitude.

Treating the ordinary members of the slaveholding class rather than the
sectional leaders, James O. Breeden explores the reaction of previously
complacent Southern medical students to the crisis over Brown's fate. He
also examines how the aftermath affected local, state, and sectional politics. Students are not always the most reliable protesters, Breeden observes;
an exodus of post-baccalaureate students from schools outside Philadelphia did not occur, some secessionists returned, and about half the Southern medical students stayed put. Yet the episode disclosed just how confused and divisive the South was in responding to the challenge that Brown
presented. In the long run, however, departure from the Union would cap-
tivate the imaginations of most white Southerners.

In their carefully reasoned explorations of Northern reactions, Peter
Knupfer and Wendy Venet further reveal that even those most thoroughly
opposed to the use of arms were compelled, by the character of Brown's

actions, to add to a violent outcome. Venet demonstrates that the female members of the reform movement had more trouble than their husbands and male allies in reconciling their antislavery ideals with Brown's intentions. Despite their largely Quaker and pacifistic leanings, most of the female reformers concluded that the larger aim of black liberty justified Brown's deeds. Peter Knupfer reveals the complexities that existed within the ranks of moderate and conservative voters in the North. They too opposed war, though for secular rather than pietistic reasons. John Brown's raid and his execution obliged these partisans to face the prospect of an antislavery, Republican victory in 1860, the result of which would almost surely be a civil war. Yet even they were unwilling to accept the Southern interpretation of Brown's raid, dismissing Southern outrage over the Northern sympathy for Brown as "silly and dangerous," to use Knupfer's words. Debates about who John Brown was and what he represented helped to promote, rather than hinder, Northern antipathy to slavery and Southern threats of disunion. In the final section of the volume, Seymour Drescher shows how the later reaction in European and British newspapers to Brown transformed his representation from a "fanatic" and "madman" into a stoical and Christ-like figure.

Some of the writers in these pages suggest that Brown's influence can be overdrawn: a civil war would have come about anyhow. A counterargument, however, would stress that, intentionally or not, Brown emboldened Northerners into identifying their personal manhood and sectional loyalty with anti-Southern resistance, and others into seeing a blustering, infuriated South as the cause of agitation and chaos, even though Brown had not really threatened anyone very effectively. Although the might-have-beens of history can never be permanently resolved, in the last essay Charles Joyner delineates the powerful impact of Brown's actions and personality upon his contemporaries. Departing from conventional historiography, Joyner combines an expressive approach with anthropological techniques. His essay shows how a singular event like John Brown's raid can become part of a sequential course toward the climax of war by a logic arising from antiphonal, almost scripted, responses between adversaries. By their reactions against the motions of their opponents, sectional leaders and their constituents escalated the conflict to the ultimate separation of the Union. Contingencies of one sort or another might have diminished the rising sectional temperature, but choices grew ever more limited under the pressure of events. As a whole, then, the present collection reveals the way in which a singular, complex, and ingenious agitator profoundly touched the life of a nation and how the very depth of Brown's despondency helped to shape his own creative vocation as a martyr who aspired to free a nation from a moral yoke and a race from its hideous bondage.

Notes

I acknowledge with much gratitude the invaluable assistance and advice of Paul Finkelman, Peter Wallenstein, Robert McGlone, David Hackett Fischer, and William W. Freehling, who reviewed this essay for the University Press of Virginia.

1. Quoted in Tilden G. Edelstein, "John Brown and His Friends," in *The Abolitionists: Means, Ends, and Motivations,* ed. Hugh Hawkins (Lexington, Mass., 1972), p. 122.

2. William A. Phillips, "Three Interviews with Old John Brown," *Atlantic Monthly* 44 (Dec. 1879), p. 739.

3. "Address at Cooper Institute, New York, Feb. 27, 1860," in Basler, ed., *Works of Lincoln,* 3:541. At various points in the text, I make use of some of the materials to be found in my 1985 essay, "John Brown's Antinomian War" (see abbreviations used in notes).

4. Redpath, *Public Life,* p. 13.

5. See Nevins, *Emergence,* 1:5–27 and 70–112. See also Stephen B. Oates, "John Brown and His Judges: A Critique of the Historical Literature," *CWH* 17 (Mar. 1971): 19–20; Potter, "Paradox." For an interesting assessment of Brown's mental health and the problems it posed for his captors, see Craig Simpson, "John Brown and Governor Wise: A New Perspective on Harpers Ferry," *Biography* 1 (Fall 1978): 15–38.

6. Stephen B. Oates, *To Purge This Land with Blood: A Biography of John Brown* (New York, 1970). In "John Brown and His Judges," Oates takes note of these shifts in historiography (pp. 5–24).

7. Robert McGlone, "The 'Madness' of Old John Brown: The Problem of Psychiatric Diagnosis in History," paper presented at the annual meeting of the American Studies Association, Miami Beach, October 1988. Although my study *The House of Percy: Honor, Myth, and Melancholy in a Southern Family,* shortly to appear, treats the issue of depression and creativity chiefly in their literary rather than ideological manifestations, McGlone's argument that Brown's creative impulse partly derived from his bipolar depressive condition predates my narrative here. Some years ago he shared with me his views in the form of an abstract of the 1988 paper cited above. McGlone's forthcoming *Apocalyptic Visions: John Brown's Witness against Slavery,* a study of Brown's psychology, provides much more detail than the sketch offered here and will elaborate his position.

8. John Brown to Franklin B. Sanborn, Feb. 24, 1858, in Sanborn, ed., *Life,* pp. 444–45.

9. See Frederick K. Goodwin and Kay Redfield Jamison, *Manic-Depressive Illness* (New York, 1990), pp. 342–67, esp. p. 344. A quarter of the poets anthologized in the *New Oxford Book of English Verse: 1250–1950* who lived during the eighteenth century, the so-called Age of Reason, were subject to manic-depressive illness. See also Nancy C. Andreasen, "Creativity and Mental Illness: Prevalence Rates in Writers and Their First-Degree Relatives," *American Journal of Psychiatry* 144 (Oct. 1987): 1288–92; Kay Redfield Jamison, "Mood Disorders and Patterns of Creativity in British Writers and Artists," *Psychiatry* 52 (May 1989): 125–34; and Anthony Storr, *Churchill's Black Dog, Kafka's Mice, and Other Phenomena of the Human Mind* (New York, 1988).

10. See Oates, *With Malice toward None: The Life of Abraham Lincoln* (New York, 1977), pp. 31 and 462–63; William H. Herndon and Jesse W. Weik, *Abraham Lincoln: The True Story of a Great Life,* 2 vols. (New York, 1892), 1:130; and Howard I. Kushner, *Self-Destruction in the Promised Land: A Psychocultural Biology of Suicide* (New Brunswick, N.J., 1989), p. 141.

11. Charles Royster, *The Destructive War: William Tecumseh Sherman, Stonewall Jackson, and the Americans* (Baton Rouge, 1992), pp. 99–101.

12. Entry for April 2, 1864, William Kauffman Scarborough, ed., *The Diary of Edmund Ruffin*, 3 vols. (Baton Rouge, 1972–89), 3:383–84; see also 3:705, 893–95, 948–49, and 950–51n, as well as 1:268–71, and 2:20, 106, 120, 139, 379, and 531. In addition, see Edmund Ruffin, *Incidents of My Life: Edmund Ruffin's Autobiographical Essays*, ed. David F. Allmendinger, Jr. (Charlottesville, Va., 1990), p. 11.

13. See Lynda Lasswell Crist and Mary Seaton Dix, eds., *The Papers of Jefferson Davis, 1856–1860*, 6 vols. (Baton Rouge, 1989), 6:196n6; William C. Davis, *Jefferson Davis: The Man and His Hour* (New York, 1991); and Paul D. Escott, *After Secession: Jefferson Davis and the Failure of Confederate Nationalism* (Baton Rouge, 1978), pp. 260–63. See also Clifford Dowdy, *Experiment in Rebellion* (New York, 1946), pp. 32, 70, 143, 205, 304, 346, and 359.

14. See Thomas E. Schott, *Alexander H. Stephens of Georgia* (Baton Rouge, 1988), pp. 9, 17, 22, 58–59, 134–35, 189–90, 453, and 501–3.

15. See Bertram Wyatt-Brown, "Conscience and Career: Young Abolitionists and Missionaries," in *Anti-Slavery, Religion, and Reform: Essays in Memory of Roger Anstey*, ed. Christine Bolt and Seymour Drescher (Folkestone, Eng., 1980), pp. 183–206; Raimund Goerler, "Family, Psychology and History," *Newsletter Group for the Use of Psychology in History* 4 (1975): 31–38; Merton L. Dillon, *Elijah P. Lovejoy, Abolitionist Editor* (Urbana, Ill., 1961); Perry Miller, "John Greenleaf Whittier: The Conscience in Poetry," *Harvard Review* 2 (1964): 8–24; James Brewer Stewart, *Joshua R. Giddings and the Tactics of Radical Politics* (Cleveland, 1970); Robert H. Abzug, *Passionate Liberator: Theodore Dwight Weld and the Dilemma of Reform* (New York, 1980); and Lewis Perry, *Childhood, Marriage, and Reform: Henry C. Wright, 1797–1870* (Chicago, 1980).

16. See Ralph Volney Harlow, *Gerrit Smith: Philanthropist and Reformer* (New York, 1939), p. 2.

17. Harlow, *Gerrit Smith*, p. 3; J. C. Furnas, *The Road to Harpers Ferry* (New York, 1959), p. 355. See also John R. McKivigan and Madeleine Leveille, "The 'Black Dream' of Gerrit Smith, New York Abolitionist," *Syracuse University Library Associates Courier* 20 (Fall 1985): 62–63. I am grateful to Professor McKivigan for calling my attention to this unusually valuable article.

18. See, for instance, Boyer, *Legend*, pp. 17 and 160; Nevins, *Emergence*, 2:93–95; Louis Filler, *The Crusade against Slavery, 1830–1860* (New York, 1960), p. 269; and Rossbach, *Conspirators*, pp. 227–28. Gerrit Smith's public disclaimer in 1867 was reprinted in Octavius Brooks Frothingham, *Gerrit Smith: A Biography* (1878; repr. New York, 1969), pp. 253–60.

19. See Sigmund Freud, "Mourning and Melancholia" (1917), in *The Collected Papers of Sigmund Freud*, ed. Ernest Jones, 5 vols. (London, 1948–50), 4:152–70; see also Kushner, *Self-Destruction in the Promised Land*.

20. Oates, *With Malice toward None*, pp. 14, 60, and 103–4; Benjamin P. Thomas, *Abraham Lincoln: A Biography* (New York, 1952), p. 11. On childhood depression, see Felix Brown, "Bereavement and Lack of a Parent in Childhood," in *Foundations of Child Psychiatry*, ed. E. Miller (London, 1968), pp. 435–55.

21. Davis quoted in William C. Davis, *Jefferson Davis*, pp. 9 and 24–25; Stephens quoted in Schott, *Alexander H. Stephens*, p. 9.

22. David L. Allmendinger, *Ruffin: Family and Reform in the Old South* (New York, 1990), pp. 3–7, 10–14, and 176–85.

23. Harlow, *Gerrit Smith*, p. 5.

24. John Brown to Henry L. Stearns, July 15, 1857, in Redpath, *Public Life*, pp. 26–27.

25. See John Bowlby, *Separation: Anxiety and Anger* (New York, 1973), p. 273.

26. John Brown to Henry L. Stearns, July 25, 1858, in Redpath, *Public Life,* p. 27.

27. Albert Rothenberg, *Creativity and Madness: New Findings and Old Stereotypes* (Baltimore, 1990), and "Creativity, Articulation, and Psychotherapy," *Journal of the American Academy of Psychoanalysis* 11 (Jan. 1983): 55–84; Arthur Koestler, *The Act of Creation* (1964; repr. New York, 1975), pp. 316–17.

28. John Brown to Henry L. Stearns, July 25, 1858, in Redpath, *Public Life,* p. 30. See also Victor Nell, *Lost in a Book: The Psychology of Reading for Pleasure* (New Haven, 1988), p. 213.

29. Phillips, "Three Interviews," p. 740.

30. John Brown to Henry L. Stearns, July 15, 1857, in Redpath, *Public Life,* pp. 1, 27, and 28.

31. Ibid., pp. 28–29.

32. Brown, "Bereavement and Lack of a Parent in Childhood," p. 439.

33. Jacob Bishop Perkins to Ralph Perkins, n.d., no. 75, folder 3, Simon Perkins Collection, Western Reserve Historical Society, Cleveland. Brown was living in western Pennsylvania at the time of his marriage to Dianthe Lusk. See Mary Land, "John Brown's Ohio Environment," *Ohio Archeological and Historical Quarterly* 57 (Jan. 1948): 30–32; John S. Duncan, "John Brown in Pennsylvania," *Western Pennsylvania Historical Magazine* 11 (1928): 50; and Ernest C. Miller, "John Brown's Ten Years in Northwestern Pennsylvania," *Pennsylvania History* 15 (1948): 25–26.

34. Salmon Brown, "My Father, John Brown," *The Outlook,* Jan. 25, 1913, p. 215. See also Ruth Thompson, quoted in Sanborn, ed., *Life,* pp. 94–95 and 104.

35. Ruth Thompson, quoted in Sanborn, ed., *Life,* p. 93.

36. Katherine Mayo, interview with Jason Brown, n.d. [1908], in the Oswald Garrison Villard Collection, Lowe Library, Columbia University (hereafter Villard Collection).

37. Katherine Mayo, interviews with Mrs. Danley Hobart, Dec. 2, 1908; with Ransom Sanford, Dec. 20, 1908; with Benjamin Kent Waite, Dec. 26, 27, 1908; and with George Abraham Griswold, Jan. 4, 1909, Villard Collection.

38. Katherine Mayo, interview with Mrs. Annie Brown Adams, Oct. 2–3, 1908. See also interview with Mrs. Henry Pettengill, Dec. 20, 1908: John Brown, Jr., told Mrs. Pettengill that "Father was never good to my mother," or so Katherine Mayo reported. Both interviews are in the Villard Collection.

39. See Milton Lusk, affidavit on Brown's sanity, Nov. 11, 1859, Henry A. Wise and Family Collection, Library of Congress (hereafter Wise Collection). Oates, p. 418, claims these affidavits are in the John Brown Papers, also at the Library of Congress.

40. John Brown to Owen Brown, Aug. 11, 1832, in Ruchames, ed., *Revolutionary,* pp. 49–50. See also John Brown to Seth Thompson, Aug. 13, 1832, in Boyer, p. 250. By this time Brown's father, Owen, always "eccentric," had himself become a recluse: Richard J. Hinton, "Old John Brown and the Men of Harpers Ferry," *Time* (July 1890), p. 733.

41. Katherine Mayo, interview with Andrew Wilson, Universalist minister in Ravenna, Ohio, Dec. 24, 1908, Villard Collection; see also her interviews with Ransom M. Sanford, Dec. 20, 1908, and with John Whedon, Dec. 1, 1908, and Jan. 1909[?], as well as Silvano Arieti and Jules Bemporad, *Severe and Mild Depression: The Psychotherapeutic Approach* (New York, 1978), pp. 139–40.

42. Katherine Mayo, interview with Andrew Wilson, Dec. 24, 1908, Villard Collection; again, see also her interviews, cited just above, with Ransom M. Sanford and with John Whedon.

43. James West Davidson and Mark Hamilton Lytle, *After the Fact: The Art of Historical Detection,* 2 vols. (1982; repr. New York, 1992), 1:130.

44. Boyer, *Legend*, p. 438.

45. Quoted in the reminiscences of Lora Case, in Emily E. Metcalf, "Historical Papers," Sept. 4, 1904 [copy], Villard Collection; Case is also quoted in Oates, *Purge*, p. 369n11. In addition, see Land, "John Brown's Ohio Environment," pp. 24–47.

46. Judg. 7.3; Deut. 20.8; quoted in Villard, *Biography*, p. 51; in Quarles, *Allies*, p. 25, and in Sanborn, ed., *Life*, p. 125.

47. S. N. Goodall, affidavit, Nov. 18, 1859, Wise Collection. See also Quarles, *Allies*, pp. 23 and 24.

48. John Brown, Jr., quoted in Sanborn, ed., *Life*, pp. 22 and 92–93.

49. Eleanor Atkinson, "The Soul of John Brown: Recollections of the Great Abolitionist," *American Magazine* (October 1909), p. 636; clipping in Villard Collection.

50. Richard J. Hinton, *John Brown and His Men* (New York, 1894), p. 603.

51. A notebook, dated sometime in 1855, quoted in Villard, *Biography*, p. 53.

52. Reported by Judge James Hanway in 1880, quoted in ibid., p. 153.

53. Quoted in ibid., p. 54.

54. Katherine Mayo, interview with Jason Brown, n.d. [1908]; see also her interview with Salmon Brown, Oct. 13, 1908, both in the Villard Collection. See, in addition, Oates, *Purge*, pp. 135 and 137; Villard, *Biography*, pp. 158–65 (Salmon Brown is quoted on p. 165), and 459; David L. King, affiant, Nov. 15, 1859, Wise Collection.

55. Rossbach, *Conspirators*, pp. 104–5.

56. Ibid., pp. 9–11.

57. See Michael Fellman, "Theodore Parker and the Abolitionist Role in the 1850s," *JAH* 61 (Dec. 1974): 666–84; John Weiss, *The Life and Correspondence of Theodore Parker* (Boston, 1864); and Octavius Brooks Frothingham, *Theodore Parker* (Boston, 1874).

58. See Tilden G. Edelstein, *Strange Enthusiasm: A Life of Thomas Wentworth Higginson* (New York, 1970).

59. Harold Schwartz, *Samuel Gridley Howe: Social Reformer, 1801–1876* (Cambridge, Mass., 1956), pp. 237–46.

60. Rossbach, *Conspirators*, pp. 270–71.

61. Theodore Parker to Francis Jackson, Nov. 24, 1859, in Ruchames, ed., *Revolutionary*, pp. 258; Rossbach, *Conspirators*, pp. 11.

62. Frederick Douglass, *Life and Times of Frederick Douglas, Written by Himself* (1892; repr. New York, 1962), p. 320.

63. David J. Gue to John Floyd, Aug. 20, 1859, in Villard, *Biography*, p. 410, and see, in general, pp. 407–12.

64. Potter, "Paradox," pp. 212 and 213.

65. Woodward, "Private War," p. 45.

66. On John Brown, Jr., and his absence from the Harpers Ferry force, see Robert McGlone, "Rescripting a Troubled Past: John Brown's Family and the Harpers Ferry Conspiracy," *JAH* 75 (Mar. 1989): 1191–93.

67. Katherine Mayo, interview with Salmon Brown, Oct. 11–13, 1908, Villard Collection; Franklin B. Sanborn, *Memoirs of John Brown* (Concord, Mass., 1878), pp. 89–97, repr. in Edward Stone, ed., *Incident at Harpers Ferry* (Englewood Cliffs, N.J., 1956), pp. 219–20; Villard, *Biography*, pp. 424 (where he also quotes Salmon Brown) and 427, and, for the quote from Brown, p. 461. Robert McGlone, however, correctly observes that Salmon Brown had his own reasons to excuse his absence from Harpers Ferry ("Rescripting a Troubled Past," p. 1190). On John Brown's lying about his motives for delay, see John Brown to Heman Humphrey, Nov. 25, 1859, in Ruchames, ed., *Revolutionary*, p. 157.

68. Katherine Mayo, interview with Salmon Brown, Oct. 11–13, 1908, Villard Collection.

69. See William C. Davis, "The Personality of Jefferson Davis," paper presented at the annual meeting of the Southern Historical Association, Atlanta, 1991; see also Simpson, *Wise,* p. 203.

70. See Hinton, *John Brown,* pp. 298, 300, and 302–5; Allan Keller, *Thunder at Harper's Ferry* (Englewood Cliffs, N.J., 1958), pp. 123–28; Villard, *Biography,* p. 438; Oates, *Purge,* p. 294; and Osborne P. Anderson, *A Voice from Harper's Ferry* (Boston, 1861), pp. 35–37.

71. Woodward, "Private War," pp. 63–64.

72. Villard, *Biography,* p. 433.

73. See Quarles, *Allies,* pp. 94–101, 109–10, 133–37, and 171.

74. See Elijah Avey, *The Capture and Execution of John Brown: An Eyewitness Account* (1906; repr. New York, 1971), p. 16; Villard, *Biography,* pp. 432–38.

75. Quoted in Villard, *Biography,* p. 457.

76. John Brown to Mary Ann [Day] Brown, Nov. 10, 1859, in Villard, *Biography,* pp. 540–41.

77. See M. D. Faber, *Suicide and Greek Tragedy* (New York, 1970), pp. 17–18.

78. John Brown to Heman Humphrey, Nov. 25, 1859, in Ruchames, ed., *Revolutionary,* pp. 157–58; see also Oates, "John Brown and His Judges," p. 20n55. On the topic more generally, see M. D. W. Jeffreys, "Samsonic Suicide or Suicide of Revenge among Africans," *African Studies* 11 (1952): 118–22.

79. See Anthony Storr, *The Dynamics of Creation* (New York, 1972), p. 92.

80. Quoted in Villard, *Biography,* pp. 508–9. See also Edward Brown, affiant, to Henry A. Wise, Nov. 5, 1859; Harvey Baldwin, affiant, Nov. 1, 1859; Edwin A. Wetmore, affiant, Nov. 19, 1859; Jonathan Metcalf, affiant, n.d.; James N. Weld, affiant, n.d.; S. N. Goodall, affiant, Nov. 17, 1859, all in the Wise Collection.

81. See Seymour S. Kety et al., eds., *Genetics of Neurological and Psychiatric Disorders* (New York, 1983); Elliot S. Gershon, "Validation of Criteria for Major Depression through Controlled Family Study," *Journal of Affective Disorders* 11 (Sept.–Oct. 1986): 125–31; Elliot S. Gershon and J. I. Numberger, Jr., "Inheritance of Major Psychiatric Disorders," *Trends in Neuroscience* 5 (July 1982): 241–42; and Thomas C. Caramagno, *The Flight of the Mind: Virginia Woolf's Art and Manic-Depressive Illness* (Berkeley, 1992).

82. McGlone, "The 'Madness' of Old John Brown." See, for instance, records of patients at the Pennsylvania Hospital, Pennsylvania Hospital Historical Library, Philadelphia; McKivigan and Leveille, "The 'Black Dream' of Gerrit Smith," pp. 68–69.

83. Thomas Wentworth Higginson to Louise Storrow Higginson, Oct. 27, 1859, in Mary Thatcher Higginson, ed., *Letters and Journals of Thomas Wentworth Higginson, 1846–1906* (1921; repr. New York, 1969), p. 85.

84. William Phillips, "Three Interviews," p. 739, and quoted in Michael Fellman, *Inside War: The Guerilla Conflict in Missouri during the Civil War* (New York, 1989), p. 17; Wendell Phillips quoted in James Brewer Stewart, *Wendell Phillips: Liberty's Hero* (Baton Rouge, 1986), p. 204; see also Edelstein, "John Brown and His Friends," in Hawkins, ed., *The Abolitionists,* p. 125.

85. See Aileen Kraditor, *Means and Ends in American Abolitionism: Garrison and His Critics on Strategy and Tactics, 1834–1850* (New York, 1969); Bertram Wyatt-Brown, "William Lloyd Garrison and Antislavery Unity: A Reappraisal," in *Articles on American Slavery: Antislavery,* ed. Paul Finkelman (New York, 1989), pp. 511–30; and James Brewer Stewart, "The Aims and Impact of Garrisonian Abolitionism, 1840–1860," in ibid., pp. 413–25.

86. Quoted in David B. Davis, *The Slave Power Conspiracy and the Paranoid Style* (Baton Rouge, 1969), p. 60.

Part II
Northern Supporters of Brown

2

PAUL FINKELMAN

Manufacturing Martyrdom: The Antislavery Response to John Brown's Raid

No one can say
That the trial was not fair. The trial was fair
Painfully fair by every rule of law,
And that it was made not the slightest difference.
The law's our yardstick, and it measures well
Or well enough when there are yards to measure.
Measure a wave with it, measure a fire,
Cut sorrow up in inches, weigh content.
You can weigh John Brown's body well enough,
But how and in what balance weigh John Brown?

Stephen Vincent Benèt[1]

JOHN BROWN'S RAID in October 1859 initially left opponents of slavery almost as confused as the people in Virginia. *The Liberator,* for example, referred to the raid as "misguided, wild, and apparently insane," but "well intended." Its editor, William Lloyd Garrison, reminded readers of his long opposition to violence, "even in the best of causes." He then added, however, that "no one who glories in the revolutionary struggle of 1776" could "deny the right of the slaves to imitate the example of our fathers."[2]

Most Republican opponents of slavery were less equivocal. The majority of party leaders publicly denied any connection to the raid; many Republican papers called Brown a madman. Lincoln bragged that the Democrats had failed to "implicate a single Republican" in the "Harper's Ferry enterprise." David Davis, Lincoln's friend, advisor, and a future Supreme Court justice, wrote his son, "What a mad affair that was at Harper's Ferry!" Even William H. Seward, who was perceived as the leader of the radical wing of his party, moved quickly, "clearing his skirts effectually of John Brown."[3]

Most anxious to distance themselves from Brown were the "Secret Six" who financed the raid. Five of them panicked; only the Reverend Thomas Wentworth Higginson remained calm, and active, following the raid. Four of Brown's backers immediately went into hiding or left the country.[4] Gerrit Smith, another of the six conspirators, at first reacted serenely, and even

41

considered writing editorials in support of Brown. Within a few days, however, he was "paralyzed" by revelations of his relationship to Brown.[5] This
paralysis turned to terror as lawyers warned him of the fate that awaited
him in the South. Smith was "at times *sublime* in his willingness to be offered up in defence of his principles & then filled with terror at the thought
of the *tortures* which he fully believed would be practiced upon him when
he reached the South & soon he was *fixed* in the belief that he was a *doomed
man* & that he could look from hour to hour for the officers who were to
take him to the scene of torture & death."[6] Gerrit Smith's sudden trip to an
asylum was clearly not contrived. He may not have been insane, but he was
surely deeply depressed and abnormally fearful.

Relatively quickly, however, antislavery Northerners abandoned some of
these early reactions to Brown's raid. Brown's financial backers gradually
came out of hiding, and Gerrit Smith discharged himself from the asylum
he had voluntarily entered. Members of the antislavery community soon
realized that John Brown was potentially the most significant martyr to the
cause since Elijah P. Lovejoy. William Lloyd Garrison predicted that hanging Brown would in the end be "a terrible losing day for all Slavedom,"
while Ralph Waldo Emerson concluded that Brown was "the new saint
awaiting his martyrdom, and who, if he shall suffer, will make the gallows
glorious like the cross."[7] Henry Ward Beecher gloried in the prospect of
Brown on the gallows: "Let Virginia make him a martyr! Now, he has only
blundered. . . . But a cord and gibbet would redeem all that, and round up
Brown's failure with a heroic success." Brown himself endorsed this view,
writing "good" above a newspaper report of Beecher's speech.[8] Even before
the court sentenced him, Garrison concluded that Brown "will be hung."
This, Garrison believed, provided a great opportunity for the antislavery
movement. He thought "it would be a master-stroke of policy to urge *the
day of his execution* as the day for a general public expression of sentiment
with reference to the guilt and danger of slavery." After the death sentence
had been carried out, Garrison further asserted that "John Brown executed
will do more for our good cause, incomparably, than John Brown pardoned."[9]

At least a few Republicans also reevaluated the importance of Brown's
escapade. Shortly after the raid Horace Greeley predicted that Brown's actions would "drive the slave power to new outrages" and make the "irrepressible conflict . . . ten years nearer." In mid-November John A. Andrew, a
rising star in the Republican party and future governor of Massachusetts,
chaired a meeting to aid Brown's family. At this gathering Andrew refused
to commit himself on the wisdom of Brown's raid but declared that "John
Brown himself is right."[10]

Self-Conscious Martyrdom

He had no gift for life, no gift to bring
Life but his body and a cutting edge,
But he knew how to die.[11]

These speeches and meetings were the beginning of Brown's canonization. Indeed, Brown himself carefully cultivated his martyrdom in prison and in the courtroom. Before his sentencing he electrified the North by declaring: "Now, if it is deemed necessary that I should forfeit my life for the furtherance of the ends of justice, and mingle my blood further with the blood of my children and with the blood of millions in this slave country whose rights are disregarded by wicked, cruel, and unjust enactments,—I submit; so let it be done!"[12] The Reverend William Henry Furness wrote of "Brown's perfect words" and wondered, "Has anything like it been said in this land or age, so *brave, wise, considerate* all said—Slavery & Freedom brought face to face, standing opposite." Another minister declared, "What a text John Brown has given us," a text he planned to use "next Sunday all day" and "a good deal this winter."[13]

By the time Brown gave this speech, decisions by Governor Henry Wise and other Virginia officials had already made him something of a martyr. The authorities in Virginia contributed to Brown's martyrdom in three ways. First, they forced him to stand trial while he was still recovering from wounds received when he was captured. Thus Brown lay on a pallet in the courtroom throughout his trial, giving the impression that Virginia was rushing him to judgment when he was physically unable to conduct his defense.

Virginia authorities compounded this political blunder by accelerating the pace of the trial. The presiding judge, Richard Parker, refused to delay the proceedings for even a day, so that Brown's attorneys could arrive. Northerners interpreted this impatience as both unjust and reprehensible. Parker likewise conducted the rest of the trial with a bias and haste that played into the hands of Brown's supporters. Brown and those who sought to exploit his trial could not have asked for a judge or a set of proceedings better suited to epitomize "justice" under the slaveocracy.

Finally, Virginia officials erred in allowing Brown access to the North through interviews and correspondence. The prisoner used his sojourn in jail to write hundreds of letters, justifying his crusade to the North and to the world. By the time of his execution many of Brown's eloquent letters had thus been published throughout the North. Moreover, Brown played his role as the soon to be martyred philanthropist self-consciously, and with consummate skill. As he told his brother shortly after his sentencing, "I am worth inconceivably more to hang than for any other purpose."[14]

Those who corresponded with Brown, or met him in prison, were over-whelmed by his sense of purpose, his righteousness, and his charisma. When the wife of Massachusetts Judge Thomas Russell visited Brown in jail, she was overcome by his stoic resolve, "his integrity, high purpose, courage, and singleness of heart," and "for the rest of her life she would think of him—as many others would think of him—as one of the most noble ideal-ists the country had ever known."[15]

If Brown was certainly the best and most persuasive advocate of his own martyrdom, the Virginia authorities also played their parts well—meting out a hasty and harsh justice that helped Brown become an abolitionist saint. However, with the execution of Brown those responsible for his phys-ical martyrdom were removed from the scene. Brown was dead, and Vir-ginia authorities gave up his body for burial by his family. Without a con-certed effort to keep Brown's martyrdom alive his memory might have passed quickly from public consciousness; Brown would have been just another abolitionist who had suffered for his willingness to help slaves.[16] The task of elevating Brown from executed insurrectionist to martyred saint consequently fell on his family, friends, and supporters. Fortunately for his supporters, at the time of his death the organized antislavery move-ment was prepared to canonize Brown as a crucified martyr for the cause of the slave. Abolitionists knew they must do something to capitalize on his death. Proposals ranged from a massive funeral in Boston to a rather ghoul-ish plan to send Brown's body on a tour of the North. In the end, though, abolitionists rejected these ideas in favor of more traditional methods of giving speeches, writing books, producing memorabilia, and self-con-sciously creating legends of Old Man Brown.

Speeches about the Martyr

> In Charlestown meanwhile, there were whispers of rescue.
> Brown told them,
> "I am worth now infinitely more to die than to live."
> And lives his month so, busily.
> A month of trifles building up a legend
> And letters in a pinched, firm handwriting
> Courageous, scriptural, misspelt and terse,
> Sowing a fable everywhere they fell.[17]

Within days of the raid some abolitionists were contemplating a rescue. However, no one ever acted on these unrealistic plans.[18] Even if Brown could have been rescued, such a result would have destroyed the propa-ganda value of his martyrdom, as many of his followers well understood. Indeed, there is strong evidence that Brown himself opposed a rescue.

Shortly after his arrest Brown apparently decided that he would die a martyr's death for the cause of antislavery. When Samuel Pomeroy, a veteran of bleeding Kansas, visited him in jail, Brown greeted his old friend by quoting Christ: "In prison ye come unto me," suggesting that Brown already had visions of himself as a crucified martyr. When Pomeroy proposed a rescue, Brown rejected his help, telling him, much as he had told his brother, "I am worth now infinitely more to die than to live."[19]

Many antislavery leaders, moreover, had already realized that a martyred Brown, lying silent in his grave, would serve well the cause of antislavery; a fugitive Brown hiding in the North or in a Canadian exile would be far less useful. Accordingly, even before the trial was over most abolitionists were concentrating on the process of turning Brown into a martyr. James Redpath, who rode with Brown in Kansas, eagerly awaited the moment when "Old B was in heaven" so that he could write a biography of the martyred abolitionist to further the cause.[20]

Only days after the Harpers Ferry raid, George Baker asked his political ally Gerrit Smith to "publish an *Address to the People,* in the *Tribune* &c on the subject of Brown's operations and condition." Baker hoped that a stirring essay by Smith would help make "the people of the North be aroused to sympathy for him." As early as October 25, Wendell Phillips was asked to discuss the incident in a lecture previously scheduled for the New York Lyceum.[21] Phillips needed no encouragement. On November 1, he spoke in Brooklyn on the "Lesson of the Hour," attacking the prosecution of Brown and declaring that the Catholic Church's "Inquisition" had been a "heaven-robed innocence compared with the trial . . . that has been going on in startled, frightened Charlestown."[22]

The antislavery community praised "exceedingly" Phillips's "beautiful and stirring speech."[23] From late November to mid-December Northerners commemorated both the trial and the execution with public prayers, church services, marches, and meetings. Even before Brown was sentenced to death, the executive committee of the American Anti-Slavery Society anticipated this outcome and took steps to capitalize on it, resolving "to observe the tragic event" of Brown's execution "by public meetings and addresses, private conferences, or any other justifiable mode of action."[24] On December 2, the day of his execution, meetings throughout the North proclaimed Brown's martyrdom and condemned the sinfulness of slavery. Bells tolled, sermons were delivered, speeches were read, and resolutions adopted. Fourteen hundred people gathered in Cleveland; abolitionists filled Boston's Tremont Hall to capacity; a one-hundred-gun salute was fired off in Albany; and in countless other cities and towns people turned out to commemorate the day and mourn Brown's death.[25]

On December 4, the first Sunday after the execution, numerous ministers spoke of Brown's death. The Reverend Nathaniel Hall of Dorchester told his congregants that "the American Pulpit can have but one theme to-day. To decline, for any other, that given in the public tragedy whose shadow is yet upon us, would be to turn away from the very call of God, as heard in his providence,—heard in the awakened minds and quickened sensibilities of a people." In Chicago the Reverend William W. Patton compared Brown to the biblical prophets who "were slain by incensed kings for their faithful political preaching." Like many in the North, Patton could "condemn therefore as a matter of judgment, the expedition in which John Brown came to his end," yet still "find reason not only to sympathize with his desire to overthrow slavery, but also to acquit the man of evil intent and even to admire him as in spirit one of the few heroes of history."[26]

Public meetings condemning Brown also took place in the North.[27] Although larger in size than the pro-Brown meetings, these pro-Union, anti-Brown, rallies were fewer in number, and far less frequent, than those supporting Brown. Moreover, the continuous outpouring of sentiment in favor of Brown overshadowed these anti-Brown gatherings. On December 15, Wendell Phillips addressed a meeting at Cooper Union in New York City. Another occurred in Philadelphia the same day. These and similar meetings reflected the widespread Northern revulsion toward those who had hanged Brown. Brown's image as a martyr was shaped by the apparent unfairness of his trial, his letters from jail, his stoic behavior at the gallows, and the efforts of antislavery activists to exploit his execution for the greater cause. This was, of course, what Brown had expected. It is why he understood that he was far more valuable to the cause of antislavery as a dead martyr than as a living fugitive or a jailed convict.

The Struggle for John Brown's Body

> John Brown's Body lies a-mouldering in the grave
> He will not come again with foolish pikes
> And a pack of desperate boys to shadow the sun.
> He has gone back North. The slaves have forgotten his eyes.
> John Brown's body lies a-mouldering in the grave.
> John Brown's body lies a-mouldering in the grave.
> Already the corpse is changed, under the stone,
> The strong flesh rotten, the bones dropping away.[28]

With Brown's execution an inevitability, antislavery activists began to discuss how to exploit it. In mid-November Henry C. Wright suggested to Wendell Phillips that Brown's body be taken to Mt. Auburn Cemetery in Cambridge, Massachusetts, where "an *appropriate* monument might there be erected to him." Wright thought that existing antislavery funds might be used for this purpose, and if they did not suffice money could easily be raised from "thousands who would count it an honor to contribute" to bringing Brown to Mount Auburn and "to erect a monument there with some suitable inscription." In Wright's opinion, antislavery speakers could readily raise such funds.[29]

Wright may have felt slightly uncomfortable with his suggestion, since it involved plans for the disposition of the body before the prospective corpse was dead. He asked Phillips to "pardon" him his indelicacy, but, after all, Brown "has lived for one object, ie: to arouse the people of this Nation" on the *"Danger* of slavery and their duty in regard to it." He further argued that Brown's "work is finished. He has gained his object. He *triumphs* by the gallows. Death *is swallowed up in history."* Wright clearly saw Brown as America's Christ, declaring that "the sin of this Nation will be taken away by the Blood of Brown." But there the analogy ended, for Wright expected Brown's burial, not his resurrection, to be the focal point of the martyrdom. Thus, he urged Phillips to "write to Brown & get him to bequeath his body to the American A[nti-]Slavery Society," or to Phillips, William Lloyd Garrison, or Garrison's publisher, Francis Jackson. Almost as an afterthought, Wright suggested that Phillips also notify Brown's *"wife* & family about it."[30]

Wright was not the only abolitionist to appreciate the value of John Brown's body. Another correspondent urged Phillips to appoint some "wide awake man," unknown as an abolitionist, indeed preferably a "known Democrat," to "go at once to Virginia and get the Body of Brown at any price within any reasonable bounds." The body could then immediately be "put into a metal coffin enclosed except the face in ice." In this way Brown's body could be taken to "all our principal cities and even the minor ones" to "let the face and hands with rope be seen and even his clothes." Such a procession through the North would not only raise money but have great propaganda value.[31]

Apparently in full agreement with these Barnum-like proposals, Phillips went to New York to meet with Brown's widow immediately after the execution. He sought to persuade her to have the body shipped to Cambridge "and buried with impressive funeral solemnities at Mount Auburn." This, Phillips believed, would be a proper antidote to a "great Union Saving Meeting" scheduled for Faneuil Hall by politicians who wanted to attack Brown and the abolitionist cause. Lydia Maria Child, among others, worked with Phillips in trying to bring Brown's body to Mt. Auburn Cemetery.[32]

Ultimately, though, Mary Brown decided that her husband's body should be sent to North Elba, in upstate New York, for a private burial. She received the body in Harpers Ferry, accompanied by J. Miller McKim, the head of the American Anti-Slavery Society's office in Philadelphia, and Hector Tyndale. When the train carrying the body reached Philadelphia, a large crowd of supporters and opponents had gathered, and authorities feared a riot.

An empty hearse diverted most of the crowd while the coffin containing Brown's body was secretly transferred to a ship that took it to New York, where Phillips again attempted to convince Mary Brown to bury her husband's remains at Mt. Auburn, in Cambridge. When she refused, Phillips and McKim instead accompanied her to the family home in North Elba. Church bells rang, and crowds turned out along the route up the Hudson valley toward Brown's final resting place. At Troy, where the funeral party spent the night, Joel Tiffany, an abolitionist preacher at an independent church, gave a eulogy for Brown, and the next day the entourage proceeded to North Elba.[33] On December 8, Brown's body was interred there, less than eight weeks after he seized the arsenal at Harpers Ferry. J. Miller McKim officiated, while Wendell Phillips delivered the eulogy.

Phillips's eulogy stressed an old theme—one that had marked a speech given at the time of his entry into the antislavery movement in 1837. In that speech at Faneuil Hall, Phillips had compared America's first antislavery martyr—the printer Elijah Lovejoy, who had been killed by a proslavery mob—to Dr. Joseph Warren, who died leading the American revolutionaries at Bunker Hill. In his eulogy, Phillips once again evoked Warren's sacrifice, arguing that just as Bunker Hill had led to American liberty from Britain, so too would the Harpers Ferry raid lead to liberty for the slaves of America.[34] This quiet ceremony was all the Browns wanted, and probably all they could have coped with.

Not only the Brown family but some abolitionists as well were pleased with the way the funeral turned out. William Lloyd Garrison wrote McKim, expressing his "profound gratification that you and Wendell were able to take care of the body and attend the funeral." Phillips himself was thrilled at having a role in the ceremony and gracefully accepted Mary Brown's decision to have a private ceremony in upstate New York, even though he would have preferred a more public demonstration that would have aided the cause.[35]

Others in the antislavery movement, however, who were not privy to Mary Brown's opposition to a more public ceremony, were dissatisfied with Brown's last rites. Thaddeus Hyatt, the former president of the National Kansas Committee, admonished Phillips that the public had been "so let down by *sneaking* proceedings," which seemed to "forbid any further demonstrations of a public character." It is not clear whether Hyatt knew that a riot might have taken place if Brown's body had been carried through Philadelphia as part of a procession. Nor did he seem to be in the least bit concerned about the wishes of Mary Brown and her surviving children. Rather, Hyatt fumed, unless Brown had "made such a request as positively to preclude" a "public demonstration," there should have been one, or so he believed. He of course doubted that Brown had made such a request.[36]

Two days later Hyatt further berated Phillips for burying Brown quickly and in a remote place. This, he declared, was "just what every doughface desired to have done and just what has most gratified the murderers of John Brown." Hyatt claimed that he had received over five hundred letters, containing over eleven hundred dollars, in the three weeks before Brown's execution and bemoaned the fact that Brown's body was sent to North Elba before more could be raised. "Now suppose we had done what ought to have been done: Enclosed John Brown's body in a metallic case in which it might have been kept for an indefinite time—taken it to the Church of the Puritans and there amid imposing and solemn ceremonies given opportunity for the natural & heartfelt expression which every live man here felt burning with him!" Such a ceremony could have been followed by others "in every prominent City of the Union." Apparently forgetting that his correspondent was himself a master of propaganda, Hyatt lectured Phillips: "The facts of human nature are sufficient for us—men in multitudes are moved by just such means as the dead bodies of those whom they revere." He sadly concluded that although this had been just such an opportunity, "we have lost it: a worse loss than the battle of Harper's Ferry." In a stinging rebuke of his antislavery ally, Hyatt told Phillips that "another John Brown it seems was needed to take charge of John Brown's mortal remains."[37]

Even with Brown's body already in a remote grave, it appeared to some that there was still an opportunity to use the dead for the cause of the living. A black resident of Danbury, Connecticut, hoped that the antislavery movement would build a monument to Brown somewhere between Philadelphia and Boston, because he was "the first martyr for freedom" in America.[38] George Stearns, one of Brown's secret financial backers, had more elaborate plans. Suspecting that no one would claim the bodies of Brown's black compatriots, Shields Green and John Anthony Copeland, Stearns and his wife asked the Reverend Samuel J. May of Syracuse to contact J. Miller McKim in Philadelphia. Stearns thought McKim should claim the bodies of both men and investigate the possibility of burying them in Pennsylvania, until they could later be reinterred at Mount Auburn, where "a suitable monument" could be built to Brown's "memory and that of his noble associates." Stearns believed it important to prevent people from saying, "We honoured the White but forgot the Colored Brethren."[39]

What Stearns did not know was that antislavery men in Philadelphia had already written to Governor Wise asking for the bodies of Green and Copeland.[40] Although Wise had promised that he would allow the bodies of the executed men to be claimed by their relatives or, in the case of Green and Copeland, by their white friends, he either went back on his word or allowed others to assume authority. Immediately after they were hanged, Green and Copeland were buried, but their remains were subsequently exhumed and conveyed to the medical college at Winchester, Virginia, for dissection. Although numerous whites in the North tried to get the bodies returned, they were unsuccessful. On December 29, in his home of Oberlin, Ohio, three thousand turned out for a funeral for Copeland, even though there was no body to bury.[41]

Creating the Legend

> The North that had already begun
> To mold his body into crucified Christ's
> Hung fables about those hours—saw him move
> Symbolically, kiss a negro child,
> Do this and that, say things he never said
> To swell the sparse, hard outlines of the event
> With sentimental omen.[42]

Three days after the hanging the *New York Tribune* published the first of many erroneous reports about Brown and the execution. According to the *Tribune,* "As he stepped out of the door a black woman, with a little child in arms, stood near his way. . . . He stopped for a moment in his course, stooped over, and with the tenderness of one whose love is as broad as the brotherhood of man, kissed it affectionately." Virtually all scholars agree that the event did not in fact take place. Some fifteen hundred troops guarded Brown, and their commander had ordered all civilians to remain in their homes. Thus, none but individuals with official approval and soldiers witnessed the execution. Representative of scholarly opinion is Jules Abels, who declared that the kissing scene "did not happen and moreover could not have happened" because of the presence of troops guarding Brown.[43]

This dubious anecdote presents two puzzles: why was it written, and who wrote it. At first glance it has the flavor of blatant propaganda. But the manner of its initial publication was hardly designed to have a strong impact on the readers of the *Tribune.* The *Tribune* of December 5, the first Monday after the Friday execution, was filled with stories about Brown's last day, with a lead story by the "special correspondent" from Charlestown. The story of Brown kissing the child was buried in the last of the many reports from Charlestown, appearing at the bottom of page eight of the paper. Most readers of the *Tribune* probably never read that far. Nevertheless, despite its implausibility, this story soon captured the Yankee imagination.

With each retelling the drama of the story grew. In his eulogy Wendell Phillips briefly mentioned the incident but changed its location to the site of the gallows itself. Later that month Whittier immortalized the scene in a poem published in the *New York Independent:*

> John Brown of Osawatomie,
>   They led him out to die;
> And, lo!—a poor slave mother
>   With her little child pressed nigh.
> Then the bold, blue eye grew tender,
>   And the old, harsh face grew mild,
> As he stooped between the jeering ranks,
>   And kissed the negro's child!

Lydia Maria Child also contributed a poem about the event, describing how Brown saw a slave child, "And, fondly stoopin o'er her face / He kissed her for her injured race."[44]

Shortly after the execution Thomas Drew described in great detail the scene in a sympathetic volume that consisted mostly of letters to and from Brown and his companions and newspaper articles about Brown. Early in 1860 James Redpath described the incident in his "authorized" biography of Brown. Redpath's description came, word for word, from the *Tribune* (but without attribution or quotation marks). However, Redpath elaborated on the story still further by describing yet a second slave woman with a child in her arms. According to Redpath, the woman declared "God bless you, old man; I wish I could help you, but I cannot," and as Brown looked at her "a tear stood in his eye."[45] This was clearly fiction, designed to create myth. By 1863 Currier & Ives had embraced the expanded version of the myth, profiting from it by selling a colored lithograph of the scene.

The source of this story is unclear. Jules Abels traces it to Edwin H. "Ned" House, "a highly imaginative reporter," whereas Boyd Stutler, a collector of Brown letters, and historian Richard O. Boyer both attribute it to Henry Steel Olcott, an assistant editor of the *Tribune,* who sought to sensationalize the Brown execution.[46] But all three agree that it did not, indeed could not, have taken place, because when Brown left the jail he was surrounded by soldiers and no civilians were near him. This is certainly a reasonable analysis of what appears to be an apocryphal story.

Yet another explanation of the story is at least plausible. Shortly after the execution, J. Miller McKim asked Charles G. Fulton of Baltimore to investigate what had actually happened. Fulton first discovered that a Dr. Rollings of the *Illustrated News* had said that "Capt. Brown had stopped on his way to the wagon to kiss a black child in a woman's arms."[47] This is essentially the same story attributed to Olcott and House. Rollings thus appears to be a third source for the myth.

However, Fulton did not end his investigation with Rollings. He also interviewed others who had been at the execution, and from these conversations he concluded that the story had some basis in fact. Fulton believed that Brown had kissed the child of a slave owned by the jailer, John Avis, before Brown actually left the jail. According to Fulton, this child "had frequently been in his cell" during his incarceration and that as he was leaving the jail Brown "stopped and bid her farewell and kissed the child." Fulton further reported that Captain Avis had told him that Brown had refused a minister at the scaffold and had declared he would "prefer to be summoned in his last moments by a poor weeping slave mother with her children." Avis quoted Brown as saying that this "would make the picture at the gallows complete."[48] Indeed, even before Fulton sent his report to McKim, others had quoted Brown as saying he did not want a minister present, but only a slave woman and her children. *The Liberator* reported that Brown had told Avis that instead of a minister he wanted to be followed to the place of execution by "a family of little negro children, headed by a pious slave mother."[49]

Fulton's explanation of the event is plausible. Brown was on surprisingly good terms with his jailer, Captain Avis, and it is reasonable to assume that if Avis had slaves they would have ambled in and out of the jail at will. Brown would certainly have come to know them in the month between his sentencing and execution. If Fulton's explanation is correct, then the reporting of the event was exaggerated, but not made up entirely out of whole cloth. Moreover, it seems likely that Brown did say he would prefer to be followed to the gallows by a slave mother and her children, for this would have been in keeping with his problack views and his hatred of ministers who supported slavery. It is not difficult to imagine how, in complete good faith, Brown's statement about a slave mother and her children following him to the gallows, combined with the possibility that he indeed kissed Avis's slave inside the jail, evolved into the story of his kissing a slave child in the jail yard.

Whatever actually happened, the picture painted by Phillips, Whittier, Redpath, and countless others was clearly distorted. It was, however, a picture that helped guarantee Brown's status as a martyr, especially as it was well suited to the sentimental tendencies of Victorian Americans. Furthermore, it served as a marvelous counterpoint to the grim note Brown had left the jailer, Avis, predicting that "the crimes of this *guilty, land: will* never be purged *away*, but with Blood." Thus, the violent and apocalyptic side of Brown (with which many abolitionists were never very comfortable) was juxtaposed against a softer, more romantic memory of the martyr. Lydia Maria Child, for instance, was overcome by the stories of his last moments. "There was nothing wanting in the *details* of his conduct. There was a grand simplicity and harmony throughout. I reverenced him for refusing to be prayed over by slave holding priests; and how my heart jumped toward him, when I read of his kissing the little colored child, on his way to the gallows."[50]

If the story of kissing the slave child presented a literary and apocryphal picture of Brown, real pictures—photographs, lithographs, and paintings — were also part of the process of ensuring Brown's martyrdom. Almost immediately after Brown's death Thomas Drew published a short volume on the raid that included a photograph of Brown. Drew happily noted that "the portrait which accompanies this work is pronounced by Captain Brown's New England friends as the best ever taken. It is lithographed by Bufford, in the very best style of the art, from a photograph by Whipple, and will be recognized by all who were familiar with the features of the original, as a faithful delineation of the features of him."[51] For Drew, who saw his publication as a profit-making venture, the picture was a major selling point of the book.

Others were interested in simply selling pictures of Brown and his family both for profit and to support Brown's widow and children. Even before the execution Thaddeus Hyatt realized that photographs of Brown might be sold to raise money for the family. Hyatt believed he could raise as much as $8,000 from the sale of Brown photographs, something Lydia Maria Child thought was "admirable" and would "prove highly successful." She wanted to purchase "every form of his likeness that can be devised, and have no corner of my dwelling without a memorial of him. The brave, self-sacrificing noble old man."[52] Other antislavery entrepreneurs sought photographs of Mary Brown, to be sold for the benefit of the widow. One businessman thought he could make hundreds or even thousands of dollars for Mary Brown through such an enterprise, while another did not predict how much would be made but did have the endorsement of the abolitionist leader Joshua Leavitt. By the spring of 1860 sales of pictures of Brown were brisk, with profits going to a John Brown Fund, set up to support his family. Supporters of Brown from Europe, as well as America, sought his portrait.[53] Before the end of 1859 a bust of Brown had been sculpted, and by July 1860 a painting of Brown "meeting the slave mother and child on the steps of the jail" was available for exhibition to raise funds for the artist and the Brown family.[54]

In addition to painters and photographers, public speakers and publishers also sought to keep Brown's memory alive. In late November someone whose wife made her living reading poetry asked Wendell Phillips to find a poem about Brown that could be read "throughout the free states," and suggested that Phillips get his "poetic friends in and around Boston" to compose the verses. A royalty would go to the author, and 20 percent of the "net proceeds" to Brown's widow. A few days before the execution a newspaper publisher offered five hundred dollars for the exclusive right to Brown's last written statement, the sum to be given directly to Mary Brown. In addition, he was willing to pay her expenses if she went to Virginia.

Reflecting the widespread desire to help Brown's widow and children—and at the same time the equally widespread belief that Mary Brown was incapable of managing her finances—the publisher suggested that the money be put into a fund to purchase a farm for the Brown family in order to guarantee their support.[55]

Writing the Gospel

He did not go to the college called Harvard, good old Alma Mater as she is. . . . But he went to the great university of the West, where is sedulously pursued the study of Liberty, for which he had early betrayed a fondness, and having taken many degrees, he finally commenced the public practice of Humanity in Kansas, as you all know. Such were *his humanities,* and not any study of grammar. He would have left a Greek accent slanting the wrong way, and righted up a falling man.

                                              Henry David Thoreau[56]

Ventures involving poems and portraits were only a small part of the movement to make use of Brown's death. Abolitionist papers carried stories about the whole experience for months after the executions of Brown and his comrades were over, but they had a relatively small circulation, and like all such newspapers, a relatively short life. The best way to keep the memory of the martyred Brown alive was through a volume about his life. Such a book could find its way into more Northern homes than would newspapers or photographs. Profits from it would, moreover, help support Brown's widow and children. For the antislavery movement there seems never to have been a question about whether such a volume should be written. The only question was who the author would be.

While Brown was in prison, Lydia Maria Child became involved in a letter-writing war with Governor Henry Wise and Margaretta J. (Chew) Mason, the wife of Senator James M. Mason of Virginia. Child asked Governor Wise for permission to visit Brown, because "he needs a mother and sister to dress his wounds, and speak soothingly to him." Although Wise consented to this, Brown himself would have no part of it. His lawyer wrote that Brown "*don't* want *women* there to unman his heroic determination to maintain a firm and consistent composure."[57] The tension between "manly" heroism and "feminine" sentimentality was clear—and yet both concepts were necessary for the creation of the myth of Brown.

Even though Child never visited Brown in jail, the *New York Tribune* published her letters to Brown and Wise, which brought great publicity to the cause of John Brown. In addition to sending these letters, she continued to speak and write on his behalf and to raise money for his family. Child was also involved in trying to bring Brown's body to Mt. Auburn Cemetery for burial. By December, Child was one of the most prominent people in the movement to aid Brown's family and keep Brown's memory alive. When she briefly left her home in December, she returned to find herself "perfectly overwhelmed with letters about John Brown from all parts of the country," managing in the next week to answer only thirty of the letters she had received.[58] All these activities convinced Child that she had not only the duty to write a biography of Brown but also the *right* to do so.

Thus, shortly after the execution Child decided to write a biography of Brown. Apparently she had the preliminary approval of Mary Brown, as well as the support of J. Miller McKim.[59] Such support was important for two reasons. First, Mary Brown had many of her husband's letters and papers, which were essential for the project. Second, without Mary Brown's approval, and the backing of her advisors among the antislavery leadership, the book would not be an authorized biography, and that might hurt sales.

By the end of November, however, Child had changed her mind. She told friends that James Redpath was already doing the same thing, "so I withdraw." This explanation was felt to be insufficient, and Child's friend Eliza Follen urged her to write a memoir of Brown in spite of Redpath's book.[60] But as Child later explained to the antislavery editor Sidney Howard Gay, this was not possible:

> I *intended* to write, and mentioned my intention to a few intimate friends. My motive was to help the families of the sufferers at Harper's Ferry, by giving the whole of the proceeds. Before I began to make arrangements, I was informed by a relative of John Brown that Redpath was already far advanced in the work, and that he was also doing it for the benefit of the family. Knowing him to be a personal friend of John Brown and his sons, and respecting him for the manly way in which he publicly stood by them at the first outbreak of this . . . affair I thought it would not be delicate for me to enter into competition with him. Moreover, he, being on the ground first, would necessarily exhaust the freshness of the facts, and satiate the curiosity to a degree that would injure the sale of a second book on the same subject. Therefore, as I had no other object but to benefit the family, I relinquished my project.[61]

Whether this is exactly what happened is not entirely clear. Apparently a number of antislavery leaders, including Wendell Phillips and George Stearns, convinced Mary Brown that James Redpath, and not Child, should write the biography of her husband. Mary Brown may also have concluded that whoever wrote a volume about her husband, it should not be Child.[62] Since Child was on excellent terms with Phillips and Stearns, the recommendation against her writing the book could hardly have been personal. It may have, however, been tied to issues of style and gender. Child's friend Eliza Follen urged her to write the book because "no *man* will do it as you will."[63] But this may have been precisely the problem. Brown was a man of action and violence. The sympathetic and sentimental Child, whose "heart jumped" at the thought of Brown kissing a slave child, hardly had the kind of temperament necessary to write about a man who had ordered the decapitation of Southerners in Kansas along the Pottawatomie Creek. Indeed, Brown had "reanimated the spirit of Yankee idealism by violence." Brown's raid "endowed antislavery with a virility that its long association with Sunday school ethics, missions to the 'heathen,' women's causes of temperance and equality, and the New England 'priestcraft' had seemed to deny." In doing so, he made it implausible that someone like Child, "a temperamental romantic,"[64] should write his biography.

Redpath, however, had been with Brown in Kansas and probably knew the truth about what happened at Pottawatomie Creek.[65] Child doubtless would have been horrified and repelled had she known of Brown's role in the massacre, but Redpath was not. For this reason alone he was probably better suited to write the "official" biography of Brown. He could easily ignore the truth about Pottawatomie, while at the same time not be upset by it.

Redpath also personally knew all the men connected with the Harpers Ferry Raid. In addition, he had recently published a book on slavery, *The Roving Editor: or Talks with Slaves in the Southern States* (1859), dedicated to "Captain John Brown, Senior, of Kansas." Shortly after the Harpers Ferry raid, Redpath had spoken out firmly and forcefully on Brown's behalf. He was one of the first antislavery men to declare Brown's raid a victory, because "his mission [was] to render slavery insecure," and this he certainly had done. As Redpath declared, "Never before, among modern nations, did seventeen men produce so terrible and universal a panic as Old Brown at Harper's Ferry." In this speech Redpath directly confronted the violence of the raid, which few in the abolitionist community were able to do. Redpath attacked the Virginians for "blowing off the face of a man who cried for quarter; the firing at a messenger protected by a flag of truce," and for "boxing up the body of the son of John Brown, to hurry it off to a medical dissection."[66] As the nation moved toward a violent civil war, Redpath seemed well equipped to write about the violence of fighting slavery.

Not surprisingly, perhaps, Mary Brown concluded that "there seemed to be no one else but Mr. Redpath."[67] But she may not have been happy with this result. Late in the book-writing process Mary Brown again sought to interest Child in doing a Brown biography. By this time there was also a story, circulating in antislavery newspapers, that Child had assembled a group of Brown documents in preparation for the biography but had somehow been convinced to give them to Redpath, who then wrote the biography of Brown using Child's materials.[68] Child, however, refused to consider starting a new Brown biography, even at Mary Brown's request. She may have been personally hurt by Mary Brown's vacillations and thus have wanted nothing further to do with the biography project. But Child may also have honestly felt that a second biography would be counterproductive. Child told Richard Hollowell, as she had told Sidney Howard Gay, that her only interest in the project had been to raise money for the Brown family. This she felt, would be accomplished by Redpath's book, and thus there was no need for her to write one.[69]

Child also noted that she initially abandoned the project "before I had begun to make the slightest arrangement" for the book, because she "was informed that Mr. Redpath was already writing it." It appears that whatever investment Child had in a Brown biography, that investment was one of emotion, rather than time and effort. Child further asserted that she acquiesced in Redpath authoring the book because she believed he had access to more information about Brown than she did. All she had was the information in the newspapers, "which were equally open" to Redpath, whereas Redpath "had the advantage of having been in Kansas with Capt. Brown and of being well posted in respecting *that* portion of his adventurous life." Child thus denied the newspaper stories to the effect that she had given all her Brown documents to Redpath, because she in fact "never *had* any." The only Brown letter Child had access to was one owned by her niece. When Redpath began his book, he asked Child to allow him to see this letter. "Knowing that Redpath was a friend of Capt. Brown and of his family," Child thought it would "not be delicate" to "stand in his way, especially as *he* also intended to write for the benefit of the family."[70]

Not everyone in the antislavery movement was happy with this result. Even as Redpath's book was in production J. Miller McKim expressed his lingering doubts about Redpath's "veracity" and asserted that "Mrs. Child was more competent than Mr. Redpath to write the book." McKim's views of Redpath were apparently no secret, and understandably Redpath was not pleased with them. Personalities, however, would not prevent McKim from selling Redpath's book through the antislavery office in Philadelphia, especially since Mary Brown would get a "large per centage of the profits."[71]

The Brown family cooperated with Redpath, who wrote the biography in great haste. Although there were "some mistakes" in the volume, Mary Brown thought it "done well" especially "considering the time he had to write it": the mistakes would be corrected in a later edition. In January 1860, with Redpath's book about to appear, Mary Brown wrote to McKim in hopes that he would overcome his differences with Redpath. While McKim had favored Child, Mary Brown pointed out to him that she had chosen Redpath on the advice of many abolitionists, including Child herself.[72]

Redpath's book, which appeared in early January 1860, was a huge success. There were over ten thousand prepublication sales in New England alone, and the book sold forty thousand copies in the first few months. By 1872 it was in its forty-first edition. Much of the royalties went to the Brown family, although some of the profits were used in the abortive plan to rescue the last of the convicted raiders. Money from later editions went to the John Brown Monument Fund.[73]

While denied the opportunity to write Brown's official biography, Lydia Maria Child nevertheless managed to contribute to the Brown family and the memory of her martyred hero. In 1860 she published the letters she had written to, and received from, Governor Wise and Margaretta Mason. Some three hundred thousand copies of this small volume were quickly sold, bringing money both to Child and to the Brown family. Child considered these letters to be her "most notable antislavery doings," in part because "they had an immense circulation all over the free states, and were blazoned by all manner of anathemas in the Southern papers."[74] It was not the money these letters earned that pleased Child. Rather, it was that the letters helped keep alive John Brown's memory.

"His Soul Goes Marching On"

He was one of that class of whom we hear a great deal, but, for the most part, see nothing at all—the Puritans. It would be in vain to kill him. He died lately in the time of Cromwell, but he reappeared here. Why should he not? Some of the Puritan stock are said to have come over and settled in New England. . . . They were neither Democrats nor Republicans, but men of simple habits and straightforward, prayerful; not thinking much of rulers who did not fear God, not making many compromises, nor seeking after available candidates.

Henry David Thoreau[75]

Despite the assertions of some historians, few American abolitionists devoted their energies "eagerly bidding for a martyr's crown," in hopes that they could convince their fellow citizens of the evils of slavery.[76] On the contrary, they were generally a hopeful, although sometimes naive, collection of reformers. They lived in an age of sentimental faith in humankind and progress. Many were pacifists and thus disinclined to advocate violence. They believed that reform could come peacefully, through moral suasion and agitation.

John Brown was in many ways like his fellow abolitionists. He quoted the Bible they knew and loved. Although his personal theology may have been a bit idiosyncratic, and unorthodox, he believed in a living God who would soon intervene on behalf of justice.[77] And, despite his rough demeanor, he understood sentimental approaches to reform. Nor, until the very end of his life, did he seek martyrdom. Indeed, his actions in Kansas and later at Harpers Ferry reveal a man determined to preserve his own life, even when it meant deliberately taking the lives of others: the executions at Pottawatomie Creek were not the work of men willing to accept martyrdom. Ultimately, too, it was miscalculation and a failure of Brown's own leadership, and not any prior design, that led to his capture at Harpers Ferry. Once captured, he simply used his position as best he could. He accepted martyrdom—indeed reveled in it—only when he saw that it was the only useful option he had. In other words, Brown allowed himself to become a martyr only when his death was inevitable.

The abolitionist movement likewise helped mold Brown into a martyr only when it became clear that there was no other alternative. Initially Brown's friends and backers had hoped for a rescue—but, this was impossible, a matter of wishful thinking.[78] Death seemed to be the *only* end for Brown. Martyrdom, then, was the only sensible course of action. Abolitionists accepted this and proceeded to act on it with skill and intelligence. In the space of a few weeks Brown evolved from an apparent madman to a martyred hero, being shaped in the image of Christ. Thus, as Frederick Douglass told his readers, "The Christian blood of Old John Brown will not cease to cry from the ground long after the clamors of alarm and consternation of the dealers in the bodies and souls of men will have ceased to arrest attention."[79]

The making of Brown into a martyr also required at least some understanding that he was, in very important ways, fundamentally different from other abolitionists, and also other martyred reformers. As Bertram Wyatt-Brown has observed, Americans have "ordinarily adopted peaceful means in dissent. Anti-institutional objectives and heretical ideas have usually taken rhetorical, religious, and pacifistic forms."[80] In this respect, Brown was different: he did not oppose violence and force, and he was willing to use such tactics to bring an end to bondage in America. His raid stunned the antislavery community, in part because Brown was not averse to violence and death, while most of his friends and backers were nonresistants and pacifists.

In many ways Brown was the harbinger of the future. He helped fuse the sentimentality of the antebellum age with the very unsentimental era that followed. In a very real sense, Brown prepared the antislavery movement for the shift from an age of Christian love and peace to one of Christian visions of an apocalypse and Old Testament notions of a vengeful God.[81] Within a year after the raid, for example, Wendell Phillips, always uncomfortable with nonresistance, moved in a new direction. Phillips collected "a bodyguard of young admirers like Oliver Wendell Holmes, Jr. (a distant relative), George W. Smalley, and [Thomas Wentworth] Higginson, who were joined by various militant blacks." A "neighborhood club of German" immigrants provided a full-time guard for his house. During this period "Phillips let everyone know that he now carried a gun," and one of his most prized possessions became a pike once owned by Owen Brown. With his pistol and Harper's Ferry pike, Phillips seemed to endorse the violence of John Brown with his deeds, just as he had in his speeches. Phillips characterized Brown a "regular Cromwellian, dug up" and the embodiment of "true manhood."[82] Now Phillips and other antislavery men and women began to emulate this "true manhood" by canonizing Brown, the apostle of a vengeful, Old Testament God.

Brown also forced William Lloyd Garrison, the apostle of nonresistance, to reconsider his position. At a meeting in Tremont Temple, Garrison endorsed slave rebellions and echoed Wendell Phillips's allusions to the American Revolution. In early December Garrison wrote: "Brand that man as a hypocrite and dastard, who, in one breath, exalts the deeds of Washington and Warren, and in the next, denounces Nat Turner as a monster for refusing longer to wear the yoke and be driven under the lash." He later declared, "Give me, as a non-resistant, Bunker Hill and Lexington and Concord rather than the cowardice and servility of a Southern slaveholder."[83]

Black abolitionists were more comfortable with Brown's violent legacy; "the Harpers Ferry affair had given a new vitality to the movement to bear arms." Blacks not only accepted but truly venerated Brown's martyrdom. They only wanted to make sure that his death would not ultimately be in vain. Responding to the question, "How shall American slavery be abolished?" Frederick Douglass declared, "The John Brown way."[84] As Daniel Littlefield notes in his essay in this volume, "Brown stood out because the others fought for white men, while he, a white man, had fought for blacks."

The refutation of Brown's alleged insanity was part of the process of realizing that violence might indeed be necessary to overcome slavery. Frederick Douglass, who had once fought the slave system quite literally with his bare hands, understood the use of force and violence when necessary. Thus he was particularly eloquent in fending off charges of Brown's insanity. As Douglass recognized, if Brown was viewed as insane, then he could not be a martyr. But, more important, Douglass understood that to use violence against slavery was not insane, although it was perhaps not always practical. For rhetorical purposes, Douglass called on Americans to consider their own heritage and to reject "the charge of insanity against a man who has imitated the heroes of Lexington, Concord, and Bunker Hill." Perhaps Douglass's greater insight into the importance of Brown's raid, however, was his realization that the age of sentimentality was over. "It is an effeminate and cowardly age," Douglass asserted, "which calls a man a lunatic because he rises to such self-forgetful heroism, as to count his own life worth nothing in comparison with the freedom of millions of his fellows."[85] Douglass understood that the age of heroism—a bloody and horrible heroism—was at hand.

By transforming Brown into a martyr, the antislavery movement helped prepare the North for a future that would create hundreds of thousands of martyrs. On the eve of the war Elizabeth Cady Stanton told the New York Anti-Slavery Society that she was prepared to "consecrate" her own five sons "to martyrdom, to die, if need be, bravely like a John Brown."[86] Indeed, hundreds of thousands of Northern mothers would soon see their sons die. Testimony to the success of those who venerated John Brown was heard when those same sons, resplendent in Union blue, marched off to war singing, "John Brown's body lies a-moulderin' in the grave, but his soul goes marching on."

Notes

I would like to thank Catherine Clinton, Seymour Drescher, Charles Joyner, Robert McGlone, James B. Stewart, Peter Wallenstein, Ronald Walters, and Bertram Wyatt-Brown for their comments on this article.

1. Stephen Vincent Benèt, *John Brown's Body* (1928; repr. New York, 1954), p. 52.
2. *The Liberator,* Oct. 21, 1859, p. 166.
3. David Davis to "Dear Son," Oct. 23, 1859, Davis Papers, Chicago Historical Society; see also Oates, *Purge,* p. 310. For the comment on Seward, see Lydia Maria Child to Lucy Osgood, Apr. 6, 1860, Box 1, Child Papers, Cornell University. Child did not blame Seward for his actions because she realized they were intended "obviously for purpose to fish for a nomination." But she did object to his praise for "that reprobate Daniel Webster." This, she felt, was going too far.
4. See Rossbach, *Conspirators,* pp. 223–28. The "Secret Six" were the Reverend Thomas Wentworth Higginson, Dr. Samuel Gridley Howe, the Reverend Theodore Parker, Franklin B. Sanborn, Gerrit Smith, and George L. Stearns.
5. George Putnam to Wendell Phillips, Nov. 1, 185[9], Box 24, Crawford Blagden Collection of the Papers of Wendell Phillips, Houghton Library, Harvard University, bMS Am 1953, quoted with the permission of Harvard Library (hereafter Phillips Papers).
6. George Putnam to Wendell Phillips, Nov. 9, 1859, Box 24, Phillips Papers.
7. Garrison writing in *The Liberator,* Oct. 28, 1959; Emerson quoted in Oates, *Purge,* p. 318.
8. Oates, *Purge,* p. 327.
9. William Lloyd Garrison to Oliver Johnson, Nov. 1, 1859, and Garrison to "An Unknown Correspondent," Dec. 18, 1859, both in Louis Ruchames, ed., *The Letters of William Lloyd Garrison,* 6 vols. (Cambridge, 1975), 4:660–61 and 664–65.
10. Greeley is quoted in Villard, *Biography,* p. 476, and see also pp. 559–60. For Andrew's comment, see [Thomas Drew], *The John Brown Invasion, an Authentic History of the Harper's Ferry Tragedy* (Boston, 1860), p. 97. See also Villard, *Biography,* pp. 559–60.

11. Benèt, *John Brown's Body,* p. 53.

12. "John Brown's Last Speech in Court, November 2, 1859," in Ruchames, ed., *Revolutionary,* p. 134.

13. William Henry Furness to "My Dear Friend" [J. Miller McKim?], Nov. 3, 1859, May-McKim Antislavery Papers, Cornell University (hereafter May-McKim Papers). For the minister's remarks, see William Henry Fish to Wendell Phillips, Box 13, Phillips Papers. Fish was the agent of the American Anti-Slavery Society for Cortland, New York: see *The Liberator,* Nov. 18, 1859.

14. John Brown to Jeremiah [Brown], Nov. 12, 1859, in Ruchames, ed., *Revolutionary,* p. 142.

15. Quoted in Oates, *Purge,* p. 344. See also the description of the Russell visit in Villard, *Biography,* pp. 545–46.

16. Indeed, numerous abolitionists, such as Calvin Fairbank, Thomas Brown, and Alanson Work, suffered virtually unknown in Southern prisons for helping slaves escape.

17. Benèt, *John Brown's Body,* p. 56.

18. Franklin Sanborn (writing under the alias Frederick Stanley) proposed a rescue to Wendell Phillips: [Sanborn] to Phillips, Oct. 22, 1859, Box 25, Phillips Papers. But this was only one of many plans. Among the more bizarre was the suggestion of Lysander Spooner that abolitionists kidnap Governor Henry Wise and exchange him for Brown. Other plans included an invasion of Charlestown to rescue Brown (see Boyer, *Legend,* pp. 16–18). Abolitionists were also concerned with the safety of those members of Brown's band who were not captured. On November 9, for example, J. Miller McKim received the cryptic telegraphic message: "Cotton has been sent," indicating that some of the conspirators had arrived safely in the North. Later in the month George H. Hoyt, who served as Brown's attorney, reported that Barclay Coppoc had been sent to Canada and that Owen Brown was safely in Ohio, although at the time Hoyt did not know the whereabouts of Charles Plummer Tidd. See the telegram of J. W. L. Barnes to J. Miller McKim, Nov. 9, 1859; and George H. Hoyt to "My dear Friend" [McKim], Nov. 18, 1859, both in May-McKim Papers.

After Brown's execution two of the jail conspirators, Edwin Coppoc and John E. Cook, did escape but were caught. Their escape was planned by a friend who became a prison guard in order to help them. Thomas Wentworth Higginson also planned a small invasion of Virginia to rescue two others, Aaron Dwight Stevens and Albert Hazlett. Although a considerable number of men were armed and brought to Pennsylvania, weather conditions combined with the rough terrain of the region made the rescue impossible, and reluctantly those involved abandoned the project. See Villard, *Biography,* pp. 570–80.

19. Quoted in Villard, *Biography,* p. 546. On Brown's decision to embrace martyrdom, see Rossbach, *Conspirators,* pp. 223–35.

20. James Redpath to Thomas Wentworth Higginson, Nov. 13, 1859, quoted in Rossbach, *Conspirators,* p. 226.

21. George E. Baker to Gerrit Smith, Oct. 22, 1859, Box 2, Gerrit Smith Papers, Syracuse University; Theodore Tilton to Wendell Phillips, Oct. 25, 1859, Box 30, Phillips Papers.

22. Wendell Phillips, *The Lesson of the Hour: Lecture of Wendell Phillips Delivered at Brooklyn, N.Y., Tuesday Evening, November 1, 1859* (n.p., [1859]), pp. 20–21.

23. Joseph Seldon to Wendell Phillips, Nov. 2, 1859, Box 26, Phillips Papers; William Henry Fish to Phillips, Nov. 2, 1859, Box 13, Phillips Papers. Similar comments on Phillips's speech can be found elsewhere in the Phillips Papers: see W. W. Wright to Phillips, Nov. 13, 1859, Box 33; H. Stredit to Phillips, Nov. 14, 1859, Box 29; and George Sterling to Phillips, Nov. 19, 1859, Box 29.

24. *The Liberator,* Nov. 4, 1859. See also William Lloyd Garrison to Oliver Johnson, Nov. 1, 1859, in Ruchames, ed., *Letters of William Lloyd Garrison,* 4:660–61.

25. See Villard, *Biography,* pp. 560–61; Oates, *Purge,* pp. 353–55.

26. Nathaniel Hall, "The Man,—The Deed,—The Event: A Sermon Preached in the First Church, Dorchester, On Sunday, December 4, and Repeated December 11, 1859," in Nathaniel Hall, *Two Sermons on Slavery and Its Hero-Victim* (Boston, 1859), p. 23; William W. Patton, *The Execution of John Brown: A Discourse, Delivered at Chicago, December 4th, 1859, in the First Congregational Church* (Chicago, [1859]), pp. 5 and 10.

27. For example, see *Great Union Meeting of Philadelphia, December 7, 1859* (Philadelphia, 1859); *Report of the Proceedings Connected with the Great Union Meeting Held at the Academy of Music, New York, December 19th, 1859* (New York, 1859). For more discussion of the Northern reaction against Brown, see Peter Knupfer's "A Crisis in Conservatism: Northern Unionism and the Harpers Ferry Raid," in this volume.

28. Benèt, *John Brown's Body,* p. 58.

29. Henry Clarke Wright to Wendell Phillips, Nov. 19, 1859, Box 33, Phillips Papers.

30. Ibid.

31. W. J. Jarvis to Wendell Phillips, [Nov. 30, 1859], Box 18, Phillips Papers.

32. Lydia Maria Child to David Lee Child, Dec. 5, 1859, Box 1, Child Papers, Cornell University.

33. Mary Brown to Edward Fitch Bullard, Jan. 24, 1860, as copied by Bullard in his letter to "Mrs. Parsons," Apr. 30, 1881, May-McKim Papers.

34. The text of Phillips's eulogy can be found in Ruchames, ed., *Revolutionary,* pp. 266–67; his speech comparing Lovejoy to Warren is available in Wendell Phillips, *The Freedom Speech of Wendell Phillips, Faneuil Hall, December 8, 1837* (Boston, 1890), and in Wendell Phillips, *Speeches, Lectures, and Letters* (Boston, 1881), pp. 1–10.

35. William Lloyd Garrison to J. Miller McKim, Dec. 17, 1859, in Ruchames, ed., *Letters of William Lloyd Garrison,* 4:663. Gerrit Smith and his secretary, George Putnam, were also pleased that Phillips accompanied Brown's body and Mrs. Brown to North Elba: see Putnam to Phillips, Jan. 19, 1860, Box 24, Phillips Papers. For Phillips's reaction, see James B. Stewart, *Wendell Phillips, Liberty's Hero* (Baton Rouge, 1986), p. 203.

36. Thaddeus Hyatt to Wendell Phillips, Dec. 5, 1859, Box 17, Phillips Papers.

37. Thaddeus Hyatt to Wendell Phillips, Dec. 7, 1859, Box 17, Phillips Papers.

38. James W. Pine to Wendell Phillips, Dec. 22, 1859, Box 23, Phillips Papers.

39. George L. Stearns to Miller McKim, Dec. 15, 1859, May-McKim Papers. Stearns referred to these men as "Garner" and Copeland, but undoubtedly meant Green by the former.

40. A. M. Green, J. P. Campbell, and Jeremiah Asher to Governor Henry Wise, Dec. 3, 1859; letter reprinted in *The Liberator,* Dec. 23, 1859, p. 203.

41. *John Brown Year,* pp. 137–38.

42. Benèt, *John Brown's Body,* p. 56.

43. *New York Tribune,* Dec. 5, 1859, p. 8; Abels, *Man on Fire,* pp. 367–68.

44. John Greenleaf Whittier, "Brown of Osawatomie," reprinted in Ruchames, ed., *Reader,* p. 295; Lydia Maria Child, "The Hero's Heart," reprinted in Richard D. Webb, ed., *The Life and Letters of Captain John Brown* (London, 1861), pp. 317–18.

45. See [Drew], *John Brown Invasion,* p. 67. (Although the volume was published in 1860, Drew finished his book in December, 1859.) For Redpath's comments, see Redpath, *Public Life,* p. 397. The story was also repeated by the American Anti-Slavery Society in its annual report (*John Brown Year,* p. 127) and, with the additions by Redpath, in Webb, ed., *Life and Letters of Captain John Brown,* pp. 317–18.

46. Abels, *Man on Fire,* p. 368; Richard O. Boyer to Velma W. Sykes, March 13, 1973, Sykes Papers, Library of Congress.

47. Charles G. Fulton to J. Miller McKim, Dec. 14, 1859, May-McKim Papers.

48. Quoted in ibid.

49. *The Liberator,* Dec. 12, 1859, p. 195.

50. Brown's final written statement is in the John Brown Papers, Chicago Historical Society. The full text reads: "Charlestown, Va, 2d, December 1859. I John Brown am now quite *certain* that the crimes of this *guilty, land: will* never be purged *away,* but with Blood. I had *as I now think: vainly* flattered myself that without *very much* bloodshed; it might be done." For Child's comments, see Lydia Maria Child to Sarah Maria Parsons, Dec. 25, 1859, Box 1, Child Papers, Cornell University. She later published a poem about the incident, "The Hero's Heart."

51. [Drew], *John Brown Invasion,* [p. 3].

52. Lydia Maria Child to "Peter and Susie" [J. Peter Lesley and Susan (Lyman) Lesley], Nov. 20, 1859; Child to Thaddeus Hyatt, Nov. 17, 1859, in Child, *Correspondence,* 1137, 1138.

53. See Dr. D. F. Brown to Mrs. John Brown, sent in care of J. Miller McKim, Nov. 22, 1859; Joshua Leavitt to Morris Spring, Esq., Nov. 17, 1859; J. K. Ingalls to J. Miller McKim, May 7, 1860; and Mary Ireland to J. Miller McKim, Belfast, Ireland, Apr. 26, 1860, all in May-McKim Papers. See also Hazel Catherine Wolf, *On Freedom's Altar: The Martyr Complex in the Abolition Movement* (Madison, 1952), pp. 128–29.

54. See Wolf, *On Freedom's Altar,* pp. 128–29; Louis Ransome to Wendell Phillips, July 5, 1860, and Sept. 15, 1860, both in Phillips Papers. Interest in Brown portraits continued after the Civil War began. In 1864 Washington G. Snethen, an antislavery legal scholar, came upon two pencil sketches of Brown and one of his sons, allegedly drawn by John E. Cook, one of those hanged after the Harpers Ferry raid. Snethen declared that "no gold could buy [the pictures] were they mine," but unfortunately they belonged to his publisher. He hoped Phillips could arrange for their purchase by a public gallery, if indeed they were authentic. See Washington G. Snethen to Wendell Phillips, June 11, 1864, Phillips Papers.

55. On the poem, see George Roberts to Wendell Phillips, Nov. 23, 1859, Phillips Papers; for the publisher's proposal, see Marcus Spring to J. Miller McKim, Nov. 29, 1859, May-McKim Papers.

56. Henry David Thoreau, *A Plea for Captain John Brown: Read to the Citizens of Concord, Massachusetts, on Sunday Evening, October Thirtieth, Eighteen Hundred Fifty-Nine* (Boston, 1969), p. 3.

57. Quoted in Villard, *Biography,* pp. 479–80. Brown suggested that Child "might instead 'give 50 cents to his wife and three daughters'" (quoted in Quarles, *Allies,* p. 144).

58. Lydia Maria Child to Edward Fitch Bullard, Dec. 19, 1859, and Child to Lucy Osgood, Dec. 25, 1859, both in Child Papers, Cornell University.

59. Mary Brown to J. Miller McKim, March 6, 1860; McKim to Mrs. John Brown, Jan. 2, 1860, both in May-McKim Papers.

60. Lydia Maria Child to "Peter and Susie" [J. Peter Lesley and Susan (Lyman) Lesley], Nov. 20, 1859, and Eliza Lee Follen to Child, Dec. 7, 1859, in Child, *Correspondence,* 1138 and 1144.

61. Lydia Maria Child to Sidney Howard Gay, Dec. 25, 1859, in Child, *Correspondence,* 1162.

62. Mary Brown to J. Miller McKim, March 6, 1860, May-McKim Papers.

63. Eliza Lee Follen to Lydia Maria Child, Dec. 7, 1859, in Child, *Correspondence,* 1144.

64. Wyatt-Brown, "Antinomian," p. 125; the phrase "a temperamental roman-

tic" is used by Blanche Glassman Hersh, *The Slavery of Sex: Feminist-Abolitionists in America* (Urbana, Ill.: 1978), p. 12.

65. Brown steadfastly denied responsibility for the Pottawatomie massacre, and his supporters accepted his stance without question. Likewise, all of the early, sympathetic biographers of Brown either believed this to be true, or like Redpath, who should have known the truth, fudged the issue. But Brown's denials were in fact equivocal: "I did not do it," he declared, "but I approved of it." Whether he was actually the executioner will never be known; if he was not, then that dubious title falls to his sons, Salmon and Owen. But no one doubts that Brown was in command at the time. (See Wyatt-Brown, "Antinomian," pp. 118–19.) Within two weeks after the execution, a Broadway play, *Ossawattomie Brown,* appeared, which blamed the Pottawatomie massacre on Brown's enemies (Abels, *Man on Fire,* p. 390).

66. Redpath speech, reprinted in *The Liberator,* Nov. 4, 1859, p. 173.

67. Mary Brown to J. Miller McKim, March 6, 1860, May-McKim Papers.

68. Lydia Maria Child to Richard P. Hollowell, [Dec. 19, 1859], copied into a letter of Hollowell to Mrs. John Brown, Jan. 4, 1860, copy in May-McKim Papers. The contents of this Child letter áre *not* part of the Child microfiche collection (Child, *Correspondence*).

69. Ibid.

70. Ibid.

71. J. Miller McKim to Mrs. Mary Brown, Jan. 2, 1860, May-McKim Papers.

72. Mary A. Brown to J. Miller McKim, Jan. 10, 1860, May-McKim Papers. On the Brown family's cooperation, see Annie Brown to J. Miller McKim, Dec. 27, 1859, May-McKim Papers. In this letter John Brown's daughter described Mrs. Redpath's visit to North Elba, collecting documents for her husband's book. Annie Brown found no fault with Mrs. Redpath, except that "she used a good deal too much of that abominable stuff called flattery." See also Mary Brown's same letter to McKim.

73. *The Liberator,* Dec. 23, 1859, p. 202; Redpath, *Public Life,* preface to 41st ed. (Sandusky, Ohio: 1872), p. 5; Villard, *Biography,* p. 573.

74. Lydia Maria Child, *Correspondence between Lydia Maria Child, Governor Wise, and Mrs. Mason* (Boston, 1860). See also Milton Meltzer et al., eds., *Lydia Maria Child: Selected Letters, 1817–1880* (Amherst, Mass.: 1982), pp. 332–33, and Child to Samuel J. May, Sept. 29, 1867, in Child, *Correspondence,* 1794.

75. Thoreau, *A Plea for Captain John Brown,* pp. 3–4.

76. Wolf, *On Freedom's Altar,* p. 4, takes the opposite position.

77. On Brown's unorthodox theological stance, see Wyatt-Brown, "Antinomian," pp. 118–20.

78. Some of the more fanciful schemes, including Lysander Spooner's suggestion that abolitionists kidnap Virginia Governor Henry Wise, are discussed in Rossbach, *Conspirators,* pp. 230–35.

79. Frederick Douglass, "To My American Readers and Friends," *Douglass' Monthly,* November 1859, reprinted in Philip S. Foner, ed., *The Life and Writings of Frederick Douglass,* 5 vols. (New York: 1950–75, 2:464. For a discussion of Brown and insanity, see Robert McGlone, "John Brown, Henry Wise, and the Politics of Insanity," in this volume.

80. Wyatt-Brown, "Antinomian," p. 98.

81. As Wyatt-Brown has noted, "Only John Brown actually brought insurrectionary action and antinomian ideals together as a conscious, aggressive, and dynamic part of the abolitionist movement" (ibid., p. 103).

82. Quoted in James Brewer Stewart, *Wendell Phillips, Liberty's Hero* (Baton Rouge, 1986), pp. 206–7. See also pp. 214–15.

83. Quoted in Quarles, *Allies,* p. 152, and in Abels, *Man on Fire,* p. 385.

84. See Quarles, *Allies,* pp. 155–56; Douglass is quoted at p. 156.

85. Douglass, "Capt. Brown Not Insane," *Douglass' Monthly,* November 1859, reprinted in Foner, ed., *Life and Writings of Frederick Douglass,* 2:458. Others made similar observations about the spirit of the age. As Francis Lieber wrote a friend, "Brown died like a man and Virginia fretted like an old woman" (quoted in Abels, *Man on Fire,* p. 379).

86. Hersh, *Slavery of Sex,* p. 100.

3

DANIEL C. LITTLEFIELD

Blacks, John Brown,
and a Theory of Manhood

No EVENT OF A SIMILAR nature for many years had produced a more marked sensation," the *Weekly Anglo-African* reported concerning the December 2, 1859, response of Boston blacks to the execution of John Brown. "Most of the colored men closed their places of business, and many wore crape on their arms, rosettes in mourning, &c. It was also observed as a day of fasting, prayer and religious worship." The Twelfth Baptist Church on Southac Street had three services that day, in the morning, afternoon, and evening. Blacks in Pittsburgh, closing their businesses between ten and three, convened for worship at eleven o'clock at the African Methodist Episcopal Church. They met again that evening.[1] The fiery and controversial Reverend Henry Highland Garnet, described by one newspaper as having done more than anyone else "to excite the colored people at the North," presided over services in New York's Shiloh Church. He decreed that henceforth "the Second day of December will be called 'MARTYR'S DAY,'" a suggestion other congregations embraced.[2]

There were also public, interracial gatherings. An evening meeting at Tremont Temple attracted hundreds and "was probably the largest gathering of the kind ever held in Boston." Cleveland's Melodeon Hall hosted its own commemoration, attracting an audience "considerably checkered—alternate black and white, like the finger-board upon a piano." And solemn congregations in Poughkeepsie's two black churches did not prevent "a large number of colored persons" from also attending a meeting at Concert Hall. Hartford, Connecticut, sponsored no public ceremonies, though the dull, hazy morning accurately captured the gloomy sentiments of most of the seven hundred blacks there. A black man hired to drape City Hall's figure of justice in mourning during the night was discovered and the black suit removed.[3]

John Brown's attack on Harpers Ferry galvanized the nation and captured the particular imagination of blacks. Beyond its immediate significance, however, this bold act capped nearly three decades of tensions between black and white abolitionists, and within the black community itself, about widely held views of race and slavery and about the relationship between manhood and violence. If, as Merton Dillon argues, abolitionists, who had once pictured blacks as "fierce, wronged warriers about to break their bonds," transformed them in the years after 1830 into "pathetic, helpless victims" in need of white benevolence, it was an image clearly at odds with the prospect of their assuming the "manly" duties and obligations of citizenship.[4]

Brown's raid took place in a culture that equated boldness and heroic violence with masculinity.[5] It was a culture, moreover, that had a racial bias. It claimed as racial traits the qualities of boldness, violence, and masculinity, and the capacity for self-government necessary to citizenship. The Unitarian minister and militant abolitionist Theodore Parker expressed this conceptual nexus in prideful speeches and sermons throughout his career.[6] The Anglo-Saxon, Parker wrote in 1854, was noted for "his restless disposition to invade and conquer other lands; his haughty contempt of humbler tribes which leads him to subvert, enslave, kill, and exterminate; his fondness for material things, preferring these to beauty; his love of personal liberty, yet coupled with most profound respect for peaceful and established law; his inborn skill to organize things to a mill, men to a company, a community, tribes to a confederated state; and his slow, solemn, inflexible, industrious, and unconquerable will." These characteristics were not all laudable but, withal, he thought, Anglo-Saxons were "the best specimen of mankind . . . in the world."[7]

In contrast, most white Americans, including abolitionists, viewed the black, in George M. Fredrickson's words, as an "inept creature who was a slave to his emotions, incapable of progressive development and self-government" and lacking "the white man's enterprise and intellect."[8] The preeminence of emotion over intellect was not necessarily bad, however. Nineteenth-century romantic racialists believed that each of the various ethnicities, nationalities, or racial groups—they seldom distinguished among these concepts precisely—had its own peculiar gift to contribute to the human family: its own "genius" or national character. That of blacks was sensuality, sensitivity, gentleness, deep feeling, and an extraordinary capacity for forgiveness and long-suffering. "Even [in his] wild state," Parker assured the Massachusetts Anti-Slavery Society in 1858, the African was "not much addicted to revenge."[9] This characterization, as Dillon suggests, was at odds with an earlier, eighteenth-century view of blacks as potentially violent savages, quick to take offense, and prone to pitiless retaliation.[10] In some ways and places this view still abided in the nineteenth century, sometimes dormant, lurking below the surface but liable to resurrection when it suited the needs or fears of slavery's supporters or opponents. Its survival created an underlying tension in the thinking of white people toward blacks (and, indeed, in attitudes of blacks about themselves), thereby complicating an already confused mix of ideas. But the prevailing conviction regarding black docility, ironically appropriated partly from proslavery literature in the service of antislavery, fit the requirements of a romantic age that, in contrast to eighteenth-century rationalism, elevated heart over head.[11]

The attributes assigned to blacks were also applied to women, and blacks and women were thus equated. "In all the intellectual activities which take their strange quickening from the moral faculties—which we call instincts, intuitions," one booster commented, "the negro is superior to the white man—equal to the white woman. It is sometimes said—that the negro race is the feminine race of the world."[12] Under the best of circumstances, some thought (Parker among them), blacks' essentially soft, feminine characteristics might counter the hard, masculine traits of Anglo-Saxons in America. In particular, blacks, like women, were considered more susceptible to Christianity, a great virtue among reformers who based their appeal on Christian morality. But abolitionists were not consistent. While they argued that blacks and whites diverged in sensibilities, it was essential to their cause that they also portray blacks as no different from white people—in aims, aspirations, emotions, perhaps even capabilities—if they were to evoke among whites adequate sympathy for the plight of the slave. Thus, when a black abolitionist accused Parker of accepting the stereotype of the meek black, Parker responded with an expression of faith: he fondly hoped that blacks would rise and achieve "their freedom by the only method which the world thoroughly and heartily accepts, and that is, by drawing the sword and cleaving the oppressor from his crown to his groin, until one half falls to the right, and the other half falls to the left." "I have said many times," Parker concluded, "I thought the African would not be content to be a slave always; I wish he would not a single day more."[13]

Because Brown's raid dealt with slavery, and involved African Americans as well as whites, it inevitably served as a lens through which whites and blacks alike would perceive black masculinity. It was, however, an imperfect lens: rather than clarify views of black manhood, the raid revealed fissures both in the ideology of race and masculinity and in alliances between black and white abolitionists. Indeed, the admiration some blacks had for Brown may well have masked, or mystified, the involvement of their own race in the raid and the availability of other models of black masculinity, ranging from romantic racialist ones of Jesus-like forbearance, at one extreme, to the vengeful image of Nat Turner at the other.

From the Atlantic to the Pacific, blacks held meetings in Brown's honor. They compared him to the great captains of history, like Oliver Cromwell, and to revolutionary patriots, like George Washington. For some who knew him he was an angel "entertained unawares"; for others he was a John the Baptist or a Jesus Christ; and for some he was a model without peer or precedent. When blacks compared him to men of the revolutionary generation, however, they often introduced a racial dimension. Brown stood out because the others fought for white men, while he, a white man, had fought for blacks.[14]

The revolutionary comparison also introduced the issue of violence itself, for many abolitionists, white and black, were nonresistants—Christian anarchists and pacifists who believed any force, even that exercised by governments, to be immoral. One might argue that this ideological outlook was stronger among whites than among blacks. But for those who followed the most prominent white abolitionist of the age, William Lloyd Garrison— whose devotion to the cause blacks had little reason to doubt—it was an anchor of the philosophical platform that governed their activities, and the abolitionist movement was one of the few contexts in which blacks and whites could normally cooperate.[15] Baptist minister and former fugitive J. Sella Martin therefore cautiously broached an opinion in Boston, Garrison's stronghold, and in Garrison's presence, that could have sparked controversy. Denying any senseless feeling of rage, he nevertheless declared that, with respect to Harpers Ferry, he was "prepared, in the light of all human history, to approve of the *means*" as "in the light of all Christian principle, to approve of the *end*." In his view, Fourth-of-July orators sanctioned both. Moreover, he found "an endorsement of John Brown's course in the large assembly" who had gathered to lament his execution. "I look at this question as a peace man. I say, in accordance with the principles of peace, that I do not believe the sword should be unsheathed, I do not believe the dagger should be drawn, until there is in the system to be assailed such terrible evidences of its corruption, that it becomes the *dernier resort*. And, my friends, we are not to blame the application of the instrument, we are to blame the disease itself. . . . So John Brown chose the least of two evils. To save the country, he went down to cut off the Virginia cancer."[16] Applauded, Martin evoked no dispute. Garrison responded by distancing himself from some of Brown's sentiments and by arguing that Brown intended a peaceful mission to Virginia. He alluded perhaps to Brown's last speech before the court, in which Brown alleged that he had never intended insurrection or to arm slaves against their masters. He had intended, Brown said, merely to run slaves off to freedom in Canada as he had done in Kansas—a statement he later repudiated.[17] Yet, Garrison concluded, "If a tax on tea justified revolution, did not the souls of men and women?" Garrison was a man of peace and a nonresistant; still, he was "emboldened to say success to every insurrection against slavery, here and elsewhere."[18]

Ironically, the militant Henry Highland Garnet, whose 1843 call upon the slaves to rise had split the Colored Convention in Buffalo, New York (and, incidentally, had also influenced John Brown) adopted a more moderate tone at the Shiloh Church in 1859. He was "not a man of blood," held "human life to be sacred, and would spare even a man-stealer, if he stood not in the bondman's path to freedom." But his hope that slavery would end peacefully was "clouded," and he was full of praise for John Brown.[19] Blacks in Providence, Rhode Island, resolved on similar praise.[20]

Yet some expressed greater ambivalence. Albany's blacks admitted disagreement as to the wisdom of Brown's actions while lauding his intentions. In New Bedford, Massachusetts, one minister supported resolutions endorsing Brown but demurred from his "fanaticism." The following speaker, however, pointedly "ignored the idea that John Brown was a fanatic, and compared him with the martyrs, who in ancient times had laid down their lives for Christ's sake." But at Garnet's meeting in New York the disagreement was less subtle:

> Rev. Wm. Goodell was introduced, and expressed himself encouraged by the signs of the times—lauded John Brown's zeal, but deprecated physical force. This exception called to his feet Rev. J. N. Gloucester, who eloquently endorsed Mr. Brown's course. Mr. Goodell replied, "Our weapons are not carnal—our means are moral, ecclesiastical and religious." Rev. Sampson White asked, "Why do we venerate the name of George Washington? In the struggle of release from what was termed English oppression, did the advocates of American liberty take the position, 'our weapons are not carnal'? Not at all—but 'Resistance to tyrants is obedience to God' was their motto. I have an arm—God has given me power, and whenever and wherever my God given rights are invaded, I shall feel it my duty to use it."[21]

In grappling with the necessity of using violence to end slavery, blacks were going against two distinct strains of American political and social thought prominent among their allies and others: the Garrisonian idea that moral suasion alone was sufficient to bring slavery to its knees, making bloodshed not only objectionable but unnecessary; and the romantic, racialist notion that blacks by temperament and outlook were docile and unsuited to violent protest. Blacks were probably less inclined to accept the latter belief anyway, but they were attracted to the militant abolitionism of the 1830s because it furnished one of the few avenues through which their frustrations with American society could be channeled. It also provided a context within which they could cooperate with white supporters who believed that both slavery and black citizenship were moral issues on which the nation ought not to compromise.

But the alliance was not without conflict. In making slavery a moral issue, white abolitionists often adopted an idealism that made them less practical than their black counterparts. White abolitionists tended to be concerned with ethical concepts, whereas black abolitionists wanted concrete progress. Consequently, blacks were more willing to take pragmatic steps toward achieving their goals rather than (to mix a metaphor) insisting on the whole loaf or nothing. Some of the differences derived from divergent views of slavery and freedom. For whites, slavery and freedom were opposites to which they attached absolute value judgments: the one was bad; the other good. For blacks, however, slavery and freedom were relative concepts. Their American experience had conditioned them to perceive a continuum between the two: degrees of freedom and degrees of slavery. A favored slave might have a great deal of liberty within the institution of slavery, while, because of discrimination, most free blacks still suffered many of the ill effects of slavery even in freedom. Whites focused their attack on slavery; blacks desired an assault on prejudice and discrimination as well. In theory, white abolitionists agreed, but since prejudice and discrimination existed in their own ranks—sometimes recognized, sometimes not—they could not entirely see eye to eye with blacks. Many whites viewed abolition either as the culmination of their fight, thus ignoring slavery's complexities and underestimating its ramifications, or as part of a grander struggle for freedom, including temperance and gender discrimination, thereby deemphasizing its importance. "One group saw slavery too narrowly," Ronald G. Walters comments; "the other almost missed seeing it for looking too widely." More intimately involved with the institution, blacks had greater singleness of purpose, and they saw a connection between slavery and prejudice. Most blacks regarded abolition as only the beginning of struggle, so long as their social proscription continued. White abolitionists often seemed more worried about their own souls than about the slave, a luxury that black abolitionists could not afford. For whites slavery was an abstraction; for blacks it was a reality.[22]

White abolitionists also tended toward arrogance and paternalism. They told blacks to adopt the puritan ethic, to work hard, to be industrious and accumulate property, but then condemned black attempts to reap the rewards of hard work. Any concern that blacks had for material well-being white abolitionists criticized as cheap, tawdry, and self-seeking. Thus, for example, when white abolitionist Sarah Grimké visited black abolitionist Samuel Cornish, who had a respectable middle-class home, she condemned it as "like the abode of sanctimonious pride and pharisaical aristocracy." Another white abolitionist who visited Cornish came away with the same opinion.[23] These and other incidents revealed the extent to which many white abolitionists objectified blacks, rather than treating them as ordinary human beings with interests similar to those of white people. Increasingly, therefore, blacks began to form their own separate institutions or organizations to deal with issues that peculiarly affected them. Indeed, anticipating the course of black militants in the late 1960s, Cornish suggested that whites work within the abolitionist movement to abolish slavery while blacks worked in their own societies to end discrimination.[24] Blacks sought to secure economic opportunity, promote social mobility, acquire the franchise, and ensure civil rights, as well as to establish black identity. They rejected white abolitionists' condemnation of independent black activity as racist, although the issue caused dissension among blacks, too.[25]

Black separatism, of course, did not necessarily mean lack of respect for white efforts. Blacks' perspectives embraced variant visions for black liberation, particularly if the stance was aggressive, and such stances were few and far between. Thus black intellectual John S. Rock announced: "The only events in the history of this country which I think deserve to be commemorated are the organization of the Anti-Slavery Society and the insurrections of Nat Turner and John Brown."[26] Consequently, even when they disagreed with him, blacks endorsed Garrison and his brand of abolitionism. They applauded his condemnation of colonization. They supported his newspaper. Blacks in Philadelphia praised Garrison in 1851 for having "pointed out to us the hope of immediate and unconditional liberty." Likewise, blacks in Boston and New York held memorial services to eulogize white, antislavery editor Elijah P. Lovejoy after an antiabolitionist mob killed him in Alton, Illinois, in 1837. Blacks lauded white abolitionists who spoke before a Massachusetts legislative committee opposing slavery in the District of Columbia. And Samuel Cornish addressed delegates to a meeting of the American Anti-Slavery Society in 1838 as "wise men of the nation . . . great and good men . . . the salt of the earth, the leaven which preserves our nation, morally and politically, and which will wipe off America's reproach and eventually be America's glory."[27]

But blacks were caught between conflicting loyalties when, in the 1840s, white abolitionists split among themselves. Garrison and his supporters wanted radical reforms that went well beyond the simple abolition of slavery: they desired fundamental changes in society and government. They rejected political action, disdained organized religion, and sought to depend solely on moral suasion to bring about a series of interrelated reforms, including temperance and women's rights. Garrison's opponents, centering around the wealthy Tappan brothers (Arthur and Lewis) of New York, were more conservative. They adopted a more pragmatic approach, fearing that agitation for women's rights and other such issues would deflect the

movement from its primary goal. They also made use of established religious organizations and the existing political system. The dispute was as
much about factional influence as about strategic ordering or fidelity to
principle, however, each side accusing the other of similar misdeeds.

As conflict between the two factions became more vicious, blacks increasingly saw the arguments as needlessly splitting the group on which
they had placed their best hopes. In their view, the dispute was beside the
point. As John Lewis, of New Hampshire, wrote his local Garrisonian society in 1840, "As a colored man, and a representative of my people, I feel it
a duty to make the advocacy of the [antislavery] cause the paramount question." He indicated that he would no longer attend meetings to debate
divisive issues, though he would still be available for antislavery lectures.
But Garrisonians, failing to recognize the point, criticized him as hungry
for publicity.[28]

In the 1840s, then, many blacks adopted a more militant and separatist
bent; and the Fugitive Slave Act and Dred Scott Decision of the 1850s—the
one facilitating slave recapture and the other declaring that blacks were not
United States citizens—caused despair and disillusionment among even the
most optimistic. Despite their general regard for Garrison, many deserted
his standard. Several went so far as to consider emigration—for reasons
other than the legislative compromise that caused many fugitives to flee
the threat of reenslavement. Legislation passed during the 1850s reinforced
the perception of many of the need for a distinct black nationality. Even
Frederick Douglass, who stood against the tide of radicalism in the 1840s,
broke with Garrison at the end of the decade. A staunch integrationist,
Douglass himself flirted ever so briefly with emigration in 1861. The mood
of impatience among blacks was something that John Brown perceived.
After all, he had black friends and associates, and he read and contributed
to black newspapers.[29]

Oswald Garrison Villard, grandson of the abolitionist and Brown's first
serious biographer, argued that Brown "was by nature unable to sympathize with the Garrisonian doctrine of non-resistance to force" and by the
1850s was "all impatience with men who only talked and would not
shoot."[30] Nor was Brown the only white man to be pushed toward action in
the decade of conflict before the Civil War. The strife in Kansas during the
middle of the decade caused restlessness even among some who retained a
theoretical commitment to nonviolence. Political conditions drove romantic racialists among the "Secret Six" who supported Brown's activist stance
to forsake their avowed devotion to pacifism. They were willing to test the
efficacy of violence among blacks as a way to resolve their conflicting views
to the effect that force was not a natural part of blacks' makeup but that
they would not be worthy of citizenship without this capacity.[31] Blacks

themselves occasionally accepted elements of romantic racialist thought, a black correspondent referring to one of Brown's colored companions, for example, as "a fine looking dark mulatto, six feet high and well proportioned, with superb African features and a considerable admixture of European boldness and intellectuality."[32] But they seldom took seriously these notions of their innate passivity. Nevertheless, they were equally anxious to prove themselves by heroic postures, and not merely verbal ones.

John Brown argued that America would respect the blacks' willingness to fight. Indeed, it might be the only way to prove their manhood or humanity. Moreover, there was a need to demonstrate that several aspects of romantic racialism were wrong. Blacks were neither docile innocents nor pliable dolts. Black activist Charles H. Langston interpreted Brown's raid in just that fashion: as a vindication of blacks' humanity. Brown went South to "put to death . . . those who steal men and sell them, and in whose hands stolen men are found."[33] There was one problem with that argument, however. John Brown was a white man and, contrary to his expectations, blacks had not flocked to support him. J. Sella Martin, at pains to explain this black reluctance, found it in Brown's conservatism: he had been unwilling to follow the logic of his movement and shed sufficient blood, and he therefore "left slaves uncertain how to act." Condemned in the North as cowardly, slaves "were not cowards, but great diplomats. When they saw their masters in the possession of John Brown, in bonds like themselves, they would have been perfect fools had they demonstrated any willingness to join him. They have got sense enough to know, that until there is a perfect demonstration that the white man is their friend—a demonstration bathed in blood—it is all foolishness to co-operate with them." The black man's record in America's past wars was ample evidence of his capacity and willingness to fight, provided he had something for which to fight.[34]

Yet almost a quarter of the raiders were black, and the ease with which the black presence at Harpers Ferry was often overlooked was a source of irritation, then and later. Henry Ward Beecher, two months after the event, and while John Brown still lived, had already written blacks out of the record. In a remarkable sermon at Plymouth Church, Brooklyn, on October 30—a sermon later revised for publication and therefore the subject of some reflection—he charged the affair to seventeen white men who went South without blacks' asking and found among them an unwelcome reception. Nevertheless, they had terrified Virginia. "Seventeen white men surrounded two thousand, and held them in duress."[35] For blacks, Beecher's emphasis was misplaced. It was the black men who accompanied John Brown, and the black men in their midst, who caused Virginians to quake. "Mr. Beecher must have read the papers," complained a black editorial, "must have read that there were twenty-two invaders, seventeen white and five black. Why does he omit all mention of the latter? Were they not men?"[36]

In the view of many white people, of course, consistent with the implications of romantic racialism and also suggested by the arguments of John Brown, they were not. They had been too few and they had acted, if at all, under white direction. They could therefore be safely, or should be wisely, discounted. Beecher, along with most of the class he represented, including supporters of John Brown, had serious doubts about black character and capability. "It is the low animal condition of the African that enslaves him," Beecher reasoned; to gain their freedom blacks had to acquire "truth, honor, fidelity, manhood." But they were not ready yet:

> Now, if the Africans in our land were intelligent; if they understood themselves; if they had self-governing power; if they were able first to throw off the yoke of laws and constitutions, and afterwards to defend and build themselves up in a civil state; then they would have just the same right to assume their independence that any nation has.
>
> But does any man believe that this is the case? Does any man believe that this vast horde of undisciplined Africans, if set free, would have cohesive power enough to organize themselves into a government, and maintain their independence? If there be men who believe this, I am not among them.[37]

Consistent with his racial outlook, Beecher interpreted incidents of mental acuity, the yearning for liberty, and skillful flight from slavery to achieve it (which is to say, any evidence of manhood) as resulting from racial admixture. Consequently, had he acknowledged their presence at all, the fact that most of the blacks who accompanied John Brown had white genes would scarcely have caused him to modify his general opinion about black incapacity.

Still, Beecher obviously respected action and, although they shifted the emphasis, so did many blacks. Some, however, rejected the notion that violent upheaval, especially in face of superior forces, was the best evidence of manhood. One black commentator wondered, for example, whether Henry Ward Beecher would have viewed Brown's course as so hopelessly misguided had it been directed in the cause of whites. Blacks deserved white support because they were human beings denied the common rights of man, whether they plotted against their masters or not. Humanity, the commentator thought, was indivisible, and the idea of separate criteria based on blood, color, class, or nationality was objectionable. Blacks need not vindicate their humanity by bloodshed.[38] H. Ford Douglas even played on the romantic racialist stereotype. "If muscle is evidence of the highest manhood," he perorated, "you will find any of the 'short boys' of New York, any of the 'plug-uglies' and ugly plugs of Tammany Hall, better qualified to be President" than one of the current aspirants in 1860. Blacks exhibited the *highest* elements of manhood, Christian patience and long-suffering tolerance.[39] For others, however, it was "high time, when white men fight and die for our rights, we should learn to act for ourselves."[40]

The twin concerns about "discipline" and "cohesive power" that pre-occupied Henry Beecher also engaged John Brown. In Brown's satirical "Sambo's Mistakes"—constructive criticism offered to blacks through one of their newspapers, the *Ram's Horn* in 1848 or 1849—he complained, among other things, about their lack of unity, their unwillingness to resolve minor differences for the sake of concerted action. He also ridiculed their submissiveness and ability to suffer insults, finding therein no grace or virtue, no nobility—no manhood. He moved to correct these defects when he formed the United States League of Gileadites in Springfield, Massachusetts, in 1851. A self-defense organization, designed to help blacks protect themselves against slave catchers authorized by the Fugitive Slave Act, Brown began his "Words of Advice" for the group with the motto "Union is Strength." "Nothing so charms the American people," he declared, "as personal bravery." Moreover, in typical nineteenth-century fashion, he in-terpreted that quality in male terms. (Recalling Shirley Chisolm's comment in 1972, however, addressed to the Congressional Black Caucus of pri-marily male politicians, that she was the only one among them who had "balls" enough to run for president, it might be wrong to confine that attitude to the nineteenth century.)[41] Harriet Tubman, one of the blacks who adhered to his cause and whose intrepidity Brown respected, Brown referred to as a male: "*He Hariet* is the most of a *man* naturally; that *I ever* met with."[42] Until blacks were willing to stand up for their rights, though, they clearly deserved no respect—but he was ready to show them the way.

While blacks, including historians W. E. B. Du Bois and Benjamin Quarles, stressed Brown's belief in racial equality, his attention to "disci-pline" had some of the same racial content of Beecher's and at Harpers Ferry amounted to anxiety. This solicitude, argues historian Craig Simpson, ex-plains his "mysterious indecisiveness" after he captured the arsenal. If he recalled advice at all, Brown might have been guided by that of black clergy-man James N. Gloucester, who told him that "the colored people are *impul-sive* . . . they need sagacity . . . to distinguish their proper course." Religious and self-righteous, Brown knew he had the proper wisdom. Simpson con-tends that Brown did not think a slave revolt could succeed without white leadership, that such an attitude is implicit in "Sambo's Mistakes" and "Words of Advice," and that it is supported by comments of his daughter Annie. Of course, Brown's reflections in "Sambo's Mistakes" merely echoed the self-criticism in black newspapers and other publications, with some of which at least he ought to have been familiar. (He subscribed to Frederick

Douglass's paper, for example.) Whether he thought a similar statement from him would have more effect is moot. The case is stronger for "Words of Advice" because he assumed leadership in forming the Gileadites. Whether or not blacks needed *white* leadership (his study of the Haitian rebellion would not have supported *that* conclusion), they certainly needed leadership.[43]

On various occasions Brown offered leadership positions to blacks, though they did not always accept. No blacks would accept the presidency of his provisional government formed at Chatham, Ontario, even though some were nominated. Osborne Anderson stated that Brown also offered command positions at Harpers Ferry to blacks, who declined for lack of experience. It is true, however, that Brown was somewhat distrustful and, while willing to have black leaders as figureheads, he wanted to exercise firm control. The reason was not so much that he doubted the success of a black revolution without white leadership, all else being equal. Rather, he feared the direction such a revolution might take. Brown acted out of a firm commitment to American political values and Christian morality. The first caused him to view the Chatham document not as a rejection of the American political system but as its purification. He did not see himself as committing treason: he maintained a firm devotion to the flag, the government, and a particular historical tradition of the United States. He merely wanted to purge American society of slavery—an ill inconsistent with what he considered the country's highest ideals. Consequently, he rejected an attempt of Chatham delegates to remove Article 46 of the provisional constitution, which reaffirmed his allegiance to the American flag. He could not participate on any other grounds. Furthermore, he dismissed with disdain a suggestion that the conspirators wait until the country was involved in a foreign war before they acted. The Stars and Stripes had served patriots in their struggle to win freedom for white men; he intended the same standard to "do duty" for blacks.[44]

But black objections to service under the American flag could only fan Brown's suspicions of black autonomy and emphasize his perception of the need for rigid direction. Opposition rapidly collapsed when he threatened to wash his hands of the whole project. His leadership style of coercive, psychological manipulation basically had nothing to do with racial considerations, for he used the same ploy at the Kennedy farm in Maryland when the raiders objected to his plan to seize the federal arsenal. Still, the short disjuncture at Chatham indicated divergent viewpoints between blacks and Brown and thus underlines the degree to which his thinking and theirs did not totally coincide. Some Canadian blacks, for example, had begun to feel that they should regard themselves as British subjects rather than American refugees, and while they maintained a commitment to the slave, they did not necessarily desire the same tie to the government they had fled. Blacks in the United States were equally disenchanted with their national government, particularly after the Dred Scott Decision robbed them of citizenship, and some felt absolved of allegiance. But Brown intended to impose, not convoke, a consensus. Changed conditions might change outlooks, as the Civil War revealed. Nevertheless, it is notable that Brown's proposals did not cause Martin Delany, a participant at the convention, to forsake his emigrationism. Blacks had their agendas; Brown had his own.[45]

In terms of Brown's commitment to Christian morality, his daughter Annie's comments regarding his attitude toward blacks are instructive: "He expected . . . that if they had intelligent white leaders that they would be prevailed on to rise and secure their freedom without revenging their wrongs, and with very little bloodshed."[46] Brown could not have studied Haiti without being aware of the terrible atrocities there, which he obviously wanted to avoid. The reaction to his Kansas massacre may have reaffirmed his intention. In short, he was caught on the horns of a dilemma between his belief that blacks ought to demonstrate their manhood by physical resistance and his fears about the possible consequences of their passions unleashed. He was not sure he could control them. Thus his plea to Frederick Douglass: "I want you for a special purpose. When I strike, the bees will begin to swarm, and I shall want you to help hive them."[47]

In view of his indecision at the Ferry, it is doubtful he would have known what to do had large numbers of slaves come forward. It would have taken a Frederick Douglass or a Harriet Tubman to take control: both would have recognized the need for either a bloody, violent action to galvanize the slaves, or swift, elusive action to encourage them. Brown would do neither, though, in addition to which many blacks already disapproved of his plan. Douglass did not think it was workable, and Tubman, reputedly sick, may not have thought so either, as it ultimately developed. She is said to have been recruiting support for the raid while Brown was in Maryland making final preparations; she assumed the plan was to run off slaves and did not know of his final dispositions. It is difficult to imagine her sitting waiting to be surrounded, even if she had agreed to take the arsenal in the first place. Henry Highland Garnet reportedly also opposed as much of the plan as he learned about.[48] J. Sella Martin, speaking at a commemorative service in London in 1863, remarked that none of the blacks who had heard of the project had thought it a good one or likely to succeed, however much they appreciated Brown's willingness to sacrifice.

By comparison with Brown's self-sacrifice, blacks also felt lacking. A member of the Chatham convention who wrote to say that he would not come to Harpers Ferry indicated that he was disgusted with himself "and with the whole negro set, God damn em!"[49] Douglass engaged in equal self-flagellation. Defending himself against a charge that he had broken a pledge to appear, he said that he had "not one word to say" in extenuation of his "character for courage." He had "always been more distinguished for running than fighting—and, tried by the Harper's Ferry insurrection test," was "miserably deficient in courage." But he had never promised to be there.[50]

Blacks recognized that Brown was right in his assertion that Americans respected courage, even the foolhardy kind, and while blacks rejected, they could not avoid the connection made between forthright (to the point of physical) opposition to oppression and the perception of manhood or humanity. In the aftermath of the affair, therefore, some took pains to highlight black involvement. For historians this sometimes took the form of counterfactual arguments focusing on the failure of the raid to attract more blacks. Quarles and Du Bois both blamed this shortcoming (and Du Bois emphasized if he did not exaggerate the number of active black participants) on the raid's postponement in 1858. Adherents at Chatham were discouraged, and scattered to other interests. Quarles mentions, for example, that Martin Delany, a Chatham delegate in 1858, was away in Africa in 1859. But Delany appears never to have committed himself to the raid, and plans for his African trip were already well underway at the earlier date. These black historians also suggest, as Osborne Anderson reported, that even in 1859 Brown moved sooner than anticipated, before others who were expected could arrive.[51]

But this suggests that a few more men would have made a significant difference. No one implies that he awaited hundreds; nor could hundreds have come undetected. It might be argued that even a few more men would have made a greater impression of strength and caused slaves to join him. But this does not appear likely. The townspeople already overestimated Brown's numbers, if they bothered to figure at all. Fearing a slave insurrection, they fled to the surrounding heights, seeming "not to notice a few of the very Negroes they dreaded cowering in their midst, as terrified as any of the whites."[52] Or, it might be argued, with a larger force Brown would have been able to fight his way out of his entrapment. But he still would have needed to act more quickly than he was apparently inclined to do.

For many white people, Brown was simply insane, a consideration that easily explained his foibles. But blacks (and Brown himself) rejected that explanation out of hand. "The newspapers and able editors may talk as they will about the insanity of Capt. Brown," one black snorted, "but to us there is something sacred in the madness of this old man." J. Sella Martin agreed. "If he was mad," Martin declaimed, "his madness not only had a great deal of 'method' in it, but a great deal of philosophy and religion."[53] Blacks (and whites, too, who rejected the insanity plea) were consequently at pains to find some rationale for his actions.

The initial attack, of course, went more or less according to plan. It was on the following day, however, in face of growing opposition and lagging support, that Brown refused to act, allowing himself to be surrounded and trapped. Black survivor Osborne Anderson said that Brown "appeared to be somewhat puzzled" and that his "tardiness" in leaving town as previously agreed "was sensibly felt to be an omen of evil by some of us" and led to the raiders' defeat.[54] Historians have therefore focused on what Oates calls Brown's "mysterious" delay. Du Bois argued that Brown was not indecisive at the Ferry; rather, he was waiting the delivery of guns supposed to be brought by Charles P. Tidd, who dallied, which prevented a retreat into the mountains as originally planned to draw off slaves. Brown never expected to begin the foray with many blacks, knowing that he must first gain their confidence by a "successful stroke." The idea was that only after an initial success would blacks come in droves.

In Du Bois's demonology, the soldier of fortune Hugh Forbes figures in the 1858 failure; Charles Tidd in that of 1859. Quarles suggests that Brown tarried at the Ferry for expected reinforcements from the local populace: much antislavery sentiment existed in western Virginia, and Brown expected to gather slaves and antislavery whites to his standard. While he waited, however, he miscalculated the speed with which the militia reacted, disregarded advice from his subordinates about the need to depart, and finally could not extricate himself from the encirclement. But Simpson, while agreeing that Brown hoped to be joined by slaves and antislavery whites, argues that he proved nevertheless psychologically unable to act. This irresolution proceeded from a failure of nerve concerning the possible cost in blood of the type he had condoned at Pottawatomie if the slaves actually rose. Brown said when he took the town that if the citizens resisted he was prepared to burn the place and "have blood." But, actually facing the prospect, he quailed and spent more time trying to gain the understanding of his slaveholding prisoners than threatening to destroy them for their transgressions.[55] In preference to sacrificing others, he ultimately preferred to sacrifice himself. This much blacks appreciated. An interest in the number of blacks involved, therefore, had much to do with the issue of sacrifice—in the commitment of blacks to their own freedom.

Anderson, the only black raider to survive, reported that "many colored men gathered to the scene of action" and that "a number were armed for the work" and fought at various locations. Frederick Douglass, who was not there, says fifty slaves collected. But historian Quarles, who has no reason to minimize black participation, confirms the presence of only twelve slaves, captured and taken to the armory by Brown. Du Bois, basing himself largely on Anderson, stated that about fifty people participated, of whom at least seventeen were black.[56] It is not entirely clear whom he was counting, but presumably he meant fifty people in addition to the raiders. (He also said that between twenty-five and fifty slaves at the arsenal were armed.) If the twelve slaves taken to the armory are added to the five black raiders (Du Bois argued that six or seven of the raiders were black), that adds up to seventeen. Of the twelve slaves, however, only two seem to have made any voluntary contribution; the rest followed orders without apparent enthusiasm and deserted at the first opportunity. However many slaves there were, and however brave or timid, they were not stupid. They could count, and what they saw did not add up to victory. Contemporary Virginia whites, pleased at the poor black turnout, charged it either to prevailing goodwill and mutual affection between master and slave, to the ease with which restless slaves could abscond to freedom already, or, in the most racist explanation, to congenital black docility. Blacks were a "good-humored, good-for-nothing, half-monkey race," as one expressed it.[57] They certainly could not be expected to fight.

When the dust had settled and all the available facts were out, what had happened at the Ferry was in some ways what blacks would have expected to happen, even if the events were adventitious. The first person killed by the raiders was black; the first person killed among the raiders was black. Hayward Shepard, a free black porter and baggage handler at the railroad station, was shot as he turned away when ordered to halt. It was dark and the raiders did not know his color. But the sniper who shot Dangerfield Newby the next day (with a six-inch spike rather than a ball or bullet) as he and two other raiders retreated from a bridge almost certainly did know his color, and his white companions were not hit. That is to say, he was targeted and they were not. Newby had come down simply to free his wife, whose master had broken a promise to sell her to him, and he carried her letter in his pocket. Instead, his body ended up brutalized, his ears were cut off as trophies, and his wife and family were sold farther south.[58]

Blacks knew that they could not rise without forethought and careful planning, and Brown provided neither. Moreover, what ideas he had he was reluctant to share with those he expected to aid him. He disregarded the opinions of Northern blacks when they contradicted his own, and if he anticipated help from nonslaveholding whites he did not tell them so. Simpson argues, Du Bois assumes, and Anderson states that some slaves did know of Brown's plans, but they could not have known the details, for these were denied even the raiders until they gathered at the Kennedy farm—and they caused dissension when they were revealed.[59] When the raid was carried out, few people, whether black or white, knew what to expect. Contemporary blacks therefore concentrated on the inadequacies of the plan and on the heroism of those blacks who did participate. "There has been a systematic attempt to underrate the bravery of the colored men who fought with Brown at Harper's Ferry," a Canadian black complained. Northern whites were blind to everyone except "Brown and seventeen [*sic*] white men." One black admirer went so far as to reverse the usual order of things and state that "black men fought at Harper's Ferry, and John Brown aided them."[60] He did not intend to diminish the leading figure, however, for blacks were more than willing to give Brown his due.

Indeed, even among blacks the preoccupation with Brown was such that his colored companions were sometimes slighted. One observer noted that in the widespread proposals to succor Brown's family, the plight of his black followers was seldom mentioned, although, as he suggested, at least one, Lewis Leary, had a family in need. A black self-critic used comments similar to Brown's in "Sambo's Mistakes" to contrast unfavorably the frivolous young men "with gold chains, perfumed hair, and gloved hands, and young women with that upon their heads which is alike unbecoming to their complexions and unworthy of their adornment" as Christians with the devotion and dedication of John Brown. "Would to God we could find under the dark skin the heroic energy, the unselfish love, the glowing spirit of martyrdom that consumed that loving and unselfish spirit!" In fact, the quiet self-sacrifice of Shields Green equaled that of John Brown. After listening, in August 1859, to Brown and Frederick Douglass debate the issue of the proposed raid at Chambersburg, Pennsylvania, and in the face of Douglass's refusal to go along, Green decided to put aside his doubts and go with the "ole man." At the Ferry when, in the midst of an obvious disaster, he was offered the chance to escape, he again chose to stick with Brown.[61]

These details were perhaps not common knowledge at the time, but blacks did attempt to publicize the fortitude and calm deportment of both Green and John Copeland as each met his death on the scaffold. Copeland's letters from jail, with their tone of brave resignation, equation of his own action with that of George Washington, pointed recollection of Crispus Attucks's death in the Boston Massacre, and earnest expression of confidence in the justice of his cause, were printed, as was his comment on the way to the gallows that he would rather die than be a slave.[62] Neither he nor Green would speak at the trial, their silence standing in eloquent contrast to the self-serving statements made by their codefendants. Copeland impressed even the judge and prosecutor, the latter commenting that if it had been possible to recommend a pardon for anyone, he would have chosen Copeland. Ironically, Copeland's death was the most excruciating (he strangled slowly), and the ropes were lengthened thereafter. At least a few blacks resolved to set aside October 16, the first day of the raid, and December 16, the day Green and Copeland died, as well as December 2 (the date of John Brown's execution), as days of remembrance.[63]

On short notice, three thousand people attended a funeral in Oberlin, Ohio, for John Copeland, although his body remained in Virginia to be dissected by medical students. At the same time, they began planning a monument to Green, Copeland, and Leary, the latter two, having lived in the area, being celebrated as townsmen. Because the three martyrs were *"representative men,* of whom every colored person in the land" had reason to be proud, the people of Oberlin were prepared to share the burden of fund-raising with others, and blacks in Boston and elsewhere took up the challenge.[64] William C. Nell, for example, sought to respond to colored American interest in their racial kinsmen and simultaneously to help surviving relatives and the monument fund by publishing histories of the three who were to be honored. He did not complete the project but published at least one of a proposed series of newspaper "sub-sketches"—one on Shields Green that was particularly moving. Never a resident of Oberlin and originally included mistakenly by the monument committee, Green was retained because of his manly conduct. He was the first black recruited for the Ferry, and, Nell noted, "fully redeemed the characteristic pledge upon his business card [as a clothes cleaner in Rochester, N.Y.]: 'I make no promise that I am unable to perform.' "[65] Fund-raising did not meet expectations and the scale of the memorial had to be reduced, but Oberlin did succeed in erecting one.

In 1881 Frederick Douglass, perhaps unaware of the cenotaph at Oberlin, or feeling it inadequate, or simply to make a point, suggested that if a statue were erected to John Brown, Shields Green should have a prominent place upon it. He meant thereby to honor the loyalty and courage of his old friend and to equate Green's deeds to Brown's. Eight years later, though, when Douglass's son proposed that blacks erect a monument to John Brown, he ran afoul of the militant, race-conscious editor T. Thomas Fortune, who thought that Nat Turner was more worthy of black men's pennies. Given that white men already had monuments to John Brown, in parchment if not stone, he was unlikely to be forgotten. Moreover, much as he respected John Brown, Fortune thought that blacks should honor blacks. A black editor had counterpoised Nat Turner to John Brown earlier (in 1859) when he offered their approaches as contrasting choices in the road to slavery's inevitable destruction: the bloody course of Turner or the relatively bloodless path of Brown.[66]

The two editorials, separated by thirty years of varying circumstances, captured essential aspects of the conundrum Brown posed for blacks. A man of conviction who gave his life for a vision of freedom and equality, he had nevertheless ultimately subordinated the liberty of blacks to the lives of whites. "Had Captain Brown's sympathies not been aroused in favor of the families of his prisoners," bemoaned Osborne Anderson, "a very different result would have been seen."[67] Turner, the black revolutionary, had no such qualms: he would slay all who stood in the way of freedom. This attitude doubtless informed the fury of those blacks who objected so vehemently to William Styron's 1960s' portrait of Nat Turner as a man undone by affection for a young white girl.[68] It might indeed be true that the image they received was not the one Styron intended; that he viewed Turner as not undone but transcendent in his rage and humanity. (Rage aside, however, that is the way Harriet Beecher Stowe viewed Uncle Tom—nonetheless a well-known term of opprobrium in the 1960s.) For some blacks, Styron's representation was unmanly; it was counterrevolutionary; it negated the call for "any means necessary."[69]

Yet Brown's vision of ultimate interracial harmony, as the 1859 editorial made clear, was the more appealing to black Americans. Nat Turner, the editor suggested, posed the spectre of black domination and racial strife. Of course, racial strife already existed, and black domination, a bugaboo justifying black oppression, was neither practicable nor, the editor implied, desirable, even among blacks. What blacks appreciated in Turner was the willingness to fight and die for his own and to provide, in the process, a model of emulation unalloyed by ambiguity. Blacks could have no doubt about his relevance to their history or his place in their pantheon of heroes. It might be true, as Frederick Douglass, Jr., argued, that "character and good acts" were worthy of recognition and perpetuation regardless of a person's color. It might even be true, which Douglass did not say, that because Brown had a choice and chose for blacks, he had greater call on their esteem. Nor could his sensitivity to the feelings of women and children be held against him. But there was also a good case for Fortune's response that "the absence of race pride and race unity" made "white men despise black men all the world over."[70] Black worship of John Brown, however worthy he might be, did nothing to answer that concern.

Indeed, Martin Delany's cooperation with Brown came back to haunt him in his own attempt to build a race movement under black leadership. When he formed the Niger Valley Exploring Party to seek out an African homeland in 1858, he became caught up in rivalries among blacks and whites over who should control this emigration scheme. The conflict was exacerbated by his difficulties in securing economic backing for his planned African expeditions. A secular black nationalist, Delany was forced to seek aid from the American Colonization Society, whose aims and white leadership he deplored and whose African stepchild, Liberia, he had attacked as a tool of whites. Moreover, he rejected their concern with Christianization, feeling that religion sapped black independence. Whites in the ACS, recognizing a long-standing black opposition to their organization, sought to achieve their aims of "civilization and Christianization" in Africa through the expatriation of black colonists (and the removal of blacks from America) by forming the African Civilization Society. (Some whites were members of both groups.) The new organization used black figureheads like Henry Highland Garnet, who was president of the society; it also sought to subsume the Niger Valley Exploring Party. Trying to maintain as much independence of action as possible and denied formal ACS backing, Delany nevertheless sailed to Africa on their economic resources. In England, after his return from Africa, he subsequently competed for financial backing of an African settlement with white representatives of the African Civilization Society who attempted to claim his organization as theirs. Although English sympathizers eventually decided that a black man claiming to represent black interests had more credibility than white men who did the same, the experience intensified Delany's belief that blacks should lead blacks.[71] In addition, it became painfully clear that too close a tie to white people could weaken a call for black unity and black leaders.

When Delany and others tried to make this point against Garnet in connection with a Haitian emigration scheme, however, the incisive minister responded:

> The fault that you have charged me with is that I have accepted an appointment of agent of Haytian emigration from . . . a *white man*. . . . You are indignant at the acknowledgment of the leadership of a *white man* in any work that particularly concerns *black men*. Now, sir, . . . I see by the newspapers that in the convention held in 1848 [*sic*] at Chatham, C.W., one *John Brown* was appointed leader—commander-in-chief—of the Harper's Ferry invasion. There were several black men there, able and brave; and yet John Brown was appointed leader. The unfortunate Stevens moved for the appointment, and *one Dr. Martin R. Delany seconded the motion*. Now, sir, tell me where I shall find your consistency, as John Brown was a *very* white man—his face and glorious hairs were all white.[72]

Garnet's comment was inaccurate in detail but effective in direction. He had appropriated for blacks a white man's vision, knowing that the aim was shared if the method was not, and knowing, too, the sensitivities and ambiguities the name John Brown evoked among blacks.

Even black radicals in the 1960s maintained a traditional black appreciation for the martyr, H. Rap Brown writing that "John Brown was the only white man I could respect and he is dead."[73] But for some blacks no white man, no matter how committed, could view their plight like another black, no matter how flawed. Even though John Brown came closer to the mark than most, he could still be found wanting. It does not matter that many who would criticize had not the gall to go as far as he had gone. Frederick

Douglass commented that colored people more than others criticized him for not joining Brown's quest, and yet, more often than not, these were the very ones who had remained respectfully remote while Brown lived.[74] But all the more need for a black man to go the distance. Shields Green might be said to equal John Brown. Nat Turner had gone beyond him.

John Brown's image nonetheless endures among blacks, and not only in the United States. When Haitian soldiers set up roadblocks to search for handguns in Port-au-Prince in May 1992, they placed one at the corner of John Brown and Martin Luther King Avenues.[75] In America, meanwhile, Denmark Vesey's portrait was installed in Charleston's Gaillard Municipal Auditorium, marking the recognition of his unrealized insurrection as a part of local lore—a herald of Martin Luther King's dream of a day when men would be judged by character rather than color, or an acknowledgment of modern political realities, or both. It caused controversy, periodically renewed, but Vesey's was a plot that died aborning. Some even argue that there was no plot at all—but either way it was relatively safe.[76] Not even a black governor, however, has ventured to name a Virginia street after Nat Turner (though there may be one somewhere) or to put his portrait in any Virginia public place. Turner, like Brown, failed, but he did move from thought to action, and the implications of his action remain frightening. Turner's image as avenging angel clearly is more palatable to blacks than to whites. When white opponents talked of John Brown inciting the murder of women and children, black supporters in particular retorted that that is what slavery did. It might be nice to end slavery peacefully. It might be necessary to end it violently. Philosophically, Brown embraced either tenet, although emotionally, after Kansas, he leaned toward the first. Nat Turner had no such ambivalence; indeed he had no such choice.

Brown, like abolitionists generally, struggled against his history and culture. He was an extreme personification of the abolitionist impulse, embodying the conflicting strands of their contradictory beliefs, including a principled commitment to the ideal of human equality, together with a strong suspicion, if not an outright conviction, of black inferiority. For those who, like Theodore Parker, assumed that Anglo-Saxons were "the best specimen of mankind" that had "ever attained great power in the world," blacks could not help but suffer by comparison. Even if one argued for their superior virtue, or that a composite of the two groups would make a better person still, blacks remained somehow lacking. Of course, the Irish received nearly equal deprecation; and when Parker spoke about warfare necessitating enlistment of "Americans, Negroes, Irishmen," he distinguished the last two from the first. But neither the exclusion nor the company provided blacks much comfort. His doubts about black equality notwithstanding, Parker spoke as feelingly against the discrimination faced by Northern blacks as he condemned the servitude of Southern blacks.[77] In his own terms, he made perfect sense.

By our lights, most abolitionists were racists, particularly if we accept Joel Kovel's definition. "Far from being the simple delusion of a bigoted and ignorant minority," he says, racism "is a set of beliefs whose structure arises from the deepest levels of our lives—from the fabric of assumptions we make about the world, ourselves, and others, and from the patterns of our fundamental social activities."[78] Yet, if we distinguish between those who added hate, aspersions, and despicable acts to their core beliefs and those who questioned their ideological environment, *racist* is much too inclusive and simplistic a term. Perhaps *racialist* is better. Life in a racially based culture determined that Americans of whatever disposition would be confronted with a certain set of assumptions, even if they didn't all think the same way; that they would have certain common points of reference, Brown no less than others. Blacks were both docile and bloodthirsty, and despite Brown's desire to disprove the first premise he was ultimately hampered by his fear of the second. He tried to dissolve his doubts in the ferocity of his actions; yet, in the end, they rose to plague him. He was a man who started a fight then stopped to think about it: his biggest battle was an internal one, and that he could not win. But his struggle with himself and with his culture commended him to blacks. It was ennobling.

The struggle of blacks was different. They were part of the same culture, but viewed it from a variant perspective. As Christians, they could appreciate the value of a moral stance that prized restraint; as realists, they saw the overwhelming obstacles to successful insurrection; as human beings, they were not always willing to lay down their lives for simple pride or self-esteem to no practical effect, though many did so, and many others applauded such acts. Ultimately, though, they were "damned if they did" and "damned if they didn't." In case of violent upheaval they were aggressive and unprincipled savages; in case of acquiescence they were meek and ignorant savages. White Americans might appreciate heroic violence, but in their adversaries, particularly of "lesser breeds," they admired it best after its failure. Noble savages are nearly always dead ones. They are at least devoid of power and safely under control.

But the predisposition to privilege heroic action was as much a part of black as of white American character, and blacks had more at stake in its exhibition. Boston abolitionist Samuel Gridley Howe, engaged in self-recrimination for not having acted forcefully enough to prevent the 1854 rendition to Virginia of fugitive slave Anthony Burns, noticed " 'a comely colored girl of eighteen' who happened to be standing near him as Anthony Burns passed. She stood watching the column with 'clenched fists . . . flashing eyes and tears streaming down her cheeks, the picture of indignant despair.' When he noticed how upset the girl was, Howe tried to comfort her. He told her not to cry; Burns wouldn't be hurt. Immediately, the black girl turned to him and screamed: 'Hurt! I cry for shame he will not kill himself. Oh why is he not man enough to kill himself!' "[79]

Nat Turner, like Malcolm X at a later date, represented black manhood—the evidence that blacks, like others, were prepared to die for their freedom (and thus merited honor, respect, and the rights of citizenship). It would be better, of course, for them and their children if they could *live in* freedom. Martin Luther King perhaps represented that hope; moreover, he illustrated that peaceful protest could also be militant; that nonviolence did not mean docility. Nineteenth-century blacks knew this too, but they did not have the means to build a mass movement based upon this idea—certainly not in the South, where King eventually worked, and where nonviolent protest, no less than violent, could be suicidal.[80] For violence to be other than futile there must be a chance for success. At the very least it has to be admonitory, instilling fear or caution so that its objects will hesitate to tempt fate in the same way again. Brown, to many blacks, represented hope but also futility—a futility, moreover, rooted in fear of blacks. For his part, Turner represented hope and a warning.

Notes

I wish to thank James Barrett, Vernon Burton, Paul Finkelman, Jeffrey Hanes, Robert Johannsen, Craig Simpson, and Ronald G. Walters for useful comments on early drafts of this paper. Walters, in particular, made pertinent suggestions that helped me sharpen the focus. Needless to say, I alone am responsible for any lingering imprecision or faulty conceptualization. The University of Illinois Research Board provided funds for research assistance, and J. Peter Ripley forwarded invaluable references to John Brown in the microfilm version of the Black Abolitionist Papers—a more extensive collection than that of the printed volumes. Stephen Hoffius furnished important information concerning Denmark Vesey's portrait. Lyn Rainard provided material regarding the Southampton Insurrection Marker, as well as logistical support during various of my visits to Virginia.

1. *Weekly Anglo-African,* Dec. 17, 1859, Black Abolitionist Papers, microfilm: roll 12, exposures 21491 and 21498 (hereafter cited in the form of *WAA,* Dec. 17, 1859, BAP, 12: 21491 and 21498).

2. Garnet is quoted in Quarles, *Allies,* 70. On "Martyr's Day," see *WAA,* Dec. 10, 1859, BAP: 12, 21474. Even before the execution took place, some had suggested the day be memorialized. See, for example, *WAA,* Dec. 17, 1859, BAP: 12, 21498, where Pittsburgh blacks, on Nov. 29, 1859, "*Resolved,* That in the event of the execution of John Brown upon the 2d of December, the anniversary of that day be hereafter perpetually observed among us as a day of humiliation and fasting."

3. *WAA,* Dec. 17, 1859, BAP: 12, 21491 and 21499; Dec. 31, 1859, BAP: 12, 21565; Dec. 24, 1859, BAP: 12, 21425, respectively.

4. Merton L. Dillon, *Slavery Attacked: Southern Slaves and Their Allies, 1619–1865* (Baton Rouge, 1990), p. 174.

5. Although what I mean here is, I think, self-evident, there is an important corpus of literature relating to violence in American culture, ranging from Hugh David Graham and Ted Robert Gurr, eds., *The History of Violence in America: Historical and Comparative Perspectives* (New York, 1969), which contains a number of valuable essays, to David B. Davis, *Homicide in American Fiction, 1798–1860: A Study in Social Values* (Ithaca, 1957) and *From Homicide to Slavery* (New York, 1986). There are also a number of works concerned specifically with abolitionism, violence, and its character in that context, including Lawrence J. Friedman, "Antebellum American Abolitionism and the Problem of Violent Means," *Psychohistory Review* 9 (Fall 1980): 23–58; John Demos, "The Antislavery Movement and the Problem of Violent Means," *New England Quarterly* 37 (December 1964): 501–26; William H. Pease and Jane H. Pease, "Confrontation and Abolition in the 1850s," *JAH* 58 (March 1972): 923–37; Lewis Perry, *Radical Abolitionism: Anarchy and the Government of God in Antislavery Thought* (Ithaca, 1973); Sylvan S. Tomkins, "The Psychology of Commitment: The Constructive Role of Violence and Suffering for the Individual and His Society," in *The Antislavery Vanguard,* ed. Martin Duberman (Princeton, 1965), pp. 419–51; and Bertram Wyatt-Brown, "John Brown, the Weathermen, and the Psychology of Antinomian Violence," *Soundings* 58 (Winter 1975): 425–41. But what I have in mind perhaps most closely relates to the issues addressed in Bertram Wyatt-Brown, *Southern Honor: Ethics and Behavior in the Old South* (New York, 1982), in that I am concerned, at least in part, with the relationship between violence and honor. As Wyatt-Brown expresses it in a preface to an abridged version of the above book, entitled *Honor and Violence in the Old South* (New York, 1986): "Secessionist leader James Jones argued that even if the overwhelming power of the North were to defeat a Southern struggle for independence, the Southerners would have at least 'saved our honour *and lost nothing'*" (p. viii). American society in general and Southern society in particular perceived blacks as devoid of honor, while at the same time understanding and appreciating the vindication of honor and manhood through violence.

6. See *The Collected Works of Theodore Parker,* ed. Francis P. Cobbe, 14 vols. (London, 1863–1870). In "A Sermon of War," preached June 7, 1846, in opposition to the Mexican conflict, for example, he said: "I know the Mexicans cannot stand before this terrible Anglo-Saxon race, the most formidable and powerful the world ever saw; a race . . . which, though it number less than forty millions, yet holds the Indies, almost the whole of North America. . . . I cannot forbear thinking that this people will possess the whole of the continent. . . . But this may be had fairly; with no injustice to any one; by the steady advance of a superior race, with superior ideas and a better civilization . . . by being better than Mexico . . . more free and manly" (4:23–24). Here, of course, Parker seems to equate manliness with forbearance, but only because he thinks that in this case Anglo-Saxon aims can be accomplished without recourse to their already proven capacity for violence. In 1859, toward the end of his life, he was still playing the same tune: "I have often spoken against war, and tried to discourage that 'excessive lust for land,' that aggressive and invasive spirit, which is characteristic of both the American and British people. It is clear that the strongest races will ultimately supplant the feebler, and take their place, as the strong grasses outroot the weak from the farmer's meadow" (12:328). Reginald Horsman traces the development of this "racial arrogance" in *Race and Manifest Destiny: The Origins of American Racial Anglo-Saxonism* (Cambridge, Mass., 1981).

7. Quoted in George M. Fredrickson, *The Black Image in the White Mind: The Debate on Afro-American Character and Destiny, 1817–1914* (New York, 1971), p. 100.

8. Ibid., p. 101.

9. "The Present Aspect of Slavery in America, and the Immediate Duty of the

North," speech delivered before the Massachusetts Anti-Slavery Convention, Jan. 8, 1859, in *Collected Works,* 6:289.

10. These ideas are expressed most succinctly in Boston merchant John Saffin's proslavery verse, published in 1701, which contradicts nearly all the basic assumptions about blacks that informed the nineteenth-century romantic outlook:

> Cowardly and cruel are those *Blacks* Innate,
> Prone to Revenge, Imp of inveterate hate.
> He that exasperates them, soon espies
> Mischief and Murder in their very eyes.
> Libidinous, Deceitful, False and Rude,
> The spume Issue of Ingratitude.
> The Premises consider'd all may tell,
> How near good *Joseph* they are parallel.

(Quoted in Winthrop D. Jordan, *White over Black: American Attitudes toward the Negro, 1550–1812* [Chapel Hill, 1968], pp. 199–200.) This invective summarized English sentiments that had existed since the sixteenth century; its composition therefore was, in Jordan's words, "no trick at all." See ibid., pp. 3–43, for early English attitudes regarding blacks.

Revolution and continuing internal conflict in Haiti fueled ideas about black savagery, violence, and incapacity for self-government—fanning Southern white fears and putting black and white abolitionists alike on the defensive. The situation there could be interpreted as evidence that blacks, like all people, desired freedom and would eventually seize it, or that the abolition of slavery would lead to tragedy, depending on one's perspective. It also served both to perpetuate old racial notions and to support new ones. For the significance of Haiti for blacks and Northern and Southern whites, see Alfred N. Hunt, *Haiti's Influence on Antebellum America: Slumbering Volcano in the Caribbean* (Baton Rouge, 1988), esp. pp. 107–88.

11. See Fredrickson, *Black Image in the White Mind,* pp. 97–129, and Ronald G. Walters, *The Antislavery Appeal: American Abolitionism after 1830* (New York, 1978), pp. 54–69, for romantic racialism and the shift away from eighteenth-century rationalism. Both Fredrickson and Walters also address the relation between ideas about blacks and women that I discuss in the following paragraph.

12. Fredrickson, *Black Image in the White Mind,* pp. 114–15.

13. Quoted in Walters, *Antislavery Appeal,* p. 58.

14. See *WAA,* Dec. 10, 1859, BAP: 12, 21476; Dec. 17, 1859, BAP: 12, 21491; *The Liberator,* Dec. 9, 1859, BAP: 12, 21449; *WAA,* Dec. 17, 1859, BAP: 12, 21493.

15. Walters, *Antislavery Appeal,* pp. 12–18. Benjamin Quarles, *Black Abolitionists* (New York, 1969), indicates differences in the ideological outlook of black and white abolitionists, the tensions between them, and the effect on blacks of the 1840s' split in the abolitionist movement (see esp. pp. 42–67).

16. *The Liberator,* Dec. 9, 1859, BAP: 12, 21449–50.

17. Brown's last statement is reprinted, among other places, in Sanborn, ed., *Life,* pp. 584–85, which includes Brown's statement of clarification. See also Andrew Hunter, "John Brown's Raid," *Publications of the Southern History Association* 1 (1897): 171–72; John Brown to Andrew Hunter, Nov. 22, 1859, in U.S. Congress, Senate, *Report of the Select Committee to Inquire into the Late Invasion . . . at Harpers Ferry,* 36, 1, no. 278, pp. 67–68; and Simpson, *Wise,* p. 205. During questioning shortly after his capture, Brown also disclaimed any intention to spark an insurrection. In response to Ohio Congressman Clement L. Vallandigham's query about whether he expected a general slave uprising consequent upon his successful taking of the arsenal, Brown

replied "No, sir; nor did I wish it. I expected to gather them up from time to time and set them free." He denied as well any attempt to carry slaves off or that to free them would oblige the destruction of whites. His "only object" was "to free the negroes." See *The Life, Trial and Execution of Captain John Brown* (New York, 1860), pp. 48–49. A transcript of Brown's inquisition is also printed in Sanborn, ed., *Life*, pp. 562–70.

18. *WAA*, Dec. 17, 1859, BAP: 12, 21492. Various historians have indicated the extent to which abolitionists, including Garrison, were pushed toward the necessity for violence as a condition of slave liberation. An early expression is in Herbert Aptheker, "Militant Abolitionism," *Journal of Negro History* 26 (October 1941): 438–84. For a later manifestation, see Dillon, *Slavery Attacked*, esp. pp. 201–41. Martin would have known, of course, that Garrison had always conceded the slaves' theoretical right to rebel, even though he rejected the wisdom or encouragement of rebellion (ibid., p. 163).

19. *WAA*, Dec. 10, 1859, BAP: 12, 21474. For Garnet's speech and its effects at Buffalo and subsequently, see Carter G. Woodson, ed., *Negro Orators and Their Orations* (Washington, D.C., 1925), pp. 150–57; Howard H. Bell, *A Survey of the Negro Convention Movement, 1830–1861* (New York, 1969), pp. 77–78; and Richard K. MacMaster, "Henry Highland Garnet and the African Civilization Society," *Journal of Presbyterian History* 48 (Summer 1970): 97–98—all of whom emphasize, in Bell's words, that Garnet "did not advocate an insurrection." Other authors, however, stress the call to violence and the potential for insurrection in Garnet's words: see Joel Schor, *Henry Highland Garnet: A Voice of Black Radicalism in the Nineteenth Century* (Westport, Conn., 1977), pp. 54–60; Steven H. Shiffrin, "The Rhetoric of Black Violence in the Antebellum Period: Henry Highland Garnet," *Journal of Black Studies* 2 (Sept. 1971): 45–56; Jane H. Pease and William H. Pease, "Black Power—The Debate in 1840," *Phylon* 29 (Mar. 1968): 26, and "Negro Conventions and the Problem of Black Leadership," *Journal of Black Studies* 2 (Sept. 1971): 34; and Charles H. Wesley, "The Negroes of New York in the Emancipation Movement," *Journal of Negro History* 24 (Jan. 1939): 98–99. Both Schor (*Henry Highland Garnet*, p. 60) and Oates (*Purge*, p. 61) suggest the extent of Garnet's influence on Brown and report the story that Brown published Garnet's speech at his own expense. Quarles (*Allies*, p. 67) also sees an influence but thinks the story that Brown had the speech printed "unlikely considering the absence of copies of such a publication and Brown's constant need of money."

20. *WAA*, Nov. 19, 1859, BAP: 12, 21374.

21. See, respectively, *WAA*, Dec. 10, 1859, BAP: 12, 21473; Dec. 17, 1859, BAP: 12, 21494; Dec. 10, 1859, BAP: 12, 21475.

22. Personal communication from Ronald G. Walters, July 3, 1992. See also Jane H. Pease and William H. Pease, *They Who Would Be Free: Blacks' Search for Freedom, 1830–1861* (Urbana, Ill., 1990), pp. 3–16; Leon F. Litwack, *North of Slavery: The Negro in the Free States, 1790–1860* (Chicago, 1961), pp. 214–46; and Dillon, *Slavery Attacked*, pp. 172–75.

23. Pease and Pease, *They Who Would Be Free*, p. 16.

24. Ibid., p. 12. The Peases state: "Cornish had suggested in 1829 that whites form abolition societies and blacks concentrate on practical social uplift," advice that seems to parallel that of black power advocates to white militants in the late 1960s to the effect that whites should work within their own communities and organizations to extirpate racism while blacks worked in their communities and organizations to build black pride and racial solidarity—problems peculiar to blacks.

25. See, for example, Leon F. Litwack, "The Emancipation of the Negro Abolitionist," in *Antislavery Vanguard*, ed. Duberman, pp. 137–55; and Quarles, *Black Abolitionists*, esp. pp. 30–56.

26. Ripley, ed., *Abolitionist,* 5:59.

27. Pease and Pease, *They Who Would Be Free,* p. 72.

28. Ibid., p. 78. Also see Walters, *Antislavery Appeal,* esp. pp. 3–33; and Aileen S. Kraditor, *Means and Ends in American Abolitionism: Garrison and His Critics on Strategy and Tactics, 1834–1850* (New York, 1969), pp. 39–177.

29. See Pease and Pease, *They Who Would Be Free,* pp. 173–232; Litwack, *North of Slavery,* pp. 244–79; Quarles, *Black Abolitionists,* pp. 197–249; Quarles, *Allies,* pp. 15–36; and Floyd J. Miller, *The Search for a Black Nationality: Black Colonization and Emigration, 1787–1863* (Urbana, Ill., 1975), pp. 93–249.

30. Villard, *Biography,* pp. 49 and 272.

31. See Rossbach, *Conspirators,* esp. pp. 182–209. The "Secret Six," who provided financial support for Brown's activities in Kansas and at Harpers Ferry, were Franklin Benjamin Sanborn, Theodore Parker, Samuel Gridley Howe, Thomas Wentworth Higginson, Gerrit Smith, and George Luther Stearns.

32. *WAA,* July 7, 1860, BAP: 12, 22569. Wilson J. Moses, *The Golden Age of Black Nationalism, 1850–1925* (Hamden, Conn., 1978), pp. 15–55, discusses romantic racialism in black thought.

33. *WAA,* Dec. 3, 1659, BAP: 12, 21444. See also Quarles, ed., *Blacks,* p. 12.

34. "Speech of Rev. J. S. Martin," *The Liberator,* Dec. 9, 1859, BAP: 12, 21450.

35. James Redpath, *Echoes,* p. 258.

36. *WAA,* Dec. 10, 1659, BAP: 12, 21477.

37. Quoted in Redpath, *Echoes,* pp. 276 and 270, respectively. Beecher's belief in the superior qualities of those of mixed blood is revealed, for example, in his statement that "the more enlightened and liberty-loving among the Southern slaves, bear too much of their masters' blood not to avail themselves of any opening to escape" (quoted in ibid., p. 266).

38. *WAA,* Dec. 3, 1859, BAP: 12, 21430. Newspaper correspondent and Brown supporter James Redpath made essentially the same point: "When the Freedom of Kansas was in danger, Mr. Beecher spoke bullets,—sixteen a minute, and half-ounce balls at that; he truly said that rifles were a moral agency, and that one might as well preach to buffaloes as to Border Ruffians; but now, when Slavery is in danger, he deprecates the assault on it, discovers 'a right way' and 'a wrong way'; and draws distinctions so critical and nice that he who runs may read that this champion of Liberty in Kansas is only a *white* man after all. He has not yet come out to be a universal man, and to sympathize equally with all men, irrespective of races or conditions of life" (*Echoes,* pp. 6–7).

39. *The Liberator,* July 13, 1859, BAP: 12, 22591–92. Douglas actually said "better qualified to be President than Abraham Lincoln," the subject of his critical address, but to introduce Lincoln in this context might be misleading because of a tendency to attach more significance to the name in hindsight than it held at the time, even though Lincoln was already honored in some quarters.

40. *WAA,* Jan. 7, 1860, BAP: 12, 21733. Detroit blacks, reaching the same conclusion, resolved that "the long lost rights and liberties of an oppressed people" were "gained in proportion as they act in their own cause, [and] therefore we are now loudly called upon to arouse to our own interest": *WAA,* Dec. 17, 1859, BAP: 12, 21497.

41. See Norman Mailer, "The Evil in the Room," *Life,* July 28, 1972, p. 39.

42. Quoted in Oates, *Purge,* p. 242; and in Du Bois, *John Brown,* p. 249. A copy of "Sambo's Mistakes" can be found, among other places, in Villard, *Biography,* pp. 659–61, who also extensively quotes "Words of Advice," pp. 50–51.

43. See Simpson, *Wise,* pp. 20, 367, with whose interpretation I basically agree; Gloucester is quoted in Quarles, ed., *Blacks,* p. 4. In the case of Haiti, Alfred Hunt

indicates that even white Southerners had a good opinion of Toussaint L'Ouverture, based on his exercise of strong leadership—especially, from their point of view, in forcing freedmen to work the plantations (*Haiti's Influence on Antebellum America,* pp. 84–106).

44. See Du Bois, *John Brown,* pp. 254–66; Quarles, *Allies,* pp. 43–51; Oates, *Purge,* pp. 243–47; and Osborne P. Anderson, *A Voice from Harper's Ferry: A Narrative of Events at Harper's Ferry; with Incidents Prior and Subsequent to its Capture by Captain Brown and His Men* (Boston, 1861), pp. 9–14. Black clergymen Thomas M. Kinnard of Toronto and Jermain W. Loguen of Syracuse (who was not present) were nominated as candidates for president of the provisional government, but Kinnard declined "after a speech of some length" and Loguen's name was withdrawn after someone suggested that he would not serve if elected. Anderson, as a congressman, was the only black officer in the provisional government, although three blacks were appointed to a fifteen-man committee to fill remaining vacancies. See Anderson, *A Voice from Harper's Ferry,* p. 12, and Quarles, *Allies,* pp. 49–50.

45. See Oates, *Purge,* pp. 278–80; Miller, *Search for a Black Nationality,* p. 143; and Bell, *Survey of the Negro Convention Movement,* pp. 117–19. Brown's indisposition to convince rather than coerce blacks to his point of view is augured in his meeting with Delany: "I have come to Chatham expressly to see you," Brown said, "this being my third visit on the errand. I must see you at once, sir, and that, too, in private, as I have much to do and but little time before me. If I am to do nothing here, I want to know it at once." His peremptory tone permitted of little negotiation. See Frank A. Rollin, *Life and Public Services of Martin R. Delany, Sub-Assistant Commissioner Bureau Relief of Refugees, Freedmen, and of Abandoned Lands, and Late Major 104th U.S. Colored Troops* (Boston, 1868), pp. 85–86.

46. Quoted in Richard J. Hinton, *John Brown and His Men, with Some Account of the Roads They Traveled to Reach Harper's Ferry* (New York, 1894), p. 260. Theodore Parker thought the same: the violence in St. Domingue "*shows what may be in America,* with no white man to help." Parker, like Brown, feared that revolution might change "black inhabitants from tame slaves into wild men" (*Collected Works,* 12:171).

47. Quoted in Frederick Douglass, *The Life and Times of Frederick Douglass: His Life as a Slave, His Escape from Bondage, and His Complete History* (1892; repr. New York, 1962), p. 320.

48. See Quarles, *Allies,* pp. 79–80, 83; *The Liberator,* Dec. 9, 1859, BAP: 12, 21451.

49. J. Sella Martin et al., *The Martyrdom of John Brown: The Proceedings of a Public Meeting Held in London on the 2nd December, 1863, to Commemorate the Fourth Anniversary of John Brown's Death* (London, 1864), BAP: 15, 27159 (quoted in Quarles, *Allies,* p. 80; and Oates, *Purge,* p. 283).

50. Philip S. Foner, ed., *The Life and Writings of Frederick Douglass,* 5 vols. (New York, 1950–75), 2:461.

51. See Du Bois, *John Brown,* pp. 280, 293–95; Quarles, *Allies,* pp. 80–82; Rollin, *Life and Public Services of Martin R. Delany,* p. 85; and Anderson, *A Voice from Harper's Ferry,* p. 27.

52. Oates, *Purge,* p. 293.

53. Quoted in *WAA,* Oct. 22, 1859, BAP: 11, 21248; *The Liberator,* Dec. 9, 1859, BAP: 12, 21451, respectively. Governor Henry Wise of Virginia also discountenanced the idea that Brown was a madman. "He is a bundle of the best nerves I ever saw; cut and thrust and bleeding, and in bonds. He is a man of clear head, of courage, fortitude, and simple ingenuousness. He is cool, collected, and indomitable" (quoted in Sanborn, ed., *Life,* pp. 571–72). Wise obviously admired Brown and thought his plan had much to recommend it: see Simpson, *Wise,* pp. 203–6.

54. Anderson, *A Voice from Harper's Ferry,* pp. 36, 38.

55. See Oates, *Purge,* pp. 291–93; Du Bois, *John Brown,* pp. 247–48, 315–20; Quarles, *Allies,* pp. 96–102; and Simpson, *Wise,* pp. 214–18.

56. Anderson, *A Voice from Harper's Ferry,* pp. 34 and 37; Douglass, *Life and Times,* p. 306; Quarles, *Allies,* pp. 98–100; and Du Bois, pp. 279 and 314.

57. Quoted in Quarles, *Allies,* p. 104.

58. See Anderson, *A Voice from Harper's Ferry,* p. 35; Thomas Featherstonhaugh, "John Brown's Men: The Lives of Those Killed at Harper's Ferry with a Supplemental Bibliography of John Brown," *Publications of the Southern History Association* 3 (1899): 295; Quarles, *Allies,* pp. 95–96; and Oates, *Purge,* p. 294. An observer reported that "one of the armorers . . . got an opportunity of a shot at him (Newby) from an upper window . . . and I never saw on any battlefield, a more hideous musket wound than his. For his throat was cut literally from ear to ear, which was afterwards accounted for by the fact that the armorer, having no bullets, charged his musket with a six-inch iron spike" (quoted in Featherstonhaugh, "John Brown's Men," p. 295). Newby's wife and children were sold into Louisiana.

59. Simpson, *Wise,* p. 206; Du Bois, *John Brown,* p. 306; and Hinton, *John Brown and His Men,* pp. 272–73.

60. See *WAA,* Feb. 11, 1860, BAP: 12, 21865; *WAA,* Dec. 10, 1859, BAP: 12, 21461, respectively.

61. Quoted in *WAA,* Nov. 26, 1859, BAP: 12, 21399; *WAA,* Feb. 4, 1860, BAP: 12, 21833, respectively. See also Douglass, *Life and Times,* p. 320; Quarles, ed., *Blacks,* p. 64.

62. See the *Oberlin Evangelist,* Dec. 21, 1859, BAP: 12, 21511; Jan. 4, 1860, BAP: 12, 21716; *WAA,* Dec. 24, 1859, BAP: 12, 21537; *The Liberator,* Jan. 13, 1860, BAP: 12, 21744.

63. See Hunter, "John Brown's Raid," p. 188; Quarles, *Allies,* pp. 134 and 137; Du Bois, *John Brown,* p. 281; and *WAA,* Dec. 24, 1859, BAP: 12, 21535; Dec. 31, 1859, BAP: 12, 21559.

64. *The Liberator,* Jan. 13, 1860, BAP: 12, 21744. See also ibid., Feb. 24, 1860, BAP: 12, 21907.

65. *Pine and Palm,* July 6, 1861, BAP: 13, 24152. See also Quarles, *Allies,* pp. 85 and 149.

66. Thomas Hamilton, editor of both the *Monthly Anglo-African* and the *Weekly Anglo-African,* made the Brown-Turner comparison in each, under the title of "The Nat Turner Insurrection": see Quarles, ed., *Blacks,* pp. 37–39, and the *Anglo-African Magazine,* December 1859, BAP: 12, 21420. The 1889 exchange between Frederick Douglass, Jr., and T. Thomas Fortune, editor of the *New York Age,* can be found in Quarles, ed., *Blacks,* pp. 75–78. Frederick Douglass, Sr., made his suggestion in a speech at Storer College, which is excerpted in Quarles, ed., *Blacks,* pp. 54–66 (the statement about Green is on p. 64).

67. Anderson, *A Voice from Harper's Ferry,* p. 61.

68. The controversy surrounding William Styron's *The Confessions of Nat Turner* (New York, 1967) can be most easily followed, perhaps, in Albert E. Stone, *The Return of Nat Turner: History, Literature, and Cultural Politics in Sixties America* (Athens, Ga., 1992). But see also John Henrik Clarke, ed., *William Styron's Nat Turner: Ten Black Writers Respond* (Boston, 1969); and John B. Duff and Peter M. Mitchell, eds., *The Nat Turner Rebellion: The Historical Event and the Modern Controversy* (New York, 1971). Although objections to the novel varied, the most strident focused on Turner's putative emasculation and the notion of his being enamored of a white female.

69. Shiffrin, "Rhetoric of Black Violence," parallels the sentiments of Henry Highland Garnet and those of black militants of the 1960s, including Stokely Carmichael, Malcolm X, Eldridge Cleaver, and H. Rap Brown. He reveals that a group of students,

when asked to identify a quotation of Garnet's, most often misassociated it with one of these modern activists. While stressing a continuity of concerns and a similarity of ideas, Shiffrin neglects to make the interesting point that even the language of Garnet sounds very much like Malcolm X's "any means necessary." In his "Address to the Slaves of the United States," which failed by one vote of being adopted as the consensus of the convention in Buffalo, New York, 1843, Garnet said, *"It is your solemn and imperative duty to use every means, both moral, intellectual, and physical that promises success"* (Woodson, ed., *Negro Orators*, p. 153). Malcolm X's phraseology, of course, is more direct, but it also is likely derivative of Garnet.

70. Quarles, ed., *Blacks*, pp. 77, 78.

71. See Miller, *Search for a Black Nationality*, pp. 170–231.

72. *WAA*, Feb. 9, 1861, BAP: 13, 23541.

73. Quoted in Quarles, ed., *Blacks*, p. 107.

74. Douglass, *Life and Times*, p. 320.

75. The *Champaign-Urbana News Gazette*, May 28, 1992. The John Brown affair forcibly impressed the people of Haiti. "On the 20th of January [1860]," one observer reported, "a mass was chimed in commemoration 'of the frightful martyrdom of the Abolitionist, John Brown, by the infamous ruffians of the Southern portion of the American Union.' The papers give the full details of the execution of Brown, and devote several columns to editorial comments, which are far from complimentary to 'le juge Parker' and the slaveholding jury of Charlestown" (*WAA*, Feb. 18, 1860, BAP: 12, 21901). Another wrote that "all Porte au Prince seemed in mourning [on the 20th]; the streets throughout the city were lined with black flags. . . . The Haytien vessels in harbor had their flags at half-mast; likewise the English and French, and those of all nations except those of the United States of America." Three thousand people, including the president's family, attended services at the National Chapel, although the president himself was indisposed and could not attend. Sympathizers reportedly collected $20,000 Haitian ($14,000 in Spanish currency) to benefit Brown's family (*WAA*, Mar. 3, 1860, BAP: 12, 21959; see also the *National Anti-Slavery Standard*, Mar. 24, 1860, BAP: 12, 22049).

76. Vesey's portrait was hung in the Gaillard Municipal Auditorium in 1976. Because no contemporary likeness of him had survived, however, his features were portrayed indistinctly. White Mayor Joseph P. Riley, speaking at the unveiling ceremony, recognized Vesey's importance in the history of the city and the need to acknowledge Charleston's black as well as white heritage. Seeking to emphasize unity, the mayor declaimed: "There have been writings of history that would attribute to Mr. Vesey actions and attempts that were not his. We should not see him as a man, as reported by some, who sought to kill, because I do not believe that was the case. . . . I find it difficult to believe his plan was to annihilate this city" (quoted in John Lofton, *Denmark Vesey's Revolt: The Slave Plot That Lit a Fuse to Fort Sumter* [Kent, Ohio, 1983], pp. vii–viii). Obviously Turner's designs admit of no such obfuscation. Vesey's portrait was later stolen from the Gaillard. See also Theodore Rosengarten, "History Alley, Memory Lane," in *Places with a Past: New Site-Specific Art at Charleston's Spoleto Festival* (New York, 1991), pp. 35–37. But in "The Vesey Plot: A Reconsideration," *Journal of Southern History* 30 (May 1964): 143–61, and *Slavery in the Cities— The South, 1820–1860* (New York, 1964), pp. 237 and 241, Richard Wade argued that no conspiracy existed.

Librarians at the Walter Cecil Rawls Library and Museum, in Courtland, Virginia, reported on July 31, 1992, that the sign commemorating Nat Turner's insurrection at Courtland (formerly Jerusalem) was also being removed for three years so that it could be recast, presumably in more acceptable language, and then reinstalled at Cross Keys, Virginia. Reputedly racist, the original plaque, located along the highway two miles west of Courtland, was not as strident as one might have supposed. Under the heading "Southampton Insurrection," it described the event as follows: "Seven miles southwest Nat Turner, a Negro, inaugurated, August 21, 1831, a slave insurrection that lasted two days and cost the lives of about sixty whites. The slaves began the massacre near Cross Keys and moved eastward toward Courtland (Jerusalem). On meeting resistance, the insurrection speedily collapsed." See *State Historical Markers of Virginia: Listing the Inscriptions on All Such Markers on the Principal Highways of Virginia, with Supplementary Data,* bicentennial ed. (Richmond, 1975), p. 119. The fact that local librarians seemed to think the marker was objectionable, whether they knew the actual wording or not, may say something about contemporary attitudes.

77. For Parker's comment, see his *Collected Works,* 4:19. See also his "Discourse to Commemorate the Rendition of Thomas Simms," April 12, 1852, in *Additional Speeches, Addresses, and Occasional Sermons* (Boston, 1867), pp. 17–105.

78. Joel Kovel, *White Racism: A Psychohistory* (New York, 1984), p. 3.

79. Rossbach, *Conspirators,* p. 37.

80. Henry Highland Garnet, for example, in his 1843 "Address to the Slaves of the United States of America," advised a kind of mass movement of militant pacifism, though he doubtless expected it to end in violence—a confusion of sentiment that permits scholars to differ over whether he called for an insurrection: "Go to your lordly enslavers and tell them plainly, that *you are determined to be free.* Appeal to their sense of justice, and tell them that they have no more right to oppress you, than you have to enslave them. . . . Do this, and for ever after cease to toil for the heartless tyrants. . . . If they then commence the work of death, they, and not you, will be responsible for the consequences. . . . You had far better all die—*die immediately,* than live slaves. . . . there is not much hope of redemption without the shedding of blood." See the reprint of Garnet's speech in Earl Ofari, *"Let Your Motto Be Resistance": The Life and Thought of Henry Highland Garnet* (Boston, 1972), pp. 149–50.

4

WENDY HAMAND VENET

"Cry Aloud and Spare Not" Northern Antislavery Women and John Brown's Raid

For abolitionists, John Brown's raid presented a call to action, a propaganda device, and an indication that their decades of agitation might be leading to the kind of immediate—albeit violent—change they had long demanded. For antislavery women, Harpers Ferry evoked special feelings. Many struggled to reconcile their pacifist views with an admiration for Brown's initiative, courage, and heroism. Their actions surrounding the raid helped to touch off a public debate over women's traditional duties as nurse and nurturer, definitions of true womanhood, and the role of women in times of national peril. The activities of one antislavery woman, Lydia Maria Child, created a furor on both sides of the Mason-Dixon line, catapulting Child into the national limelight and igniting in her new passion and commitment to antislavery. "God alone knows how many John Brown's we *may* wake up when we 'cry aloud and spare not,'" she wrote after Brown's execution. "I can not calculate the *consequences,* but my *duty* is clear to me. I *must* stand by the poor slave, come what will."[1]

Moral Suasion Reconsidered

No woman was a member of the "Secret Six," the New England philanthropists who bankrolled the Harpers Ferry insurrection. Julia Ward Howe's husband, Samuel Gridley Howe, was among them, however, and she met Brown in the 1850s. In her memoirs, published at the turn of the century when Howe was much acclaimed as a poet and suffrage activist, she remembered Brown as "a Puritan of the Puritans, forceful, concentrated, and self-contained. We had a brief interview, of which I only remember my great gratification." The precise extent to which Julia Ward Howe may have known of the planned insurrection in advance is open to question, but she later wrote that Brown's plan was to create such an uprising of slaves that their sheer numbers would cause Southerners to abolish the evil institution, "possibly without even a battle." Howe also recalled that "the whole scheme appeared to me wild and chimerical."[2] Clearly, the failed insurrection caused disruption for the Howe family, with Samuel Gridley Howe fleeing to Canada, terrified of being arrested for his role in the conspiracy. During the Civil War, Julia Ward Howe wrote the "Battle Hymn of the Republic." When set to the music of the song "John Brown's Body," it became the most stirring anthem of the Northern cause and arguably the most inspirational abolitionist work ever written.

Abigail Hopper Gibbons, a Quaker activist, also knew about the insurrection in advance because Brown spent an evening with Gibbons and her husband at their New York home several weeks before the raid. Believing the scheme was not practical, she asked what he planned to do with the women and their children. "Not hurt a hair of their heads" was Brown's reply, according to Gibbons's daughter and biographer. However much Abby Gibbons deplored Brown's violence, though, she respected his courage and motives. When her home was sacked during the New York draft riots of 1863, a John Brown pike was found in a corner of the parlor.[3]

Harriet Tubman not only knew about the raid in advance; she helped to plan it. She had met Brown in 1858 when she was in Canada sheltering runaway slaves. He quickly became her fervent admirer, calling her "General" and urging her to recruit soldiers for his army among fugitives in Canada. Apparently she complied. William Ellery Channing's poem "John Brown" suggests she brought four men to Brown's ranks. She is also said to have raised money and suggested a July 4th date for the raid, presumably because of its association with the patriots' declaration in 1776. Since she was herself a runaway slave and because she had made multiple trips to the South to liberate others, Brown hoped Tubman would accompany him on the raid, especially after Frederick Douglass declined to do so. Once the conspirators had determined a date on which to begin their insurrection, John Brown, Jr., attempted to locate Tubman, who was recuperating from a recurring illness in New Bedford, Massachusetts. Because her whereabouts were unknown to many in November 1859, her role as Brown advisor in the preceding months did not become publicly known for some time. Nor did she play a prominent role in promoting the righteousness of his cause in the aftermath of the raid. Nevertheless, for the rest of her life Tubman held Brown's attempt at liberation in high regard, believing his role in emancipation surpassed that of Lincoln.[4]

For those who did not know in advance of Brown's intentions, the Harpers Ferry episode evoked a combination of shock and exultation. Women abolitionists joined male colleagues in writing letters, organizing meetings, giving speeches, and passing resolutions applauding Brown's actions, although many also made special efforts to distance themselves from his violent methods. As Lydia Maria Child wrote after the execution, "Certainly honest John Brown, by his direct way of proceeding, has driven us abolitionists into a perplexing corner. We cannot help reverencing the *man* while we disapprove of his *measures*."[5]

White female abolitionists may have taken on a greater burden in defending Brown than their male counterparts. Many of them came from a Quaker and pacifist background; they found his violence deeply troubling. Moreover, as activist women they faced constant opposition to their work from a public consumed by images of middle-class domesticity. By entering the public sphere, they had already rejected widely accepted notions about women's appropriate role, in addition to which, as defenders of John Brown, they ignited public controversy because they appeared to be condoning violence as a means to end slavery.

The Philadelphia Female Anti-Slavery Society, which for nearly thirty years had been a force for antislavery and female activism, perhaps best reflected the views of many women. In a series of resolutions enacted at its November 16, 1859, meeting, the society and its president, Sarah Pugh, expressed sympathy with John Brown for his "intense hatred of slavery and ardent love of liberty" and their deepest consolation for the man who "stands doomed to death by tyrants who traffic in 'slaves and souls of men.'" Clearly uncomfortable with Brown's methods, the society's members viewed his insurrection as a "solemn warning" that if slavery were not abolished peacefully, it would be overthrown with violence. At the same time, they reiterated their rejection of warfare as a means to achieve goals and their commitment to moral suasion. Emphasizing the need for women to be publicly active, they believed all friends of antislavery should preach the truth in this critical hour of the nation's history.[6]

At National Hall in Philadelphia, abolitionists paid tribute to Brown after his execution. Mary Grew, a prominent member of the Philadelphia Female Anti-Slavery Society, gave a speech in which she praised Brown for realizing that God views all his children as equal. She also commended his heroism, declaring that "our dying brother had taught us a lesson of faith, dignity and unswerving courage," and wondered whether others would be willing to sacrifice their lives for such a holy cause. She cautioned, however, that "the force of bullets is soon spent, but the power of a Great Idea is eternal. There is no power like that of the spoken word of Truth."[7]

Lucretia Mott also spoke in National Hall. A Quaker minister and dedicated pacifist, she nevertheless sympathized with Brown's motives and played host to his wife, who stayed with Mott and her husband en route to Harpers Ferry before her husband's execution.[8] According to the *Philadelphia Press*, Mott declared that violence was the "natural consequence" of the sin of slavery, and she denounced those who upheld the Constitution with its recognition of the peculiar institution. According to the *Press*, audience reaction was mixed, but one sympathizer described the gathering in the best possible light: "The meeting was unprecedented in Philadelphia for numbers. Hisses abounded, but applause much more."[9]

In New York, Antoinette Brown Blackwell preached a Sunday sermon in Goldbeck's music store. The first female minister ordained in a major American denomination, she had quit her Congregational pastorate after only one year but continued to give speeches and sermons on topics about which she felt strongly. In her December 4 remarks, she emphasized that nonresistance was the appropriate position for any Christian to take but also praised Brown's heroism both during his raid and in his demeanor through trial and execution. According to one newspaper report, Blackwell then declared that if antislavery advocates like the biblical Peter were moved to fight, they should "go out like the old hero who died on Friday and was now in heaven." But backing off slightly, she added that the first step toward abolition was to convince slaveholders they must be as unselfish as John Brown had been.[10]

Abby Kelley Foster joined other members of the Worcester, Massachusetts, antislavery society in passing a resolution shortly after the abortive insurrection "that, as Abolitionists, we have no disclaimers to make, no apologies to offer." While lacking enough information to pass judgment on the wisdom of the method chosen, they nonetheless applauded Harpers Ferry rebels for their heroism and condemned the United States as a nation in which blacks were denied education, and even legalized marriage. Foster and half a dozen male colleagues offered speeches in Mechanics Hall on the day of Brown's execution. Among the more radical and uncompromising of female Garrisonians, she defended Brown's tactics by arguing that the use of force to eliminate despotism was justifiable and Christian.[11]

In Rochester, Susan B. Anthony arranged a meeting in Corinthian Hall for the evening of Brown's execution. Always more comfortable organizing public gatherings than speaking at them, she went from house to house selling tickets and taking donations, assisted by a member of the Liberty party and several Quaker friends. The fifty-cent admission fee kept rabble-rousers from entering Corinthian Hall, although the radical nature of the topic kept many respectable men and women away as well. As Anthony recalled in her diary, "Not one man of prominence in religion or politics will publicly identify himself with the John Brown meeting." Even members of the local Ladies Anti-Slavery Society declined to participate, disturbed by Brown's violence and the negative publicity surrounding the insurrection. They did, however, continue to praise the antislavery efforts of Frederick Douglass, Rochester's most famous abolitionist, who had fled to Canada and later to England, fearing his relationship with Brown before the raid would implicate him in Brown's treason. Barely three hundred attended the Brown commemoration in Rochester—two hundred according to an unsympathetic local newspaper, which also condemned keynote speaker Parker Pillsbury for implying that Brown was a greater hero than the slave-owning George Washington. When Anthony, who presided, wrote to the *National Anti-Slavery Standard,* she perhaps acknowledged indirectly the disappointing size of the audience: "Our meeting was a grand moral success."[12]

Lydia Maria Child bypassed the Brown memorial staged by white activists in Boston and instead marked the second of December with African Americans at a meetinghouse in Southac Street. She wrote about this experience in countless letters to fellow abolitionists, including one to her friend Sarah Shaw, whose son, Robert Gould Shaw, would become an abolitionist martyr himself when he was killed leading the Massachusetts 54th during the Civil War. "I could not have elsewhere found a scene so congenial to my tender state of mind," Child wrote, noting as well that the black audience firmly believed in Brown's sanity and praised the fallen leader as a "friend of their persecuted race." She also commented on the hymns "sung so plaintively," and while the prayers, she said, "sometimes degenerated into rant," many were eloquent. She was especially struck by one old man, a former slave, who announced dramatically that since it pleased God "to take away our Moses, Oh, Lord God! raise us up a Joshua!"[13]

For Child, the execution, on December 16, of Brown's fellow conspirators was a far more painful day, for these men were not reconciled to their fate. She found particularly repugnant the decision by Virginia authorities to provide lower calibre coffins for the black men than for the white conspirators, thus "carrying their savage contempt for the race . . . to the very borders of the grave!" In the spring, when the last Brown conspirators faced execution, Child was again deeply disturbed. From her neighbors in Wayland, Massachusetts, she collected three hundred signatures on a petition in an effort to spare their lives, but the campaign failed to secure mercy from the court.[14]

Sarah Grimké and Angelina Grimké Weld, who had helped to pave the way for women abolitionists by becoming the first female paid agents of the American Anti-Slavery Society in the 1830s, were living near Perth Amboy, New Jersey, in 1859–60. Cofounders and teachers at a progressive school called Eagleswood, and living in a community of reformers where issues such as the use of force by antislavery Kansans were subject to debate, they were quickly drawn in by the events at Harpers Ferry. Sarah wrote to a friend with enthusiasm, "What a glorious spectacle is now before us." A dedicated spiritualist, she reported having met Brown in the spirit world and noted her profound sympathy with the martyr. Two of Brown's African American conspirators were buried at Eagleswood, and representatives of the school had to guard the graves for fear that angry townspeople would desecrate them. Some abolitionists further believed that Eagleswood school would be an ideal location for Brown's children to be educated.[15]

Angelina Grimké Weld became ill during the time of Brown's insurrection. Although the nature of her illness is not known, it may have been exacerbated by stress of these momentous times. Long a committed non-resistant, she made no public comments about Brown's raid but wrote to a son shortly afterwards, "Things look very dark and gloomy and as I have given up all hope of . . . [slavery's] abolition except thro blood and insurrection, I feel willing it should come in my day, for the longer it is put off, the worse it will be."[16] Although many abolitionists viewed Brown's actions as proof of slavery's imminent demise, Weld foresaw the bloody struggle which would devastate her homeland.

Benevolence and True Womanhood

While some activist women carried Brown's banner at political rallies, others promoted the cause through more traditional channels. By endorsing Brown's activities as worthy of female benevolence, they kindled a public debate and aroused sectional antagonism. Several women, for example, participated in the organized effort to raise money for members of Brown's family. Begun weeks before the execution and spearheaded by Thaddeus Hyatt in New York, the effort included the sale of photographs of the soon-to-be-martyred hero. Abolitionist women such as Lydia Maria Child wrote letters to Hyatt, who made sure they were printed in Northern newspapers. A woman signing her name "Lucy" (perhaps Lucy Stone) wrote in praise of the "self-sacrificing hero of Harper's Ferry." Contributing to the fund and requesting a photograph, she closed with the words "always for the right, whether down-trodden or triumphant!" One New York woman wrote to Hyatt emphasizing the role of mothers in this period of national trial. Rather than underscoring Brown's image as determined radical, she presented him as a dedicated family man whose sacrifice made him an admirable candidate for female charity. Promising to convince all her friends to contribute as she had done, she added, "I hope all the mothers of our city will each consider it a privilege to not only have one of these photographs as a parlor adornment, but a higher and nobler one" to assist Brown's family.[17]

A number of women wrote to Brown in prison, and several attempted to visit him. One who did both was Rebecca Spring, a member of the same reform community in which the Grimké sisters lived, the daughter of the prominent abolitionist Arnold Buffum, and the wife of a wealthy philan-thropist. Accompanied by her son, Spring visited Brown twice in early November, her arrival duly noted by several newspapers. To Theodore Tilton of the *New York Tribune,* she described Brown as "noble and grand" and quoted him as saying that he faced execution calmly, for *"I do not think I can better serve the cause I love so much, than to die for it!"* Northern news-papers applauded Spring and other women for selflessly wanting to minis-ter to the wounded Brown, whereas Southern journals labeled efforts to nurture the "criminal" Brown a perversion of women's nurturing role. One such article, in reporting initially that Spring had been denied access to Brown, commented sarcastically, "We hope she will be able to survive the disappointment," adding that "all Yankees, of either sex, . . . should be at once driven from our midst." Mrs. Spring's "son" also aroused suspicion, for it was alleged that he was really the brother of Aaron Stevens, using Spring as a vehicle to gain an interview with the conspirator.[18]

Much as Spring's visit became an issue of partisan debate, she seems to have been motivated as much by charity as by the desire to create antislav-ery propaganda. Spending four hundred dollars of her own money, she provided Brown and fellow prisoner Aaron Stevens with flowers, books, clothing, medicine, even food. She wrote them letters, sent music, and eventually arranged for the burial of Stevens and Albert Hazlett at Eagles-wood. Lydia Maria Child praised Spring's initiative and generosity.[19]

Another woman who visited Brown in jail was Mary Ellen Russell, the wife of Massachusetts Judge Thomas Russell. The Russells had been friends of Brown for several years; he had stayed with them in Boston on more than one occasion. Although she never approved of Brown's violent methods, she admired him as a man of vision and idealism. Mary Ellen Russell spent several hours with the condemned man a few weeks before his execution, and, like the visit of Rebecca Spring, her journey inspired partisan feeling. A journalist for the *New York Herald* concluded that her visit was a legit-imate example of female charity, noting that she had touched Brown's heart, "and no woman could turn from him, so full of trials and sorrow." A Southern-sympathizing newspaper countered by censuring Russell, whose "presence here upon such a mission was doing violence to the feelings of our mothers, wives and sisters, and we are glad she made her stay but a short one."[20]

Brown did not encourage these visits and indeed made consistent efforts to seek assistance for his wife and children, rather than himself. When a Quaker woman wrote to him in October, both her letter and his response were illustrative. By conveying admiration for his intentions but concern about his resort to arms, she expressed a common theme among activist correspondents. While distancing herself from violence, she nevertheless saw the parallel with George Washington, who led the nation through seven years of bloodshed in the name of a tax revolt. If Americans honored Washington, she declared, "how much more ought thou to be honored for seeking to free the poor slaves." Brown replied by praising his Quaker friends and asking sympathizers to honor his memory by helping his family.[21]

Scores of other Northern women wrote to Brown, and although their letters may have gone unanswered, they were later printed in the sympathetic biography of Brown written by his friend James Redpath and published in 1860 as abolitionist propaganda. Many of the letters were deeply religious in tone, replete with recommendations of biblical passages for Brown to read and prayers for his eternal life. Others identified with Brown's wife and her impending widowhood, and his young children about to lose their father. As one correspondent assured Brown, "We shall not forget those dear to thee. We take them as a sacred legacy." Several women made specific offers to educate Brown's daughters.[22]

Other letters were more overtly activist and political in tone. Like the Quaker woman who compared Brown to Washington, correspondents invoked the founding fathers, including one Bostonian who stated that "the spirit of Washington may hail thee as a brother and a peer." Several of the letters came from African American women who thanked Brown for helping redeem the nation from what one called the "National Sin of Slavery." For all these women, John Brown was a courageous hero and a source of inspiration. One woman wrote from Brooklyn, "Does not the Commonwealth of Virginia foresee that when they have taken your life, and those of your fellow-sufferers, there will rise up twenty John Browns where there was one before, and the ghost of John Brown will haunt them till they let the oppressed go free?" Louisa May Alcott's laudatory poem was also included in Redpath's book: "No monument of quarried stone / No eloquence of speech / Can grave the lessons on the land / His martyrdom will teach."[23]

While Brown's raid thus inspired some women to give speeches, write letters, and raise money, his actions reminded others of women's prescribed role in a male-dominated society. One woman who wrote to Brown in prison that she was sickened to see "injustice triumph" also expressed frustration that her gender precluded her doing anything to help him. Elizabeth Cady Stanton conveyed similar views in a letter to Susan B. Anthony. Living in rural Seneca Falls, New York, raising a large family, speaking and writing when time allowed, she did not participate in a memorial meeting, even though Brown's actions reminded her of women's limited political role. "The death of my father and the martyrdom of that great and glorious John Brown, conspire to make me regret more than ever my dwarfed and perverted womanhood," she wrote. "In times like these, every soul should do the work of a full grown man."[24] Like most women abolitionists, Stanton had an idealized view of Brown based upon her perception of his role as the "liberator" of Kansas. Perhaps unaware of the violent nature of some of his western activities, she recalled in her memoirs that when she and Anthony visited Kansas in 1867 as part of a woman suffrage campaign, "we reached the sacred soil where John Brown and his sons had helped to fight the battles that made Kansas a free State."[25]

Mrs. Child and Mrs. Mason

The sectional debate over female benevolence and public activism ultimately focused around the antislavery writer Lydia Maria Child. The author of children's literature, self-help books, and several novels, she became a Garrisonian abolitionist and in 1833 published *An Appeal in Favor of That Class of Americans Called Africans*. The resulting negative publicity caused her to lose much of her popular audience. Like Rebecca Spring, she hoped to visit Brown, nurse his wounds, and offer words of support. Her offer, to a far greater extent than Spring's, created a storm of controversy and partisan commentary, and a heated debate over the role of women in times of public crisis.

Child was consumed by the Brown affair, writing to her friend Sarah Shaw that "I suppose *you*, like *me* . . . can think of nothing else but those prisoners in Virginia." As a pacifist, she could not condone Brown's violence; moreover, she deplored his sense of timing, noting to Shaw that the Harpers Ferry insurrection seemed particularly ill-conceived given that free settlers in Kansas seemed to be prevailing politically, winning out in the race to keep the territories free. More sympathetic than most Garrisonians toward those who sought a political solution to slavery, Child also noted that the insurrection came just as the Republican party was beginning to achieve some stature. All the same, Child deeply admired Brown, whom she described as taking "the Old Testament view of things. He is a real psalm-singing, praying Puritan, of the old stamp," and she likened his raid to the Revolutionary War's opening volley at the Battle of Concord.[26]

On October 26, Child wrote a letter to Brown, disclaiming his use of violence but offering her sympathy and lauding his "courage, moral and physical." She wanted to nurse his wounds and "speak to you sisterly words of sympathy and consolation." She also wrote to Virginia Governor Henry Wise seeking his permission to visit Brown and asking that he forward her letter. While declaring her long-time commitment to "uncompromising" abolitionism, she told the governor, perhaps disingenuously, that she would not attempt to use her visit with Brown as an opportunity for ideological debate.[27]

Although Wise responded immediately and affirmatively to Child's requests, citing her "merciful and humane . . . lawful and peaceful" mission, he also admonished her, stating that Brown's insurrection was a natural outgrowth of antislavery agitation and the sympathy of reformers such as herself.[28] Meanwhile, Brown thanked Child for her "kind letter" in his November 4th response, but assured her that he was being well cared for and asked that she direct her efforts toward the welfare of his family and followers, including his wife, three young daughters, and the two daughters-in-law whose husbands had been killed during the abortive insurrection. "I cannot see how your coming here can possibly do me the least good," he concluded and, presumably hinting at her abilities as a propagandist, wrote that "I feel quite certain you can do me *immense good* where you are."[29]

In a response to Governor Wise, published in the Northern press, Child took issue with his contention that the Harpers Ferry raid was a natural consequence of abolitionist agitation. Rather, "it was the legitimate consequence of the continual, and constantly-increasing aggressions of the Slave Power," particularly the attempts to erode the liberty of freedom-loving Americans. In recounting a history of the antislavery struggle from the 1830s, Child concluded that "because slaveholders so recklessly sowed the wind in Kansas, they reaped a whirlwind at Harper's Ferry." Strong though the attachment of Northerners was to the Union, the slave interests had weakened the Union "beyond all power of restoration."[30] To Brown she sent her assurances that his family would be well cared for and commented on a recent letter from Rebecca Spring recounting news of her visit with Brown. "What is in store for us I know not," she concluded. "But we are indeed a guilty nation." In closing, she assured Brown his efforts were not in vain and added, "Farewell, brave and generous man!"[31]

Margaretta Mason, wife of Virginia Senator James Mason, was so infuriated by Child's words that she sent a reply to the Massachusetts abolitionist. Beginning her hostile commentary with the sentence, "Do you read your Bible, Mrs. Child?" Mason proceeded to condemn her for wanting to "soothe with sisterly and motherly care the hoary-headed murderer of Harper's Ferry." Brown hoped to incite a race war, Mason continued, to butcher innocent white women and their children. Southern women were true women because they cared deeply for their slaves, sewed their clothing, nursed them in times of illness and childbirth, and carried out these duties *"in that state of life it has pleased God to place us."* If Child were a true woman herself, she would find sufficient outlets for her benevolent inclinations among the poor people of the North. Finally, Mason asked that Southerners refrain, henceforth, from reading any of Child's popular compositions.[32] Having lost her Southern readership nearly thirty years earlier, Child may have been amused by the latter comment, but she considered in detail Mrs. Mason's words and carefully crafted her own polemic in response. Later she confided gleefully to a friend, "I have answered Mrs. Mason, . . . [and] have given her such a dose of Scripture, that I think she will repent having asked me whether I read my Bible."[33]

Child waited until after Brown's execution to send her reply, which was dated December 17. After wishing Mrs. Mason well, "both in this world and the next," she defended Brown and expressed her confidence he would be judged well by the "impartial pen of History." She then proceeded to present her "dose of Scripture," including more than a dozen passages to show that slavery was dehumanizing, oppressive, and immoral. Adding to her arguments, she quoted from Southern laws making slave marriages illegal, prohibiting African Americans from testifying against Caucasians in court, and prohibiting them from being taught to read and write. She cited Southern newspaper stories about the ill-treatment of slaves, and quoted Sarah and Angelina Grimké along with a number of other native Southerners who had publicly condemned the institution of slavery. She defended the activities of abolitionists who for thirty years had attempted to reason with slaveowners. Ideally, all despotisms should be defeated by moral persuasion, Child warned, but those that do not yield "*must* come to an end by violence. History is full of such lessons." Accentuating the positive, she pointed to the British West Indies as an example of a place where a strong economy had been created by cash labor after slavery's abolition.[34]

Finally, Child turned to the subject of women's role. In response to Mrs. Mason's admonition to engage in benevolent activities instead of abolition, she replied that "it would be extremely difficult to find any woman in our villages who does *not* sew for the poor, and watch with the sick, whenever the occasion requires." Although exaggerating, she claimed that Northern women paid their domestic servants a generous wage so that they could afford to purchase nice clothing instead of receiving it as charity. Northern women also helped those less fortunate in times of illness and childbirth, Child assured Margaretta Mason, adding pointedly, "After we have helped the mothers, *we do not sell the babies.*" She closed by informing Mason of the loss of her Southern readership many years before and expressing her belief that she stood in good company, along with Channing, Bryant, Lowell, Emerson, Stowe, and others.[35]

Unbeknownst to Child, Governor Wise gave her correspondence with him to the *New York Tribune,* prompting the antislavery writer to direct a letter explaining her motive in seeking an audience with Brown.[36] Because the *Tribune* had published the Child/Wise/Brown correspondence in November, she decided to send the newspaper her exchange with Margaretta Mason. Mrs. Mason had already released her own letter to the Virginia press. In 1860 the American Anti-Slavery Society published the entire set of letters under the title *Correspondence between Lydia Maria Child, Gov. Wise and Mrs. Mason, of Virginia.* The pamphlet sold three hundred thousand copies, the largest readership in Child's long literary career. Many years later, she called this publication "the most notable of all my anti-slavery doings." She was probably correct. Three hundred thousand copies was a tremendous printing for that time, and the exchange was also reprinted in many newspapers.[37]

Jean Fagan Yellin has aptly called this publication "Child's major contribution to the ongoing debate over definitions of true womanhood."[38] It is also important to note that her exchange with Mason provoked responses from both Northern and Southern correspondents. While the views of these writers differed widely, virtually all commentators discussed the issue of Child's gender. The antislavery press was predictably laudatory, with *The Liberator* applauding Child's public activism by calling her "a noble representative of Northern women" who had no equal in Virginia or anywhere else south of the Mason-Dixon line.[39] The antislavery press also defended Child against the criticism of others by reprinting critical reviews of her activities and occasionally including editorial comment.

Several antiabolitionist writers addressed letters to Northern newspapers accusing Child of being a weak female who was merely the tool of male abolitionists. In one letter to the editor of the *Boston Transcript,* an individual signing his or her name "x.y." condemned Child as an unsuccessful "Florence Nightingale of Wayland [Massachusetts]" who failed to carry out her plan to visit John Brown. *The Liberator,* in reprinting the letter, condemned its author for this "dastardly fling" and for cowardice in failing to sign the document. The antislavery weekly then reprinted the exchange of letters between Brown and Child as an explanation of why she did not visit the Charlestown jail. The *National Anti-Slavery Standard* reprinted another letter, this one from the *New Haven Register,* in which the writer accused abolitionists of using Child as a means through which to garner national press coverage. According to its author, by putting forth propaganda under the names of "silly women" such as Child, abolitionists hoped "that what comes from the gentler sex will be more apt to make an impression than if it went in the name of [Wendell] Phillips or [William Lloyd] Garrison, [William H.] Seward or [Horace] Greeley." The writer argued Child really had no intention of actually visiting Brown; indeed the entire incident was created merely to generate political capital.[40] This letter was reprinted without comment.

The *Standard* reprinted one letter from a Richmond newspaper that was sympathetic toward Child's benevolent inclinations, while also noting that her "kindness and affection" were misplaced. A Norfolk, Virginia, newspaper suggested Child's motive in attempting to visit Brown was the desire to aid his escape, perhaps by hiding him in her crinoline. Newspapers in the deep South were even more caustic, if the story reprinted from the *New Orleans Picayune* is any indication. Calling Child an "unsexed termagant," this newspaper accused her of being more interested in trying to stir up Northern fanaticism than in nursing the criminal Brown. Her public stance amounted to nothing more than the usual abolitionist harangue about Northern patience and Southern aggression. The newspaper's most virulent criticism of Child, however, was based upon her gender. The antislavery writer did not deserve the job of nurse, noted this scathing article, because Child lacked the "soft touch and . . . eyes that beam with gentlest sympathy"; rather, this woman with her "shrewish treble" spouted only "hyena hatreds." In short, Child might be forgiven her abolitionist polemic, wrong though it was, but she could not be forgiven for being both an activist female and one who made claims to be a "ministering angel."[41]

Lydia Maria Child wrote about her reactions to this criticism in numerous letters to her friends. To Sarah Shaw she commented on the dozens of letters she had received, some from slave states being "violent and filthy beyond belief," thus reinforcing her conviction regarding slavery's degrading impact on the white people of the region. Nor was she swayed by the arguments of those Northerners who warned that abolitionist extremists must respect the government's constitutional obligations to protect slavery, dismissing the letter of one "old fogy," to whom she had recently replied. The attacks on her gender appear not to have fazed Child, who as a veteran of nearly thirty years of antislavery agitation had become accustomed to all manner of criticism from any number of sources. Like most of the abolitionists, she was self-righteous about the cause and her role in it. Indeed, Child believed that God guided her hand in her public comments to Brown. In a letter to Maria Weston Chapman early in 1860, she wrote: "I believe the Lord put it into my heart to write that letter to him, on purpose that I might be whirled aloft by the excitement, and so command a large audience."[42]

John Brown's raid did indeed inspire Lydia Maria Child, who strongly believed that the national crisis called for women's public activism. She set an example for others with a series of new antislavery volumes. In addition to the publication of her correspondence with Mason and Wise and a poem for Redpath's biography of Brown, she wrote several antislavery tracts in the coming months, a prolific achievement for a woman on the threshold of old age. In *The Duty of Disobedience to the Fugitive Slave Act: An Appeal to the Legislators of Massachusetts,* Child warned New Englanders: "As sure as there is a Righteous Ruler in the heavens, if you continue to be accomplices in violence and fraud, God will *not* 'save the Commonwealth of Massachusetts.'" In *The Patriarchal Institution,* she presented a compendium of statements from Southerners, laws upholding slavery, and newspaper articles. She thereby hoped to refute the claims that slaves were quite content in bondage and their lives were better than those of Northern workers, along with the myth of the "chivalrous and high-minded character" of white Southerners. *The Right Way the Safe Way* was Child's treatise describing emancipation in the British West Indies and indicating the superiority of a system of free labor over slavery.[43]

Heroines, Hecklers, and Histrionics

Although Child and Mason garnered more newspaper coverage than any female figures in the Brown imbroglio other than the martyr's widow herself, several others became unwitting players in the sectional controversy over women's roles. One was Miss C. C. Fouke, daughter of a Harpers Ferry tavern keeper, who allegedly threw her body between a mob and Brown conspirator Will Thompson on the second day of the insurrection, thus preventing his murder by vigilantes in the local hotel. *The Liberator* and other Northern newspapers praised this act of bravery and proclaimed the Virginia woman an abolitionist heroine, comparing her efforts to those of Pocahontas and Florence Nightingale. In order to clarify her role in the affair, Fouke wrote a letter to the *St. Louis Republican,* which was also reprinted elsewhere. She did indeed shield Thompson, Fouke wrote, but she did so because she feared mob violence, wanted to protect an ailing sister-in-law who was resting in the next room, and believed Thompson should be tried in the courts. Fouke wanted to assure her readers that she did not sympathize with Thompson's cause. Drawing the veil of Southern womanhood around her, she was emphatic in announcing that she had protected the insurgent *"without touching him."*[44] Ultimately, though, Fouke's efforts to intercede on Thompson's behalf were for naught. Several men dragged him out of the hotel, shot him in the head, and dumped his body in the Potomac River.[45]

Women continued to play a role in the sectional propaganda war surrounding Harpers Ferry long after Brown was dead. The *Richmond Enquirer* printed an article, reprinted as well in the Northern press, announcing that a Yankee schoolteacher had been fired from a position teaching French and music at a local women's academy. Apparently she had rebuked several students for having criticized John Brown and for expressing the belief that he deserved hanging. The *Enquirer* then took aim at educated Northern women and abolitionists by complaining that "Yankee school-teachers . . . come South to make money," and "cannot keep a discreet tongue in their head. Abolition is in them, and it will gush out one way or another." Condemning female activism, the Richmond newspaper speculated that the former teacher would "make capital out of the occurrence somewhere down in Maine or Massachusetts."[46]

Because so many female abolitionists were also active in the woman's rights movement, it is not surprising that their public support of Brown had repercussions for organized feminism. When the New York State Woman's Rights Convention met on February 3–4, 1860, a letter was presented from a representative of Georgia. A petition demanding political rights for women had been sent to a "distinguished member of our Senate," who showed great interest in it, but only after having deleted the word "black." Then came word of the "treasonable and murderous invasion of John Brown," which, coupled with the "sympathy felt for him and the honors paid to his memory, has extinguished the last spark of fraternal feeling for the people of the North. We now look upon you as our worst enemies."[47] Since support for the woman's rights movement was severely limited in the South even before the Brown episode, the loss of interest by one Georgia legislator was hardly a major setback; nevertheless, this letter shows the depth of sectional feeling about Brown.

During the secession winter and spring of 1860–61, women abolitionists demonstrated their belief that the national crisis called for female activism by stepping up their lecturing engagements. They joined male colleagues in making speeches throughout the Northern and Midwestern states. Denouncing slavery and promoting separation from the Southern states, they invoked John Brown. Abby Kelley Foster eulogized the antislavery martyr in a speech in Cleveland, likening him to a hero from another time of national peril, the Marquis de Lafayette. At the Fourth Annual New York State Anti-Slavery Convention in Albany, February 4–5, 1861, Elizabeth Cady Stanton declared that she would rather see her sons die for the cause of abolition than give into the power of slavery. "I would consecrate them all to martyrdom, to die, if need be, bravely, like a John Brown, on the accursed soil of Southern despotism, boldly declaring that Jesus died to give to the nations of the earth a blood bought liberty."[48]

Audiences at such lectures often reacted with hostility. Rowdies variously disrupted the speeches by heckling, turning out the lights, even burning images of the speakers in effigy. Stanton was convinced that the national hysteria surrounding Harpers Ferry accounted for this public intolerance. What she failed to realize was that by advocating secession, these speakers alienated Americans who genuinely feared the destruction of the Union. By invoking John Brown, they reminded the public about the violence that could result from the controversy over slavery. By being publicly active and also female, they further alienated those who, in this time of national crisis, were profoundly uncomfortable with challenges to women's traditional role.[49]

In 1904, when she was more than eighty years old, Susan B. Anthony penned a letter to a friend in Chicago. "You will remember Dec. 2d was the day John Brown was hung," she wrote. "It is just forty-five years ago. We then had a celebration, or a funeral service we might say, in Corinthian Hall in this city [Rochester]." Anthony went on to describe in detail the speeches, the family members who attended, the audience.[50] For her and for others, the memories of Brown's raid were fixed indelibly in their minds. Many recognized the event as their Battle of Concord, as a major turning point in the fight for abolition. The event forced many of them to grapple with their traditional pacifism, in tandem with the desire to see slavery overthrown even by violent means. On a more general level, it led them to debate the issue of women's roles in times of public crisis. As the road to Harpers Ferry led on to war, so these debates would continue.

Notes

1. Lydia Maria Child to Sarah Shaw, Dec. 28, 1859, by permission of Houghton Library, Harvard University, in Child, *Correspondence,* 1169.

2. Julia Ward Howe, *Reminiscences, 1819–1899* (Boston, 1900), pp. 254–55.

3. Sarah Hopper Emerson, ed., *Life of Abby Hopper Gibbons, Told Chiefly through Her Correspondence,* 2 vols. (New York, 1897), 1:261.

4. See Sarah Bradford, *Harriet Tubman: The Moses of Her People* (New York, 1961), pp. 117 and 133–37; Earl Conrad, *Harriet Tubman* (New York, 1969), pp. 114–18 and 122–27; Ripley, ed., *Abolitionist,* 5:222.

5. Lydia Maria Child to Sarah Shaw, Dec. 28, 1859, in Child, *Correspondence,* 1169.

6. *National Anti-Slavery Standard,* Nov. 26, 1859.

7. Ibid., Dec. 10, 1859; *New York Tribune,* Dec. 3, 1859.

8. Otelia Cromwell, *Lucretia Mott* (Cambridge, Mass., 1958), p. 169.

9. *Philadelphia Press,* n.d., reported in the *National Anti-Slavery Standard,* Dec. 10, 1859. See also the *New York Tribune,* Dec. 3, 1859.

10. *New York Tribune,* Dec. 5, 1859.

11. Quoted in *The Liberator,* Nov. 4, 1859; *National Anti-Slavery Standard,* Dec. 10, 1859; the *Worcester Daily Transcript,* Dec. 3, 1859. See also the *Massachusetts Weekly Spy,* Dec. 7, 1859.

12. Ida Husted Harper, *The Life and Work of Susan B. Anthony,* 2 vols. (Indianapolis, 1898), 1:181. See also Nancy A. Hewitt, *Women's Activism and Social Change: Rochester, New York, 1822–1872* (Ithaca, 1984), pp. 188–89; the *National Anti-Slavery Standard,* Dec. 10, 1859; and the *Rochester Union and Advertiser,* Dec. 3, 1859, in Patricia G. Holland and Ann D. Gordon, eds., *The Papers of Elizabeth Cady Stanton and Susan B. Anthony* (Wilmington, 1989; microfilm), ser. 3. For a discussion of Frederick Douglass and his relationship with the local Ladies Anti-Slavery Society, see Amy Kirby Post to Frederick Douglass, Feb. 13, 1860, Post Family Papers, University of Rochester Library.

13. Lydia Maria Child to Sarah Shaw, Dec. 22, 1859, Child, *Correspondence,* 1157.

14. For Child's comment regarding the coffins, see ibid. See also Milton Meltzer, *Tongue of Flame: The Life of Lydia Maria Child* (New York, 1965), p. 148.

15. See Catherine H. Birney, *The Grimké Sisters: Sarah and Angelina Grimké* (Boston, 1885; repr. New York, 1970), pp. 282–83. See also Gerda Lerner, *The Grimké Sisters from South Carolina: Pioneers for Woman's Rights and Abolition* (New York, 1975), pp. 338–39; and Katharine Du Pre Lumpkin, *The Emancipation of Angelina Grimké* (Chapel Hill, 1974), pp. 212–14. On Dec. 19, 1859, Lydia Maria Child wrote to Edward Bullard: "The present report is that they [Brown's children] are to be educated by Mr & Mrs Weld at the Eagle[s]wood Seminary. I should judge that the influence there would be extremely good" (Cornell University Library, courtesy of the Department of Rare Books, Anti-Slavery Manuscript Collection, in Child, *Correspondence,* 1151).

16. Lumpkin, *Emancipation of Angelina Grimké,* pp. 213–14.

17. *New York Tribune,* Nov. 21 and 28, 1859; see also Nov. 15, 1859.

18. See the *New York Tribune,* Nov. 10 and 18, 1859; the *Independent Democrat* and the *Baltimore American,* n.d., quoted in the *National Anti-Slavery Standard,* Nov. 19, 1859; see also Nov. 12, 1859.

19. See Lydia Maria Child to Francis Jackson, Dec. 18, 1859, Bowditch Family Papers, Essex Institute, Salem, Mass., in Child, *Correspondence,* 1150; Lydia Maria Child to Susan Lesley, Dec. 25, 1859, J. Peter Lesley Collection, American Philosophical Society Library, in ibid., 1163; Lumpkin, *Emancipation of Angelina Grimké,* p. 212; and the *New York Tribune,* Nov. 18, 1859.

20. *New York Herald,* Nov. 7, 1859. For the censure of Russell, see the *Independent Democrat,* n.d., quoted in the *National Anti-Slavery Standard,* Nov. 19, 1859. See also Oates, *Purge,* pp. 202–3, 272, and 343–44.

21. *National Anti-Slavery Standard,* Nov. 12, 1859.

22. Quoted in Redpath, *Echoes,* p. 423. See also pp. 420 and 424–25, and Redpath, *Public Life,* p. 415.

23. Quoted in Redpath, *Echoes,* pp. 422, 419, 417–18, and 98, respectively.

24. Quoted in ibid., pp. 416–17. See also Elizabeth Cady Stanton to Susan B. Anthony, Dec. 18, [1859], Stanton Collection, Library of Congress.

25. Elizabeth Cady Stanton, *Eighty Years and More: Reminiscences, 1815–1897* (New York, 1898), p. 245.

26. Lydia Maria Child to Sarah Shaw, Nov. 4, 1859, in Child, *Correspondence,* 1131.

27. Lydia Maria Child to John Brown, Oct. 26, 1859, in Milton Meltzer and Patricia G. Holland, eds., *Lydia Maria Child, Selected Letters, 1817–1880* (Amherst, Mass., 1982), pp. 324–25; Lydia Maria Child to Henry Wise, Oct. 26, 1859, in ibid., pp. 325–26. See also the *National Anti-Slavery Standard,* Nov. 12, 1859; and the *New York Tribune,* Nov. 8, 1859.

28. Henry Wise to Lydia Maria Child, Oct. 29, 1859, Miscellaneous Bound Collection, Massachusetts Historical Society, in Child, *Correspondence,* 1127. See also the *National Anti-Slavery Standard,* Nov. 12, 1859; and the *New York Tribune,* Nov. 8, 1859.

29. John Brown to Lydia Maria Child, Nov. 4, 1859, Boyd Stutler Collection, West Virginia Department of Culture and History, in Child, *Correspondence,* 1132. See also the *New York Tribune,* Nov. 12, 1859; and the *National Anti-Slavery Standard,* Nov. 19, 1859.

30. Lydia Maria Child to Henry Wise, after Oct. 29, 1859, Child, *Correspondence,* 1128. See also the *New York Tribune,* Nov. 19, 1859; and the *National Anti-Slavery Standard,* Nov. 26, 1859.

31. Lydia Maria Child to John Brown, Nov. 16, 1859, in Meltzer and Holland, eds., *Lydia Maria Child, Selected Letters,* pp. 327–28.

32. Margaretta Mason to Lydia Maria Child, Nov. 11, 1859, Miscellaneous Bound Collection, Massachusetts Historical Society, in Child, *Correspondence*, 1134. See also *The Liberator*, Dec. 31, 1859; and the *National Anti-Slavery Standard*, Jan. 7, 1860.

33. Lydia Maria Child to Lucy Osgood, Dec. 25, 1859, Cornell University Library, courtesy of the Department of Rare Books, Anti-Slavery Manuscript Collection, in Child, *Correspondence*, 1164.

34. Lydia Maria Child to Margaretta Mason, Dec. 17, 1859, in Child, *Correspondence*, 1148. See also *The Liberator*, Dec. 31, 1859; and the *National Anti-Slavery Standard*, Jan. 7, 1860.

35. Ibid.

36. *New York Tribune*, Nov. 12, 1859.

37. Lydia Maria Child to Samuel J. May, Sept. 29, 1867, in Meltzer and Holland, eds., *Lydia Maria Child, Selected Letters*, p. 333; see also Child to Horace Greeley, Dec. 18, 1859, ibid., p. 474; and *Correspondence between Lydia Maria Child and Gov. Wise and Mrs. Mason, of Virginia* (New York, 1860).

38. Jean Fagan Yellin, *Women and Sisters: The Antislavery Feminists in American Culture* (New Haven, 1989), p. 62.

39. *The Liberator*, Nov. 11, 1859.

40. *Boston Transcript*, n.d., reprinted in *The Liberator*, Nov. 18, 1859; *New Haven Register*, n.d., reprinted in the *National Anti-Slavery Standard*, Mar. 31, 1860.

41. Richmond *Herald*, n.d., reprinted in the *National Anti-Slavery Standard*, Nov. 6, 1859; *Norfolk (Va.) Argus*, n.d., reprinted in ibid., Nov. 12, 1859; *New Orleans Picayune*, n.d., reprinted in ibid., Dec. 17, 1859.

42. Lydia Maria Child to Sarah Shaw, Dec. 22, 1859, in Child, *Correspondence*, 1157; Child to Maria Weston Chapman, Jan. 11, 1860, by courtesy of the Trustees of the Boston Public Library, Department of Rare Books and Manuscripts, Anti-Slavery Collection, in ibid., 1181.

43. *The Liberator*, Nov. 30, 1860; see also Redpath, *Public Life*, p. 348; Lydia Maria Child, *The Patriarchal Institution, As Described by Members of Its Own Family* (New York, 1860), p. 53; and Lydia Maria Child, *The Right Way the Safe Way* (1862; repr. New York, 1969).

44. *The Liberator*, Nov. 11, 1859; see also the *National Anti-Slavery Standard*, Nov. 19, 1859; the *Boston Transcript*, n.d., reprinted in ibid.; and the *St. Louis Republican*, n.d., reprinted in the *New York Tribune*, Dec. 7, 1859.

45. See Oates, *Purge*, pp. 296–97.

46. *Richmond Enquirer*, Dec. 2, 1859, reprinted in the *New York Tribune*, Dec. 7, 1859, and in the *National Anti-Slavery Standard*, Dec. 17, 1859.

47. "Proceedings of the New York State Woman's Rights Convention, Feb. 3–4, 1860," in Holland and Gordon, eds., *Papers of Elizabeth Cady Stanton and Susan B. Anthony*, ser. 3; see also *The Liberator*, Mar. 2, 1860.

48. See the *Cleveland Weekly Review*, Mar. 16, 1861, reprinted in the *National Anti-Slavery Standard*, Apr. 6, 1861; Elizabeth Cady Stanton, "Free Speech," lecture delivered at the Fourth Annual New York State Anti-Slavery Convention, Feb. 4–5, 1861, in the scrapbooks of Elizabeth Cady Stanton, Vassar College Library, Special Collections.

49. Theodore Stanton and Harriot Stanton Blatch, eds., *Elizabeth Cady Stanton as Revealed in Her Letters, Diary, and Reminiscences*, 2 vols. (New York, 1922), 1:180. For a broader discussion of women's roles during the secession crisis, see my discussion in Wendy Hamand Venet, *Neither Ballots nor Bullets: Women Abolitionists and the Civil War* (Charlottesville, Va., 1991), ch. 2.

50. Susan B. Anthony to Ella S. Stewart, Nov. 30, 1904, Susan B. Anthony Collection, Chicago Historical Society.

Part III
Northern and Southern
Opponents of Brown

5

PETER KNUPFER

A Crisis in Conservatism: Northern Unionism and the Harpers Ferry Raid

"THE HARPERS FERRY STORY, judged on its merits, proves little or nothing of immediate significance, either political or social," Henry Raymond wrote in his *New York Times* in late October 1859. "It neither establishes the predominance of Abolitionism at the North, nor the security of Slavery at the South. Its related meanings lie far deeper than the surface of events, and will only be developed with time."[1] Unlike later historians of the sectional conflict, Raymond thought that the raid on Harpers Ferry had not foreclosed the country's options. To this conservative Republican editor, events had reaffirmed Northern fidelity to the Union and left "the peace of the Union ... very much in the hands of the South. If the South will frankly unite with the Conservative North in keeping the whole question of slavery out of Congress and beyond the national interference—in leaving it, that is, to the laws of nature, and the practical good sense of the people—the *émeute* at Harper's Ferry will prove, indeed, a 'blessing in disguise' to the whole country."[2]

In fact, the Harpers Ferry raid occurred just as elements in the South were indeed attempting to "unite with the Conservative North" to put aside the slavery question. In October 1859 the North was still in the midst of a major realignment of political forces stemming from the collapse of the Whig party and the rise of the Know-Nothing and Republican rivals early in the decade. Conservatives, especially those in the Ohio River valley and the commercial centers of the East, held out hope of creating a national union organization to overpower sectional militants in the Democratic and Republican parties. The raid on Harpers Ferry provided them with an opportunity to discredit radicals in both sections and proclaim themselves as the only "safe," conservative, party of national reconciliation.

The problem with creating such a national coalition was that practically every politician in the North professed to be "conservative" and opposed to disunion. But several obstacles prevented the amalgamation of this widespread sentiment. One problem was the confusion of party labels, especially among groups opposed to the Republican party. Although people in each party might agree that the Union was in danger from sectional agitation and that violence and party spirit were eroding public respect for the republic's vital institutions, they also blamed one another for starting the conflict. Another reason for the fragmentation of conservative sentiment was the fundamental shift in the nature of American nationalism in the 1840s and 1850s. Spatial and economic expansion and integration had raised the stakes of power, thereby sharpening the division of Northern public opinion about how to deal with the ongoing sectional crisis. A full understanding of the North's response to the Harpers Ferry raid must recognize that this intensified sectional dynamic, while integral to the North's perceptions of the raid's significance, was the subtext for a complex and vehement quarrel among Northerners. For if the raid led Southerners to debate more deeply how to protect slavery, it also led Northerners to argue over how to preserve the union.

The Republicans represented one approach to the problem. Their understanding of the Union stemmed from the party's critique of slavery. The party's consensus on "no more slave states" required a much more vigorous assertion of federal power than the preceding generation had been comfortable with. And the party's rock-solid opposition to secession indicated that it would regard disunion as insurrection. Republicans further believed that the way to end the agitation over slavery was to defeat the slave power in a peaceful but direct confrontation. In the upcoming local, state, and national elections the party hoped to reach moderate and conservative voters by promoting itself as the only organization strong enough to suppress the spiraling violence and disorder of sectional politics.[3]

Against the Republicans stood a diverse, factionalized opposition whose beliefs might be characterized as "constitutional unionist." This opposition represented the cluster of beliefs and interests that had created and sustained the second American party system. The group included those national Democrats who remained loyal to Illinois Senator Stephen Douglas; still-unattached conservative Whigs of the Clay/Webster school who were reluctant to move into a sectional organization; and members of the American party. Their solution to the slavery issue was to set it aside by reviving the economic issues that had so successfully shaped the partisan conflict of the 1830s and early 1840s. Although this group agreed with the Republicans that the agitation over the slavery question by sectional militants threatened the Union, it did not believe that a political confrontation with the South would resolve anything. As self-described conservatives, the constitutional unionists offered the prescriptions of the founding generation, which had warned that sectional parties were more dangerous than sectionalism or partyism alone.

The constitutional unionists were themselves divided between the national Democratic party and the fragments of its now-moribund opponent, the Whig party. Old partisan animosities had kept these groups separated during the sectional struggle. Already divided into Northern and Southern factions, the Democrats urgently sought the votes of centrists in the lower North and upper South by touting the shopworn rhetoric of Union nationalism and popular sovereignty. Reeling from the divisive effects of the dispute over slavery in Kansas, the regular Democratic organization faced a chorus of opposition from discontented Southerners, who, backed by the Buchanan administration, demanded the ousting of Douglas as titular party leader and the imposition of a federal slave code in the territories. At the same time, national Democratic leaders were furiously at work to cement the party's broken wings into an effective coalition for the upcoming 1860 election. The next session of Congress would be the arena for Northern and Southern contention over the Democratic nomination at Charleston the following May.[4]

Whigs and Americans yet outside the Republican ranks had been trying for seven years to rebuild their national coalition into a united opposition to the Democrats. Politicians in this group blamed the Democrats for having stirred up sectional passions by repealing the Missouri Compromise in 1854. The Whig/American contingents, having designated themselves the "Opposition" by 1858, looked for leadership to Senator John J. Crittenden of Kentucky, former president Millard Fillmore, the Whig/American candidate in 1856, and the commercial elites of New York City, Boston, Baltimore, and Philadelphia. The correspondence and public utterances of these leaders reveal considerable concern over the so-called reserved vote of conservatives, whose regular attendance at the ballot box had fallen off since the demise of the Whig party and who remained susceptible to the increasing Republican emphasis on Whig economic issues like the tariff.[5]

The fluidity of party coalitions from 1858 to 1860 made it impossible to predict the outcome of the next general election. For a brief moment in 1858, Republicans and Northern Democrats united to defeat the Buchanan administration's policy of forcing a proslavery constitution on Kansas. When that dalliance ended, the Opposition and the Republicans carried on discussions aimed at forging a coalition against the Democrats. Fledgling Republican organizations had cropped up in some border states, especially Missouri, and some Republican strategists, including Horace Greeley of the *New York Daily Tribune*, had been pressing the party to moderate its radical image from the 1856 campaign and adopt a pro-Southern strategy for 1860.

In the months preceding Brown's raid, the Opposition had mounted strong and occasionally successful challenges to the Democratic party in the border states, as well as in North Carolina and Tennessee. Republicans either had to defeat this rising conservative sentiment or compromise with it in an anti-Democratic coalition.[6]

Students of electoral politics at the decade's end generally agree that John Brown's raid crippled the budding national union movement by ending any hope of a united opposition to the Democratic party.[7] On the one hand, Southern Oppositionists, thrown on the defensive for even considering an alliance with any Northern organization, were further isolated because they were less inclined than their Northern friends to court the Democratic party, their traditional enemy. On the other hand, Northern Oppositionists, already estranged from the Republicans by the latter's pronouncements about a "house divided" by an "irrepressible conflict" between the North and the South, reckoned that the Republicans would themselves be abandoned by a conservative electorate.[8] Lacking an effective coalition partner in either section in the election of 1860, the Opposition would wither and die, its feeble attempt at third-party politics, the Constitutional Union party, having failed utterly.

But did the Harpers Ferry raid wreck the national union movement? Did it encourage the Opposition to attack the Republican party, now tainted by complicity in the raid? Or was the rift between the Opposition and the Republicans a matter of tactical choices among voters and leaders who otherwise shared a common attachment to a common concept of the Union? Perhaps the uniting of the Opposition with the Republicans failed to occur as the result simply of calculated gambles by both camps that separate organizations were more likely to succeed than an amalgamated one. Yet it is also possible that the attempt at fusion was stillborn because Northerners were turning away from the looser, confederationist notions of the Madisonian constitutional tradition toward the muscular nationalism championed by the Republican party. Arguably, the raid and its aftermath encouraged the Opposition to strike out on its own and make a third-party effort to wield the balance of power in Congress and in the presidential elections in the coming year. In that sense, many conservatives saw the further estrangement of the Republicans from the Opposition to be a good thing.

The resounding defeat of the conservative Constitutional Union and national Democratic parties in 1860 would demonstrate how badly Northern Oppositionists had misread the strength of constitutional unionism in the North. Just as the raid and its aftermath revealed tactical differences among Southerners about how to protect slavery, so did it uncover Northern differences about how to preserve the Union, differences that the Republicans would more effectively reconcile and use to their advantage than would their opponents. For the key to Republican recovery from the setback of Harpers Ferry was the extent to which the party's leadership could demonstrate how an antislavery policy could be squared with the defense, and not the breakup, of the Union.

*   *   *   *   *

The immediate reaction and furious aftermath to the raid boded poorly for the Republicans, however.[9] The party had been trying to polish its unionist credentials when the raid occurred, because further sectional conflict, especially if traced to the party or its more vocal antislavery supporters, could hurt its bid to control the House of Representatives in the Thirty-sixth Congress and to win the presidency in 1860. But the images of emancipation, insurrection, race war, and disunion were too powerful to suppress. Abolitionists beatified Brown; Southerners demonized abolitionists. Both groups predicted disunion. Prominent Republicans deplored Brown's tactics while praising his courage and conviction and blamed the "Pro-Slavery Democracy" for the Kansas atrocities that had induced him to act.[10] Democrats had a field day, charging responsibility for the raid directly to the Republican high command. Southern attitudes hardened into a firm resolution that fence sitters and moderates were just as culpable and threatening as the most radical abolitionists. Symbolic of Southern disenchantment after the raid, 350 Southern students at two medical colleges in Philadelphia withdrew, to the cheers of governors and citizens in Virginia, North Carolina, and Georgia.[11] As one Northern hunker observed to Jefferson Davis, "All things considered, the Insurrection at Harpers Ferry is a fortunate thing: It brought on the Crisis *in time* and will enable the true men of the Country to put down & *for ever* the Republicans and their Confederates."[12] Even the *Baltimore Sun,* usually the soul of border-state moderation, editorialized breathlessly a week before Brown's execution that the South could not live "under a government, the majority of whose subjects or citizens regard John Brown as a martyr and a Christian hero, rather than a murderer and robber."[13]

The Thirty-sixth Congress, meeting three days after Brown's execution, sank into a sectional gridlock, members even brandishing loaded weapons. Southern Democrats blocked the Republican agenda in the House, and the two sides quarreled over the speakership for almost two months. A Senate committee investigated the Harpers Ferry incident in hopes of uncovering subversives. Finding none, the committee contented itself with publishing a mass of evidence and harassing reluctant witnesses.[14] "Paranoia continued to induce paranoia," C. Vann Woodward writes of the raid's aftermath, "each antagonist infecting the other reciprocally, until the vicious spiral ended in war."[15]

In this volatile atmosphere the nation entered the campaigning season for the crucial general election of 1860. Yet it was not as clear then as it seems now that conservative hopes of a national union coalition were destroyed by the raid; at least, national Union men did not act as if the raid had destroyed their plans. In fact, John Brown's actions had raised the issue of law and order, an issue conservatives believed rightly belonged to them, thus giving them a ready-made weapon with which to bludgeon Republicans and lead voters away from Democratic and old Whig ranks. An outpouring of Union sentiment in the North, if added to recent electoral gains in the upper South, could signal to the Opposition that it might be able to make an independent bid for the balance of power in the country.

Perhaps the most important cheering sign to conservatives hoping for a powerful national union party was the widespread denunciation of Brown in the North, which the Opposition read as a gauge of the deep conservative sentiment of the country. Even the mildest support for Brown drew instant, harsh criticism. Men of commerce and property—and Southern connections—got up the usual Union meetings in cities across the North. Huge crowds in Philadelphia, New York City, and Boston roared approval as dozens of prominent speakers pledged to stand by the South. The New York merchants' "Vigilant Association," charged with investigating the origins of the raid, issued a "manifesto" claiming that a secret "Central Association" had attracted abolitionists who were "long contemplating a war of races."[16]

Prominent Republican leaders became easy targets. William Henry Seward caught the most fire for his famous statement a year earlier in Rochester, New York, that an "irrepressible conflict between opposing and enduring forces . . . means that the United States must and will, sooner or later, become either entirely a slaveholding nation or entirely a free-labor nation." Seward had already alienated constitutional unionists in 1850, when he claimed that a "higher law than the constitution" sanctioned resistance to slavery and to any compromises with it. When considered in light of Abraham Lincoln's vivid evocation in June 1858 of a "house divided" over slavery, Seward's statements stood as the clearest indication yet that the new Republican party and its leaders were willing to confront rather than compromise with the institution. To conservatives of all parties and sections, such statements were tantamount to a declaration of war against the "Union as it is"—a Union founded with the idea that sectional partisanship would be fatal to the constitutional order. Revelations soon after Brown's arrest to the effect that prominent abolitionists had bankrolled the raid only intensified the denunciations of Republicans in general and abolitionists in particular as agitators who had preyed upon Brown's sense of victimization in Kansas in order to get him to instigate a slave revolt.[17]

This argument, however, reversed cause and effect and minimized Brown's responsibility for the raid. To constitutional unionists, Brown was not just an abolitionist. He was a *murdering* abolitionist propelled into his terrible design by the parlor revolutionaries of Northern abolitionism. In their view, Brown didn't have to convince abolitionists to go along with him; instead, they planted in the mind of an already passionate and vengeful man the idea that the raid would inflame a long-delayed but ultimately irrepressible conflict between the sections. According to the Democratic *Providence Post,* Brown was a sane fanatic, like William Lloyd Garrison (only braver). He "has been for years a man of blood—a highway robber and murderer. And he was undoubtedly moved to the commission of his crime at Harper's Ferry by no more honorable or noble motive than *hatred* to slaveholders. All that can be said in excuse of his conduct is, that he did not perceive his obligations to the community in which he lived. He had given way to his passions—constantly fed and fired by Republican orators and writers—until he was incapable of judging of his own position and duty."[18] The *Post,* along with fellow conservative newspapers like the *Boston Courier* and other constitutional unionists like Amos Lawrence of Boston, called unsuccessfully on Virginia's Governor Henry Wise to spare Brown from the noose. Wise would thereby defuse Northern sympathy for the old man, deprive abolitionists of a martyr, and announce to the world that slavery's safety was so certain and Virginia's sense of justice so tempered with mercy that the state could afford to dispose of Brown quickly and get on to other and more important matters.[19]

Democrats and various elements of the Opposition harped on the themes of lawlessness and institutional disintegration. Such complaints resonated with Northerners weary of sectional and partisan strife. Practically all Northerners had reached the conclusion that sectional conflict was undermining the country's institutions at an alarming rate. But solutions to the problem were not as easy to devise. Had the raid occurred a decade earlier, when sectional issues—but not sectional parties—threatened the nation, it would probably have blended into the background of crime and disorder that characterized the public prints in Jacksonian America. Even in 1859 the papers routinely reported border incidents with Mexico that came close to renewed war with the United States; filibustering expeditions to Cuba and Central America; mob violence and vigilantism in Baltimore, New Orleans, and New York City; the ongoing war between the Buchanan administration and the Mormon colony in Utah; and the usual "agony columns" with their train of accidents, murder, and mayhem.[20]

Lawlessness and violence also had long been associated with sectional conflict: the forced rescues of fugitive slaves, the brutal attack on Senator Charles Sumner on the floor of the Senate in May 1856, the bloody civil war in Kansas Territory—all demonstrated the violent reflexes stimulated by sectional tensions. "It is now incorporated in the national ethics of the entire country that there is no obligation upon citizens to enforce laws not entirely comporting with their interests, or the peculiar notions of right which each may happen to cherish," a southern Whig complained. Lashing out at the "slave-driving Democracy" and "black Republicanism" as threats to public order, one of Millard Fillmore's friends fumed that "we talk of the anarchy and confusion prevailing in Mexico, but we overlook the infamy and treason in Utah, and the disgraceful conduct of the Representatives in Congress. The John Brown raid on Harpers Ferry, and the lynching and tarring and feathering now taking place in the South, for a mere expression of opinion, is disgraceful to our annals." Indeed, even a cursory survey of the major newspapers in the late 1850s reveals a general fear that the country was spinning out of control, a fear that the controversy over slavery had intensified and broadened.[21]

To the constitutional unionists, violence was the inevitable consequence of attempting to resolve through politics a problem that only the uncontrollable forces of population and economic competition could settle. Having made their careers in a political system that had encouraged this belief, and having presided over several decades of economic growth that had intertwined the two sections' economic systems more firmly, constitutional unionists thought that the cure of confrontation was worse than the disease of slavery itself. In politics, this meant that only symptomatic relief—the suppression of slavery agitation by common agreement of the major political parties—would preserve "the Union as it is."[22]

Constitutional unionists saw no underlying "irrepressible conflict" at work in Brown's raid because they saw no natural incompatibility between freedom and slavery within the present Union. The slaves were content; they had not rebelled. Northerners had reaffirmed their faith in the Constitution's protections for slavery. Moreover, the country's history of prosperity and of national expansion had demonstrated the mutual reciprocity of slave and free-labor systems. New York Unionists declared in mid-December "our unalterable purpose to stand by the Constitution *in all its parts,* as interpreted by the Supreme Court of the United States; and we hereby denounce as unpatriotic and untrue, revolutionary and dangerous, the idea of an irrepressible conflict existing between the two great sections of our beloved Union. On the contrary, we maintain that the North and South were created for each other; that there is a natural and necessary affinity between them by parentage, history, religion, language, and geographical position; and that even their different climates and different forms of industry add strength to this bond of Union, by enabling them to supply each other's wants."[23] Speaking at a Union meeting in Philadelphia on December 7, 1859, Isaac Hazlehurst reminded the crowd that "our path of duty is plain. Fidelity to all sections and at all times, and obedience to the constituted authorities of the land, will make the Union perpetual. With our Union as it is, and thorough fraternal feeling between its various parts, we may present ourselves to the world as a grand nationality, fostering its own labor and developing its own resources."[24]

Repeated references to the mutuality of economic interest between the North and the South as a "grand nationality, fostering its own labor and developing its own resources" spoke to an important theme in conservative interpretations of the country's political and economic development. Hazlehurst and his intellectual kinsmen in the professional classes of the North and the border states were articulating a vision of interlocking, regulated labor systems working to develop the country's material resources under the sponsorship of vigorous national authority. In this view, slave and free labor were not antagonistic but complementary, for both suited the moral, geographical, and racial makeup of their respective sectors of the country. Constitutional unionists, whether in the North or the South, viewed the growing integration of the national economy as a sign of progress, not of decay.

With the continued protection afforded by the Constitution, slaveholders could rest assured that a federal policy of fostering economic development would redound to the benefit of all. Alexander H. H. Stuart, soon to be a leader in the Constitutional Union party, pointed this out to the Richmond Agricultural Society in late October. Talk of an "irrepressible conflict" between the sections denied the wisdom of the framers, he argued. Only *similar* labor systems compete with each other. Northerners and Southerners, prompted by profit not by philanthropy, had developed labor systems attuned to the needs of their communities and sections. Typical of conservative thinking by this time, Stuart's view of political economy tried to emphasize the unity of interest created by diverse economic systems. The rational self-interest of everyone, applied and articulated gradually through time, had produced this unique blending of peoples and economic systems.[25] The constitutional framework encouraged the further incorporation of free- and slave-labor systems into this unique American blend. But the evolutionary process would only continue with the suppression of sectional extremists and demagogic politicians and the return to a Whiggish policy of federally sponsored economic development.

The raid therefore demonstrated to constitutional unionists the stability of slavery, if not the moderation of slaveholders. Conservatives approved of the disciplined, well-regulated tempo of plantation agriculture, for not only did it produce efficiently for Northern merchants, manufacturers, and consumers, but it also created an obedient black population. The failure of slaves to join the raid, when considered alongside Southern threats of disunion, enabled conservatives to continue to accept slavery while condemning slaveholding militants for disregarding clear evidence that both Northerners and blacks remained faithful to their obligations.

Whig/American constitutional unionists saw little reason after the Brown affair to merge with like-minded Democrats, however. If the agitation over slavery, and not slavery itself, was responsible for the raid, these conservatives could hardly support either of the parties that had used the slavery issue as a route to national power. Despite the creeping conservatism of the Republicans, constitutional unionists could not trust a party whose leaders had campaigned on the fundamental antagonism between free and slave labor. Nor could they support Republicans whose guarded reaction to Brown's raid and subsequent execution suggested that the party still wanted to mollify its radical constituencies. Convinced that the raid had thoroughly discredited Seward and estranged conservative Republicans, the Washington correspondent of the *New York Express* crowed in late October that "every day gives fresh indications that the Opposition Party *outside* of the Republican ranks, can control the next election, by holding the undoubted balance of power."[26] As one of Senator Crittenden's correspondents put it, "I think that the Harpers Ferry affair will do much to bring out the Conservative element; and it will detract no little from the Republican party."[27] The Opposition could now make a concerted effort to separate the Republican leadership from the mass of its followers and draw the latter into a national party. Finally, the concentration of old Whig and American strength in the lower North and border states propelled them toward forging their own third party instead of continuing their efforts to form a united national opposition with the Republicans against the Democrats. As Michael Holt and Daniel Crofts have pointed out, the continued existence of strong, competitive party systems in the border states up to and through the election of 1860 indicated to the Southern Opposition that it could rely on its own resources and power base to challenge the Democratic party.[28]

It is not surprising, then, to see Whig/American constitutional unionists gathering in Washington in mid-December 1859 to launch plans for a Union party and call for presidential nominations from the states. The Brown raid had not driven these elements into the Democratic party, nor had it suppressed their movement. Instead, the strength of conservatism in the North, as opposed to its weaknesses and divisions, convinced them that they now had an opportunity to revive the moribund Whig party as a conservative Union party under the platform pronounced by Henry Clay in the aftermath of the Compromise of 1850: "The Union, the Constitution, and the enforcement of the Laws." Furthermore, the Constitutional Union party recognized that a quick launch of their party might co-opt old Whig and American voters in the North who might be tempted to vote Republican. By calling an early nominating convention and leaving the choice of candidates to individual state organizations, the party hoped to encourage Northern conservatives to make common cause with the movement before the Republicans were to meet in Chicago on May 16. But aside from this nod in the direction of Northern Oppositionists, the Constitutional Union party concentrated on the conciliation of Opposition sentiment in the South, where Oppositionists faced Democratic accusations of infidelity to slavery and Southern rights. The "fanatics," a "Southern gentleman" wrote from Philadelphia on December 5 to the *Daily National Intelligencer,* were vastly outnumbered in the North, "but one of these raving maniacs creates more splutter than one hundred sober-minded conservative citizens. . . . The South are led to believe that they and their institutions have no friends in the free States, and they seem to ignore the large anti-Republican party that exists in every free State of the Union."[29]

But "anti-Republican" elements in the North were mostly members of the Democratic party. The new Constitutional Union party would not make overtures until very late in the election campaign to the party they blamed for the sectional conflict. To the Constitutional Union party, the Democrats consisted of two elements: conservatives (some of them former Whigs temporarily voting Democrat), who were susceptible to the blandishments of the Opposition, and factious partisans and disunionists, who had made common cause in the slavery question and were beyond redemption. The former would recognize their natural coalition partners and come over to the Union party, abandoning the latter group to sink in its own treason and ambition. Millard Fillmore made this point frequently, both publicly and privately; the Democrats' revival of the slavery agitation through the repeal of the Missouri Compromise was the real source of the sectional conflict, and Democrats were determined to stand on that act now and forever. To old Whigs like Fillmore, Brown was an agent of larger, more sinister forces set loose by sectional interests. "You have been at the South and you can best appreciate the feeling excited by John Brown's foolish and criminal invasion of Virginia," Fillmore wrote to Dorothea Dix. "He doubtless believed what these insane fanatics at the North have taught, that the slave would rise in mass and join his insurrectionary standard." Both sides had broken the compromise settlement of 1850 and had thus involved the country in a war over Kansas. The result was the creation of "a party, fired with a fanatical zeal against the imaginary wrongs of slavery, and stimulated by the hope of partizan success, that seems to endanger every thing which I hold sacred in our political institutions."[30] Throughout

the coming year, despite growing evidence that many Northern conservatives were listening to Republican professions of Union conservatism, Fillmore remained adamant in his opposition to the Republicans and the Democrats.[31] Instead, he and other Constitutional Union leaders expected
Democratic conservatives to abandon what they sneered was the "ultra fire-
eating disunion democracy" as a stinking mass of corruption and support
the new third party.[32]

The Constitutional Unionists' constant professions of conservative
strength in the North were, however, leading the party away from organizing that sentiment for the upcoming election. The refusal of conservative
Opposition congressmen to support either a Republican or Democratic
candidate for Speaker illustrated this complacency about the state of public
opinion. American and old Whig conservatives thought that an independent party, perhaps centered around the Southern Opposition in Congress
and emanating from a conservative Speaker of the House, could attract
national support.[33] And the decision to substitute "Constitutional" for "national" in the party's name further indicated the party's heightened sensitivity to Southern fears of consolidation.[34] Such overconfidence would
prove self-defeating; the Constitutional Union organization managed to
build an anti-Republican fusion ticket in only one Northern state.

*   *   *   *   *

The failure of the Constitutional Union party left the field in the North to
the Democratic and Republican parties. The Democratic party remained as
the most potent expression of constitutional unionist sentiment in 1859
and 1860. The party's traditional policy on slavery—local option, or popular sovereignty—had blended well with the party's long-standing cham-
pionship of the egalitarian and populist impulses of a rootless and highly
mobile culture. But under the impact of sectional pressures a loose set of
nostrums about self-government in the West became a hard, structured
doctrine locked into its own inner contradictions. The party of strict construction and limited government was by the mid 1850s a law-and-order
party demanding the rigid enforcement of the Fugitive Slave Act and the
conquest of Cuba.[35]

The Harpers Ferry raid and its aftermath increased this willingness to
apply public power to public issues. Democrat Caleb Cushing, in a fiery
speech to a Boston Union meeting, depicted the horrors of civil war if
recriminations and dark conspiracies by fanatical abolitionists were allowed to continue. He urged his listeners to block attempts to interfere with
other states. "For, gentlemen, when we look forward to the consequences
of a disruption of this Union, is the North then to invade the South for the

purpose of carrying on an armed prosecution of these projects of inter-ference with the institutions of the South?"[36]

Democrat Stephen Douglas moved quickly to reinforce the federal gov-ernment's power to enforce the laws. He introduced an antisedition mea-sure for stopping interstate conspiracies and for protecting property in the territories. Speaking to crowded Senate galleries on January 23, 1860, Doug-las defended this new form of intervention in both the territories and the states as a natural and necessary exercise of the federal government's re-sponsibility to maintain the domestic tranquility against "this system of sectional warfare." Douglas's resolution called for a bill in favor of "protect-ing each State and Territory of the Union against Invasion by the authori-ties or inhabitants of any other State or Territory, and for the suppression and punishment of conspiracies or combinations in any State or Territory, with intent to invade, assail, or molest the government, inhabitants, prop-erty, or institutions of any other State or Territory of the Union."[37]

Targeting national-minded conservatives in both sections, Douglas chal-lenged the Buchanan administration's handling of the raid's aftermath. On November 25, Governor Wise had written an excited appeal to President Buchanan to "take steps to preserve peace between the States" before a rumored rescue of Brown could go forward from sanctuaries in New York, Pennsylvania, and Ohio. The president's reply on November 28 prefigured his position in the secession winter of the following year: the Constitution gave him no authority to "'take steps' for this purpose." Buchanan's vac-illation was Douglas's opportunity to prove that slavery was safer under the regular administration of the Constitution than under the faltering ap-plication of the instrument by James Buchanan.

Buchanan was not the only target of Douglas's proposal. The Illinois Democrat took special pains to argue that conspiracies must be ferreted out by the courts. "You must punish the conspiracy, the combination with intent to do the act, and then you will suppress it in advance." What "com-bination" was responsible for the Harpers Ferry raid? "I have no hesitation in expressing my firm and deliberate conviction that the Harper's Ferry crime was the natural, logical, inevitable result of the doctrines and teach-ings of the Republican party, as explained and enforced in their platform, their partisan presses, their pamphlets and books, and especially in the speeches of their leaders in and out of Congress." Republicans made war on slavery, Douglas declared, by preying on the passions and prejudices of Northerners and Southerners. Dismissing Republican disavowals of the Brown raid, Douglas called on them to "repudiate and denounce the doc-trines and teachings which produced the act."

Douglas and his supporters further reiterated the general constitutional union argument that a diversity of labor systems strengthened rather than weakened the Union. Building on the arguments he had repeatedly made during his debates with Abraham Lincoln in 1858, Douglas claimed that slaveowning was a matter of choice. "If the theory of the Constitution shall be carried out by conceding the right of the people of every State to have just such institutions as they choose, there cannot be a conflict, much less an 'irrepressible conflict,' between the free and the slaveholding States." Furthermore, talk about a "house divided" by an "irrepressible conflict" denied decades of prosperity produced by the mutual dependence of these systems. Harpers Ferry, in his mind, represented the natural outgrowth of Republican moralizing about the unmitigated evil of slavery.[38]

Douglas's desire to bring law and order to the territories and to interstate relations reflected not only his disgust with President Buchanan's lack of resolve in the Brown affair or his conviction that the Republicans were ultimately to blame for the raid. It also stemmed from his ongoing campaign to formalize popular sovereignty, the heart of the party's policy on slavery. Brown's raid occurred just after Douglas had published an article in *Harper's Monthly* magazine, which tied the loose and flexible policy of popular sovereignty to the anchor of constitutional traditions.[39] Douglas's desire to give constitutional respectability to popular sovereignty mirrored the general trend toward more structured, ideological, and constrained discourse near the end of the 1850s.

But popular sovereignty in Kansas had proved a lawless doctrine. Douglas himself had inadvertently encouraged this state of affairs with his Freeport Doctrine, which attempted to maintain some maneuvering room for the territories by denying that the Dred Scott Decision prevented a territory from repelling slaveholders. Douglas's move, then, sought to dignify popular sovereignty with enough historical and intellectual respectability to make it a viable conservative, unifying platform for 1860. Douglas's defense of these measures was an antisecession, pro-Union defense that tried to press back the rising slavery agitation of Southerners.[40]

It is not clear that Douglas's moves mollified Southerners already disappointed by his opposition to the proslavery Lecompton constitution of Kansas. His assaults on the Republicans offered reassurance that a Douglas administration would, in effect, suppress that party. Some Southern Democrats remained loyal to him and the national organization.[41] But his speech on his sedition bill, like the resolution itself, also hit at disunion conspiracies. And Douglas's defense of popular sovereignty merely confirmed Southern belief that at heart he was a free-soiler.[42]

The rumored complicity of Republicans with the Harpers Ferry raid should have given Douglas's maneuvers stronger chances of success in attracting Constitutional Unionists to his side and in building influential delegations for the upcoming convention in Charleston. In the state and local elections of late fall and winter 1859, the party showed moderate gains in New York, New Jersey, Massachusetts, and Maryland, but not enough to offset Republican control of key positions in some of those states.[43] In an earlier era, a ready-made issue like Harpers Ferry could have made Douglas invincible, but too many other divisive forces were at work in his party and in the nation. Most important, the Republican party was proving its ability to meet the challenge posed by the raid, in its drive to legitimize its platform and expand its constituencies.

Although the Republican party repeatedly denied that it sought the breakup of the Union or unlawful interference with slavery, it still had not shed the radical image projected in its 1856 campaign. In that year, the Republicans denounced slavery as barbaric, put forward a platform full of antislavery and anti-Southern bombast, and campaigned not as the party of Union, but as the party of the North. Since then, Republicans had moved assertively toward the political center, seeking to convert conservative Whigs and nativists reluctant to join a sectional organization.[44] By the time John Brown entered Harpers Ferry in October 1859, the Republicans were competing with the Democrats at all levels of the political system for the "floating" votes of uncommitted conservatives. The Lecompton fight and the Republicans' moderated tone and shift of emphasis toward economic issues in the aftermath of the Panic of 1857 helped the party win important local and congressional elections in 1858 and stand poised for victory in the upcoming presidential election in 1860.

The Republicans' moderation in tone was accompanied by an internal debate over whether a Southern strategy to conciliate old-line Whigs and Americans would best demonstrate the Republicans' fidelity to the Union. Horace Greeley had been a vocal advocate of such an approach. He was delighted by the appearance of Republican support in the border states and by the tentative alliance of Republicans and border-state men in the fight against the proslavery Lecompton constitution.[45] Republican conservatives, men like Thomas Corwin of Ohio, Frank and Montgomery Blair of Maryland, and Edward Bates of Missouri, were heartened by the possibility of such a united Opposition. They had concluded that the party's rekindled romance with Whig economics and its retreat from overt sectional appeals had certified its "safety." Their test of the party's legitimacy rested on its acceptance of peaceful, constitutional processes and its respect for traditional political institutions.[46]

Through the late summer of 1859, conservative Republicans crusaded for a united Opposition to the Democrats. Bates in particular saw his star rising as the only man capable of broadening the party's base of support. The border-state press often linked Bates's name with that of John Crittenden or John Bell as a united Opposition ticket for 1860. In April 1859

Bates issued a public letter that briefly deprecated any agitation of "the Negro question" and went on at length about economic and foreign policy issues.[47] Like the Fillmore men, Bates saw the Kansas-Nebraska Act as the germ of Harpers Ferry, and he hoped that his bid for the presidency would alienate radical Republicans while conciliating a larger number of moderates in all parties, North and South. Nor did Bates and his friends believe that Harpers Ferry had doomed his candidacy; through December, Bates's conservative supporters worked for his nomination.[48] Thomas Corwin, recruited by Republicans for the crucial congressional races of 1858, reported from Ohio in late October 1859 that "I have been constantly on the stump fighting the heresies of Republicanism and the delusions of Democracy. The former, I trust, in Ohio, are thoroughly expurged from the creed of that party, and the latter, I hope, are somewhat damaged. I find the public mind of Ohio opening to a more catholic view of national affairs, especially on the dangerous question of slavery."[49]

In addition, conservative Republican newspapers tried to sound a conciliatory note in response to the raid. Brown had acted alone and without Republican prompting or involvement, the *New York Times* declared. Proslavery violence in Kansas had made him insane and had filled him with the desire for revenge. For his subsequent folly in Virginia, Brown deserved the full measure of punishment the law allowed. Meanwhile, Henry Raymond complained, partisan excesses were at least partly responsible for giving the raid far more attention than it deserved. "If we are not really the blindest people that ever existed; and judicially set apart for destruction," Raymond declared, "we ought now to begin to see that the most important political work we have to do is to combine as one people in the resolve to put this tremendous social question of slavery out of the reach of partisan agitators." And speaking of "partisan agitators," Raymond tried to minimize the damage done by Seward's "irrepressible conflict" speech by claiming that unfortunate passages in Seward's remarks did not truly reflect the New York senator's opinion on the sectional crisis.[50] Others similarly distanced themselves from Seward but expressed more sympathy for Brown, while simultaneously pointing to slavery as the ultimate source of the trouble. Horace Greeley remarked on October 19 that "believing that the way to Universal Emancipation lies not through insurrection, civil war, and bloodshed, but through peace, discussion, and the quiet diffusion of sentiments of humanity and justice, we deeply regret this outbreak." Brown and his band "dared and died for what they felt to be the right, though in a manner which seems to us fatally wrong. Let their epitaphs remain unwritten until the not distant day when no slave shall clank his chains in the shades of Monticello or by the graves of Mount Vernon."[51]

Other Republicans voiced similar sentiments, if in stronger and more forceful language. Wisconsin's James R. Doolittle told the Senate in early December that the party was "opposed to this whole system of lawlessness and violence which has led to filibustering from the United States into Nicaragua; to filibustering from Missouri into Kansas, which has been followed by this filibustering by Brown from Canada into Virginia." The party, he told Southerners, would use "all legal and proper means within the Constitution" to "put down this filibustering." The Harpers Ferry raid carried a warning to traitors, Michigan's Zachariah Chandler lectured. "Dare raise your impious hands against this Government, against our Constitution and laws and you hang."[52]

And while conservative Republicans lamented Seward's proclamations about an "irrepressible conflict," they found more credible the firm resolve and disciplined principle enunciated by Abraham Lincoln at the Cooper Institute in New York City on February 27, 1860. Lincoln's eventual nomination suggested to conservatives that this old Whig and disciple of Henry Clay would remain sensitive to the limitations imposed by his new office and his party. Like Douglas, Lincoln sought to palliate conservative opinion by devoting most of his address to establishing the constitutional and statutory lineage of a free-soil policy. Responding to Douglas's *Harper's* article and aware of the heightened importance of conservative votes in the aftermath of the Brown raid, Lincoln and his supporters argued that the Republicans were a safe, pro-Union party. Criticizing Southerners and their Northern allies for trying to suppress free speech, Lincoln vigorously defended the party's right to speak out against slavery. But he denied that the party comprised a veritable army of John Browns anxious to destroy Southern institutions and declared the Republicans' intention to stand by the Union and suppress *any* insurrection. In effect, Lincoln capped conciliatory pressures building within the party and opted for a potent mixture of antislavery sentiment and nationalist conservatism, effectively shutting off any possibility of a Southern strategy. The speech ironically transposed Lincoln's and Seward's positions in the party—with Seward shifting to the right to become the party's leading spokesman for conciliation in the upcoming face-off with the fledgling Confederacy.[53]

These developments meshed well with other Republican attempts to downplay the "unfortunate" misconstruction of Sewardite notions about irrepressible conflicts. They reassured Northerners that the party's antislavery core was wrapped in a comforting concern with maintaining order. The Republican platform for 1860 thus offered a balanced mixture of conservative and antislavery sentiment by coupling attacks on disunionism with a defensive tone about preserving the constitution and the country against the "revolutionary" and "subversive" doctrine of slavery expansion. The same section that denounced "the lawless invasion by armed force of the soil of any state or territory, no matter under what pretext, as among the gravest of crimes" also pledged fidelity to state rights.[54] At the same time, Republicans held out the possibility of supporting a constitutional amendment guaranteeing federal noninterference with slavery in existing slave states.

Republicans also counterattacked against Democrats and Constitutional Unionists. They derided the Union meetings by pointing to the cotton connections of the sponsors and ridiculed Constitutional Union leaders for "timidity," "irresolution," and "indecision—qualities which of all others are least to be trusted in an emergency."[55] The alarmist rhetoric of the meetings, with its apprehensions of race war, praise of slavery's benign and beneficial effects, and demands for the suppression of antislavery speech, played into Republican hands. Here, the latter replied, was the prime example of the slave power's increasing influence over Northern civic life. As Allan Nevins has pointed out, the stock conservative tactic of calling Union meetings and stirring up sentiment among the country's influential professional and commercial classes failed to check the movement of Northern public opinion toward a grim, Unionist determination to crack down on *any* insurrectionary conspiracy whatever its origin.[56]

But the Republicans' successful counterattack against constitutional unionist criticisms came at a price: the final abandonment of a Southern or border-state strategy in order to focus its efforts on winning the electoral votes of crucial Northern swing states.[57] Reaching this conclusion required relinquishing the cherished belief that a political party's "nationality" was determined by its incorporation of diverse interests from all sections and classes into an organization that suppressed divisive sectional issues. Lincoln's Cooper Institute address had attempted to minimize the Republicans' sectional nature by arguing that the absence of a Southern Republican party should be traced to the South's clampdown on free speech. Yet the fact remained that significant voting blocs in the South, including backcountry yeomen farmers and commercial interests in border-state towns like St. Louis and Louisville, had put up stiff resistance to secessionism.[58] The Republicans stood for a new meaning of the term "nationality": adherence to principles and policies regardless of their conformity to the range of sectional and socioeconomic interests in the country. The party opted for a conservative *Northern* strategy for 1860; they would combine their assertive opposition to disunion with a firm resolve to carry out an antiextensionist program.

Of even greater assistance to the Republican campaign was the hysterical reaction to the raid in the South. Recent Southern talk of reviving the slave trade encouraged Northerners to question Southern motives. If Northerners had dismissed the slave trade movement as the hobby of a few fanatics, why were Southerners not drawing the same conclusions from the Brown affair?[59] A wide range of Northern commentators pointed out repeatedly that not a single slave had joined the insurrection, that Northerners vigorously denounced the raid and supported Brown's punishment, and that the prompt suppression of the affair by federal troops and with the cooperation of authorities in both free and slave states were all proof that slavery was safe. Even the proslavery *New York Express,* noted for its blunt, race-baiting, and nativist editorial views, pointed out that slaveholders were safer in Virginia than were ordinary citizens on the crime-infested streets of New York. Southern threats of disunion seemed not only silly but downright dangerous when considered in such a light.[60] Southerners, though, treated such sentiments contemptuously, telling Northern conservatives that the real price of Union would be "protection for slavery." The Southern dismissal of Northern conservatives undermined Democrat and Opposition efforts at coalition building and helped legitimize Republican claims that the real origins of Harpers Ferry lay in slavery itself.[61]

In short, Republicans found that they could turn the liabilities of the raid into an asset. By the middle of 1860, as the presidential campaign gained momentum, Republicans played on economic issues and unionism to attract conservatives to their ranks. By that time, Brown's fate had faded into the background, given the focus on electoral politics, the fight over the speakership, and especially the division of the Democratic party at Charleston and Baltimore. As the election approached, a divided conservative opinion was supporting four candidacies for the presidency, each of whom tried to trumpet his "safe" qualities. A year after the raid, the *New York Times* could claim that Lincoln was truly "a conservative, devoted to the Union, considerate equally of every section, and of every State, and resolved faithfully, and with firmness, to maintain the Constitution in all its parts." Lincoln's victory in November announced that his party, the party of a new, muscular, and assertive Union backed by the might of growing northern majorities, had won the struggle for Northern loyalties.[62]

*   *   *   *   *

The realigning of parties in advance of the election of 1860 revealed Northern differences about how to maintain the Union—and that disagreement in turn demonstrated that Northern unionism had undergone striking shifts of emphasis in the 1850s. The Harpers Ferry raid sharpened the crisis in Northern conservatism because it raised issues that set conservatives against each other and encouraged the Republicans to confine their campaign to the North. The Republican decision to concentrate on vital Northern states was more than an election tactic or a necessary reaction to institutional imperatives of the electoral system, however: it reflected the Republicans' identification of the Union with conceptions of free labor, material progress, and a vigorous federal role in safeguarding Northern economic interests.[63] And the Opposition's decision to launch a third-party movement stemmed in turn from its identification of the Union with a political economy of diverse laboring and production systems that the government could promote but not actively discourage. Many constitutional unionists could equate antislavery politics only with disunion. Like Henry Clay, who pledged to renounce the Whig party if it "is to be merged into a contemptible abolition party" and thereby "adopt doctrines utterly subversive of the Constitution and the Union," constitutional unionists of any party were temperamentally and ideologically unsuited for a firm alliance with the Republican party, no matter how often prominent Republicans invoked the memory of the Great Compromiser.[64] Nor could the Opposition find much to like in a Democratic party whose Northern wing touted a "do-nothing" philosophy about economic development and whose Southern wing threatened disunion if the federal government did not promote slavery.

The division of Northern unionism, revealed so sharply in the aftermath of the Harpers Ferry incident, heralded the waning of the old Madisonian constitutional union tradition. Territorial expansion and the increasingly complex integration of agricultural, commercial, and industrial sectors were forging a nation-state out of the unorganized and unwieldy fragments of the old federal republic. This process of spatial and economic consolidation profoundly influenced politics and culture as older institutions tried to accommodate the strain. Blending elements of Jacksonian unionism with an enticing vision of a complex and powerful continental empire, American nationalism in the 1850s broadened the reach of political majorities once viewed as properly restrained in their jurisdiction over "local" institutions. Slave and free interests both demonstrated their willingness to use a weak and pliable federal government to implement a more assertive and less compromising conception of the Union as the vanguard of powerful economic interests.[65] The metamorphosis of unionist thought in the 1850s raised the stakes in the controversy over slavery. The progressive identification of the Union with the nation suppressed the post-founding generation's understanding of the two as separate but related entities. The Union had been simply the government, grafted onto the nation and constructed so as to cultivate the voluntary consent of succeeding generations. Its legitimacy rested on its ability to withstand internal divisions. The second party system had served, briefly, as one institutional defense against sectional tensions so that for a time party conflict preserved the old Union.[66]

The hardening of Northern unionism also influenced the evolution of

American conservatism during a period when self-described conservatives dominated public life. Antebellum conservatives were most concerned about the maintenance of institutional cohesion and the development of a unique American civilization that they thought the Union should foster. With important qualifications, conservatives joined in the widespread celebration of material progress that accompanied the growth of a market-oriented entrepreneurial ethos in the mid-nineteenth century. They assumed that change must still occur within a framework of flexible yet sturdy social and political institutions. Be they recognized political parties, the church, social classes, the workplace, or schools, such institutions established multiple sources of authority that restrained the human tendency to "extremes." Institutions therefore mediated conflicts and forced people to recognize the complexities of life in a diverse community. Conservatives tied the fortunes of society to historical institutions—especially the law— but made few concessions to the idea that institutions could actually alter human nature. Therefore, the essence of antebellum conservatism was its defense of institutions against the dissolving influence of what conservatives called "isms": the fanatical, radical mind-set that placed adherence to a single idea above an ordered, hierarchical, and regulated community life. In their minds the Union symbolized the greatest of such institutions not because it harkened back to some mystical, organic origin, but because it was the penultimate act of conservative statesmanship: the deliberate, practical creation of a unifying political system that imposed limits on political strife.[67] Before the onset of the political crisis of the 1850s, conservatives commonly identified their objective as the preservation of the Union as it is.

The problem for conservatives in all parties by the time of Brown's raid was that "politics seemed to enter into everything," disrupting the evolution of American civilization by setting historic institutions against each other. The "machine that would go of itself" contained parts that clashed and injured one another. From the pulpit, the stump, the press, and the plantation came fierce denunciations of citizens in the other section, a sign that traditional sources of authority—the ministry, parties, editors, merchants, and the planting class—were being pulled into the sectional contest. Instead of providing a flexible, differentiated set of institutional responses to sectional conflict, the political system in the 1850s seemed to be focusing ever more narrowly on the one issue that had the capability of destroying the old federal union.[68]

Antebellum conservatives had been particularly sensitive about the consequences of political "agitation" in a developing nation. "The mode of saying may be often more offensive than that which is said," a conservative clergyman observed in a Thanksgiving-day sermon, "and there is a mode

which does not conduce to union, because its tendency is to destroy fraternal feeling."[69] By 1859, however, growing numbers of Americans were less
interested in cultivating fraternal feeling through gentle language and the
toleration of dissent than they were in quieting the noise of partisan warfare
by forcing the other side to shut up. The toughening of popular sensibilities
brought with it ideological rigidity and an intensified concern about revolution and disorder; it lessened the appeal of conciliation by contrasting passivity and submissiveness with determination and conviction.[70]

Apprehensiveness about the consequences of confrontation was especially evident in the Harpers Ferry controversy. A notable feature of the
public discussion in the North was its focus on neither the details of the raid
nor the basic facts of Brown's complicity but instead on the obscure origins
of the incident—namely, the relationship between violent speech and violent action.[71] Seeking to blame demonic "agitators" and partisans for the
raid, Northerners moved further away from Brown and closer to what they
believed were the dark and sinister conspirators who had egged him on in
his mad career. The heightened concern about lawlessness as the natural
result of both violent speech and rampant partisanship indicates that the
quarrel over John Brown's raid had completed the process of subsuming the
sentimental, affective, and individualistic traits of American nationalism
and culture, and had replaced them with a stern acceptance of confrontation and perhaps violence as the only alternatives to disintegration and
chaos. The furious attacks against the clergy, writers, and poets who manufactured Brown's martyrdom confirmed the decline of the old New
England intelligentsia and the rise of a more conservative and less sentimental set of values among educated elites. That some Northerners who otherwise little sympathized with abolitionism expressed open admiration for
Brown's noble demeanor and his remarkable courage hardly suggested a
rising humanitarian sentiment for blacks (whose mourning for Brown was
usually ridiculed in the press, when it was noticed at all). Instead, as George
Fredrickson has argued, it signalled a growing approval of strong, decisive,
and violent action. The raid and its aftermath accelerated the decade-long
trend toward cultural consolidation in mainstream Northern political, professional, and intellectual circles.[72] This concern about a democratic society's threshold of tolerance for radical or violent opinions had been an
important theme of the sectional crisis from the gag-rule debates of the late
1830s through the caning of Charles Sumner after his violent speech denouncing slavery and slaveholders. And it would escalate in the controversy
that broke out in December 1859 over Hinton Helper's antislavery tract, *The
Impending Crisis of the South,* which denounced slavery as an economic
catastrophe from the viewpoint of Southern nonslaveholding whites.[73]

The debate over the unresolvable issue of Brown's sanity illustrates this pattern of thinking in Northern reactions to the raid. All sides in the discussion, regardless of party affiliation, assumed a direct link between violent speech and violent behavior and worked with the same definition of "fanaticism": attachment to one idea or principle at the expense of a realistic, reasoned understanding of the plurality of ends in public life. Judged by the discussion in the press throughout the fall and winter of 1859–60, the idea that Brown had acted purely on his own initiative was inconceivable. Depending on the commentator, Brown was egged on either by propaganda about an "irrepressible conflict" issued by Republican leaders;[74] or by instruction in the virtues of vigilantism and border ruffianism by Democratic leaders;[75] or by the outrages of proslavery propagandists in Kansas and the South.[76] According to the *New York Journal of Commerce,* it was "easy to trace the connection between cause and effect—between the teachings of the leading spirits of Republicanism, and the practice of their willing instruments, in carrying out the spirit of the doctrines thus inculcated. If the latter is less prudent than their leaders, it is by no means certain that they are more responsible before the bar of public opinion."[77]

The issue, then, was *whose* violent speech incited Brown, and how responsible Brown was for his own actions. As the staid old Whig journal the *Washington Daily National Intelligencer* put it three days after Brown was apprehended, although the incident appeared to be the act of a lone fanatic, there was a rationality to it in the fact that "behind it lies a basic adaptation of means to ends, even though the means seemed all out of proportion to the ends desired. Whether the raid resulted from blind fanaticism separate from events, or from calculated desire for revenge against wrongs perpetrated by aggressors in another quarter, . . . it remains none the less true that the very inception of such a quixotic enterprise indicates the prevalence of a morbid sentiment on the subject of slavery, growing out of the antagonisms which form so large part in the political discussions of the day."[78]

Northern reactions to Brown's raid, then, should be understood in the light of the political conflict and general social malaise in the late 1850s. The major political parties were deeply involved in the process of broadening and consolidating conservative and moderate support. The raid and execution of Brown and his company fell upon this maturing realignment of parties like a wet blanket and paralyzed the existing factions before they could reformulate their alliances among new political friends. The raid not only contributed to the emotional fury of 1860 but also helped to assure that Republican strategy in 1860 would retain its sectional basis; the party would not "go national" but would instead focus on vital free states at the expense of Southern Republicans and Unionists in Missouri, Kentucky, and North Carolina.

The raid affirmed to Southerners not that disunion and war were inevitable but that a Republican victory would mean disunion and war. In that sense, the raid only reinforced long-standing premonitions about the probable results of a Republican victory. Southerners feared not consolidation, but absorption. Fears of consolidation hearkened back to the populist, limited-government rhetoric of Jacksonian democracy and the policy of nonintervention. But Southerners had not been immune to the ongoing cultural consolidation of the country. They had willfully used the federal government to expand slavery into the West, to force Northerners to return fugitive slaves, to obtain a Supreme Court decision extending constitutional guarantees to slavery in areas under federal jurisdiction, and now, in 1859, to demand a federal slave code for the territories and federal protection for slaveholders sojourning through free states with their chattel. Willing to apply federal force to these projects, Southerners now faced the consequences of such a strategy: the possibility that a constitutional majority would check, and then reverse, this trend. The combination of Northern sympathy for Brown, the rise of the Republicans, and the publication of Helper's tract proved to Southerners that such a majority was forming and would flex its muscles, both in and outside of the South, in the election of 1860.

The rapid economic development of the country in the 1850s both reinforced and accelerated the trend toward uniformity and cultural rigidity in American life. The sectional conflict hardened the country for confrontation late in the decade, so that even constitutional unionists, who celebrated the diversity and flexibility of the old federal system and the second-party system, found themselves contributing to a climate of hostility to dissenting viewpoints and the give-and-take of compromise. John Brown's raid hurried along this process and failed to check the Republican drive for power. A Republican victory at the expense of a national coalition with the Opposition would, in effect, complete the demise of the second party system and its most vital attribute: national political parties committed to walling out the slavery issue from national party politics.

Notes

1. *New York Times,* Oct. 27, 1859.

2. Ibid., Oct. 29, 1859.

3. See Don E. Fehrenbacher, *Lincoln in Text and Context: Collected Essays* (Stanford, 1987), pp. 55–56; Richard H. Sewell, *Ballots for Freedom: Antislavery Politics in the United States, 1837–1860* (New York, 1976), pp. 344–58.

4. See Roy F. Nichols, *The Disruption of American Democracy* (New York, 1948), pp. 266–71; Joel Silbey, *A Respectable Minority: The Democratic Party in the Civil War Era, 1860–1868* (New York, 1977), pp. 28–29 and 116–26.

5. See, for example, George Lunt to John Crittenden, Jan. 10, 1860, John Jordan Crittenden Papers, Library of Congress (hereafter Crittenden Papers); and "K" to the *Washington Daily National Intelligencer,* Dec. 5, 1859 (printed on Dec. 7). In a speech at a Boston Union meeting on December 10, Democrat Caleb Cushing urged Boston conservatives to mobilize the "more than one-half the registered voters of Massachusetts" who "obstinately and persistently refuse to exercise the elective franchise" (reported in the *Washington Daily National Intelligencer,* Dec. 12, 1859). On Whigs and Americans, see Daniel Walker Howe, *The Political Culture of the American Whigs* (Chicago, 1979), esp. pp. 210–37; and Tyler Anbinder, *Nativism and Slavery: The Northern Know-Nothings and the Politics of the 1850s* (New York, 1992), pp. 246–78.

6. See the criticisms by the Buchananite *New York Journal of Commerce,* Mar. 17 and 23, 1858, of a rumored alliance of Republicans, old Whigs, and anti-Lecompton Democrats. For a succinct statement of the situation, see William L. Barney, *Battleground for the Union: The Civil War and Reconstruction* (Englewood Cliffs, N.J., 1990), pp. 96–97, and the discussion of Republican strategy in Richard H. Abbott, *The Republican Party and the South, 1855–1877: The First Southern Strategy* (Chapel Hill, 1986), pp. 11 and 13–16.

7. See Barney, *Battleground for the Union,* p. 97; Daniel Crofts, *Reluctant Confederates: Upper South Unionists in the Secession Crisis* (Chapel Hill, 1989), pp. 67–72; and John Burgess Stabler, "A History of the Constitutional Union Party: A Tragic Failure," (Ph.D. diss., Columbia University, 1954), ch. 11.

8. "Was there ever a politician who has so completely overshot the mark as Seward?" one Unionist wrote to John J. Crittenden in early December. "His Rochester speech was aimed at *you*. It hurt you, no doubt for the time being—by creating an impassable gulf between your friends & his. But the recoil of the gun has *killed* Seward. If the Opposition should drop differences & unite behind you, we can beat the Democracy. If they don't, the Democracy will beat the Opposition": John O. Sargent to Crittenden, Dec. 12, 1859, Crittenden Papers. See also W. P. Boyd to Crittenden, July 17, 1858, and Anthony Kennedy to Samuel Smith Nicholas, June 7, 1859, both in ibid.; and see Edmund Pechin to A. R. R. Boteler, Nov. 19, 1859, A. R. R. Boteler Papers, Perkins Library, Duke University (hereafter Boteler Papers).

9. The political impact of Brown's raid and execution is assessed in Oates, *Purge,* pp. 310–24 and 354–61; Nevins, *Emergence,* 2:70–131; Emerson D. Fite, *The Presidential Campaign of 1860* (New York, 1911), pp. 1–32; Potter, *Impending,* pp. 356–84; and Quarles, *Allies,* pp. 114–69.

10. See the speech of Massachusetts Senator Henry Wilson to New York Republicans, Oct. 25, reported in *New York Times,* Oct. 26, 1859. Two New York Republican newspapers, the *Post* and the *Courier & Enquirer,* traced the raid to slavery's inherently unstable and violent character. See the discussion in the *New York Times,* Oct. 10, 1859, and the letter by "Salus Populi" in the same issue.

11. The *Washington Daily National Intelligencer,* Dec. 22 and 23, 1859, carried Philadelphia press reports of this incident.

12. Richard Brodhead to Jefferson Davis, Dec. 24, 1859, in Lynda Lasswell Crist and Mary Seaton Dix, eds., *The Papers of Jefferson Davis,* 6 vols. (Baton Rouge, 1971–), 6:270.

13. Baltimore *Sun,* Nov. 28, 1859, quoted in Potter, *Impending,* p. 384.

14. The "Mason Committee" report is in the *United States Senate Committee Reports, 1859–1860,* 2:1–25; Southern maneuvers can be traced in Potter, *Impending,* pp. 385–404.

15. Woodward, "Private War," p. 68; a similar analysis can be found in Potter, *Impending,* p. 356.

16. Union meetings across the mid-Atlantic states are described in the *Washington Daily National Intelligencer,* Dec. 9, 12, 21 and 30, 1859; the *New York Express,* Dec. 6, 1859; and in Nevins, *Emergence,* 2:105–7. See also the association's manifesto in *New York Times,* Oct. 27, 1859, and the discussion in Philip Foner, *Business and Slavery: The New York Merchants and the Irrepressible Conflict* (Chapel Hill, 1941), pp. 156–58.

17. The administration paper, the *Washington Constitution,* ran a series of articles, Oct. 20–22, 1859, accusing Seward of direct complicity in the raid. See also the *New York Herald*'s exploitation of the issue in its mid-October numbers, especially Oct. 19.

18. Quoted in the *Washington Daily National Intelligencer,* Nov. 1, 1859.

19. The *Providence Post* and *Boston Courier,* n.d., both quoted in ibid.; see also Nevins, *Emergence,* 2:91–93.

20. The country's plague of crime is reported in Allan Nevins, *Ordeal of the Union,* 2 vols. (New York, 1947), 1:65–71; David Grimsted, "Rioting in Its Jacksonian Setting," *AHR* 77 (April 1972): 361–97; and Edward Pessen, *Jacksonian America: Society, Personality, and Politics* (Homewood, Ill., 1969), pp. 67–69.

21. See the Madison, Georgia, *Weekly Visiter,* n.d., quoted in the *Washington Daily National Intelligencer,* Nov. 1, 1859. H. Cowpen to Millard Fillmore, San Francisco, Feb. 1, 1860, Millard Fillmore Papers, State University of New York—Oswego (hereafter Fillmore Papers, SUNY). For the political expression of this general sense of malaise and inefficacy, see "The Lessons of Violence," *Washington Daily National Intelligencer,* Oct. 29, 1859, as well as Mark Summers, *The Plundering Generation: Corruption and the Crisis of the Union, 1849–1861* (New York, 1987).

22. For a discussion of this definition of constitutional unionism, see Peter Knupfer, *The Union as It Is: Constitutional Unionism and Sectional Compromise, 1787–1861* (Chapel Hill, 1991), esp. pp. 3, 165, and 168–70.

23. Call to Union meeting, in the *Washington Daily National Intelligencer,* Dec. 21, 1859.

24. Quoted in ibid., Dec. 9, 1859.

25. Stuart's speech is reprinted approvingly and in full in the *Washington Daily National Intelligencer,* Nov. 5, 1859. For a similar analysis, see Reverdy Johnson's defense of Douglas's article on popular sovereignty, in ibid., Nov. 10, 1859. See also "Address of the National Union Men of New York, to their Fellow Citizens of the United States" [Jan., 1860], in Fillmore Papers, SUNY. See also Howard C. Perkins, "The Defense of Slavery in the Northern Press on the Eve of the Civil War," *JSH* 9 (November 1943): 501–31.

26. *New York Express,* Oct. 29, 1859; the paper harped on this theme throughout the upcoming state election. See also the issue of Dec. 14, 1859, on the attempted reorganization of the American party to attract "moderate" Republicans.

27. Mortimer D. Hay to John Crittenden, Feb. 4, 1860, Crittenden Papers.

28. Michael Holt, *Political Crisis of the 1850s* (New York, 1978), pp. 226–36; Crofts, *Reluctant Confederates,* pp. 67–72.

29. "K" to *Washington Daily National Intelligencer,* printed Dec. 7, 1859. On the Constitutional Union party, see Stabler, "History of the Constitutional Union Party," and John Vollmer Mering, "The Slave-State Constitutional Unionists and the Politics of Consensus," *JSH* 43 (August 1977): 395–410.

30. Millard Fillmore to "Miss Dix," Mar. 5, 1860, Millard Fillmore Papers, Houghton Library, Harvard University.

31. See Fillmore's letter to the New York Union meeting, which was printed in the *Washington Daily National Intelligencer,* Dec. 30, 1859. The manuscript copy, dated Dec. 18, is in the Fillmore Papers, SUNY. Fillmore's correspondents belabored this theme. "You ascribed the present political troubles to their *true cause*—the repeal of the Missouri Compromise," wrote one. "But for this, we should not have had the

Kansas difficulties or a republican party, nor would the slavery question have been the all absorbing & exciting question it now is—the great Whig issues, the tariff, moderate internal improvements, the honest & economical administration of government & perhaps some others, would have had a proper attention. We should have had no John Brown raids, & no Helpers books would have been necessary" (R. H. McCurdy to Millard Fillmore, Jan. 30, 1860, ibid.).

32. George P. Fisher to John Crittenden, Jan. 7, 1860, Crittenden Papers; see also J. W. Bryce to A. R. R. Boteler, Dec. 2, 1859, Boteler Papers.

33. On the Southern Americans and the speakership, see W. Bryce to A. R. R. Boteler, Dec. 2, 1859; and John Wilson to Boteler (private & confidential), Dec. 12, 1859, both in Boteler Papers; Crofts, *Reluctant Confederates,* pp. 72–75; and Ollinger Crenshaw, "The Speakership Contest of 1859–1860: John Sherman's Election a Cause of Disruption?" *Mississippi Valley Historical Review* 29 (Dec. 1942): 323–38.

34. William Cabell Rives to John Crittenden, Jan. 9, 1860, Crittenden Papers.

35. On Democratic conservatism, see Jean H. Baker, *Affairs of Party: The Political Culture of Northern Democrats in the Mid-Nineteenth Century* (Ithaca, 1983), pp. 143–260; Bruce Collins, "The Ideology of the Antebellum Northern Democrats," *Journal of American Studies* 11 (April 1977): 103–21; Larry Gara, *The Presidency of Franklin Pierce* (Lawrence, Kans., 1991); and Nichols, *Disruption of American Democracy.*

36. Speech of Caleb Cushing, Dec. 10, 1859, reported in the *Washington Daily National Intelligencer,* Dec. 12, 1859.

37. Robert W. Johannsen, *Stephen A. Douglas* (New York, 1973), p. 724; *Congressional Globe,* 36th Cong., 1st Sess., Jan. 16, 1860, p. 448. See also Catharine M. Tarrant, "To 'Insure Domestic Tranquility': Congress and the Law of Seditious Conspiracy, 1859–1860," *American Journal of Legal History* 15 (Apr. 1971): 113–16.

38. *Congressional Globe,* 36th Cong., 1st Sess., pp. 552–55, quotations at pp. 552, 553, and 554.

39. "The Dividing Line between Federal and Local Authority: Popular Sovereignty in the Territories," *Harper's Monthly,* Sept. 1859, pp. 422–24.

40. See Johannsen, *Stephen A. Douglas,* pp. 707–14; Damon Wells, *Stephen Douglas, The Last Years, 1857–1861* (Austin, Tex., 1971), pp. 183–93; and Baker, *Affairs of Party,* pp. 188–89.

41. See Joel Silbey, *The Partisan Imperative: The Dynamics of American Politics before the Civil War* (New York, 1985), pp. 122–26.

42. On Douglas's continuing belief that free farmers, not slaveholders, would possess the territories, see Collins, "Ideology of the Antebellum Northern Democrats," pp. 106–8.

43. Nichols, *Disruption of American Democracy,* pp. 267–68.

44. William E. Gienapp, *The Origins of the Republican Party, 1852–1856* (New York, 1987), pp. 305–448.

45. Abbott, *Republican Party and the South,* pp. 5–13; Sewell, *Ballots for Freedom,* pp. 344–54.

46. On conservative Republicans, see Eric Foner, *Free Soil, Free Labor, Free Men: The Ideology of the Republican Party before the Civil War* (New York, 1970), pp. 186–225; and Sewell, *Ballots for Freedom,* pp. 304–8.

47. Edward Bates to J. Philips Phoenix et al., Feb. 24, 1859, printed in the *New York Daily Tribune,* Apr. 16, 1859; see also Howard K. Beale, ed., *The Diary of Edward Bates, 1859–1866,* in the *Annual Report of the American Historical Association for the Year 1930* (Washington, D.C., 1930), pp. 1–9 and 36–46.

48. Beale, ed., *Diary of Edward Bates,* pp. 61–71.

49. Thomas Corwin to J. J. Miller, Esq., n.d., reprinted in the *Washington Daily National Intelligencer,* Oct. 27, 1859.

50. *New York Times,* Oct. 27 and Nov. 5, 1859.

51. *New York Daily Tribune,* Oct. 19, 1859.

52. *Congressional Globe,* 36th Cong., 1st Sess., Dec. 7, 1859, pp. 34 and 36.

53. The speech may be found in Basler, ed., *Works of Lincoln,* 3:522–50; see also the discussion in Sewell, *Ballots for Freedom,* pp. 350–54; and in Fehrenbacher, *Lincoln in Text and Context,* pp. 55–56. Seward trimmed his sails to the breezes of conservatism, too. In a frantic speech to the Senate two days after Lincoln's, he pleaded for a reconciliation between the "capital" states of the South and the "labor" states of the North; Fehrenbacher, *Lincoln in Text and Context,* p. 56; Sewell, *Ballots for Freedom,* p. 358; *Congressional Globe,* 36th Cong., 1st Sess., Feb. 29, 1860, pp. 910–14.

54. Fite, *Presidential Campaign of 1860,* p. 125; Henry Steele Commager, ed., *Documents of American History,* 6th ed. (New York, 1958), pp. 363–65.

55. *Lowell (Mass.) Daily Journal and Courier,* Sept. 9, 1860, in *Northern Editorials on Secession,* ed. Howard C. Perkins, 2 vols. (New York, 1942), 1:32.

56. "The Union meetings gave no reassurance because they could give no guarantees," Nevins comments. "They demonstrated what was obvious, that right-thinking northerners deplored any outrage; but who could check wrong-thinking northerners?" (*Emergence,* 2:106).

57. Abbott, *Republican Party and the South,* pp. 13–14.

58. See the letter from a Southern "Whig conservative" in Richmond to the *Washington Daily National Intelligencer,* Dec. 6, 1859; see also Crofts, *Reluctant Confederates.*

59. See the *Philadelphia American,* n.d., quoted in the *Washington Daily National Intelligencer,* Nov. 1, 1859.

60. *New York Express,* Oct. 19, 1859; see also the *Washington Daily National Intelligencer,* Oct. 19, 1859. The strength and reliability of Northern conservatism and the "fidelity of the negro race" were prominent themes in the press soon after the event; see the survey of the press in the *Washington Daily National Intelligencer,* Nov. 1, 1859, the editorial in ibid., Dec. 6, 1859, from which the above quotation is taken.

61. On Southern demands for protection, see the editorial in the *Richmond Enquirer,* Oct. 27, 1859.

62. *New York Times,* Oct. 17, 1860, quoted in Foner, *Business and Slavery,* p. 186. Foner (*Free Soil, Free Labor,* pp. 132–48) and Sewell (*Ballots for Freedom,* pp. 362–63) emphasize the victory of antislavery elements over conservatives for control of the Republican party in the late 1850s. Yet the incompatibility of radicalism and conservatism in the party could be papered over by both groups' common opposition to secession. Moderates, including Lincoln, were less concerned about defining abstractions like the nature of the Union than were either conservatives anxious to keep an eye southward or radicals apprehensive about caving in to the demands of the conciliators. Lincoln could afford to therefore take a comfortable middle ground by avowing his determination to defend the *government* and the laws against treason. Lincoln's aversion to old unionist thought became more evident during the Civil War. See Mark E. Neely, *The Fate of Liberty: Abraham Lincoln and Civil Liberties* (New York, 1992), pp. 3, 22, and 232; and Paul Finkelman, "Civil Liberties and the Civil War: The Great Emancipator as Civil Libertarian," *Michigan Law Review* 91 (May 1993): 1353–81.

63. See Thomas Alexander, "The Civil War as Institutional Fulfillment," *JSH* 47 (Feb. 1981): 3–31; and Foner, *Free Soil, Free Labor,* pp. 9–10.

64. Quoted in the *Washington Daily National Intelligencer,* Nov. 27, 1850. For a different interpretation, one that stresses the affinities between Clay's and the Republicans' unionism, see Robert Remini, *Henry Clay: Statesman for the Union* (New York, 1991), pp. 8, 51, 447, 643–44, 692, and 786; and Mark E. Neely, Jr., "American

Nationalism in the Image of Henry Clay: Abraham Lincoln's Eulogy on Henry Clay in Context," *Register of the Kentucky Historical Society* 73 (January 1975): 31–60.

65. See John Higham, *From Boundlessness to Consolidation: The Transformation of American Culture* (Ann Arbor, 1969), pp. 22–23; Paul Nagel, *One Nation Indivisible: The Union in American Thought, 1776–1861* (New York, 1964), pp. 82–124; Major L. Wilson, *Space, Time, and Freedom: The Quest for Nationality and the Irrepressible Conflict, 1815–1861* (Westport, Conn., 1974), pp. 211–37; Charles M. Wiltse, "From Compact to Nation State in American Political Thought," in *Essays in Political Theory Presented to George H. Sabine*, ed. Milton J. Konvitz and Arthur E. Murphy (Ithaca, 1948), pp. 153–78; and J. R. Pole, *The Idea of Union* (Alexandria, Va., 1977), esp. pp. 111–12.

66. See Silbey, *Partisan Imperative*.

67. This discussion of conservatism depends heavily on the following sources: Warren Susman, "The Nature of American Conservatism," in Warren Susman, *Culture as History: The Transformation of American Society in the Twentieth Century* (New York, 1984), pp. 57–74; Higham, *From Boundlessness to Consolidation;* Noel O'Sullivan, ed., *Revolutionary Theory and Political Reality* (New York, 1983); Robert Nisbet, *Conservatism: Dream and Reality* (Minneapolis, 1986); Michael D. Clark, *Coherent Variety, The Idea of Diversity in British and American Conservative Thought* (Westport, Conn., 1983); and George Fredrickson, *The Inner Civil War: Northern Intellectuals and the Crisis of the Union* (New York, 1968), p. 23. For a different view, see Rush Welter, *The Mind of America, 1820–1860* (New York, 1975), pp. 105–28. Good contemporary sources on the Constitution, mediating institutions, and their psychological effects are Francis Lieber, *Manual of Political Ethics Designed Chiefly for the Use of Colleges and Students at Law,* 2 vols. (Boston, 1838), and *On Civil Liberty and Self Government* (Philadelphia, 1859); and George Ticknor Curtis, *The Strength of the Constitution* (Boston, 1850). For a conservative Republican's view, see Thomas Corwin, "The American Citizen, His Duty," speech at Plymouth Church, Brooklyn, reported in the *New York Times,* Nov. 30, 1859.

68. See William E. Gienapp, " 'Politics Seem to Enter into Everything': Political Culture in the North 1840–1860," in *Essays on American Antebellum Politics, 1840–1860,* ed. John J. Kushma and Stephen Maizlish (College Station, Tex., 1982), pp. 15–69; Michael Kammen, *A Machine That Would Go of Itself: The Constitution and American Culture* (New York, 1987); David Herbert Donald, *An Excess of Democracy* (Oxford, 1960); and especially Phillip S. Paludan, "The American Civil War Considered as a Crisis in Law and Order," *AHR* 77 (October 1972): 1014.

69. The Reverend Dr. Hawes, of Calvary Church, New York, quoted in the *Washington Daily National Intelligencer,* Oct. 30, 1859.

70. Kenneth Stampp, *And the War Came: The North and the Secession Crisis, 1860–61* (Chicago, 1965), pp. 1–12.

71. With few exceptions, the Northern press provided full coverage of Brown's capture, his trial, interviews, and speeches, and his execution. The correspondence implicating abolitionists, along with the mass of documentation about his plans for a revolutionary government and a slave insurrection, were published verbatim in most of the newspapers. Such press coverage was remarkable for a medium dominated by partisanship and social prejudice. It also suggests that the widespread agreement in the North about the facts of the event and its outcome on the gallows permitted Northerners to shift the controversy toward more abstract and ultimately unresolvable issues. The Senate select committee concluded that the raid was "simply the act of lawless ruffians, under the sanction of no public or political authority," and recommended no special preventive legislation. See discussion in the *Congressional Globe,* Senate, 36th Cong., 1st Sess., June 15, 1860, p. 3006.

72. See Fredrickson, *The Inner Civil War,* pp. 44–50; and Higham, *From Boundlessness to Consolidation,* pp. 23–24. Fillmore's home-town newspaper, the *Buffalo Commercial Advertiser,* moved slowly into Republican ranks following the Brown raid, expressing reluctant admiration for the old man's courage. Constitutional unionist newspapers frequently criticized Northern clergy for eulogizing Brown. See, for example, "The Growth of Sectionalism," *New York Express,* Dec. 2, 1859. A similar conflict of sentiments (although not among the same alignment of groups) occurred over the visit in 1852 of the Hungarian revolutionary, Louis Kossuth. Kossuth was a man of action, a liberator, an apostle of liberal nationalism, whose charisma alternately attracted and alienated American intellectuals and politicians: see Donald Spencer, *Louis Kossuth and Young American: A Study of Sectionalism and Foreign Policy, 1848–1852* (Columbia, Mo., 1977).

73. For a discussion of the debate in Congress over Helper's book, see Michael Kent Curtis, "The 1859 Crisis over Hinton Helper's Book *The Impending Crisis:* Free Speech, Slavery, and Some Light on the Meaning of the First Section of the Fourteenth Amendment," *Chicago-Kent Law Review* 68 (1993): 1113–78.

74. *Washington Constitution,* n.d., extracted in the *New York Times,* Oct. 21, 1859. The *New York Express* wasted no time; its headlines on Oct. 18, 1859 screamed: "Alarming News from Virginia: The Irrepressible Conflict Begun!"

75. *Albany Evening Journal,* n.d., quoted in the *New York Times,* Oct. 21, 1859.

76. See the *New York Times,* Oct. 21, 1859, which attributed the raid to Brown's desire to avenge the wrongs perpetrated on his family and property by "the Pro-Slavery Party in Kansas." And see the report of the October 28 speech by Joshua Giddings in Philadelphia, *New York Express,* Oct. 29, 1859.

77. *New York Journal of Commerce,* Oct. 19, 1859.

78. *Washington Daily National Intelligencer,* Oct. 21, 1859.

6

PETER WALLENSTEIN

Incendiaries All:
Southern Politics and
the Harpers Ferry Raid

FROM THE PERSPECTIVES of planters and their spokesmen in the late 1850s, the South was under siege. From their drawing rooms and gin mills, their editorial offices and legislative seats, they perceived threats on all sides. In fact, they faced a triple threat. The most obvious—to them at the time and to historians since—came from the North; there, a vocal minority, abolitionists, were demanding an end to slavery itself, and a substantial majority, antislavery even if not abolitionist, calling for an end to the expansion of slavery. In addition were two potentially significant threats to slavery that both originated in the South—the first from the slaves themselves and the other from whites who did not own slaves. Worse yet was the possibility of connections between these internal and external enemies. Moreover, proslavery Southerners felt weakened by their own lack of unity.

John Brown's raid at Harpers Ferry, Virginia, in mid-October 1859 revealed the entire constellation of dangers. A small band of men—most of them white, some black—entered the South from the North and attacked the federal arsenal and armory at Harpers Ferry. Hoping to elicit support from slaves and nonslaveholding yeomen alike, the raiders brought pikes for the slaves and firearms for the whites. In this shift of tactics from moral persuasion to military violence, they heightened the slaveholding South's perceived need to come up with a unified response.[1]

In the weeks and months that followed the raid, Southerners responded in varied ways to the latest attack on their region's peculiar institution. Some of these reactions were private, though collective; others took place in the realm of formal politics. Some were impassioned; others, calculating. Many participants, moreover, acted with an eye to the upcoming 1860 presidential election, as contenders and factions jockeyed over prospective nominations and platforms. Together, the spectrum of responses demonstrated a range of interpretations of the nature of the raid and what it said about the South, the North, and the future of the nation, interpretations that were articulated in both private letters and public speeches.

Evidence and Inference: The Early Reports

The day after the raid ended, with Brown and most of his men captured or killed, the *Richmond Dispatch* offered its preliminary assessment of the "strange events" at Harpers Ferry. Early rumors that the raiders were pursuing "a plan for freeing slaves" had been, the paper noted, "generally discredited." Rather, some people suggested, the raid was "a movement among discontented operatives who wanted an increase of wages." Before long, however, "the most conclusive information" forced a general interpretation "that the whole affair was the conception and work of a party of Abolitionists from distant states." Surely, the *Dispatch* noted, this was a "mad and hopeless" enterprise. Early, inflated estimates that hundreds of "incendiaries and slaves" had been involved dropped to fewer than thirty "incendiaries" and no slave volunteers at all, thereby allowing the *Dispatch* to dismiss the whole affair as "a miserably weak and contemptible" one. The "poor devil" Brown "had prepared for business on a large scale" and "assumed the pompous title of 'Commander-in-Chief of the provisional government'" that he planned to establish. The raid and the raiders thus became objects of derision.[2]

Nonetheless, the raid itself, observers agreed, was bad enough. And what did it mean? How should it be understood, and how confronted? The outlines of the discourse of the weeks and months that followed could already be seen in the tenor of newspaper editorials in Virginia's capital city that first week after Brown and his men took temporary control of the arsenal and armory. Even as the *Dispatch* derided the raid, it warned of its seriousness. Evidence already pointed toward a conspiracy that went far beyond the twenty-two men directly involved: all those arms, presumably supplied by the "Freedom Shriekers" of the North, suggested a wider threat. Abolitionists "think they do God service by running off slaves, and resisting the laws, and shedding blood in furtherance of their crazy notions. But there is a method in their madness." And "they have, no doubt, their agents in every Southern State." Moreover, "if such a scene can occur in Harper's Ferry, what other village in the Southern States has any security?"[3]

Worse than the raid itself—the men, their acts, and their arms—were the implications of a collection of maps and letters that Brown left behind at his headquarters the night his band moved on Harpers Ferry. The maps marked various portions of the South—particularly areas with slave majorities in South Carolina, Georgia, Alabama, and Mississippi—where Brown presumably hoped his intended conflagration would spread. Correspondence gave evidence that at least some among the North's leading abolitionists had known in advance about the raid, had approved of it, and had helped finance it. Moreover, a letter purportedly written by one Lawrence Thatcher from Memphis pointed directly toward the triple threat. Thatcher assured Brown not only of "an immense number of slaves ripe and ready at the very first intimation to strike a decided blow"—in fact, he wrote, "a bold stroke of one day will overthrow the whole state" of Arkansas—but also of a considerable "number of whites ready to aid us."[4]

Responding to early reports, the *Richmond Enquirer* warned: "The extent of this iniquitous plot cannot be estimated by the number of men . . . killed or captured at Harper's Ferry." The range of places from which these men had come—from Maine to Kansas—showed *"an extent of country embracing the whole Northern section of the Union, as involved in the attempt at instigating servile insurrection in Virginia."* Moreover, said the *Enquirer*, Brown's band brought with them large quantities of pikes, revolvers, rifles, and ammunition, which in turn forced the question: *"From whence came the money to buy these things?"* The answer "would reveal the extent of the conspiracy." Continuing in this vein, the paper mused on "the known economy of our *Northern Brethren*" and marveled that "so large a sum has been furnished for the pillage of our property and the murder of our persons." Clearly, "the Northern fanatics mean more than words, and are determined to wage with *men and money* the 'irrepressible conflict' to its bitter end." The funds "at the disposal of these wretches" offered a direct measure of Northerners' "hatred [of] the South." Looking to an ominous future when the Republicans might have won the White House, the paper warned that, this time, "the Federal Government was . . . in hands faithful to the Constitution, but another year may place that aid in the hands of our assailants."[5]

The *Richmond Whig* differed little from the *Dispatch* or the *Enquirer* in assessing the news from Harpers Ferry. It, too, spoke of *"insurgents . . . hailing from so many different Northern States"* and of "voluntary contributions [from] Abolitionists *throughout the Northern States.*" Accordingly, the raid "only proves the utter blindness and recklessness of Abolition fanaticism, and the necessity of constant vigilance on the part of the Southern people." The *Whig* named leading abolitionists as "all schemers and conspirators against the lives and property of the Southern people, and the peace of the Union."[6]

The *Whig* also spelled out the central importance of Northern responses to the raid. It hoped and professed to "believe that the great body of the Northern people look upon these Abolition conspiracies with almost as much horror as we do." But it demanded confirmation: "We shall . . . look to the action of the Northern people in reference to the incendiary proceedings at Harper's Ferry with no little anxiety." As the paper further declared:

> If the Union is to last, and civil war averted, the masses of the Northern people must . . . set their seal of eternal condemnation upon these bold, bad men, and their dangerous, incendiary counsels. If they do not, and that promptly, the Harper's Ferry conspiracy will constitute the beginning of an "irrepressible conflict" between the North and the South, *which can only end in an utter destruction of the Federal Government, and in oceans of fraternal blood.* Should this Harper's Ferry conspiracy not have the effect of opening the eyes of the masses of the Northern people to the practical tendencies and enormities of Abolitionism, and should it fail of inducing them to repudiate the whole tribe of Abolition leaders and agitators in their midst, we shall then despair of the Republic, and look only for long years of civil war with all its calamities and indescribable consequences.

The paper demanded that Northerners condemn the raid and its supporters "and thus show to the people of the South that the great body of the citizens of the North, of all parties and persuasions, have no sympathy with these Abolition incendiaries and will in no manner tolerate either their diabolic teachings or their diabolic conspiracies."[7]

Although many Northerners supplied demonstrations of the kind that these Southerners were seeking, more did not. Proslavery Southerners demanded Northern unanimity in condemnation of Brown—much as they had demanded unanimous support of the Fugitive Slave Act—and, once again, they were disappointed. On top of that, they perceived with fear and revulsion the wave of sympathy for John Brown that followed his execution on December 2. As North Carolina Senator Thomas L. Clingman later observed, nothing had made a "stronger impression on the minds of the Southern people . . . than the manner in which the acts of John Brown were received in the North. Instead of the indignation and abhor[r]ence which his crimes ought naturally have excited, there were manifestations of admiration and sympathy."[8] Virginia authorities had meant, in hanging Brown, to dishonor him; instead, many Northerners responded to his execution by honoring him. In death he became a martyr. Thus "John Brown's body" was not limited to Northerners in its symbolic power, as, for example, when Union soldiers later sang about it as they marched to war against the Confederacy. Precisely because of Southern perceptions of Northern responses to it, "John Brown's body" had great political significance in the South as well.

A "Reign of Terror" and a Quest for Unity

Across the South, whites displayed a range of responses to the unfolding news of Harpers Ferry and its aftermath in the North. Some people reacted much as had Thomas Jefferson, with his cries about "a firebell in the night" at the time of the crisis over Missouri four decades before. Southerners of the "firebell" approach felt sickened at the prospect that the nation was coming unraveled. By contrast, those of the "fire-eater" persuasion not only welcomed the unraveling but did what they could to promote it. Upon hearing of the raid, Edmund Ruffin, for one, confided to his diary his hope that it would be tied to the abolitionists, for "such a practical exercise of abolition principles is needed to stir the sluggish blood of the South."[9] Differ as they might, though, the two groups agreed that prospects for continuing the Union seemed less promising in December than they had in September.

Some Southerners' actions came under color of law, but others were entirely extralegal, as vigilance committees went about their work across the South. More than one Northern newspaper kept a column headed "Reign of Terror" to cover items from the South, and William Lloyd Garrison published a book with that title in 1860. An occasional disaffected Southerner used the same term, among them a former state senator from South Carolina, who went on in January 1860 to describe Charleston with distaste as "a focus of slave traders, disunionists and lynching societies which possess it entirely."[10]

Planters liked to think that the other major groups in the South would not challenge their interests and their rule. In scores of Southern counties—including those indicated on John Brown's maps—a majority of voters owned slaves. In the entire states of South Carolina and Mississippi, approximately half of all voters owned slaves. Moreover, many other voters either aspired to become slaveholders or feared the consequences of emancipation and thus gave their support to the institution. Even in Virginia, where Nat Turner's 1831 uprising had led to a strong effort in the legislature to enact a gradual end to slavery, the system seemed secure from imminent attack by western whites in the late 1850s.[11]

And yet the arithmetic offered pause. From their positions of relative power, proslavery whites looked out on the triple threat and saw themselves vulnerable. In every Southern state, people who did not own slaves—slaves themselves, free blacks, and nonslaveholding whites—outnumbered the members of slaveholding families by more than three to one (see fig. 6.1). In most states across the Deep South, slaves outnumbered each of the other two groups, slaveowners and nonslaveowners alike, while in the Upper South, people who were neither slaves nor slaveowners proved the largest group. Across the region, then, members of slaveowning families made up the smallest of the three groups. And planter families (those owning at least twenty slaves each) comprised only a small minority of a small minority. Even in Mississippi and South Carolina, where planters made up 19 or 20 percent of all slaveowners, only 4.1 percent of all residents, slave and free, were white members of planter families.[12] In Mississippi, the num-

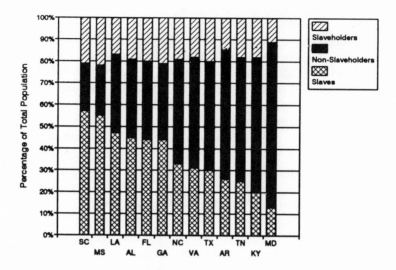

Figure 6.1. The social structure of the Southern states, 1860

ber of white families that owned slaves approached 50 percent, and in South Carolina it may even have reached that proportion. In Kentucky, by contrast, nonslaveholders outnumbered slaveholders by at least three to one; the same was true in Maryland, Missouri, Arkansas, and Tennessee. The disparity was far more than two to one in Virginia, North Carolina, and Texas, and, although smaller, it was substantial even in Louisiana, Alabama, Florida, and Georgia (see fig. 6.1). In the Appalachian South, moreover, tens of thousands of whites had long felt aggrieved at plantation political dominance on issues ranging from voting rights and legislative apportionment to taxes and expenditures on education or transportation.[13] In Southern cities, Yankees and immigrants jostled with slaves and free blacks, and, whether they felt affinity or aversion for one another, any among them might take action against slavery.[14]

Even if a successful attack by nonslaveholding whites against slavery appeared improbable at the voting booths or in the legislatures, other kinds of threats could not be so readily dismissed. Some whites disliked slavery out of a sense of companionship, or for religious or other reasons. Some disliked it because it drove down their own pay and limited rather than fostered their prospects; some who might have supported slavery turned against it when their chances of becoming slaveholders themselves seemed to fade. For some whites in the South, in short, slavery was a threat or an abomination, whether because of what it did to whites or because of what it did to blacks. Proslavery forces would do what they could to cow or cajole fellow whites into following their lead. Yet, as one South Carolina spokesman for slavery and secession wrote about nonslaveholding whites some weeks after the Harpers Ferry raid, "I mistrust our own people more than I fear all of the efforts of the Abolitionists."[15]

Slaveowners liked to believe their own idealized version of master-slave relations, according to which slaves were contented, not rebellious. At the same time, incidents of surly, even violent, behavior had to be explained. The favored explanation had it that the slaves had been "tampered with." It was, after all, possible for someone to "succeed in corrupting a slave, in swerving him from allegiance," at which point loyalty could no longer be assumed, and slavery must depend on more overt coercion.[16] From slaves' perspective, of course, news of Harpers Ferry might offer encouraging evidence that they had allies somewhere out there. Continued slavery might thus become both more onerous to slaves and more dangerous to their owners. According to the proslavery perspective, this was all so avoidable, so unnecessary and unfortunate.

Northerners consequently came to be viewed as dangerous aliens, "abolition emissaries." As for the burden of proof, one newspaper editor urged that all "strangers from the North" be considered "as *prima facie* an incendiary," who themselves bore the responsibility of proving otherwise. Resolutions drawn up at a North Carolina courthouse the week before Christmas articulated an apprehension that the area was "infested with itinerant Abolitionists, who, under various disguises[,] are endeavoring to sow the seeds of dissatisfaction among our slave population." The meeting accordingly "resolved that all strangers, particularly those from non-slaveholding States, who come in our midst *under suspicious circumstances,* although claiming to be in pursuit of peaceful occupation, shall be subjected to the most rigid scrutiny, and if there is probable cause to believe they are abolition emissaries they shall be taken up and made to undergo a searching examination and be dealt with accordingly."[17]

Residents of the South whose loyalty to slavery could not be relied upon seemed to exist everywhere: slaves, yeomen, and Northerners; teachers, preachers, and peddlers. Moreover, the forces of abolition could operate without being physically present, for the mails could carry "incendiary" materials, including copies of North Carolina native Hinton Helper's antislavery book *The Impending Crisis* and the Republican *New York Tribune.* Vigilante groups nabbed people possessing copies of such materials, the incendiary nature of which they readily demonstrated by casting the literature into public bonfires.[18]

Another group that posed a threat to slavery was black Southerners who were not slaves. If William Seward and Abraham Lincoln warned that the nation could not long survive half slave and half free, a Southern variant had it that the region's peculiar institution was jeopardized if black residents were divided between slave and free. Free blacks, in the view of many whites, had too little freedom to satisfy themselves but too much not to threaten slavery; whatever their behavior, they embodied the seditious notion that blacks could be something other than slaves. John Brown's followers included free blacks; moreover, Nat Turner's earlier "slave rebellion" had included free as well as slave rebels. Thus, from across the South in 1859–60 came calls to squeeze the free black population, by forcing its members either out of the state or into slavery. As one white South Carolinian wrote in the aftermath of Harpers Ferry, "A free negro in a slave country is a natural incendiary."[19]

At state and local levels alike, many Southerners reached for the patrol and the militia to bring matters back under control. A South Carolina planter characterized Harpers Ferry as "no insurrection but an invasion of abolitionists and free negroes." In any case, the patrol would monitor more closely the behavior of slaves and would seek to prevent "emissaries" from "tampering with" them. And the militia would be prepared for attacks from any source—slaves themselves, a band like Brown's, or even federal forces.[20]

Across the South then, in a myriad of actions at the local level, the "reign of terror" went on. The raid at Harpers Ferry proved an event that, as one historian has put it, "led Southerners to hang peddlers and piano tuners, and to see abolitionists swarming everywhere."[21]

And yet these Southern responses could embody divergent messages. John Brown called forth in the South words and actions more complex than simply a reflexive strike at apparent representatives of a hostile and threatening North. To take one example, Charles Manly, a former Whig governor of North Carolina writing in December 1859, aired his anxious readiness with the words, "I want to knock down a John Browner so bad I *dunno* what to do." Manly was no more upset by John Brown, however, than he was by the fire-eaters, those Southern radicals who, pursuing their disunionist agenda, sought to exploit the raid, the raiders, and all Northerners who celebrated one or both. His letter reflected one moderate Southerner's anger and frustration at "Fanatics" on both sides. In short, striking back at John Brown and his presumed minions could reflect a moderate's effort to hold to a middle ground as much as a radical's effort to exploit an opportunity.[22]

Harpers Ferry and Southern Legislatures

Southern state legislators considered various actions that might quarantine anyone who might have contracted the John Brown disease. The Virginia General Assembly set the tone when it appointed a joint committee to investigate the raid. In late January 1860 the committee made three general recommendations for action. One related to commerce and industry. Its spirit and substance were reflected in the language of a meeting in Amelia County urging laws that would discourage the consumption of Northern products until people in the North ended "their agitation and movements against us and our interests." Rather than passing laws, however, the committee suggested the establishment of voluntary associations, consistent with the resolutions passed at another Virginia meeting, "to use, eat, drink, wear or buy nothing under the sun from north of the Mason and Dixon line." Such actions, reminiscent of the colonies' boycotts of English goods in the years before the American Revolution, might deter Northern attacks against slavery and, in case the Union were to break up, should help prepare the South for regional self-sufficiency. The second and third proposals related to security. One sought military preparedness; the other focused on outsiders of the John Brown variety. The committee recommended the introduction of a bill for "more prompt and effectual punishment of all foreign emissaries and others, who may be found guilty of conspiring against the peace of our community, or seeking to incite our slaves to insurrection."[23]

State legislatures in Upper South and Deep South alike might appoint committees and pass resolutions.[24] But the Deep South went further. Legislatures there were inclined to take more direct action, and some even appropriated funds for military purposes. Mississippi and South Carolina, the two states where slaves formed the majority of the population, did so, as did the two states lying between them. The Georgia legislature, for example, responded to Harpers Ferry by appropriating $75,000 for military preparations, an amount nearly one-tenth the size of the entire state budget for the preceding year; South Carolina supplied $100,000. The Mississippi legislature authorized $150,000 to obtain arms for the militia, while Alabama voted $200,000.[25] Peace—an increasingly uneasy peace—might persist, but then again it might not. In the aftermath of Harpers Ferry, majorities in Deep South legislatures thus voted substantial amounts of money to begin preparations for military defense in case that fragile peace got swept away.

If such was the reaction of Southern legislators, the popular culture generated a related kind of response. A song made its way around Virginia (see fig. 6.2). It began:

> Now all you Southern people, just listen to my song,
> It's about the Harpers' Ferry affair, it is not very long.
> To please you all I do my best, I sung it in other towns,
> And while I am in Richmond, I'll tell you about old Brown.

After recounting some of the details of John Brown's raid, capture, trial, and execution, the song offered advice, first to Southern whites, then to Southern blacks.

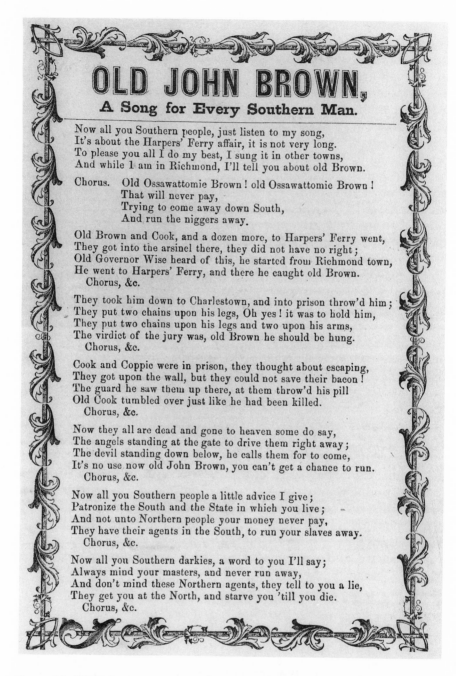

Figure 6.2. "Old John Brown, a Song for Every Southern Man," contemporary broadside. (Courtesy of the Virginia Historical Society)

Now all you Southern people a little advice I give;
Patronize the South and the State in which you live;
And not unto Northern people your money never pay,
They have their agents in the South, to run your slaves away.

Now all you Southern darkies, a word to you I'll say;
Always mind your masters, and never run away,
And don't mind these Northern agents, they tell to you a lie,
They get you at the North, and starve you 'till you die.

In the meantime, as their constituents were variously handling the affair according to their lights back home, the South's elected representatives in the U.S. House and Senate were putting on their own show.

North versus South in the U.S. Senate

The Harpers Ferry episode gave rise to a great debate in the U.S. Senate. When the Senate convened for a new session on December 5, 1859, three days after John Brown's hanging, the first order of business turned out to be a demand from Virginia Senator James M. Mason for a Congressional investigation of the raid. First, senators wrangled over whether to hold hearings on the raid at all.[26] The ensuing debate offered Southern senators a lens through which to view the North as well as a mirror in which they could peer back at the South. What did the episode tell them, they asked, about the South? And what did it say about the North?

Virginia's senators, Robert M. T. Hunter and James M. Mason, led the charge, battling Northerners throughout the session. The Virginia senators made it clear that the main issue was not John Brown's failed effort at revolution. Senator Hunter, for one, though he spoke of lethal threats to "peaceful women and helpless children," declared, "we know we can defend ourselves against such outrages as this." But what if Brown's band were a proxy for the North, a vanguard of invasion? "Much depends on what is the real state of northern feeling in regard to these matters." Did Brown's adventure find "the sympathy of the great mass of the North"? Did Brown obtain actual support for his attack? If so, then his raid "becomes a much graver question." In fact, Southern spokesmen were convinced that Brown's little band did not act on its own. Senator Mason spoke of the "outrage" that "was attempted by these vagabond instruments of people elsewhere."[27]

Northern members argued against the Southern perception that John Brown was a proxy for Northern public opinion. New Hampshire's Senator Daniel Clark, for one, rejected the notion as absurd. After John Brown "had expended his exertions for two years, what had he accomplished? He had got twenty-two men, black and white, who would go with him, and that was all. In the whole vast region of the North he could find only twenty-two men, seventeen white men and five negroes, to engage in this undertaking. Do not the Senators from Virginia see in this the eminent conservatism of the North?"[28]

Senator Mason, scoffing in turn at this construction of the event, took advantage of an opportunity he saw to place Southern slavery in a favorable light. John Brown, according to the senator, came into the Old Dominion expecting to raise thousands of troops from among Virginia slaves. His failure resulted "solely" from "the loyalty of the slaves"—and that loyalty gave the lie to abolitionists' premises. Brown brought so few men because he "acted on the theory that we know has been proclaimed over and over again by those who entertain this nefarious abolition design. He acted on the theory that the slaves are always ready for revolt; that it required nothing but to put arms in their hands to bring them to revolt." To the stark contrary, the failure of the raid at Harpers Ferry "was owing to the loyalty of the slaves, it was owing to the actual condition of slavery in the State of Virginia, to the affection, the kindness, the love which they bear to their masters and to their masters' homes."[29]

Senator Alfred Iverson of Georgia insisted that what animated his colleagues from the South was an urgent wish "that we may understand how far the northern people are effective in their opposition to slavery in the southern States." Similarly, Stephen R. Mallory of Florida sought assurances from the North that it was not irredeemably hostile toward Southern slavery. He urged Northern senators, particularly Republicans, to "assist us here in transmitting to our constituents the fact that the North is not overwhelmingly against us; that there are conservative men there; that this party does not design to drive us out of the Union." Neither Iverson nor Mallory could have obtained much solace from Senator Clark's attitude, as evinced in one of his earlier remarks. Although he asserted of Brown's raid, "I have failed anywhere and everywhere to find any sympathy for that crime," Clark followed up that syrupy concession with an abrasive—and perhaps equally extravagant—proviso that he could not say that, in his state or any near it, "there is any sympathy with the institution against which that was directed, for there is not the least."[30]

Northern members of the Senate insisted on holding up another mirror, as well, to the South, one relating to free speech and public expression. Southern spokesmen rejected the view that slavery might be a legitimate object of public discussion—that is, among its opponents—while Northerners saw it as fair game. Henry Wilson of Massachusetts, for example, speaking about a meeting of abolitionists in his state, observed that members of the audience, even though not in agreement with everything that was said, "did not interrupt the meeting, believing as they did, and as we do in our part of the country, in the absolute right of free discussion of all questions." Taking a similar approach, Maine's William P. Fessenden rejected the premise that public sentiment across the North could be gauged by what was said at a meeting, even one that was well attended. "We allow everybody to hold a public meeting that wants one, and he may say what he pleases." Moreover, according to Fessenden, "attending these meetings is a matter of amusement" as well as a reflection of interest, an indication of curiosity but by no means evidence of commitment to what was being said.[31]

Nevertheless, North and South found themselves in substantial agreement as to their underlying difference: each side understood slavery to be somehow the central issue. Speaking about Brown, Albert Gallatin Brown of Mississippi characterized what he called "the great public heart" of the North when he asked, "What, then, is it that elicits all this sympathy for him?" Senator Brown then answered his own question: the sympathy "is not for John Brown, heroic as you have said he was, but it is for the cause in which he was engaged. . . . No, gentlemen, disguise it as you will, there is throughout all the non-slaveholding States of this Union, a secret, deep-rooted sympathy with the object which this man had in view."[32]

The two sides offered counterexamples to shore up their interpretations of what had happened and their prescriptions for an appropriate response. Senator Fessenden said that he, for one, would decline to answer any question as to whether he would "abet murder and treason, and the violent seizure of the property of the United States by armed men." No more would he expect a Southern senator to reply to a question like: "Sir, had you any complicity in the attempt on the part of a portion of the people of the South, to take slaves from the coast of Africa contrary to the laws of the United States, by violence import them against the law into this country, and sell them against the law?" Mississippi's Albert Gallatin Brown offered his own scenario, which imagined John Brown making "a similar foray into Massachusetts." "Suppose an expedition should be fitted out from Virginia and Carolina, to go and capture the armory at Springfield and hold it with the avowed object of overturning the government of Massachusetts, and the whole government of the New England States, and of the North, and planting slavery there; then suppose, when you had captured the leader and gibbeted him upon the gallows, the southern people should hold meetings, religious and political, to express sympathy with the man. . . . What would be your conclusion?"[33]

Thus John Brown offered an occasion for debate on the compatibility of South and North and on ultimate questions about the nature of the Union. Speaking of his constituents, Hunter declared: "Sufficiently intelligent to understand their rights, sufficiently brave to defend them, they have proved loyal to the Government, and loyal they will remain to it so long as it remains true to its duty. When its powers shall be perverted from protection to destruction, their allegiance will cease, and with the same spirit in which they instituted this Government they will build up another." He spoke heatedly of Virginians' option "to recur to our reserved rights."[34]

Those threats did not go unanswered. For example, Senator James R. Doolittle of Wisconsin equated the radicalism of the North, such as that exemplified in John Brown's actions, with radicalism in the South, including talk of secession. The Republican party would insist, he vowed, on sustaining both the Constitution and the rights of the states, "all the States of this Union, North and South." And if his party would "neither invade the rights of the States nor suffer them to be invaded," neither would it "dissolve the Union nor suffer it to be dissolved." He wanted it clear that "if there should be such men at the South, who, like this man Brown from the North, are deluded with the idea that they can break up this Government and establish new confederacies or provisional governments for the United States," any effort to do so was treason. He concluded: "We are opposed therefore to this whole system of lawlessness and violence which has led to fillibustering from the United States into Nicaragua; to fillibustering from Missouri into Kansas, which has been followed by this fillibustering by Brown from Canada into Virginia." Regarding the quashing of all such unlawful acts, he asked his colleagues from the South, "Will you join with us? Can we rely upon you?"[35]

Much of this rhetoric, it should be noted, was equally consistent with either of two very different political persuasions and objectives. It can be read—and could have been heard, and might have been meant—as either a taunt or a plea. Legislators in each house, and from either party and either region, could choose to deride their political opponents, or they could continue, during the crisis of late 1859 and early 1860, to seek assurances and common ground.

A Contentious Conflation:
John Brown, Hinton Helper, and John Sherman

While all this was going on in the Senate, a related confrontation developed in the House of Representatives. There congressmen, divided by party and region over the House speakership, also spoke in fervent tones that combined grandstanding with genuine anger and concern. Many came to work armed. Republicans had settled on John Sherman of Ohio as their candidate, but matters had not gone smoothly. Much was at stake, even within the House, given that the Speaker appointed committees and their chairmen. Republicans would need support from outside their party ranks, for neither they nor the Democrats (bitterly divided as they were between administration Democrats and the supporters of Stephen A. Douglas) held a majority of seats, and thus a victory for either hinged on gaining the support of enough members of the American (Know-Nothing) party. From December 5 to February 1, the House went without a Speaker, for no winner emerged until the forty-fourth ballot.[36]

John Sherman's main problem was Hinton Rowan Helper, an antislavery Southerner. Helper, a nonslaveholder from North Carolina, had published a treatise called *The Impending Crisis of the South,* which consisted of a diatribe against slavery and a compilation of census data, and Sherman, along with sixty-seven other Republican members of the House, had signed an endorsement of Helper's plan to bring out an abridged version of the book, a *Compendium.* In his book Harper argued his twin theses that slavery was causing the South to fall ever further behind the North and that slavery hurt Southern white nonslaveholders. John Brown and Hinton Helper were by no means identical spokesmen for the antislavery position. Helper envisioned an all-white America, for he hated blacks as well as slavery, while Brown professed an egalitarian commitment to promoting slaves' emancipation without deportation. Helper compiled a book, while Brown proved a man of action. And yet they could readily enough be perceived as a matching pair. After all, Helper's *Compendium* carried headings like "Revolution—Peaceably if we can, Violently if we must." Especially after Harpers Ferry, and in the context of Sherman's endorsement and candidacy, Helper's book took on great symbolic significance.[37]

The Impending Crisis appeared to serve well the Republicans' propaganda purposes in the North. For one thing, it distilled its message into terms consistent with the lowest common denominator in the North's critique of the South. Fully consistent with a racist agenda of excluding all blacks from the West, slave and free alike, it emphasized the harm slavery did to whites rather than how it hurt blacks. It shored up a widespread belief that slavery was a fossil of a feudal past, out of place in the modern world, and, moreover, that it retarded the nation's (and the North's) progress and compromised its material well-being.[38]

If Helper's approach appears curious, it is in that, radical as he was in some respects, he fails to conform to the notion that abolitionists represented the vanguard of Northern public opinion—that they were more egalitarian, taking the high moral ground that slavery was evil in blighting black Americans' lives, whatever it did to whites. Helper worked from a different logic. He came from North Carolina; he was not living in Illinois or Kansas. The antislavery stance of containing slavery, which worked so well in the free-soil North and (especially) West, made no sense to someone standing where slavery already was an established institution. There, rolling slavery back appeared crucial—an immediate need, not merely an option or a possible ultimate goal. Thus, from where he stood, Helper talked abolition, not merely antislavery, rollback rather than containment.

Helper's similarities to Brown thus begin to come into focus. Both were abolitionists. One embodied the hostility felt by Southern yeomen against the peculiar institution; the other worked from the premise of such enmity; and both sought to exploit it. Each spoke to a national audience about the evils of slavery, and both appeared to attract broad-based support in the North.

Different as they were, then, *The Impending Crisis* and Harpers Ferry brought similar messages to proslavery Southerners. Regardless of whether either Brown or Helper in fact spoke for mainstream Northern public opinion, each appeared to garner widespread approval across the North, and each had declared war on slavery in the South. Each represented, at least in part, the dreaded triple threat against slavery—from nonslaveholding whites in the South, from the slaves themselves, and from outside forces. Each, too, pointed up the need and offered the opportunity to unify white Southerners against all such threats, an observation that could come from a variety of perspectives. Thus, as a letter from one Southern slaveholder put the matter in December 1859, "John Brown and Helper may do more to build up the Democratic party than anything that has happened for years."[39]

In February 1860 a Democratic Virginia legislator linked supporters of the two when he referred to "admirers of Brown and endorsers of Helper."[40] One reason for the equation of Brown and Helper was surely the hope among many Southerners and Democrats of derailing Sherman's bid for the speakership. At the same time, fine distinctions tended to vanish from view in the political heat of the winter of 1859–60. Both Brown and Helper represented serious and related attacks on a central institution of Southern society, an institution undeniably under attack. The triple threat appeared too real to try to shake off like a bad dream.

Thus it was that, while the House was debating the speakership, Senator Iverson of Georgia went wild. Charging Northern senators with duplicity, he noted that they "disclaim for themselves and their people any sympathy whatever with Brown and his acts and his intentions. And yet, sir, look at what is transpiring this very day in this very Capitol." By supporting John Sherman, the Republican party was "this day attempting to raise to the third office in this Government a man who has openly indorsed sentiments more incendiary in their character than anything that John Brown has ever uttered." Iverson continued the next day to link John Brown, Hinton Helper, and John Sherman. "When you say that you do not sympathize with Brown and his acts, when you say that you do not intend to interfere with slavery in the southern States, when you say that you intend to observe the constitutional rights of the southern people, you, at the same time, go to the polls banding together in political organizations, and elevate to political power the very men who inculcate these treasonable sentiments. Then, what are all your disclaimers worth?" Warming to his theme, the senator from Georgia raised the stakes. "And yet the Republican party propose to elevate to a high office a man who has . . . attempted to circulate a pamphlet containing the most treasonable and the most insurrectionary sentiments, . . . exciting insurrection and advising our slaves to fire our dwellings and put their knives to our throats." For such a crime, Iverson noted, John Brown had already been hanged, and anyone who endorsed Hinton Helper's book should be hanged as well.[41]

Iverson then moved on to raise the specter of secession—a full year before South Carolina took such action in December 1860. "What is the Union worth," he demanded, "when the rights and equality of the States are put at naught?" Returning to the question of Sherman's election to the speakership, he averred, "I do not pretend to say that I would dissolve the Union . . . upon the mere election of a Black Republican Speaker. . . . But when you elect a Black Republican who has counseled sedition, who has approved of treasonable sentiments, who has uttered to the slaves of the southern States the sentiment that they ought to cut the throats of their masters; when you put in power a man of that character, and show, by your elevating him to power, that you approve of his sentiments," that, for Iverson, was clearly another story. That would be grounds for secession.[42]

In the end, after all the many rounds of balloting, Sherman barely missed election. The successful candidate was one William Pennington of New Jersey, a colorless conservative Republican who had not endorsed Helper's book. Thus was compromise achieved, which meant that Senator Iverson and his colleagues did not have occasion to respond to the election of a new House speaker by withdrawing from their seats. Secession could wait.[43]

Tilt toward Disunion

Stunned by John Brown's raid, many Southerners were forced to give their commitment to the Union serious reconsideration. On hearing the news one North Carolinian admitted in December 1859 that "I have always been a fervid Union man but I confess the endorsement of the Harpers Ferry outrage and Helper's infernal doctrine has shaken my fidelity and . . . I am willing to take the chances of every probable evil that may arise from disunion, sooner than submit any longer to Northern insolence and Northern outrage."[44] Repeated countless times across the South, this response to the events of 1859—in particular, the apparent Northern "endorsement" of both Harpers Ferry and Hinton Helper—brought the Union much closer than ever before to collapse. Those events captured the attention even of the apathetic, shook the faith of unionists, and encouraged the disunionists.

Moreover, Harpers Ferry continued to supply the central symbol of danger to slavery as an institution. In June 1860 a South Carolina military officer told his men that some "John Pike Brown the Second may be in our midst aiding and counseling and urging our slaves to an immediate and bloody insurrection."⁴⁵ Increasingly, Southern voters came to see what an old warhorse fire-eater, South Carolina's Robert Barnwell Rhett, had meant when he said that the raid at Harpers Ferry was simply "fact coming to the aid of logic." More and more saw in the raid, as the Tennessee legislature put it, "the natural fruit of this treasonable 'irrepressible conflict' doctrine put forth by the great head [William Seward] of the Black Republican party and echoed by his subordinates."⁴⁶

One fire-eater, Edmund Ruffin, did what he could to recruit John Brown for a continuing appointment, after his death, as professor of secession. Ruffin attended Brown's hanging. At that time, he secured one of Brown's pikes and labeled its handle "Samples of the favors designed for us by our Northern Brethren." He then took it to the nation's capital, where he showed it off to Southern members of Congress and anyone else who would look. Gratified at the response, he secured other John Brown pikes from Harpers Ferry, labeled them, too, and shipped one off to each Southern governor. In addition to carrying his pike everywhere, Ruffin took to wearing a suit of cloth made in Virginia. One recent scholar describes Ruffin wearing his homespun, parading "with his pike to promote both southern manufacturing and a boycott of northern goods," and, in the process, "transforming himself into the symbol of secession incarnate."⁴⁷

Leading Southern politicians remained divided in late 1859 and early 1860 over whether slavery was safer in the Union or out of it, over whether secession or the survival of the Union posed for it the greater threat. Jousting desperately over the nature of Brown's band, the degree to which it represented Northern public opinion, and thus the overall meaning of Harpers Ferry were those already committed to disunion as well as those who retained some hope of averting secession. Unionists, no matter how conditional their commitment, had to pursue a strategy based on the premise that, if the South were politically unified—and the North divided—the South could continue to control the Democratic party, and the Democratic party could thus continue to control the nation. James A. Seddon, for example, complained to his friend Senator Robert M. T. Hunter in December 1859 of the South's failure to interpret the raid to better advantage. He attacked Virginia Governor Henry A. Wise and others for seeking "to make these infamous felons grand political criminals—to hold the whole North or at least the whole Republican party identified with them and to spread the greatest excitement and indignation against that whole section and its people."[48]

Seddon's indictment bears quotation at length. "The Harper's Ferry affair ought to have been treated and represented either in its best light as the mad folly of a few deluded cranks branded fanatics or, more truly, as the vulgar crime and outrage of a squad of reckless desperate Ruffians, . . . and they should have been accordingly tried and executed as execrable criminals in the simplest and most summary manner. There should not have been the chance offered of elevating them to *political* offenders or making them representatives and champions of Northern Sentiment." Rather, Governor Wise, for one, "by insisting on holding them as the chiefs of an organized conspiracy at the North, has provoked . . . the sympathy and approbation of large masses and of established organs of public opinion at the North." Thus Brown and his followers had gained tribute "as veritable heroes and martyrs, exponents and champions of the North immolated for their love of liberty and aid to the oppressed [in] Southern Slavery."[49] In short, according to Seddon's view, the wrong spin had been put on the raid. Rather than employing the incident as a device to divide the North, to promote revulsion against abolitionists, and to make more manifest the great conservative sentiment that better characterized Northern public opinion, disunionists had sought to unify the South and, in the effort, appeared to have unified the North. Unionists felt the sand slipping away from beneath their feet. They lost control of the interpretation of Harpers Ferry. They lost control of the course of events. Moreover, they found themselves abandoning the unionist position for disunionism.

The perception came to prevail in the South that John Brown spoke for the Republican party, and that the Republican party spoke for the North. The Republicans—despite their 1860 platform's repudiation of John Brown and its disavowal of any intent to tamper with slavery in the South— appeared to threaten slavery, the South's dominant economic institution and its major means of race control. The North's embrace of the Republican party in 1860 further demonstrated what many Southern voters and politicians thought they already knew, and it persuaded many others that the North as a region had declared its hostility to slavery. For many, no overt act was needed by the incoming Lincoln administration. The North had already revealed its intent.[50]

Now the radicals in the South turned the tables on the radicals in the North. One year to the day after John Brown's raid began, a letter from a South Carolinian pointed the way toward uniting the South for secession "through the publishing of strong and incendiary pamphlets that stir the sleeping South out of the lethargy fostered by the poison called love of Union." "Emissaries" now promoted secession, not abolition. And in April 1861 former Virginia Governor Henry A. Wise, seeking to force his state into secession, engineered the seizure, by an armed band of native white proslavery Southerners, of the arsenal and armory at Harpers Ferry.[51]

Thus, for a majority of voters and politicians in state after state across the South—whether following Lincoln's election or not until his call for troops to put down the "rebellion" at Fort Sumter—secession became the only option. Whether secession would prove a means of forcing a new compact for the United States, as some still hoped, or a step toward forming a new Southern nation, as others were determined, remained to be seen. Whether it would prove peaceful, only time would tell. Whether it would lead to military conflict, not only between South and North but within the South, as slaves and nonslaveholders turned against the system, would soon be known. Southerners of the fire-eater approach touted secession and a new Confederacy as a panacea for all Southern ills; those of the firebell persuasion stepped into the new political world anticipating a catastrophe.[52] The great gamble was under way.

Long Shadows

Roughly a year after John Brown's raid, capture, and execution, American voters registered their preferences among the 1860 presidential candidates. Enough Northerners chose Abraham Lincoln to give him an outright victory in the electoral college. All seven states across the Deep South opted to respond by seceding. The first to do so was South Carolina, majority slave and always in the vanguard of such movements. South Carolina resolved on this course of action regardless of whether other states followed—and six other states did follow, even before Lincoln took office. That forced the issue. Then came Fort Sumter, Lincoln's call for troops, the secession of four more states, and Civil War. As figure 6.3 shows, slavery continued to be the key to southern political behavior: the first tier of states to secede typically had populations that were about 45 percent slave; the second tier, about 30 percent. States with populations no greater than 20 percent slave remained in the Union.[53]

Perhaps—just perhaps—the events of the winter and spring of 1860–61 would have unfolded much as they did even if John Brown had never thought of going to Harpers Ferry. A handful, more or less, of converts to secession, if that is all that can be credited to the raid, would not have changed the outcome of the conventions in Alabama in January 1861 or in Virginia three months later. Many whites across the South drew what assurance they could from the fact that no slaves and no nonslaveholders

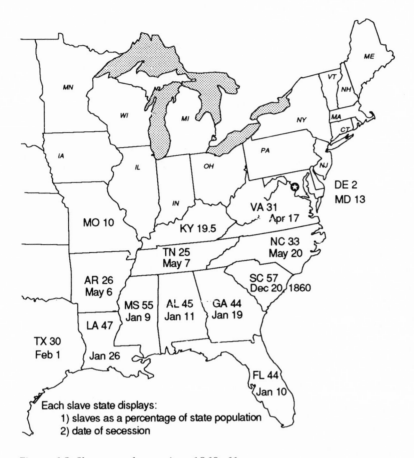

Figure 6.3. Slavery and secession, 1860–61

rushed to join John Brown after he moved on Harpers Ferry. Yet the growing perception, particularly in the Deep South, of an equation between
John Brown and the Republican party surely prepared voters and politicians alike to view Lincoln's election—already evidence of the equation of
the Republican party with the North—as grounds in and of itself for secession. Northern responses to Brown's execution contributed to this developing perspective, inasmuch as Brown's martyrdom served to enhance the
danger that slavery's supporters saw in the North.

In the winter and spring of 1860–61, unionists in the North and secessionists in the South each conceived that the other was forcing the issue.
The competing images of "John Brown's body," the clashing interpretations of his raid at Harpers Ferry, did their work. Five years after that raid,
Abraham Lincoln won reelection to the presidency, on a platform calling

for a continuation of the war against secession and a Constitutional amendment that would end slavery everywhere in the nation.[54] The siege was not yet over, not yet triumphant. Nevertheless, the triple threat to slavery—from slaves, from nonslaveholding Southern whites, and from the North—was closing in, heralding a transformation of Southern as well as national politics.[55]

Once the killing fields of the Civil War had claimed their countless dead, and emancipation was proclaimed and implemented, and Reconstruction took its course through the postwar era, Harpers Ferry no longer loomed as the great event it had seemed when it burst on the national scene in late 1859. By the late 1860s, a decade after Harpers Ferry, too many other great events had joined it in history and legend alike for it still to cast much of an independent shadow. The image of John Brown and his raid on Harpers Ferry no longer took center stage when political leaders and their constituents wrangled over current questions of public policy. After all, questions of slavery and secession no longer demanded answers.

What remained, though, were those many other social and political issues that had come to be connected with the raid and its interpretation: relations across race and class lines within the South, relations between South and North within the nation. The quest for control of black Southerners by white, and the quest for liberation from that control, would continue for generations. Americans' tribal past continued to shape the present: no apocalyptic raid at a federal facility—not even an apocalyptic war—could bring an end to that. Nonetheless, in all likelihood, the raid helped to bring about the war, and the war surely shaped the contours of change.

Notes

1. See Woodward, "Private War," pp. 41–68; Oates, *Purge,* pp. 229–306; Wyatt-Brown, "Antinomian," pp. 97–127; and Simpson, *Wise,* pp. 203–18.

2. *Richmond Dispatch,* Oct. 19, 1859.

3. Ibid.

4. Quoted in Woodward, "Private War," pp. 63–64; see also Oates, *Purge,* p. 279; *New York Times,* Oct. 22, 1859.

5. *Richmond Enquirer,* quoted in the *New York Times,* Oct. 22, 1859.

6. *Richmond Whig,* quoted in the *New York Times,* Oct. 22, 1859.

7. Ibid.

8. Quoted in John C. Inscoe, *Mountain Masters, Slavery, and the Sectional Crisis in Western North Carolina* (Knoxville, 1989), p. 212.

9. Diary entry for Oct. 19, 1859, quoted in Henry T. Shanks, *The Secession Movement in Virginia, 1847–1861* (Richmond, 1934), p. 237.

10. William Campbell Preston to Waddy Thompson, Jan. 27, 1860, quoted in Steven A. Channing, *Crisis of Fear: Secession in South Carolina* (New York, 1970), pp. 30, 36n. See also William Lloyd Garrison, *The New "Reign of Terror" in the Slave-*

holding States, 1859–60 (New York, 1860); and William L. Barney, *The Secessionist Impulse: Alabama and Mississippi in 1860* (Princeton, 1974), pp. 166–80.

11. Regarding the Turner uprising and its aftermath in Virginia, see William W. Freehling, *The Road to Disunion,* vol. 1, *Secessionists at Bay, 1776–1865* (New York, 1990), pp. 178–96. It is true that tensions continued in late antebellum Virginia; for astute observations on these, see William W. Freehling, "The Editorial Revolution, Virginia, and the Coming of the Civil War: A Review Essay," *CWH* 16 (Mar. 1970): 64–72.

12. Figure 6.1 shows South Carolina's nonslaveholders outnumbering slave-holders 22 to 21 percent, but, among the 42.8 percent of all residents who were not slaves, 1.4 percent were nonwhite. Thus my calculations leave whites evenly di-vided. See also Kenneth M. Stampp, *The Peculiar Institution: Slavery in the Ante-Bellum South* (New York, 1956), p. 30. The data underlying figure 6.1 can be found in Lewis Cecil Gray, *History of Agriculture in the Southern United States to 1860,* 2 vols. (Wash-ington, D.C., 1933), 1:482; U.S. Census Bureau, *Population of the United States in 1860* (Washington, D.C., 1864), pp. 598–99 and 604; and U.S. Census Bureau, *Agriculture of the United States in 1860* (Washington, D.C., 1864), pp. 247–48. The figure first appeared in Peter Wallenstein, "Cartograms and the Mapping of Virginia History, 1790–1990," *Virginia Social Science Journal* 28 (1993): 97, and is reprinted with per-mission. It assumes that all free families were the same size and that each slavehold-ing family appeared only once in the records. For a useful warning against any effort to impose precise numbers and clear divisions on antebellum white Southerners, though, see the chapter entitled "Master-class Pluralism" in James Oakes, *The Ruling Race: A History of American Slaveholders* (New York, 1982).

13. See Alison Goodyear Freehling, *Drift toward Dissolution: The Virginia Slavery Debate of 1831–1832* (Baton Rouge, 1982).

14. See Peter Wallenstein, *From Slave South to New South: Public Policy in Nine-teenth-Century Georgia* (Chapel Hill, 1987), p. 12; and Ira Berlin and Herbert G. Gut-man, "Natives and Immigrants, Free Men and Slaves: Urban Workingmen in the Antebellum American South," *AHR* 88 (Dec. 1983): 1175–1200.

15. Daniel Hamilton to William Porcher Miles, Feb. 2, 1860, quoted in Channing, *Crisis of Fear,* p. 256. See also Carl N. Degler, *The Other South: Southern Dissenters in the Nineteenth Century* (New York, 1974), pp. 13–96.

16. Letter to *Charleston Mercury,* Nov. 11, 1859, quoted in Channing, *Crisis of Fear,* p. 41; Judge Thomas Withers, quoted in ibid., p. 39n; and see ibid., pp. 56–57.

17. Quoted in Victor B. Howard, "John Brown's Raid at Harpers Ferry and the Sectional Crisis in North Carolina," *North Carolina Historical Review* 55 (Autumn 1978): 398; and Inscoe, *Mountain Masters,* pp. 212–13, respectively.

18. See Woodward, "Private War," p. 66; Howard, "John Brown's Raid," pp. 400–407; and Michael Kent Curtis, "The 1859 Crisis over Hinton Helper's Book, *The Impending Crisis:* Free Speech, Slavery, and Some Light on the Meaning of the First Section of the Fourteenth Amendment," *Chicago-Kent Law Review* 68 (1993): 1113–79, esp. pp. 1159–67.

19. Quoted in Michael P. Johnson and James L. Roark, *Black Masters: A Free Family of Color in the Old South* (New York, 1984), p. 188. See also Howard, "John Brown's Raid," p. 410; Wallenstein, *From Slave South to New South,* p. 89; and Ira Berlin, *Slaves without Masters: The Free Negro in the Antebellum South* (New York, 1974), pp. 370–80.

20. Quoted in Johnson and Roark, *Black Masters,* p. 187; see also Kent Blaser, "North Carolina and John Brown's Raid," *CWH* 24 (Sept. 1978): 197–212, esp. pp. 205–6.

21. Ollinger Crenshaw, "The Psychological Background of the Election of 1860 in the South," *North Carolina Historical Review* 19 (July 1942): 275.

22. Charles Manly to Judge Thomas Ruffin, Dec. 15, 1859, quoted in Paul D. Escott, *Many Excellent People: Power and Privilege in North Carolina, 1850–1900* (Chapel Hill, 1985), p. 33.

23. Quoted in Shanks, *Secession Movement in Virginia,* pp. 92, 93, and 95–96.

24. For examples of such resolutions, see Avery O. Craven, *The Growth of Southern Nationalism, 1848–1861* (Baton Rouge, 1953), p. 311 (for Tennessee); Harold S. Schultz, *Nationalism and Sectionalism in South Carolina, 1852–1860* (Durham, N.C., 1950), pp. 192–94; and Percy Lee Rainwater, *Mississippi: Storm Center for Secession, 1856–1861* (Baton Rouge, 1938), pp. 104–6.

25. See Wallenstein, *From Slave South to New South,* pp. 100 and 106; Barney, *Secessionist Impulse,* pp. 112–16; Schultz, *Nationalism and Sectionalism in South Carolina,* p. 194; and Nevins, *Emergence,* 2:112.

26. Regarding Mason's demand, see Nevins, *Prologue to Civil War,* pp. 115 and 125–26; Oates, *Purge,* pp. 359–60; and the *Congressional Globe,* 36th Cong., 1st Sess., Dec. 5, 1859, p. 1. Much of the subsequent wrangling revolved rhetorically around an amendment, offered by Lyman Trumbull of Illinois, that would have broadened the focus of the investigation. Using language almost identical to that in Mason's proposal, Trumbull urged investigation of a similar but proslavery effort, "the invasion, seizure, and robbery, in December 1855, of the arsenal of the United States, at Liberty, in the State of Missouri, by a mob or body of armed men." Southern senators took great exception to the amendment, while Republicans professed bewilderment as to why the two events should not get equal attention. Senator James F. Simmons of Rhode Island rejected a carte-blanche investigation of only Harpers Ferry as displaying "a disposition to implicate public men, and implicate political parties" (*Congressional Globe,* 36th Cong., 1st Sess., Dec. 6, 1859, p. 5; and Dec. 7, 1859, p. 27).

27. See the *Congressional Globe,* 36th Cong., 1st Sess., Dec. 6, 1859, p. 9 (for Hunter), and p. 13 (for Mason). See also Henry Harrison Simms, *Life of Robert M. T. Hunter: A Study in Sectionalism and Secession* (Richmond, 1935); John E. Fisher, "Statesman of the Lost Cause: The Career of R. M. T. Hunter, 1859–87" (M.A. thesis, University of Virginia, 1966), pp. 21–24; and James Luckin Bugg, Jr., "The Political Career of James Murray Mason: The Legislative Phase" (Ph.D. diss., University of Virginia, 1950), pp. 686–745.

28. See the *Congressional Globe,* 36th Cong., 1st Sess., Dec. 6, 1859, p. 11.

29. Ibid., p. 14. For quite different treatments of this question, see Potter, "Paradox," pp. 201–18; and Merton L. Dillon, *Slavery Attacked: Southern Slaves and Their Allies, 1619–1865* (Baton Rouge, 1990), pp. 232–42.

30. See the *Congressional Globe,* 36th Cong., 1st Sess., Dec. 6, 1859, p. 14 (for Iverson), Dec. 7, 1859, p. 28 (for Mallory), and Dec. 6, 1859, p. 11 (for Clark).

31. See ibid., Dec. 6, 1859, p. 12 (for Wilson), and Dec. 7, 1859, p. 31 (for Fessenden). See also Curtis, "The 1859 Crisis over Hinton Helper's Book," pp. 1147–59.

32. See the *Congressional Globe,* 36th Cong., 1st Sess., Dec. 7, 1859, p. 33.

33. See ibid., Dec. 7, 1859, p. 32 (for Fessenden) and p. 33 (for Brown).

34. See ibid., Dec. 6, 1859, p. 10.

35. See ibid., Dec. 7, 1859, p. 36.

36. See Potter, *Impending,* pp. 385–90; Nevins, *Prologue to Civil War,* pp. 116–24; Roy Franklin Nichols, *The Disruption of American Democracy* (New York, 1948), pp. 270–76; and Ollinger Crenshaw, "The Speakership Contest of 1859–1860: John Sherman's Election a Cause of Disruption?" *Mississippi Valley Historical Review* 29 (Dec. 1942): 323–38.

37. Hugh C. Bailey, *Hinton Rowan Helper: Abolitionist-Racist* (University, Ala., 1965), pp. 61–81; Hinton Rowan Helper, *The Impending Crisis of the South: How To*

Meet It, ed. George M. Fredrickson (Cambridge, Mass., 1968), pp. ix–xix. See also Potter, *Impending,* p. 387; Howard, "John Brown's Raid," p. 419.

38. See Helper, *Impending Crisis,* pp. xxx–xlix.

39. "A Slaveholder" (a Southern Whig) to Congressman John Sherman, Dec. 10, 1859, quoted in Howard, "John Brown's Raid," p. 418n.

40. John C. Rutherfoord, quoted in Shanks, *Secession Movement in Virginia,* p. 100.

41. See the *Congressional Globe,* 36th Cong., 1st Sess., Dec. 6, 1859, p. 14, and Dec. 7, 1859, pp. 29 and 30. See also Curtis, "The 1859 Crisis over Hinton Helper's Book," pp. 1143–59.

42. See the *Congressional Globe,* 36th Cong., 1st Sess., Dec. 7, 1859, p. 30.

43. See Nevins, *Prologue to Civil War,* p. 124; Channing, *Crisis of Fear,* p. 111.

44. William A. Walsh to L. O'B. Branch, Dec. 8, 1859, quoted in Craven, *Growth of Southern Nationalism,* p. 311. See also Marc W. Kruman, *Parties and Politics in North Carolina, 1836–1865* (Baton Rouge, 1983), pp. 187–89; and Jean H. Baker, *The Politics of Continuity: Maryland Political Parties from 1858 to 1870* (Baltimore, 1973), pp. 24–31.

45. Speech of Thomas G. Bacon, June 4, 1860, in the *Edgefield (S.C.) Advertiser,* June 13, 1860, quoted in Channing, *Crisis of Fear,* pp. 265–66.

46. For Rhett's remark, see the *Charleston Mercury,* Oct. 31, 1859, quoted in Channing, *Crisis of Fear,* p. 88; Tennessee legislature quoted in Craven, *Growth of Southern Nationalism,* p. 309.

47. See Eric H. Walther, *The Fire-Eaters* (Baton Rouge, 1992), pp. 258–61; the quotations are from pp. 259, 261, and 260.

48. See James A. Seddon to R. M. T. Hunter, Dec. 26, 1859, in Charles Henry Ambler, ed., *Correspondence of Robert M. T. Hunter, 1826–1876* (Washington, D.C., 1918), pp. 280–84 (quotation from p. 281).

49. Ibid., p. 281.

50. See Daniel W. Crofts, *Reluctant Confederates: Upper South Unionists in the Secession Crisis* (Chapel Hill, 1989), pp. 70–72; Craven, *Growth of Southern Nationalism,* pp. 305–11; William J. Cooper, Jr., *Liberty and Slavery: Southern Politics to 1860* (New York, 1983), pp. 266–71; and Dwight Lowell Dumond, ed., *Southern Editorials on Secession* (Washington, D.C., 1931). For the 1860 Republican platform, see Henry Steele Commager, *Documents of American History,* 7th ed., 2 vols. (New York, 1963), 1:363–65.

51. Letter of William Tennant, Jr., to M. L. Bonham, Oct. 16, 1860, quoted in Channing, *Crisis of Fear,* p. 262; see also Simpson, *Wise,* pp. 248–50.

52. See Walther, *The Fire-Eaters,* pp. 7 and 297–302.

53. Figure 6.3 first appeared in Wallenstein, "Cartograms and the Mapping of Virginia History," p. 99, and is reprinted with permission. For a sophisticated political analysis that, while accounting for the differential between Upper South and Deep South in the developing sectional crisis, downplays the centrality of slavery and slaveholding, see Michael F. Holt, *The Political Crisis of the 1850s* (New York, 1978), ch. 8.

54. See Commager, *Documents of American History,* 1:435.

55. See Joseph T. Glatthaar, "Black Glory: The African-American Role in Union Victory," in *Why the Confederacy Lost,* ed. Gabor S. Boritt (New York, 1992), pp. 135–62; Peter Wallenstein, "Which Side Are You On? The Social Origins of White Union Troops from Civil War Tennessee," *Journal of East Tennessee History* 63 (1991): 72–103; and Richard Nelson Current, *Lincoln's Loyalists: Union Soldiers from the Confederacy* (Boston, 1992).

7

JAMES O. BREEDEN

Rehearsal for Secession?
The Return Home of Southern Medical Students
from Philadelphia in 1859

Ever since John Brown's mad attempt at Harper's Ferry, the Southern people seem to
have lost their common sense and chivalry.

Frank Leslie's Illustrated Newspaper, December 31, 1859

Such seemed to be the case indeed, as the South responded to this isolated
act of terrorism with outrage and fear. But it could hardly have been otherwise. By 1859 the South was in the iron grip of a fear-driven psychosis, the
product of four decades of sectional tension and animosity, that conditioned its relations with the outside world. Increasingly, the North was seen
as a threat to the Southern way of life and its every action greeted with
suspicion. Thus, despite condemnation of Brown's fanaticism by Northern
conservatives, the mass of Southerners interpreted it as the "secret will" of
the abolitionists, and of many Northerners. There followed a frenzy of
irrational behavior: public meetings to protest the atrocity and sound the
alarm, the formation of myriad Southern rights and local defense organizations, blacklistings and boycottings of Northern firms, and, worst of all,
vigilante and mob action against Northerners and suspected Northern
sympathizers. Lesser known, though, is the secession of some 250 southern
medical students from the schools of Philadelphia.[1]

Philadelphia was the medical center of antebellum America. Having pi-
oneered in American medical education during the colonial period, its
medical schools were the nation's best. Each year hundreds of young men
made the trek to Philadelphia to enroll in either the medical department of
the University of Pennsylvania or Jefferson Medical College. A large number of these were Southerners. In the decade preceding the Civil War over
half of the more than two thousand Southern youths annually preparing
for a career in medicine went North for their professional training, the bulk
of them entering the schools of Philadelphia or New York, Philadelphia's
principal medical rival. The former were a particular favorite, however:
through 1860 Southerners made up nearly 69 percent of the total graduates

of these institutions.[2] For reasons that are unclear, Jefferson Medical College was especially popular with students from the South. "There was something in the atmosphere of the school," one of its biographers has suggested, "that seemed to invite attendance from that great section of the country; something in the spirit of its institutions that was especially congenial to the southern temperament." Of the school's 630 matriculants during the 1859–60 session, 395 (62.7 percent) were from slaveholding states, whereas at the University of Pennsylvania Southerners were outnumbered two-to-one in the 528-member medical department.[3]

But as the fateful era of the Old South wore on, radical Southern nationalists became increasingly incensed at the thought of Southern youths leaving their region for schooling—not only those seeking training in medicine but also the additional hundreds who flocked to the superior colleges and universities of the North. This practice cost the South millions of dollars in lost revenue, exposed hundreds of young Southerners to abolitionism and kindred doctrines threatening to their region's way of life, and stamped Southern institutions with a badge of inferiority. "We certainly ought to patronize our own literary institutions in preference to those at the north," J. D. B. De Bow, the prominent propagandist of Southern nationalism railed in 1856, "when we know that our colleges and universities are equal, if not superior, to any in the United States, and not send our children to northern colleges, which are nothing other than hot-beds of fanaticism." The Southern medical profession eagerly joined the campaign for intellectual independence. In their inaugural number, in 1844, the editors of the *New-Orleans Medical Journal* exhorted: "It is in the *South* we must study *Southern Diseases.*" "Experience drawn from the icy region of the north," Samuel A. Cartwright, perhaps the most outspoken advocate of a distinctive southern practice, elaborated, was not applicable "to the diseases of the South."[4]

Indeed, if Southern medicine was unique—and some support (chiefly involving the geographical distribution of diseases and the presence of a large slave population) can be mustered for such a claim—it followed that its practitioners needed to study in Southern medical schools. The idea of a distinctive Southern medicine was not quite this simple, however, for sectionalism and self-interest have to be taken into consideration. Physicians in the South, for all the lip service they paid to the idea that medicine and politics did not mix, were no more immune from the taint of Southernism than their countrymen. James C. Billingslea, a particularly fiery Alabama physician, in an 1856 appeal for medical independence held that Northern physicians looked with contempt upon their Southern colleagues "simply because we are *slaveholders.*"[5] Moreover, most medical schools were proprietary, and their success and faculty salaries depended upon student fees.

For a curious combination of science, sectionalism, and self-interest, then, a concerted campaign was launched to persuade aspirants to a career in medicine to study at home.

While the growth of the medical schools of New Orleans, Nashville, and Louisville—attributable to their location, the quality of their faculty, and effective advertising—was impressive, the campaign to halt the patronizing of Northern schools experienced little success. Only a month before the secession from Philadelphia, the dean of the Oglethorpe Medical College bemoaned the continued exodus of Southern students to the North's " 'great emporiums' of Medical science, to swell the crowded lecture rooms, and thereby *fill the purses of Northern men,* who for the most part are *inimical* to the South and her 'peculiar institutions.' "[6] Then, suddenly, John Brown's moment of madness promised to accomplish what years of Southern pleas and propaganda had been unable to.

Prelude to Secession

No sooner had the fall term at the nation's medical schools begun in October 1859 than the news of Brown's raid rocked the nation. The initial reaction in the North was condemnation, and no more so than in Philadelphia, a city with historical Southern ties. But soon feelings of sympathy, even admiration, for Brown began to surface, the result of his courageous and inspiring behavior during his imprisonment and trial, coupled with the boisterous blustering of Virginia's Governor Henry Wise. Changing sentiment in Philadelphia was evident in heightened abolitionist fervor. As Brown's execution neared, the abolitionists staged nightly sympathy meetings for the condemned insurrectionist. Curiosity and opposition drew the Southern students to these meetings, and confrontation with the abolitionists was only a matter of time. Hostilities erupted on December 2 at a noon prayer vigil called to coincide with Brown's execution, one of a host of such observances held throughout the North. National Hall, among Philadelphia's largest meeting places, was filled to overflowing with both Brown supporters and Southern sympathizers. The Southern medical students turned out in force. Appalled at the emotional outpouring in favor of Brown, they interrupted the abolitionist speakers with cheers for Governor Wise and broke up the meeting. Only a heavy police presence prevented violence. The "miserable rowdies," as one prominent abolitionist labeled the students, then took to the streets to celebrate Brown's execution, "telling how many 'niggers' they owned."[7]

A second opportunity for violence presented itself the next afternoon when Brown's body arrived in Philadelphia by train from Harpers Ferry on its way to New York for burial. A large and noisy crowd—blacks, abolition-

ists, Southern sympathizers, and three hundred Southern medical students—assembled across the street from the train station, as no one was
allowed inside. Rumors were rife, adding to the tension. Mayor Alexander
Henry and the chief of police, fearing a riot, prevailed upon Mrs. Brown to
change her plans to send the body to a local undertaker for embalming so as
not to tarry in Philadelphia. In a ruse designed to draw the crowd away, a
covered empty box was placed in a heavily draped hearse by the police and
hurriedly driven off. In the meanwhile, the real coffin was quietly taken to
the Walnut Street wharf in a furniture wagon to continue its journey to
New York by boat.[8] Although an incident was thus averted, tensions remained perilously high.

Indeed, concerned about the message local abolitionist activity was
sending Southerners, conservatives in Philadelphia called a mass rally for
December 7 to demonstrate the city's respect for the South and support for
its constitutional rights. The daylong meeting, despite a hailstorm, drew a
huge crowd, who listened to speeches condemning the abolitionists and
expressing solidarity with Virginia and the South. At its conclusion, the
Union Meeting Committee, on behalf of the citizens of Philadelphia, presented a representative of Virginia with an American flag "inscribed with
their loyal devotion to the Union as framed" as a visible symbol of the
conservative principles that united their city and that state.[9]

Had it not been for Pennsylvania's Anti-Slavery Convention and Fair,
which held its annual meeting in the city on the heels of the Union rally,
calm might have returned to Philadelphia. But with emotions running
high on both sides, the abolitionists and the conservatives were on a collision course, and in the midst of it all were the Southern medical students.
Controversy raged from the outset. During the opening-day proceedings
on December 13, anxious city officials, fearful in part of altercations with
the medical students, first ordered the removal of a large sign that had been
hung across the street and then forced the relocation of the proceedings to a
more remote site. The high point of the three-day meeting was a lecture by
George W. Curtis, a veteran New York abolitionist, on Thursday evening,
December 15, in National Hall—an address that "focused all the feelings
accumulated since the raid."[10] Unsigned advertisements in the conservative press urged all Philadelphians who were determined that "no more
hireling incendiaries shall be permitted to make their inflammatory addresses in our loyal city" to attend a mass meeting in front of National Hall
a half hour before the lecture "to adopt such measures as the exigency may
require to prevent the dissemination of principles which are calculated and
intended to arouse a spirit of the most intense animosity in our community." Philadelphia's *Daily Evening Bulletin,* which deplored the politics of
Curtis and his admirers but defended their right to freedom of speech,

condemned the proposed rally, calling its object "plainly to create disorder."[11]

By the time the doors of National Hall were opened to the public an angry mob (said to number as many as ten thousand) had assembled in front of the building, intent upon breaking up the meeting. A contingent of Southern medical students mingled with the protesters, getting up cheers for Governor Wise ("the man who hung John Brown"), the South, and democracy, boos for Mayor Henry and Curtis, and "promiscuous groans for everybody and everything that had interfered with the intended sport of burning National Hall and scattering the persons gathered in it." While he, too, "had no sympathy" with Curtis, Mayor Henry nevertheless saw it his duty "to secure to every one the exercise of the undisturbed freedom of speech," and stationed a force of five hundred policemen around and inside the hall to hold the mob in check.[12]

Some of the protesters, however, managed to get inside, where they attempted to interrupt Curtis with hisses. They were promptly arrested for disorderly conduct. But the main agitation was outside, in front of the hall. As the mob grew in numbers and fervor, there were repeated cheers and groans, along with calls for rushing the building and burning it. Firebrands harangued the crowd for it was, in the words of one of them, "an outrage that a band of fanatics should assemble in a hall in Philadelphia and promulgate doctrines that are abhorrent to all." Inevitably, the hall was rushed, and it appeared for a moment that matters had gotten out of hand, until the police moved forward with reinforcements and repelled the rioters. Because of the quick action of the authorities, the damage was slight, largely a few broken windows, although a bottle filled with vitriol thrown through a window badly burned the face of one young woman. The lecture, described by the *Daily Evening Bulletin* as "quite moderate in tone, for an Abolitionist of these times," ended just as order was being restored. After groaning and hissing at the audience of two thousand as it filed out of the building, the mob dispersed.[13]

The abortive rally resulted in sixteen arrests, all members of the mob. Four of those arrested were Southern medical students. Like most of the others, they were charged with inciting to riot. Three were further charged with carrying concealed weapons: C. T. Henry of Georgia was armed with a Colt revolver "fully loaded"; a "billy" was found on an unidentified twenty-one-year-old student; and a "murderous looking dirk knife" was confiscated from John C. Clark of Kentucky. All sixteen were taken before an alderman and held to await a hearing the next morning, where they were arraigned and bail, ranging from $400 to $800, was set.[14]

Friction between the Southern students and authorities, it should be noted, was nothing new. Youths from the South were widely regarded, in the words of Edmund Stedman, as "poor scholars, but blustering with rum and bowie-knives."[15] Such was especially the case with medical students. Edward Warren, who would serve as medical inspector of the Army of Northern Virginia, had enrolled at Jefferson Medical College in 1850. He later recalled:

> Medical students were regarded in those days as most uncouth and un-civilized specimens of humanity, and they were popularly rated and re-viled as Southerners, and especially as Virginians. Whenever a disturbance occurred, the "students" were held responsible and they were generally treated as if they were convicts or outlaws—as the representatives of an in-ferior race and civilization. The result was a perpetual state of warfare be-tween the Philadelphians and those who had come among them to engage in the study of medicine, with the development of reciprocal senti-ments of aversion, which bore bitter fruits for both parties.

Predictably, then, the arrests at National Hall outraged the Southern stu-dents, especially as the rumor spread that "twenty-five were put in prison, in a calaboose, and otherwise insulted."[16]

The Secession of the Students

On Tuesday, December 20, 1859, a telegraphic dispatch from Philadelphia jolted the nation. "The Students from Southern States, attending the medi-cal colleges in this city," it stated in part, "held a meeting to-day, and resolved to secede in a body from these institutions and go to Southern Colleges."[17] The secession movement originated at the heavily Southern Jefferson Medical College. By early December growing concern over Phila-delphia's response to John Brown's raid had already caused some of the students to consider returning home. Reflecting the anxiety of their parents and region, they felt it was their duty to defer further study in Philadelphia "until a better feeling was restored," but an immediate display of warm feelings and sympathy from Northern classmates and the faculty persuaded the Southern students to postpone any immediate action.[18] The arrests at National Hall on December 15, however, revived secessionist sentiment. The students met and decided not to give up their studies but to apply in a body for admission to the colleges of the South.

If the students and their defenders are to be believed, no discussion with any Southern school was initiated until Saturday, December 17—two days after the incident at National Hall—when a series of three telegrams to Dr. L. S. Joynes, dean of the Medical College of Virginia at Richmond, set the exodus in motion. The first, presumably from a student, queried: "Are Southern students admitted for remainder of session?" Taken by surprise, and not having the authority to act alone, Joynes called an executive session of the faculty for that evening to discuss the unusual request. The meeting had barely begun when a second telegram was received, this one from Francis E. Luckett and Hunter H. McGuire, spokesmen for the students, pressing the earlier query: "Upon what terms will your school receive 150 from this place first of January. Answer at once." Before the discussion was concluded another telegram from Luckett and McGuire had arrived, imploring the faculty: "We anxiously await your reply. For God's sake let it be favorable—only diplomas [sic] fee. We are in earnest, confidential." Swayed by the urgency of the appeals and their own sectional sentiments, Joynes and his colleagues voted unanimously to accept the students on the terms proposed. A similar request was made of Henry R. Frost, dean of the Medical College of the State of South Carolina—and with the same result.[19]

The favorable responses of the Richmond and Charleston faculties set off a wave of secession fever, as students from the University of Pennsylvania joined those from the Jefferson Medical College in making plans to leave. On Monday, December 19, the threatened exodus was the chief topic of discussion on each campus. Reportedly, too, a representative of the students arrived in Richmond to make arrangements for the trip. Governor Wise and the citizens of the city were exultant at the prospect of the students' return home, with the result that funds to pay their travel expenses were quickly secured through appropriation and public subscription.[20]

The decision to leave was formally made at a meeting at nine o'clock Tuesday morning. Only students from the South were admitted: Northern students were not invited and the press was "met at the door by a very decided refusal." The students turned out en masse, filling Assembly Hall— where, ironically, the Anti-Slavery Convention had met just a week earlier —to overflowing. A four-person student executive committee from the Jefferson Medical College, headed by T. F. Lee of Alabama, presided over the meeting. The first order of business was the approval of a prearranged resolution from the floor calling for a committee of five to request the presence of Francis E. Luckett and Hunter H. McGuire. "These gentlemen, we believe," the resolution read, "will freely, cheerfully and fearlessly devote their efforts to bring about a proper state of feeling among Southern students." The resolution was passed unanimously, and awaiting a call, Luckett and McGuire were brought before the assembled students in a matter of minutes. Indeed, there seems little doubt but that the exodus was instigated by Luckett with the assistance of McGuire. "They were," one student recalled, "really the leaders of the secession movement."[21]

Little is known of Luckett, other than that he was a Virginian and an ardent Southerner. When Brown's raid occurred he was a physician at the Philadelphia Almshouse, who conducted a "quiz class" for the students at Jefferson Medical College. (In this age of didactic lectures and paucity of satisfactory textbooks, students were frequently forced to employ "quiz masters" to keep up with their classes.) McGuire, who was to achieve a place of honor in the annals of Southern history as Stonewall Jackson's physician, was descended from an old and prominent Virginia family. He was the son of Dr. Hugh Holmes McGuire, the founder of Virginia's Winchester Medical College, where the younger McGuire matriculated at seventeen. He completed the college's two-year curriculum in 1855 and within months was elected professor of anatomy. McGuire taught at the college and practiced medicine with his father for two years before going to Philadelphia for further training, where he enrolled at Jefferson Medical College because of its Southern leanings.[22] McGuire was soon invited to join Luckett in conducting his "quiz class." It became the city's largest, and was particularly popular with students from the South. As mentors and confidants, Luckett and McGuire were thus ideally positioned to induce the Southern youths to secede.

Their motives can only be surmised. At the time Northerners charged personal gain—that each was promised a professorship in the South, although the historical record does not bear this out. Inflamed sectional animosity seems more plausible. In April 1859 Luckett had been a prominent witness for a Southern claimant in a fugitive slave case in Philadelphia. The black, who was probably a runaway, was nonetheless set free because the commissioner for the federal district court that heard the case believed his identify insufficiently certified. An incredulous Luckett was infuriated by the decision, and the incident fueled his growing resentment toward the North. McGuire had also long been wary of the North, and John Brown's raid pushed him into the radical camp: his home in Winchester, where his mother and sisters resided, was only thirty miles from Harpers Ferry. Increasingly, both Luckett and McGuire viewed conditions in Philadelphia—the growing abolitionist sentiment, the tirades of the Republican press against the South, and the oppressive behavior of local authorities—as intolerable for Southerners. The final blow was the incident at National Hall. There were, they bristled, no grounds for the student arrests. Rather, Northerners had again shown their true colors.[23]

Immediately upon his arrival in Assembly Hall that Tuesday morning, Luckett briefly summarized the circumstances that had led to the meeting, leaving no doubt as to its purpose. He then read a number of dispatches and letters. The first was from Governor Wise, announcing that any student leaving Philadelphia for Virginia would be welcomed "with open arms." A second, erroneously attributed to the president of the Philadelphia, Wilmington & Baltimore Railroad, offered free passage to all those who desired to go South. A third promised a reception in Richmond with military honors. Two dispatches proffered drafts of $500 to defray incidental expenses. Letters from the faculties of medical schools in Virginia, North Carolina,

Georgia, and Tennessee assured the students that they "would be welcomed
... in a handsome manner." Luckett concluded, somewhat disingenuously,
that he would not seek "to dissuade" the students "from what they considered duty but instead hoped that their retirement would be made in a
dignified manner and without bravado of any kind."[24]

With the stage for secession set, the executive committee immediately
introduced six resolutions to make it a reality. A preamble framed the issue
precisely as the students wanted it seen: "We have left our homes and
congregated in this city with a view to prosecute our medical studies, and
[have] become fully convinced that we have erred in taking this step, that
our means should have been expended and our protection afforded to the
maintenance and advancement of the institutions existing in our own section, and fostered by our people." The first resolution called for mass secession, stipulating that "as many as approve of the act" withdraw from the
medical schools of Philadelphia in a body and return to the South "to
devote our future lives and best efforts to the protection of our common
rights and the promotion of our common interests." The second disclaimed "any personal animosities" and deprecated "any political agitation" in taking this step, while the third expressed gratitude to Governor
Wise and others for their "substantial encouragement and aid." The fourth
promised to "cheerfully welcome in the South" any Northern student
"who will subscribe to the preceding resolutions." The fifth called for sending a copy of the proceedings to all Northern medical colleges "for the
benefit of Southern students who may have matriculated in them." The
sixth requested that Southern papers publish the proceedings. All six resolutions were enthusiastically endorsed.

With secession duly decided upon, McGuire addressed the meeting. He
expressed his regret that such a radical step as secession was necessary, but
he considered it a duty under the circumstances. He also exhorted the students to observe "perfect order in all their deportment . . . [as] gentlemen
from the South," so that in leaving Philadelphia, where they had "received
so much kindliness," their reputations would remain unblemished. A list of
those who were set on leaving, said to number over two hundred, was read.
The opportunity was then given for others to join the movement, whereupon another fifty names were added. A motion by McGuire that the seceders leave in a body the following night at 10 P.M. in a special train was
adopted. The hour-long meeting was reportedly characterized throughout
by "great decorum and propriety." In describing the proceedings to his
congressman, a jubilant medical student from Mississippi wrote:

> I am happy to announce that I this morning attended one of the most in-
> teresting, and, you will doubtless say, the most praiseworthy meetings
> ever held in this city. It was composed of the Southern medical students of

the different colleges of this city. A number of resolutions were passed pregnant with Southern sentiments, and were signed by a great number of those present, and are still being signed by others. This meeting resulted in the determination on the part of all true-hearted Southerners to take up their line of march tomorrow evening, at ten o'clock, for the South.[25]

Not surprisingly, news of the threatened secession touched off efforts to persuade the students to stay. Because of estimates that half of its Southern membership was determined to withdraw, the Jefferson faculty were understandably active in this endeavor. Their hopes that the dean would make an early and strong appeal to the youths' better judgment were disappointed because of his reservations regarding the propriety of such a step. Indeed, when he at last agreed to address the students, his remarks "fell stillborn upon the ears." On their part, though, the faculty vigorously urged restraint. After the secession meeting, Samuel D. Gross, the school's revered professor of surgery, devoted the last fifteen minutes of his lecture "to the consideration of the subject," delivering an appeal to the students on both practical and patriotic grounds. First, he sought to demonstrate the recklessness of their proposed course and the ill effects that would befall them personally as a result. Second, he reflected on its likely disruptive influence on national harmony, predicting that the results would be disastrous. Stay at least until the end of the term, he pleaded. The students held Gross in high esteem, but in the end he was no more successful than the dean. "Although my address was well received," he recalled, "the most profound silence prevailing during its delivery, it failed of its object."[26]

Similar appeals to the students from Northern friends to finish out the school year before leaving were also spurned. Several Southern senators, who worried that the proposed course of action would add to "present political difficulties," sent a dispatch advising the student "not to mix in politics" and stay where they were. Likewise, the fathers of some of the youths, who had not been consulted about the decision to leave, telegraphed their sons, urging them "in the strongest manner" to remain. This advice, too, went unheeded. In explaining their behavior, one of the seceders later remarked: "We examined our conscience on this subject, and on its dictates acted. We did not consult our parents, our guardians, or our friends. They were too distant from us." "On this account," he went on, "many of us, at first, hesitated, and have since had occasional emotions of doubt; but when stern duty speaks to the hearts of southern men, and appeals to their judgment for their country's sake, they will ever act promptly, though northern friends may attempt to soothe and northern enemies threaten."[27]

On Wednesday, December 21, the day of their scheduled departure, the seceding students bustled about the city making preparations to leave. Plans to travel en masse to the depot failed, and the seceders instead left their boarding houses in groups of four or five. Likewise, the expected special train did not materialize, with the result that the students were thrown in with the ordinary passengers. It was also discovered that the number of seceding students (predicted to be three hundred) had been overestimated, as many who on first impulse had vowed to leave reconsidered and decided to remain—at least for the moment. Luckett and McGuire accompanied the secessionists, in addition to which a large and boisterous crowd of classmates were on hand to see them off. While the scene was spirited, there was no serious trouble, and the police force dispatched to the depot as a safeguard was not needed. "They left the city," one reporter remarked, "merely shaking its dust from their feet, and without any bravado whatever." But there were several incidents—most amusing, a few threatening. A creditor seized one of the seceders, refusing to release him until his bill had been settled, while a lady "in great distress" protested the departure of another youth who had "won her affections." One departing student was arrested for disorderly conduct. "The defendant," the arresting officer testified, "groaned the 'nigger police' of Philadelphia, and denounced the 'nigger Mayor,' and when remonstrated with for his conduct, he persisted." A townsman was arrested for using insulting language to some of the students. The excitement at the depot delayed the train for twenty minutes. When it at last pulled out from the station shortly after 11 P.M. the students staying behind cheered their departing friends and gave three cheers to "Governor Wise," "Virginia," and "the Union," following which they returned, rather noisily, to the city.[28]

Just how many Southern students left the medical schools of Philadelphia is not entirely clear, as each side has tried to present its case in the best possible light. The records of the Medical College of Virginia, which are probably the most reliable source, indicate that 244 students arrived in Richmond on December 22, although Richmond papers set the number at 268. The seceders insisted that 257 left Philadelphia on December 21, and another fifty to seventy-five followed within ten days—but other than a handful of students who arrived on December 23, having remained behind to supervise the shipping of the entire group's baggage, there is little evidence to support the contention of additional withdrawals. Because of its Southern orientation, the seceders were overwhelmingly from the Jefferson Medical College: approximately two hundred of its students left, as compared to a loss of only forty for the University of Pennsylvania.[29]

Reception in Richmond and the South

The students' first stop was Baltimore, where they were required to change from the Philadelphia, Wilmington & Baltimore Railroad to the Baltimore

& Ohio. Although the train arrived at four o'clock in the morning, a group of one hundred students from the University of Maryland School of Medicine was on hand to greet them and to extend an invitation to continue their education in Baltimore on the same terms that other schools had offered. Stirring speeches of welcome and support were given, which spokesmen for the Southern students warmly reciprocated. The secessionists were then escorted to the Baltimore & Ohio station in a festive torchlight parade led by a band. Although several chose to remain in Baltimore, most continued on their journey to Richmond.[30]

The students arrived in Washington at dawn, which precluded the grand reception promised by a number of Southern senators and representatives. "So the boys," the *New York Herald* taunted, "lost a treat that was in store for them." But a bigger one awaited them in Richmond. From Washington, the party traveled by boat some forty miles down the Potomac to Aquia Creek, the northern terminus of the Richmond, Fredericksburg & Potomac Railroad, for the last leg of the sixteen-hour journey. The president of the line provided the students with passes, and extra cars were added to the train to accommodate them. A hastily organized delegation from the Medical College of Virginia hurried to Aquia Creek to welcome the seceders to Virginia. "A perfect hurricane of voices," an unidentified Virginia newspaper reported, greeted them as their steamer approached the dock. They were emotionally and warmly welcomed, to which they responded with "three hearty cheers," and all along the route to Richmond the returning students were "enthusiastically cheered."[31]

In Richmond, the chief topic of conversation all week had been the medical students' secession. "The act is warmly eulogized by every man who refers to it," a correspondent of the *New York Herald* reported, while the *Enquirer,* Richmond's leading newspaper, urged: "Let this event be appreciated by our people; let them turn out and give a hearty old Virginia welcome to these Southern students." Indeed, a hero's welcome, planned by a joint committee from the Medical College of Virginia and the Central Southern Rights Association, was in store for the students. Two hours before their scheduled arrival the streets around the depot were blocked with spectators anxious to witness this historic event. All was ready when the train pulled into the station at 3:20 P.M.[32] A Richmond newspaper recorded the joyous scene:

> The locomotive bell announced the advent of the eagerly expected train.—Then, from extreme end of Broad street unto the Depot, a rolling cheer swept like a ringing fusillade of musketry, and at the Depot it swelled out in one grand volume, increasing in intensity as the train drew nearer and nearer.—Then the Band struck up [Carry Me Back to Old Virginny], and, when the cars passed through the multitude, the scene was such as to baf-

fle all description. Through every window of the cars uncovered heads were eagerly stretched out, and there was such waving of hats and hand-kerchiefs as only strong and vigorous arms could accomplish.[33]

The youthful secessionists were heartily greeted by students and faculty from the Medical College of Virginia, members of the Richmond City Council, a delegation from the state legislature, and representatives of local Southern rights associations. Red ribbons were pinned to the left breast of each student. Led by the Governor's Guard—a newly formed calvary troop—and the Richmond Medical College Guard, and accompanied by the welcoming committee, they marched to Capitol Square. The streets along the route were thronged with cheering well-wishers. The shouts were deafening. Even the ladies of Richmond, who were said to pride themselves on avoiding public displays, braved the brisk weather to welcome the students, enthusiastically waving their handkerchiefs in delight as the procession entered the Capitol grounds and symbolically marched around its Washington Monument. A crowd of five thousand had been waiting for hours, densely packed on the grounds in front of the governor's mansion, and, with the arrival of the procession, gave three loud cheers for Governor Wise.[34]

Wise stood in waiting at the front door. When the ovation subsided, he mounted a granite block used as a carriage step. The crowd surged forward, and cheering erupted anew, lasting for a full five minutes. A correspondent for the *New York Herald* remarked: "Never have I witnessed such a degree of enthusiasm as hailed the Governor's presence. Cheer after cheer thundered forth from the immense assemblage, in which the medical students joined heartily."[35] When order had at last been restored, the Governor addressed the students. Since Wise was on the verge of leaving office, it would be his last public speech. The wily politician accordingly seized the moment to promote his personal agenda, hoping to bolster his long-shot candidacy for the Democratic nomination in 1861. Wise spoke for over an hour. He enthralled the crowd, which frequently interrupted him with applause and cheers, even though his address was standard fire-eating fare: the importance of the preservation of the Union, but not at the expense of Southern rights and honor; the threat of abolitionism and "Black Republicanism" to the Union and the South; the need for home educational institutions and manufactures to halt Northern exploitation of the region; and the necessity of asserting Southern interests on all occasions and through every means. Skillfully playing to the students, he trumpeted: "I have no doubt that here in Richmond, science can be taught as well as it is taught in Philadelphia." T. F. Lee, who had presided over the secession meeting in Philadelphia, responded to Governor Wise's address on behalf of the students, his eagerly received remarks mirroring those of Wise: "I hope that the seeds we have sown will bear their own good fruit. We disavow disunion. We had no such purpose in coming here. Our determination was and is to aid in building up our own institutions. We will stand by them, and if we are called upon to defend our *great* institution, we do it with willing hearts."[36]

From the Capitol grounds, the procession marched the short distance to the Medical College of Virginia, accompanied by the vocal throng. Once the students were seated in the lecture room, the faculty, together with Luckett and McGuire, took their place on the lecturer's platform. Cheers greeted them. Dr. C. B. Gibson, professor of surgery and the senior most member of the faculty, welcomed the secessionists on behalf of the college. His talk opened with the well-known stanza from Sir Walter Scott's "Lay of the Last Minstrel":

> Breathes there the man with soul so dead
> Who never to himself hath said
> This is my own, my native land!
> Whose heart has ne'er within him burned
> As home his footsteps he hath turned
> From wandering on a foreign strand.

"Young gentlemen," he intoned, "the words of the poet come over us to-day, with a seriousness never before experienced. You have come 'home,' and from a 'foreign strand,' and your hearts have 'burned' as you turned your footsteps to your 'native land.'" "You are welcomed not by us only, but by *every* citizen of Richmond," Gibson continued, "the excitement occasioned by the report that you were coming, the oldest inhabitant has never seen equalled." The students responded with a resounding "Hurrah for Richmond!" At the conclusion of Gibson's welcome, James B. McCaw, professor of chemistry, informed the students that the matriculation books would be opened the next day and that those who enrolled would receive a free general ticket to the lectures for the remainder of the session, an announcement that produced another round of cheers. The playing of "Home, Sweet Home" concluded the program at the medical college.

The climax of the homecoming festivities, however, was "a grand collation" at the Columbian Hotel, Richmond's finest. The route from the medical college was again lined with cheering spectators. At the hotel, places had been set for six hundred but twice that number partook of the meal, which was "sumptuous in quality and bounteous in variety and quantity." The lengthy guest list was impressive: state and local political figures, civic and business leaders, the medical faculty and physicians of the city, presidents and officers of the various Southern rights associations, members of the press, faculties of educational institutions, and contributors to the fund formed to underwrite the day's activities. But the atmosphere was relaxed as the guests mingled easily. Rockets blazed, champagne flowed freely, and a "roseate glow," one reporter jocularly noted, "soon began to gather on cheeks before pale and haggard from travel." "Tongues were let loose," he went on; "there were speech-makers and speeches, toasts and sentiments, wit, and many a 'here's to us,' and all those things which emanate from joyful and brotherly hearts, filled with enthusiasm and patriotism." At some point the proceedings spilled into the street and became a "mass meeting." Students, professors, and members of the public made speech after speech from an upstairs window, "all breathing the sentiment of devotion to the South and the Union." The Philadelphia students were repeatedly lauded on principle and deed. They came to Richmond "not as Unionists or disunionists," one speaker proclaimed, but "to ask the education of Southern gentlemen from Southern gentlemen—to learn lessons from men who are true to the Constitution." Another rather ominously, asserted, that the youths' exodus showed the North "that we are in earnest—that we will not quietly submit to that spirit of aggression which would manifest itself in the murder of our wives and children. If the dire conflict *must* come, let it come." After some two hours the crowd finally began to disperse. The students, who had now been up for over twenty-four hours, were put up in hotels and private residences. But the day would long be remembered—by participants and spectators alike. Perhaps a Petersburg visitor put it best: "The reception of the students . . . was brilliant, enthusiastic, exhilarating, thrilling, and soul-stirring."[37]

On Friday, December 23, the band of 244 students who had arrived in Richmond the day before began breaking up. Richmond and the Medical College of Virginia was the final destination for 144 of them; the others continued on to schools further south, where they were the recipients of a second round of heroes' welcomes. Their receptions in Augusta and Charleston were typical. Thirteen enrolled at the Medical College of Georgia in Augusta, where a special meeting of the faculty and students was held to receive them. The script was largely familiar. Professor L. D. Ford, representing the faculty, touted the secession as an indication of the South's "swelling, surging indignation . . . at the invasion of the holy rights of our hearth-stones and of our very lives, by those calling themselves our fellow citizens and brethren." "You did nobly well," he commended the secessionists. Speaking for the seceding students, D. A. Mathews reiterated their desire to promote Southern institutions as the reason for leaving Philadelphia. "We have acted under a sense of duty to the South; no other motive prompted us," he avowed. But in a new twist, Mathews addressed a query often put to the seceding students: "Why can you not wait until the present session is over, and then act?" His explanation was intriguing, if perhaps not entirely convincing:

We replied, "Because now is the *time* to strike while southern men are *ready*. If we wait until you have given all these men diplomas, they will hardly do much for southern institutions when they return home; for it is well known that physicians are apt to recommend the institutions in which they graduate to their office pupils and friends generally. Every man is apt to 'hold to' for his *alma mater*. We do not wish to be bound to the North by any such influence."[38]

The twenty-eight returning students who matriculated at the Medical College of the State of South Carolina in Charleston were formally welcomed with a banquet on December 27, at which Dean H. R. Frost was the principal speaker. He praised their return home as "among the most important of the signs of the times." "It is," he asserted, "the first public step to release us from intellectual bondage on the North."[39]

Popular Reaction

Reaction to the medical secession was swift and predictable. Not surprisingly, it had a sectional bias: the act was castigated in the North and lauded in the South, as press reports reveal. Northern newspapers unanimously blamed the exodus on the Southern students themselves. In Philadelphia, for example, the *Press* maintained that they "acted more upon impulse than upon reflection," while the *Daily News* angrily asserted: "The idea that any man should flee from our City because it happens to contain a few fools, is so supremely ridiculous as to suggest the idea that these gentlemen brought a very small amount of brains with *them*." The *New-York Daily Tribune* likewise dismissed the secession as a "foolish, hasty and ill-advised movement," and in the opinion of Chicago's *Press and Tribune*, the students demonstrated "more brass than breeding, and more imprudence than sense."[40]

There was general agreement that the youths had not departed because they had been insensitively or harshly treated. Rather, Northern editors pointed to the warm feelings of Philadelphia toward the South and the general conservativism of its citizens. "It cannot be said," the *Press* argued, "that Philadelphia has been unkind to those gentlemen, or forgetting of the interests of her medical institutions. Everything that could possibly be done to make Philadelphia a complete school of medicine and to attract hither the young men from the South and the North, has been done." An editorialist in the *North American and United States Gazette* was even more direct, bluntly asking: "Can the medical students in Philadelphia complain of their being interrupted in attendance on lectures, and clinical instruction in hospitals, by any abolitionist rant or cant? Are their teachers less zealous or less instructive, or less intent on the discharge of their duties, in consequence of the lurid state of the political atmosphere?" "There can be but one answer," he thundered, "and that emphatically negative, to these questions."[41]

The real cause of the student exodus, the Northern press agreed, was dissatisfaction with abolitionist sentiment in Philadelphia in the wake of John Brown's raid, or, as Philadelphia's *Daily News* put it, the fact that "certain persons residing among us are in the habit of holding meetings, wherein they express views hostile to the peculiar institution of the South." In short, the issue was free speech. "The cause of this stampede," the *Philadelphia Sunday Dispatch* similarly held, "is because the people of this city permit the exercise of the right of speech according to the Constitution of Pennsylvania, and will not consent that persons who hold opinions different from those of the great majority shall be prevented from saying whatever they think by threats of personal violence or the use of vitriol." The *Chicago Press and Tribune* hailed "the right of decent American citizens . . . to meet in peace and discuss questions of national concern, without molestation" and attributed the departure of the medical students to their failed attempt to curb the right of freedom of speech with "a cowardly mob." New York's papers concurred. "These students," the *Times* scornfully observed, "endeavored to introduce into a Northern State one of the laws and usages of the South,—that, namely, of mobbing a speaker who uttered sentiments which they disapproved. They found themselves at once in an 'irrepressible conflict' with Northern law,—and were defeated."[42]

The seceders were also depicted as riotous troublemakers that Philadelphia was better off without. "The city police have been relieved of a constant source of solicitude," the *Sunday Dispatch* sneered. "All the disorderly Southern students, who have given so much trouble to the municipal authorities already during the season, have patriotically resolved to leave the city for the city's good, and will now inflict upon the suffering South their riot, drunkenness and folly." "Philadelphia," Chicago's *Press and Tribune* echoed, "is glad they have gone; because, from time out of mind, Southern students in our Northern medical colleges have been distinguished for the possession of those plantation practices which make them the abhorrence of all in whose society they were thrown." "Had Northern young men been guilty of similar conduct in a Southern city," the *Germantown Telegraph* asserted, "the law would have been anticipated by a coat of tar and feathers, with fifty lashes added and ejection from the place."[43]

The departing Southern youths were also subjected to the censure of ridicule and satire. Demanding the lowering of flags to half-mast, the editor of one Philadelphia paper sarcastically remarked: "Our once fair city has been covered with disgrace and shame." The reason? Philadelphia was "tainted with Abolitionism!" and "no longer a fit place for self-respecting men to dwell in," as the reaction of the medical students to the mayor's protection of abolitionists must surely prove. "These noble youth are gone," he wailed, "and we must all do the best we can." Alas, but "no longer will their cheerful tobacco smoke, and genial whiskey drinkings enliven the upper rooms of the landladies where they board! No longer will their heroic bowie knives and revolvers gleam in the gas light at the street corners and in oyster cellars! No longer will their delicate attentions gladden the hearts and purses of the demoiselles." In an equally biting vein, Chicago's *Press and Tribune* proposed:

> Let the Union-savers establish a Medical College . . . that shall be free from all Abolition taint. Let the Faculty be instructed to provide, every day, an Abolitionist to be offered up as a sacrifice to appease the wrath of the students from the South. Let the Municipality in which it is founded grant to these students the right to throw vitriol upon all public speakers who may offend their political or moral notions. Let the "subjects" in the dissecting rooms be Abolitionists and Abolitionists only, upon whom the pent up wrath of the Hotspurs may be safely expended. Let this be done. We are tired of Northern aggression and we want the Union preserved.[44]

But perhaps the cleverest satire on the medical students was a parody on Tennyson's "Charge of the Light Brigade," which initially appeared in the little known *Manayunk Reports* in suburban Philadelphia and was reprinted in the *Sunday Dispatch* on January 1, 1860.

> Charge of the Medical Lightheaded Brigade
> (Three Years after Tennyson)
>
> Right from the jaws of Death
> Rushed the mad sectionalists—
> Wretched dissectionists,
> All out of breath;
> Letting the fee go, down to the dépôt
> Rushed they—two hundred!
> Medical sawbones all—
> Heedless of jawbones all—
> Thinking of rawbones all!
> "Curse the North!" was their cry—
> Theirs not to reason why,
> But like young colts to shie,
> Lest the grim ghost of Brown
> Tumble the Union down!
> Oh, funny two hundred!
>
> Dune to the right of them
> Urging the flight of them!

Landlords to left of them,
Laundresses 'reft of them,
Debit-ties surrendered!
Warrants pursuing them,
Sheriffs undoing them—
Thus rushed the secessionists,
Rabid secessionists—
Funny two hundred!
Grinned the Professor's phiz;
Pupil's sole loss it is;
Paid was the entrance fee;
No more their gold they'd see,
Would the two hundred!
Disunion in college,
Confusion of knowledge,
Misusion of porridge
Was well for a forage,
Had fathers not wondered!

Flashed the parental damns;
Senatorial telegrams
(Hinting at youthful shams)
From Washington thundered!
Yet since Ossawatomie
Northern phlebotomy
Lures like "jacko'-lights,"
Over the border bogs!
So the pill Jacobites
Physicked the Quaker dogs—
Doses—two hundred!

Why have we wondered
That thus they blundered?
Two hundred burning
For Southern learning,
Thinking that *black* letter
Was better, far better,
Than free press and speech
Which Northern Professors teach;
So the train thundered!
North keeps the rich fund—
M. D. lose two hundred!

Charges of "tampering" were widespread in the North: "These boys were no doubt tampered with," the *Germantown Telegraph* commented, in a typical remark. The culprits were the Southern medical colleges, plus Luckett and McGuire. "The parties that have incited this exodus," according to the *Philadelphia Sunday Dispatch,* "are 'professors' in badly organized 'one-horse' colleges in Virginia, South Carolina and Tennessee, and other States." In a lengthy and highly critical editorial, the *North American and United States Gazette* labeled Luckett and McGuire abductors. "They seem to have had no misgivings," the editor charged, "to leading away, or rather abducting a large body of students under frivolous pretexts, from the very school, the Jefferson Medical, under whose wings and by the labors of whose professors alone, they enjoyed opportunities for consorting with their victims and playing on their generous sensibilities on questions alien to their medical studies, and in no way connected with their future usefulness and professional standing." The editor went on to assail "the conduct of the Faculties of the medical colleges in the southern States, who have with hardly an exception, made themselves either accomplices or accessories after the fact, in the treason perpetrated by Drs. Luckett and McGuire."[45]

Northern newspapers were unanimous in the belief that secession was bad for the students, the South, and the Union. "The result," the *Philadelphia Sunday Dispatch* contended, "will be that, long after the memory of the temporary and unnecessary excitement which exists at present among a few people shall have passed away, the medical patriots will struggle with the disadvantages of an imperfect medical education, feeling the sober truth, that in consequence of their rashness, want of proper judgment, and that tolerance of opinion which every American should show to his fellow citizens, they have made themselves quacks instead of scientific physicians." A correspondent of the *Daily Evening Bulletin* likewise remarked: "The young men will yet repent of this rash step, and live to censure those who have, for their own private gain, led them away from the best sources of professional knowledge, and disturbed the current of their thoughts from study, to the angry strifes of politics." The *New York Daily Tribune* considered the act "medically terrible" for the South. Calling the seceders "that batch of half-baked doctors," it flippantly scoffed: "If the South be determined to manufacture all her own doctors as well as cloth her deed will be its own sufficient punishment." "We fear the South will be the greatest sufferer in the end," the *Albany Evening Journal* concurred, "if they propose to do without the balance of their education. 300 ignorant Doctors let loose in the South, might be as destructive of life as a 'Brown invasion.'"[46]

The implications of the student exodus for the Union was considered

even more regrettable. Some feared that the secession might touch off a
flurry of similar behavior. "If public opinion, either south or north sanction
this outrage," as Philadelphia's *North American and United States Gazette* put
it, "what seminary of learning, we would ask, is safe for a day against disruption, if not dismemberment, for, like imitative convulsions, which are
brought on in one person by the sight of them in another, the slightest
cause, the most frivolous protest, the very mention of the thing, will suffice
to produce the catastrophe." And there was some basis for such anxiety.
Calling attention to a rumored secession from the medical schools of New
York, Chicago's *Press and Tribune* warned: "Their patriotic rage is con-
tagious." A contributor to the *Baltimore American,* who signed himself "A
Unionist," likened the medical secession to amputating a limb of national
unity: "It is time," he implored, "to counsel patience, and forbearance,
reconsideration and fraternal feeling," further pleading "Don't let us cut off
the limbs." But it was the *New York Times* that sounded the loudest alarm.
Viewing the exodus of the students as "far more significant of the intensity
of Anti-Northern feeling which now pervades the Southern States, than
any political speeches in or out of Congress could be," the editor viewed the
future with pessimism. "If these young men," he elaborated, "who must
presumably represent at least the average intelligence of the Southern
States, and who have been living in actual contact with the people of a great
and singularly conservative Northern city, think it impossible for them any
longer to maintain honorable relations with the North, what are we to
expect of the great masses of Southern men, who know the North only
through the inflammatory diatribes of their own sectional Press? If the
Union meetings of Boston, Philadelphia and New-York meet with an immediate response of this kind from a body of educated Southern men actually within hearing of their oratory, what effect can we hope they will
produce in the heart of Mississippi or Arkansas?"[47]

As one might expect, the South welcomed the secession of the medical
students as a "step in the right direction" and "a sign of the times." A
typical reaction was that of Richmond's *Daily Dispatch:* "This is a movement of the right kind, and, if it be ultimately followed by stopping all the
other drains upon Southern resources which have gone to swell the coffers
of distant sections, will inaugurate an era of prosperity and independence
for the South which will surpass the most sanguine dreams of her most
ardent friends." "Good News for Richmond and the South," the rival *Enquirer* reveled in a December 20 headline. In addition, Southern editors
uniformly insisted that the students had returned home because they had
been "inhospitably treated," the culprit being abolitionist excess. The
Southern students' abandonment of Philadelphia, the *Petersburg (Va.) Daily
Express* blustered, "is one of the legitimate fruits of the detestable excesses of

Northern fanaticism, and especially of the revolting sympathy which has been proclaimed for the fate of the traitor and murderer, John Brown." According to the *Express,* the lecture of George W. Curtis, "one of the blackest hearted abolitionists" and "an enemy of the South," was simply the latest in a lengthy list of outrages. The Southern students "could not but be excited by such a scene, under such circumstances." Augusta's *Daily Constitutionalist* was in full agreement, fuming:

> All southern men, young and old, are compelled to hear, at the North, vile aspersions on our institutions—read them in the papers and listen to them at the churches—and witness gross caricatures of them on the stage and at other places of amusement. At no former time, have these tirades of abuse of the South been more prominent or rampant than during the past few months; and it cannot be a matter of surprise that intelligent southern medical students could bear such taunts without feeling justly indignant.

The *New Orleans Daily Picayune* pronounced the action of the medical students "the practical application of a just theory of self-defence against assaults, with which current events menace us."[48]

Charges of tampering, so prevalent in the North, were unceremoniously rejected out of hand. The *Daily Picayune* equated implications that Southern medical colleges had employed agents to induce the students to leave with "the Northern fashion of 'drumming' to get customers for themselves." "That practice," it sneeringly remarked, "has never gained foothold in the South in any department of business." Augusta's *Daily Constitutionalist* transformed the charge into praise, arguing that it was not tampering but generosity that characterized the response of the Southern schools. As a result, the oppressed Southern students, some of whom "were poor, and had, by industry and economy, saved money to pay for their attendance on the lectures," were able to escape "the miss-called city of 'Brotherly Love,' and breathe again an atmosphere not poisoned or tainted with abolitionism." The much-maligned Luckett and McGuire were likewise regarded as heroes. The reaction of the *Richmond Enquirer* was representative: "Virginia and Richmond owe a debt of gratitude to Drs. Luckett and McGuire for the leading part they took in urging the step, and preparing for the comfort and accommodation of all the students."[49]

The Southern press also spurned notions that the student exodus amounted to "practical disunion." Rather, as a long overdue vote of confidence for home institutions, it promised to ease sectional tension. As the *Richmond Enquirer* put it, "the best way to preserve the Union is to be prepared, in every way, for the event of disunion." As for the Southern students, they had no desire "to see the Federal Union destroyed; they, nevertheless, wish to see Medical Colleges built up and sustained by the patronage of the South, and they feel that it is necessary that a beginning should be made." "We congratulate and thank these noble sons of the South," it exclaimed, "upon the step they have taken." Augusta's *Daily Constitutionalist* was positively ecstatic over the future of the South in the wake of the students' return: "There is something of the true metal about it—and years hence, they will have the envied reputation of inaugurating the first real measure of southern policy that will show the North and the East, our independence of schools, colleges, and of all departments of art, trade, or manufacture in the free States. We are daily approaching the time when the South will stand forth 'redeemed, regenerated, and disenthralled' from all our former dependence on the free states."[50]

In marked contrast, and for all the region's sectional suspicions and defensiveness, some Southern editors were nonetheless openly critical of the student secession. The *Baltimore Exchange* considered the withdrawal "unwise in itself, as well as particularly ill-timed . . . [and] not likely to result in any advantage to them." But, contrary to the opinion of many Northern papers, the seceders were not at fault. Rather, responsibility lay at the door of the Southern medical schools, and with Governor Wise and others who encouraged secession. "Any other body of young men who had received, under similar circumstances, the same encouragement," the *Exchange* observed, "would have acted in precisely a similar way." Nashville's *Republican Banner,* despite holding that "Southern gentlemen had no business in the Northern Colleges," also believed that the student exodus from Philadelphia was misguided. The editor was especially critical of Southern schools and civil officials who applied "inducements to these embryo doctors," asserting that "all of this appears in decidedly bad taste." He also questioned the use of public funds for the students' benefit: "The authorities of different cities go on making appropriations of money to travel and educate these young gentlemen, who are abundantly able to defray their own expenses, much more so, at least, than thousands of the constituents of those voting the appropriations, and whose hard labor helped to raise them." In much the same vein, he criticized the Southern schools for offering free tuition: "If their instructions are worth anything, they are worthy as much as their contemporaries of Philadelphia and New York. If they are first class colleges they should be able to command the attendance of these students at the regular rates."[51]

Medical Reaction

The students' secession touched off an equally heated debate in scientific circles. Again, Philadelphia reacted with wounded pride and bitterness. As in the popular press, the student stampede was attributed to tampering on the part of Southern schools. The *Medical and Surgical Reporter* assailed "the *unprofessional* conduct . . . of the faculties of those medical colleges which connived" the affair. "Such conduct between professional men, in private practice," the editor went on, "would make the offending party or parties amenable to any code of medical ethics." In rebuttal, E. D. Fenner, dean of the New Orleans School of Medicine, lashed out: "We are utterly disgusted with this talk about Southern colleges 'tampering' with . . . students at the North. It is meet that those Northern institutions which make such charges should substantiate them. . . . As the matter stands . . . the whole ground of complaint is against the Northern colleges concerned, for they have issued a gross insult and a vile slander against their Southern brethren, which they cannot prove and will not apologize for."[52] Condemnation of the students' behavior was equally widespread. "Identified as we are with the South by birth, by education, and in feeling," the editor of the *St. Louis Medical and Surgical Reporter* remarked, "we nevertheless regret this movement, believing that in point of time and manner of execution it was unwise and calculated to result only in evil." "We have no sympathy with these seceders at all," the newly launched *Louisville Medical Journal* exclaimed; "their action is all wrong, and we protest against the whole of it." The *Cincinnati Lancet and Observer* accused the Southern students of behaving "like a set of mad-caps and fanatics."[53]

The youthful secessionists also had their defenders, but unlike in the case of the popular press, and probably because of the intense competition among schools for students, support for them was not exclusively sectional. Claiming that "a poisonous miasma . . . from the political swamp of fanaticism" had infected Philadelphia with "the leprosy of treason," which had rendered it uninhabitable "not only to southerners, but any man loving the Union," the *New-York Medical Press* insisted that the Southern students "did perfectly right in leaving." As venerable a figure as Nathan S. Davis, the principal founder in 1847 of the American Medical Association, gave the withdrawal a qualified endorsement. "If this movement," he wrote in the *Chicago Medical Journal*, "is to be regarded as the result of political causes, it is to be regretted. If, on the contrary, it was the result of a returning sense of the mistake the young gentlemen committed in passing by the schools of their own states, especially for those of Pennsylvania, we cannot but commend their good judgment." The strongest approval came, of course, from the South. Illustratively, Savannah's Richard D. Arnold, one of the luminaries of the Southern medical profession, labeled the students' action "a patriotic impulse towards their native homes which stamps them as true men."[54]

With the exception of Philadelphia, which clung to the charge of tampering, the medical press considered the student secession to be the result of abolitionist agitation. "If Philadelphia applauds John Brown, *a convicted traitor, murderer, and robber,*" the outspoken *New-York Medical Press* charged, "she cannot expect to receive any support from those who have been so ruthlessly invaded." The *Cincinnati Medical and Surgical News* similarly held: "Our Southern brethren have not interfered with our institutions, whilst the North is constantly invading the rights of the South, and meddling where they have no business." The Southern medical press concurred, branding Philadelphia a particular hotbed of abolitionism. The extremist editor of the *Oglethorpe Medical and Surgical Journal,* who had taken his professional training there twenty years earlier, characterized the city as a place "where the demon of abolitionism prevents the mass of her citizens from extending even ordinary courtesies of conventional life to Southern students, notwithstanding they have for a long period of time added largely to the fame of her Medical Schools and the material wealth of her citizens." To W. K. Bowling, the similarly inflammatory dean of the medical department of the University of Nashville and the editor of the *Nashville Journal of Medicine and Surgery,* it was "a Calcutta black hole."[55]

Southerners further considered the secession an unmistakable warning to the abolitionists and to the North. As important as the student withdrawal had been in promoting home institutions, the *Southern Medical and Surgical Journal* contended, "a higher benefit, a greater good, a far more widely extended blessing will be dispensed by them, in that they strikingly warn the fanatical of Northern communities that it is to their own advantage to respect the constitutional rights of others—their warm-hearted and impulsive, but honorable and independent brethren of the South." There was also support for this sentiment outside the South. The *Cincinnati Medical and Surgical News* thought it "the duty of every *honest, union-loving* editor, no matter what the character of his paper, whether *Political, Religious or Medical,* to speak out in condemnation of the course pursued by the fanatical abolitionists of the North."[56]

The most consistently voiced reaction in the medical press to the student secession was, however, the fear that sectionalism had at last invaded science. In the North the *American Medical Gazette* ruefully remarked: "We had thought and hoped that there was one sacred spot, into which the smoke of the boiling political cauldron could not enter, and that with the question of slavery it was conceded that we of the *medical profession,* as such, had nothing to do." In the West the *Cincinnati Lancet and Observer* angrily asserted: "We are mortified and chagrined that the vexing political questions and prejudices of the day, kept alive by small and insignificant politicians of the hour, should have been permitted to enter one of the temples of our science." In the South the nationally respected *Southern Medical and Surgical Journal* lamented: "For the first time, to our knowledge, in the history of this country, have political acerbity and intolerance risen to such a height as to cumber the walks of science and to invade the personal comfort of those who would follow her peaceful pursuits. *Pax et Scientia* have been so long so naturally coupled in a harmonious association, that their severance will appear, to most minds, like the abstraction of the combining principle from chemistry or the cohesive force from the constitution of matter."[57]

Attempts to assess the effect of the secession produced much speculation. Although a spokesman for Philadelphia's medical schools, writing in the *Medical and Surgical Reporter,* insisted that it would not "in the slightest degree" affect the city's status as the medical capital of the nation, the general feeling was that a major blow had been struck for home education. The assessment of the *St. Louis Medical and Surgical Journal,* an opponent of the goings-on, is instructive: "The stampede among the medical students of Philadelphia last winter has at least had the effect of directing the attention of western and southern young men to the uncalled for neglect of home institutions, and of arousing strong feeling in favor of home education." The South ecstatically concurred, rejoicing, as one professor, William Hauser, put it, that "the hateful vassalage of Southern medical students to Northern Colleges is broken up at last." "There never has been a time so auspicious as the present," he elaborated, "for the building up of Southern Medical Colleges, and the consequent elevation of the Southern medical mind to the highest point of attainment in medical learning."[58]

At the very least, most members of the medical profession, Southerners included, hoped that the harmful effects of the incident would be minimal. The *Southern Medical and Surgical Journal* expressed the hope that, the students' secession having forcefully revealed the dangers of fanaticism, "our glorious Union may be consolidated and cemented, not only in bonds of a common interest, but as in times past, in the stronger and more reliable bonds of a common love." Likewise, in predicting that "science and art will live when all these unhappy and unnatural passions have passed away," the *Cincinnati Lancet and Observer* voiced a prominent sentiment.[59]

Not everyone, however, subscribed to pleas for union and such expressions of optimism. "The blood of old Brown, together with *all* the minions of abolitionism," the radical *Oglethorpe Medical and Surgical Journal* crowed, "can never *restore* the Northern people to the confidence and love of the South again." "In fact," the editor maintained, "John Brown rang the death-knell of the union of the American Confederation at Harper's Ferry, and henceforth the Northern and Southern sections of the North American States must ever be two distinct nations." Equally prescient, the editor of the *Ohio Medical and Surgical Journal* foresaw an inevitable struggle, "reducible . . . to the mere matter of time," between the North and South over slavery. He feared its effect on science in America, which had "scarcely doffed the swaddlings of infancy." "What we are most concerned about," he commented deploringly, "is the danger threatened to the whole profession, by the clouds gathering on our political horizon. The momentous question of the hour is not, how this or that school is to be affected by our sectional troubles, but what is to become of the whole profession."[60]

Aftermath

Southern nationalists and medical school faculties moved to exploit the windfall medical secession. Edmund Ruffin, the shrill spokesman of Southernism, called the incident "a notable & important evidence of the prevailing disposition of people of the south to separation of intercourse with the North." J. D. B. De Bow, who had long advocated Southern economic and cultural independence, was ecstatic, asserting: "The *exodus of Southern Students* recently from the Colleges of the North is a matter for public gratulation." George Fitzhugh, the militant proslavery author and a frequent contributor to De Bow's fire-eating *Review,* was equally elated. "The Southern medical students who lately deserted Northern colleges," he exclaimed, "deserve immortal honor. It is time the South should educate her sons." The *New Orleans Daily Picayune* evinced similar sentiments: "If this sudden determination of the Southern medical students in Philadelphia will but arouse a determination to educate at home, however this movement may be regarded, it will result in most happy influence for the South." Southern medical schools enthusiastically redoubled their efforts to persuade the region's youths to study at home. "There never has been a time so auspicious as the present," a professor at Savannah's Oglethorpe Medical College commented, "for the building up of Southern Medical Colleges, and the consequent elevation of the Southern medical mind to the highest point of attainment in medical learning." Insisting that "it is as much the imperative duty of Southern people to build up their own medical institutions as to foster and sustain their own manufactories," the editor of the *Atlanta Medical and Surgical Journal* protested: "It is time that we should cease to be dictated to, by Northern Medical Colleges, or Northern medical men. It is time that we should cease to look to *nationality in medicine,* any more that we should look to a *nationality in politics. . . .* We say let there be as few Southern students found in Northern Colleges as Northern students in Southern Colleges."[61]

Medical schools aggressively sought to capitalize on the surge of Southern nationalist sentiment, hoping to transform it into subsidies from public funds. Calling the moment "*a golden period* for our Southern Medical Colleges," the dean of the Oglethorpe Medical College instructively urged: "Let our Legislature *endow the unendowed* ones, and even *add* to the *endowments* of some of those which it has already aided pecuniarily, and they will do more to add to our strength and greatness than has ever been accomplished heretofore." In state after state, enabling legislation was introduced. In Virginia, for example, on December 23, the day after the arrival of the seceding students in Richmond, a bill to appropriate $30,000 to the Medical College of Virginia for capital improvements was introduced into the House of Delegates. It was supported by a petition signed by sixty-six students from the school. Despite popular enthusiasm for the medical secession, the bill moved slowly through the fiscally conservative legislature, but finally, in March, the measure passed.[62]

While such subsidies boded well for education in the region, the medical secession was not ultimately the boon to Southern intellectual independence that its supporters had hoped. To be sure, some 250 Southern students had left Philadelphia. And many of these fulfilled their promise to complete their education at a Southern school.[63] But it should also be borne in mind that an equal number of Southern students chose not to participate in the secession. Moreover, a hoped-for secession from the schools of New York failed to materialize—largely because of an absence of incendiaries like Luckett and McGuire. To make matters worse, the students who remained in Philadelphia served as visible reminders of the city's conservative character and the superiority of its medical schools—and the continuing presence of a sizable number of Southern students in Philadelphia was political hay for the Northern press. These youths were praised in Philadelphia's *North American and United States Gazette* as "by far the most respectable" element of the Southern student population, who were to be commended for refusing to abandon "the sterling institutions of which they have become matriculants." In addition, the paper contended, outside of the South, where the incident was largely viewed as an outburst of irrational behavior, once the students returned to their senses they would become "repentant of their hasty determination, and . . . reconsider their precipitate intention." Another Philadelphia paper flippantly remarked as the seceders left: "We expect to see a hundred out of the hundred and fifty living back in Philadelphia before the Ides of March are over."[64]

While this did not happen, an undetermined number of the students eventually did renounce their secession. "The attractions of a good college, an excellent faculty, and a splendid education," a representative of the Philadelphia press taunted, "were even more powerful than their desire to sacrifice themselves to their principles." Especially embarrassing to the movement's leaders was the report that some of the returning students allegedly said "that their visit to Richmond was only to enjoy a Christmas frolic, and an exhibition of Governor Wise's oratorial pyrotechnics." So frequent did reports of "retroseceders" become that Luckett prepared a formal denial and correction for the Southern press. Following "a thorough investigation of the subject," he insisted, "there is but one who has returned, and in justice to him it should be stated that he has disavowed any intention of remaining longer in Philadelphia than is requisite to settle definitely and satisfactorily, business matters of a personal and private nature."[65]

Finally, and most disappointing and damaging of all to regional interests, the next school year saw Southern students again make the trek to Philadelphia. This was not unexpected in the North. At the time of the secession the Philadelphia correspondent of the *New York Daily Tribune* had seriocomically predicted: "They will heartily regret their impetuosity, and another year will witness their return—at least we fear as much." While their numbers were noticeably lower (about a half of what they had been), Southerners made up approximately the same percentages of the Philadelphia student bodies as they had a year earlier because of significantly smaller classes. Deeply disappointed, Harvey L. Byrd, the fire-eating dean of the Oglethorpe Medical College, moaned: "We have lost all hope of arousing a love of their native land in the bosoms of men who will turn their backs upon their homes and home institutions, and that too, at the most critical period of their country's history, to patronize the institutions of their enemies; and especially, when they are in no essential respect superior to those of the South."[66]

Rehearsal for Secession?

If, as the return of Southern students to Philadelphia the following fall suggests, the medical exodus of 1859 was not a rehearsal for secession, is it to be regarded as simply an isolated incident of irrational behavior? Far from this, the stampede of the Southern students—for that was what the act really was—is significant for what it represented. First, it is indicative of the excitability of Southerners in the wake of John Brown's raid. "The very devil seems to have gotten into the students," William Gibson, the University of Pennsylvania's longtime professor of surgery, informatively exclaimed.[67] The behavior of the students simply mirrored that of their region.

Second, the crucial role of Luckett and McGuire in the students' abandonment of Philadelphia is illustrative of the growing and disruptive influence of the fire-eater in Southern society as sectional animosities flared on the eve of the Civil War. Eschewing restraint, Southerners steadily subscribed to this group's radical solution to sectionalism. Harpers Ferry was a seminal step in the triumph of the fire-eater mentality. In assessing the role of Luckett and McGuire in the medical secession, Arthur E. Peticolas, the

Medical College of Virginia's professor of anatomy, remarked to the seceders: "Many will say they instigated you to rebellion, and we lack not even in our own section of country, I fear, certain namby pamby moralists, who will analyze and criticise their conduct with no very Christian spirit." But Peticolas himself had only high praise for Luckett and McGuire. As he reminded the students, "They are entitled to your everlasting gratitude. No, gentlemen, not alone to your gratitude, but they are entitled also to share with you the gratitude of every man, woman and child in a slaveholding State; for I believe, they with you and you with them, have almost unconsciously struck the heaviest blow that has ever yet been aimed at that hideous hydra-headed monster known to us as abolition fanaticism. You owe them a debt which can never be repaid."[68] This assessment is reminiscent of that of men such as Edmund Ruffin, William L. Yancey, Robert Barnwell Rhett, Robert Toombs, Louis T. Wigfall, and Albert Gallatin Brown during the secession crisis following the election of Lincoln.

Moreover, both the insistence of the students that they were returning home to build up Southern institutions and the behavior of the region's medical schools once the secession had been announced shed important light on the campaign for regional intellectual independence from the North. In particular, the stigma of their reputedly inferior educational facilities and opportunities became increasingly intolerable in the Old South. At the time of the student exodus, Fredericksburg's *Weekly Advertiser and Chronicle of the Times* bluntly asserted: "We hope, that *henceforth no* Southern youth will be sent to the North to be educated." And a year later, as the Lower South was withdrawing from the Union, the *Southern Medical and Surgical Journal* entreated: "Let Southern Institutions of learning, like all other departments of Southern enterprize, receive now new life and additional impulse from the remodeling and regeneration which must surely follow the present national troubles and disaster, brought upon us by fanatical enemies, not only of the South, but of the whole country." At the same time, the near universal denunciation of the medical secession in the Northern popular press points up the growing loss of patience with the South in much of the country—with its blustering, its posturing, and its demands. As the incident unfolded, Greeley's *New York Daily Tribune* exhorted: "How can the Union be saved? By letting every white man South and North know, and keeping the facts before them, that the Union contains thirty millions of people, while the slave owners are only three hundred and fifty thousand! Shall this handful long be permitted to keep the millions in a state of constant uproar, excitement, and turmoil? Let us say mildly, but firmly—No!"[69] Just as the fire-eaters seduced the South with their words, those of Greeley and his kind fell on increasingly sympathetic ears in the North.

Finally, the medical secession hints at the mounting willingness of the South to resort to extremist action to protect its perceived vital interests. Threats of secession had issued from the region for years. When disunion did come, the Southern medical profession was among its strongest supporters. Regional physician rhetoric was remarkably similar to that of a year earlier, at the time of student secession. The editor of the *Atlanta Medical and Surgical Journal* was exemplary, exclaiming: "Too long have the talent of the South, and the products of her soil contributed to enrich the ungrateful and mercenary North. Henceforth let us not only plant, but cultivate in a more congenial soil; let us live and labor at home, and *for home;* and let us harvest and garner at home."[70] In the final analysis, then, if the return home of the Southern medical students in 1859 was not actually a rehearsal for secession, it is perhaps only because they acted prematurely.

Notes

1. There have been two previous, if only partly successful, treatments of this aspect of the South's reaction to John Brown: Thomas W. Murrell, "The Exodus of Medical Students from Philadelphia, December 1859," *Bulletin of the Medical College of Virginia* 51 (1954): 2–15; and Harold J. Abrahams, "Secession from Northern Medical Schools," *Transactions and Studies of the College of Physicians of Philadelphia,* ser. 4, 36 (July 1968): 29–45. John Brown and the events at Harpers Ferry have, of course, been extensively chronicled and analyzed. But two works were of particular value in the preparation of this study: Abels, *Man on Fire,* and Oates, *Purge.*

2. See Wyndham B. Blanton, *Medicine in Virginia in the Nineteenth Century* (Richmond, 1932), pp. 9–10; see also Frederick P. Henry, ed., *Standard History of the Medical Profession of Philadelphia* (Chicago, 1897), ch. 4. Although dated, the standard work on antebellum American medical education remains William Frederick Norwood, *Medical Education in the United States before the Civil War* (Philadelphia, 1944). Recommended biographies of Philadelphia's medical schools are George W. Corner, *Two Centuries of Medicine: A History of the School of Medicine, University of Pennsylvania* (Philadelphia, 1965); and Frederick B. Wagner, Jr., ed., *Thomas Jefferson University: Tradition and Heritage* (Philadelphia, 1989).

3. George M. Gould, ed., *The Jefferson Medical College of Philadelphia . . . 1826–1904: A History,* 2 vols. (New York and Chicago, 1904), 1:154. See also ibid., vol. 1, ch. 8; Henry, ed., *Standard History of the Medical Profession of Philadelphia,* pp. 217–20, and ch. 4 generally; and Corner, *Two Centuries of Medicine,* ch. 7.

4. See, respectively, J. D. B. De Bow, "Southern Educational and Industrial Development," *De Bow's Review* 20 (May 1856): 621; "Introductory Address," *New-Orleans Medical Journal* 1 (May 1844): iii; Samuel A. Cartwright, "Cartwright on Southern Medicine," *New Orleans Medical and Surgical Journal* 3 (Sept. 1846): 260. For a fuller discussion of the Southern campaign for intellectual independence, see Clement Eaton, *The Freedom-of-Thought Struggle in the Old South,* rev. ed. (New York, 1964), ch. 9. Southern medical nationalism is examined in John Duffy, "A Note on Ante-Bellum Southern Nationalism and Medical Practice," *JSH* 34 (May 1968): 266–76; James O. Breeden, "States-Rights Medicine in the Old South," *Bulletin of the New York Academy of Medicine* 52 (Mar.–Apr. 1976): 348–72; and John Harley Warner, "A

Southern Medical Reform: The Meaning of the Antebellum Argument for Southern Medical Education," *Bulletin of the History of Medicine* 57 (Fall 1983): 364–81.

5. James C. Billingslea, "An Appeal on Behalf of Southern Medical Colleges and Southern Medical Literature," *Southern Medical and Surgical Journal* 12 (Sept. 1856): 398.

6. Harvey L. Byrd, "Patronage of Northern Medical Schools by Southern Students of Medicine," *Oglethorpe Medical and Surgical Journal* 2 (Nov. 1859): 235.

7. Quoted in Mary Lesley Ames, ed., *Life and Letters of Peter and Susan Lesley*, 2 vols. (New York and London, 1909), 1:382. See also L. A. Wailes, "The First Secessionists," *Confederate Veteran* 30 (May 1922): 184; William Dusinberre, *Civil War Issues in Philadelphia, 1861–1865* (Philadelphia, 1965), ch. 4; and Horace Howard Furness, *Historical Address Delivered in Connection with the Installation of the Reverend Charles E. St. John as Minister of the First Unitarian Church of Philadelphia, 12th of January, 1908* (Philadelphia, 1908), p. 16.

8. See Wailes, "The First Secessionists," p. 185; Abels, *Man on Fire*, pp. 369–70; Oates, *Purge*, pp. 354–56; and Dusinberre, *Civil War Issues in Philadelphia*, ch. 4.

9. "Gov. Wise and the Flag of Our Union," *New York Times*, Dec. 26, 1859. See also *Great Union Meeting, Philadelphia, December 7, 1859* (Philadelphia, 1859); and Dusinberre, *Civil War Issues in Philadelphia*, ch. 4.

10. See Dusinberre, *Civil War Issues in Philadelphia*, pp. 89–90. See also ibid., ch. 4.

11. "Curtis at National Hall," *Philadelphia Daily Evening Bulletin*, Dec. 16, 1859; and "To the Public," ibid., Dec. 15, 1859.

12. "Curtis at National Hall," and "The Police Arrangements at National Hall—The Arrests," both in ibid., Dec. 16, 1859.

13. "Curtis at National Hall," ibid., Dec. 16, 1859; see also Ames, ed., *Life and Letters of Peter and Susan Lesley*, 1:382.

14. "The Police Arrangements at National Hall—The Arrests," *Philadelphia Daily Evening Bulletin*, Dec. 16, 1859; see also "The Anti-Slavery Fair, &c. . . . ," *Baltimore American*, Dec. 19, 1859.

15. Laura Stedman and George M. Gould, eds., *Life and Letters of Edmund Clarence Stedman*, 2 vols. (New York, 1910), 1:243. On the reputation of Southern youth, see also Henry Adams, *The Education of Henry Adams: An Autobiography* (Boston, 1918), pp. 56–59; and Avery Craven, *Edmund Ruffin, Southerner: A Study in Secession* (New York, 1932), p. 106.

16. See Edward Warren, *A Doctor's Experiences in Three Continents* (Baltimore, 1885), p. 129; and Abrahams, "Secession from Northern Medical Schools," p. 30.

17. Newspapers across the nation carried this dispatch. See, for example, "Meeting of the Medical Students in Philadelphia," *Richmond Daily Dispatch*, Dec. 21, 1859; "Meeting of Southern Students," *Richmond Enquirer*, Dec. 21, 1859; "Large Secession of Southern Medical Students from Philadelphia," *Baltimore Sun*, Dec. 21, 1859; "Meeting of Southern Medical Students," *Raleigh North Carolina Standard*, Dec. 28, 1859; "Latest by Telegraph," *Charleston Mercury*, Dec. 23, 1859; "Meeting of Southern Medical Students in Philadelphia," *Augusta (Ga.) Daily Constitutionalist*, Dec. 24, 1859; "Meeting of Southern Medical Students," *Memphis Daily Appeal*, Dec. 25, 1859; "By Telegraph," *Nashville Republican Banner*, Dec. 21, 1859; "By Telegraph," *Louisville Daily Courier*, Dec. 21, 1859; "By Telegraph," *Weekly Vicksburg Whig*, Dec. 28, 1859; "Desertion of Northern Colleges," *New Orleans Bee*, Dec. 21, 1859; "The News," *Cincinnati Daily Gazette*, Dec. 21, 1859; "Another Effect of the 'Irrepressible Conflict': Southern Students Quitting Philadelphia," *New York Herald*, Dec. 21, 1859; "The News," *Boston Daily Courier*, Dec. 21, 1859; and "More Dissolution of the Union," *Chicago Press and Tribune*, Dec. 21, 1859.

18. "The Stampede at Philadelphia," *New York Herald*, Dec. 22, 1859.

19. Murrell, "Exodus of Medical Students from Philadelphia," p. 10. See also "Good News for Richmond and the South," *Richmond Enquirer,* Dec. 20, 1859; "Southern Medical Students at the North," *Charleston Mercury,* Dec. 23, 1859; and "Philadelphia Students Returning," *Charleston Daily Courier,* Dec. 24, 1859.

20. "The Stampede at Philadelphia," *New York Herald,* Dec. 22, 1859; Murrell, "Exodus of Medical Students from Philadelphia," p. 10.

21. See, respectively, "Meeting of the Medical Students in Philadelphia," *Richmond Enquirer,* Dec. 24, 1859; and Wailes, "The First Secessionists," p. 185.

22. See "Stampede of Medical Students," *Philadelphia North American and United States Gazette,* Dec. 21, 1859. The best account and analysis of McGuire's life and career is Stuart McGuire, "Hunter Holmes McGuire, M.D., LL.D.," *Annals of Medical History,* n.s., 10 (Jan.–Mar. 1938): 1–14 and 136–61. The only attempt at a full-scale biography, although largely unsatisfactory, is John W. Schildt, *Hunter Holmes McGuire: Doctor in Gray* (privately printed, 1986).

23. On the fugitive slave case, see Dusinberre, *Civil War Issues in Philadelphia,* pp. 59–60. See also "The Threatened Stampede of Medical Students . . . ," *Baltimore Sun,* Dec. 22, 1859.

24. This secession meeting and its proceedings were widely reported. In addition to the sources previously cited (see note 17), I have drawn on the following news accounts in preparing the present narrative: "Practical Secession—Stampede of Southern Students," *Philadelphia Daily Evening Bulletin,* Dec. 20, 1859; "The Medical Students Going South—Meeting Yesterday Morning," *Philadelphia Press,* Dec. 21, 1859; "The Resolutions of the Medical Students," ibid., Dec. 23, 1859; "Medical Students Carrying out Non-Intercourse," *Philadelphia Public Ledger,* Dec. 21, 1859; "Southern Medical Students Quitting Philadelphia," *New York Times,* Dec. 21, 1859; "The Southern Students," *Baltimore American,* Dec. 22, 1859; and "Meeting of the Medical Students in Philadelphia," *Richmond Enquirer,* Dec. 24, 1859. The letter attributed to the president of the Baltimore Railroad appears to have been written instead by Edwin Robinson, president of the Richmond, Fredericksburg & Potomac Railroad (*Richmond Daily Dispatch,* Dec. 21, 1859).

25. Quoted in "Telegraphic," *New York Herald,* Dec. 22, 1859.

26. Samuel D. Gross, *Autobiography of Samuel D. Gross,* ed. Samuel W. Gross and A. Haller Gross, 2 vols. (Philadelphia, 1893), 1:129. See also "The Medical Students Going South—Meeting Yesterday Morning," *Philadelphia Press,* Dec. 21, 1859; "The Medical Students," *Richmond Daily Dispatch,* Dec. 23, 1859.

27. See "The Movement of the Southern Students," *New York Times,* Dec. 22, 1859; "The Southern Students at Philadelphia," *Baltimore Sun,* Dec. 22, 1859; "Latest by Telegraph," *Richmond Enquirer,* Dec. 22, 1859; and "Meeting of the Faculty and Students of the Medical College of Georgia," *Augusta (Ga.) Daily Constitutionalist,* Dec. 31, 1859.

28. See "The Medical Students Make an Exit," *Philadelphia North American and United States Gazette,* Dec. 22, 1859; "Departure of the Medical Students," *Philadelphia Press,* Dec. 22, 1859; "Arrests at the Baltimore Depot," *Philadelphia Daily Evening Bulletin,* Dec. 22, 1859; "Departure of Medical Students . . . ," *Baltimore Sun,* Dec. 23, 1859; "The Southern Students . . . ," *Baltimore American,* Dec. 23, 1859; and "Medical Students, &c. . . . ," ibid., Dec. 24, 1859.

29. See the report of Dean L. S. Joynes to Board of Trustees of the Medical College of Virginia, Mar. 14, 1860, in Murrell, "Exodus of Medical Students from Philadelphia," pp. 12–13; "Gov. Wise's Departure from Richmond—The Arrival and Reception of the Medical Students from Philadelphia," *Richmond Enquirer,* Dec. 23, 1859; "Meeting of Richmond Medical Students," ibid., Jan. 31, 1860; and "Not To Be Stopped," *Richmond Daily Dispatch,* Dec. 24, 1859.

30. See "The Philadelphia Medical Students," *Baltimore American,* Dec. 22, 1859; "Students from Philadelphia," ibid., Dec. 23, 1859; "The Seceding Medical Students from Philadelphia—Their Reception in Baltimore," ibid., Dec. 24, 1859; and "The Medical Students—Their Passage through Baltimore," *Richmond Daily Dispatch,* Dec. 24, 1859.

31. See "Arrival of the Medical Students at Washington," *New York Herald,* Dec. 23, 1859; and "The Homeward Bound," unidentified Virginia newspaper clipping, in "Return of the Southern Medical Students Home in 1859," scrapbook at the Library of the College of Physicians of Philadelphia. On the passes distributed to the students, see "Liberal Offer," *Richmond Daily Dispatch,* Dec. 21, 1859.

32. See "Reception of the Medical Students, &c.," *New York Herald,* Dec. 21, 1859; "The Return of the Medical Students," *Richmond Enquirer,* Dec. 22, 1859. See also "Preparations to Receive the Medical Students from Philadelphia," ibid., Dec. 22, 1859.

33. "The Homeward Bound," unidentified Virginia newspaper clipping, in "Return of the Southern Medical Students Home in 1859."

34. See "Southern Rights Association—Action in Reference to the Medical Students from Philadelphia," *Richmond Daily Dispatch,* Dec. 23, 1859; "Reception of the Medical Students," *Richmond Enquirer,* Dec. 22, 1859; "Reception of the Southern Medical Students at Richmond, Va.," *Philadelphia Press,* Dec. 23, 1859; "The Reception of the Southern Medical Students at Richmond," *New York Herald,* Dec. 23, 1859; and "Our Richmond Correspondence, Dec. 22, 1859," ibid., Dec. 26, 1859.

35. "Our Richmond Correspondence, Dec. 22, 1859," *New York Herald,* Dec. 26, 1859.

36. "Governor Wise's Speech, To the Medical Students," *Richmond Enquirer,* Dec. 24, 1859; see also "The Students from Philadelphia," *Richmond Whig and Public Advertiser,* Dec. 24, 1859.

37. Quoted in "Surfeited with Excitement . . . Policemen Liberally Rewarded . . . The Reception of the Students . . . ," *Petersburg (Va.) Daily Express,* Dec. 24, 1859. Details of the preceding account have been drawn from "The Homeward Bound," unidentified Virginia newspaper clipping, in "Return of the Southern Medical Students Home in 1859"; "Arrival of the Philadelphia Students," *Richmond Daily Dispatch,* Dec. 23, 1859; "The Collation at Columbian," *Richmond Enquirer,* Dec. 23, 1859; "The Students from Philadelphia," *Richmond Whig and Public Advertiser,* Dec. 24, 1859; and "The Students' Supper," ibid., Dec. 26, 1859.

38. Mathews quoted in "Meeting of the Faculty and Students of the Medical College of Georgia," *Augusta (Ga.) Daily Constitutionalist,* Dec. 31, 1859. See also "Medical Students," *Richmond Daily Dispatch,* Dec. 30, 1859; "The Medical Students," *Richmond Enquirer,* Dec. 24, 1859; "Board for the Students," *Richmond Daily Dispatch,* Dec. 2, 1859; and "The Southern Students," ibid., Dec. 26, 1859.

39. "The Seceding Students," *Charleston Daily Courier,* Dec. 28, 1859; see also "The Medical Students," *Charleston Mercury,* Dec. 26, 1859.

40. "The Return of the Medical Students," *Philadelphia Press,* Dec. 24, 1859 (and see also the *Philadelphia Sunday Dispatch,* Dec. 18, 1859); "The Students' Stampede," *Philadelphia Daily News,* Dec. 21, 1859; "The Virginia Doctors . . . ," *New-York Daily Tribune,* Dec. 27, 1859; "Calomel and Jalap," *Chicago Press and Tribune,* Dec. 22, 1859.

41. "The Medical Students Going South—Meeting Yesterday Morning," *Philadelphia Press,* Dec. 21, 1859; "Secession of Medical Students," *Philadelphia North American and United States Gazette,* Dec. 22, 1859. See also "The Return of the Medical Students," *Philadelphia Press,* Dec. 24, 1859; and "The Southern Medical Students in Philadelphia," Dec. 21, 1859, unidentified newspaper clipping in "Return of the Southern Medical Students Home in 1859."

42. "The Students' Stampede," *Philadelphia Daily News*, Dec. 21, 1859; "The Exodus," *Philadelphia Sunday Dispatch*, Dec. 25, 1859; "Calomel and Jalap," *Chicago Press and Tribune*, Dec. 22, 1859; "Flight of the Doctors," *New York Times*, Dec. 26, 1859.

43. "The Exodus," *Philadelphia Sunday Dispatch*, Dec. 25, 1859; "Calomel and Jalap," *Chicago Press and Tribune*, Dec. 22, 1859; "Exodus of the Sawbones," *Germantown Telegraph*, Dec. 28, 1859.

44. "The Esculapian Stampede," Dec. 23, 1859, unidentified newspaper clipping (Philadelphia), in "Return of the Southern Medical Students Home in 1859"; "Northern Aggression," *Chicago Press and Tribune*, Dec. 26, 1859.

45. "Exodus of the Sawbones," *Germantown Telegraph*, Dec. 28, 1859; "The Exodus," *Philadelphia Sunday Dispatch*, Dec. 25, 1859; "Abduction of Medical Students," *Philadelphia North American and United States Gazette*, Dec. 30, 1859.

46. "The Exodus," *Philadelphia Sunday Dispatch*, Dec. 25, 1859; "Carry Me Back," *Philadelphia Daily Evening Bulletin*, Dec. 22, 1859; "The Sawbones Exodus," *New York Daily Tribune*, Dec. 23, 1859; Untitled report, *Albany Evening Journal*, Dec. 21, 1859.

47. "Abduction of Medical Students," *Philadelphia North American and United States Gazette*, Dec. 30, 1859; "Northern Aggression," *Chicago Press and Tribune*, Dec. 26, 1859; "A Few Thoughts on the Movement of the Medical Students, in Philadelphia, from the South, and the Action of Southern Medical Faculties," *Baltimore American*, Dec. 26, 1859; "Practical Secession," *New York Times*, Dec. 21, 1859.

48. "The Medical Students—The Vanguard of a Grand Movement—Welcome to Virginia," *Richmond Daily Dispatch*, Dec. 24, 1859; "The Philadelphia Medical Student Stampede," *Petersburg (Va.) Daily Express*, Dec. 24, 1859; "Interesting Occasion at the Medical College of Georgia," *Augusta (Ga.) Daily Constitutionalist*, Dec. 28, 1859; "Our Medical Schools," *New Orleans Daily Picayune*, Dec. 22, 1859.

49. "Our Medical Schools," *New Orleans Daily Picayune*, Dec. 22, 1859; "Interesting Occasion at the Medical College of Georgia," *Augusta (Ga.) Daily Constitutionalist*, Dec. 28, 1859; "The Return of the Medical Students—Is It Practical Disunion?" *Richmond Enquirer*, Dec. 24, 1859.

50. "The Return of the Medical Students—Is It Practical Disunion?" *Richmond Enquirer*, Dec. 24, 1859; "Interesting Occasion at the Medical College of Georgia," *Augusta (Ga.) Daily Constitutionalist*, Dec. 28, 1859.

51. *Baltimore Exchange*, quoted in "The Stampede of the Medical Students," *New York Evening Post*, Dec. 24, 1859; "The Medical Students," *Nashville Republican Banner*, Jan. 4, 1860.

52. "The Secession of Medical Students from the Schools of This City," *Medical and Surgical Reporter*, n.s., 3 (Jan. 28, 1860): 393; E. D. Fenner, "American Medical Association—Breakers Ahead," *New Orleans Medical News and Hospital Gazette* 7 (May 1860): 213–14. On the allegations of tampering, see "The Secession of Medical Students from the Schools of This City," p. 391; and William M. McPheeters, "The Secession of Medical Students from Philadelphia," *St. Louis Medical and Surgical Reporter* 18 (Jan. 1860): 92–93. For examples of the paper war this charge precipitated, see Samuel D. Gross, "Southern Medical Students and Southern Medical Schools," *North American Medico-Chirurgical Review* 4 (Mar. 1860): 378–91; W. K. Bowling, "The 'Abducted' Babies Again," *Nashville Journal of Medicine and Surgery* 18 (Apr. 1860): 364–69; and "Southern Medical Students and Southern Medical Schools," *New Orleans Medical News and Hospital Gazette* 7 (Apr. 1860): 119–25.

53. McPheeters, "The Secession of Medical Students from Philadelphia," p. 92; "Exodus of Southern Medical Students from Philadelphia and New York," *Louisville Medical Journal* 1 (Feb. 1860): 61; "The Stampede of Medical Students from Philadelphia," *Cincinnati Lancet and Observer*, n.s., 3 (Feb. 1860): 119.

54. "The 'Deserted Village,'" *New-York Medical Press* 3 (Feb. 18, 1860): 127–28; Nathan S. Davis, "Southern Students Leaving the Medical Schools at Philadelphia," *Chicago Medical Journal*, n.s., 3 (Jan. 1860): 53; Richard D. Arnold, "Southern Medical Students in Northern Colleges," *Savannah Journal of Medicine* 2 (June 1860): 350.

55. "Southern Medical Students Deserting the Philadelphia Schools," *New-York Medical Press* 2 (Dec. 24, 1859): 860. "Editorial Department," *Cincinnati Medical and Surgical News* 1 (Jan. 1860): 31. Harvey L. Byrd, "Exodus of Southern Medical Students from Northern Colleges," *Oglethorpe Medical and Surgical Journal* 2 (Mar. 1860): 422; W. K. Bowling, "Seceding Students," *Nashville Journal of Medicine and Surgery* 18 (Feb. 1860): 171. Typical of the reaction in the Philadelphia medical press is "The Return Home of Some Southern Medical Students," *Medical News and Library* 18 (Jan. 1860): 11.

56. "Return of Southern Medical Students from Northern Colleges," *Southern Medical and Surgical Journal*, n.s., 16 (1860): 76; "Editorial Department," pp. 30–31.

57. D. M. Reese, "Sudden Stampede of Southern Medical Students from Philadelphia," *American Medical Gazette* 11 (Jan. 1860): 61; "The Stampede of Medical Students from Philadelphia," p. 120; "Return of Southern Medical Students from Northern Colleges," p. 73.

58. "News and Miscellany," *Medical and Surgical Reporter*, n.s., 3 (Mar. 10, 1860): 529; "Medical Colleges and Medical Students," *St. Louis Medical and Surgical Journal* 18 (May 1860): 279; William Hauser, "Salutatory," *Oglethorpe Medical and Surgical Journal* 2 (Jan. 1860): 323–24. For an example of New York's attempt to capitalize on Philadelphia's misfortune, see "Where to Study," *New-York Medical Press* 3 (Mar. 24, 1860): 207–8.

59. "Return of Southern Medical Students from Northern Colleges," p. 76; "The Stampede of Medical Students from Philadelphia," p. 120.

60. Harvey L. Byrd, "Patronage of Northern Medical Schools by Southern Students," *Oglethorpe Medical and Surgical Journal* 2 (Jan. 1860): 320; "Medical Students in Motion," *Ohio Medical and Surgical Journal* 12 (Jan. 1860): 252; see also "The Seceding Students," ibid. (Mar. 1860): 349–50.

61. Ruffin in William Kauffman Scarborough, ed., *The Diary of Edmund Ruffin*, 3 vols. (Baton Rouge, 1972–89), 1:384–85; J. D. B. De Bow, "Editorial Miscellany," *De Bow's Review* 28 (Feb. 1860): 243; George Fitzhugh, "Johnson, Boswell, Goldsmith, Etc.," in ibid. (Apr. 1860): 417; "Our Medical Schools," *New Orleans Daily Picayune*, Dec. 30, 1859; William Hauser, "Salutatory," p. 323; "Southern Medicine," *Atlanta Medical and Surgical Journal* 5 (1860): 446.

62. Harvey L. Byrd, "Exodus of Southern Medical Students from Northern Colleges," p. 422. For the Virginia bill, see "House of Delegates," *Richmond Enquirer*, Dec. 23, 1859; "Legislature of Virginia," *Staunton Spectator and General Advertiser*, Dec. 27, 1859; and "Medical College of Virginia," *Richmond Enquirer*, Mar. 27, 1860.

63. See "The Commencement of the Virginia Medical College," *Richmond Daily Dispatch*, Mar. 9, 1860; "Virginia Medical College," *Richmond Enquirer*, Mar. 13, 1860.

64. "The Medical Students Make an Exit," *Philadelphia North American and United States Gazette*, Dec. 22, 1859; "Departure of the Medical Students," *Philadelphia Press*, Dec. 22, 1859.

65. "Cold Day . . . Medical Students Returning . . . ," *Baltimore American*, Dec. 30, 1859. See also "Thought Better of It," *Philadelphia Daily Evening Bulletin*, Dec. 28, 1859; "The Virginia Medical Students," *New York Daily Tribune*, Dec. 29, 1859; "Return of Medical Students to Philadelphia," *New York Times*, Dec. 29, 1859. For Luckett's comment, see "Southern Medical Students," *Richmond Enquirer*, Jan. 20, 1859.

66. "The Virginia Doctors . . . ," *New York Daily Tribune*, Dec. 27, 1859; Harvey L. Byrd, "Southern Medical Students in Northern Medical Colleges—Once More,"

Oglethorpe Medical and Surgical Journal 3 (Jan. 1861): 268–69. See also Henry, ed., *Standard History of the Medical Profession of Philadelphia,* pp. 221–22; and "The Revolution," *New Orleans Medical Times* 1 (May 1861): 237.

67. Quoted in Henry, ed., *Standard History of the Medical Profession of Philadelphia,* p. 220n.

68. "Address of Dr. A. E. Peticolas to the Southern Medical Students," *Richmond Enquirer,* Jan. 3, 1860.

69. "A Move in the Right Direction," *Fredericksburg (Va.) Weekly Advertiser and Chronicle of the Times,* Dec. 24, 1859; "Editorial and Miscellaneous," *Southern Medical and Surgical Journal,* n.s., 17 (June 1861): 511–12; Untitled report, *New York Daily Tribune,* Dec. 24, 1859.

70. "Atlanta Medical College, Our Journal, etc.," *Atlanta Medical and Surgical Journal* 6 (Aug. 1861): 747.

Part IV
Beyond Sectionalism

8

ROBERT E. MCGLONE

John Brown, Henry Wise, and the Politics of Insanity

Except in the one respect in which systematized delusion flawed [John Brown's] mind, he retained a piercing vision; the foresight of a man "cool, collected, and indomitable," as Governor Wise of Virginia was soon to write.

—Allan Nevins, *Prologue to Civil War*

Ahab, in his hidden self, raved on. . . . But, as in his narrow-flowing monomania, not one jot of Ahab's broad madness had been left behind; so in that broad madness, not one jot of his great natural intellect had perished. . . . So far from having lost his strength, Ahab, to that one end, did now possess a thousand fold more potency than ever he had sanely brought to bear upon any one reasonable object.

—Herman Melville, *Moby-Dick or, The Whale*

OLD JOHN BROWN had to be crazy. That was the almost universal supposition after Brown's capture on October 18, 1859, at the federal armory at Harpers Ferry, Virginia. Sometimes rebuked for his "wild" scheme to free the slaves, sometimes depicted as a "poor demented old man" deserving clemency, Brown was everywhere the subject of widespread bewilderment. As friends and foes alike began to grasp the political ramifications of Brown's raid, his "crazy" act ignited public debate of an unprecedented nature. At Brown's trial on charges of treason, murder, and conspiracy to incite a slave uprising, the claim that he was legally insane upset the calculations of prosecutors and defense attorneys alike.

The issue arose early. As Judge Richard Parker convened the circuit court of Jefferson County on October 27, the second day of Brown's six-day trial, one of Brown's court-appointed attorneys read a telegram to the court claiming that "insanity" was hereditary in Brown's family. Given the popular assumption that madness was inherited, the telegram implied that

Brown might plead insanity and thus avoid conviction for the crimes he and his men had committed. But something more was implied. The telegram was from Asahel H. Lewis, an abolitionist newspaper editor in Akron, Ohio. Lewis worried privately that "prominent men of the north" might be implicated in a failed effort to incite "servile insurrection."[1] If Brown were insane—adjudged legally irresponsible for his actions—that judgment, Lewis apparently reasoned, would absolve his accomplices of responsibility, too. It would thereby discount any evidence that Brown represented the abolitionists whose letters to him Virginia militiamen had seized in the Maryland farmhouse where he had concealed his tiny "army" before the attack. But Lewis left these concerns unstated, appealing instead to popular, culturally defined beliefs about insanity and the applicability of those beliefs to Brown's actions. The logic of those popular ideas would establish ground rules for the political game one troubled Virginian anticipated would spring from "this Harper's Ferry imbroglio."[2]

From the outset, then, the question of Brown's sanity had political as well as legal implications. It quickly became a public issue, molding popular sentiment North and South and warping the political dynamic of sectional conflict. The Akron editor's telegram triggered a heated exercise in what might be called the politics of insanity. As Lewis anticipated, prominent Republicans seized upon the charge of insanity to deny that their party had any responsibility for the Harpers Ferry raid. Several abolitionists even tried privately to demonstrate Brown's madness to Virginia authorities, while some of John Brown's friends and financial supporters used his alleged mental instability initially to dissociate themselves from his actions. As Brown's words and conduct in prison began to win widespread admiration in the North, however, other abolitionists and supporters exalted the "Old Hero" in a world gone mad. Making the most of Brown's Northern roots and his role in the sectional strife in Kansas three years earlier, Brown's Virginia captors, in contrast, sought to use his raid and its consequences to advance the cause of "Southern rights" within the Democratic party. They insisted that Brown was sane enough to hang and that his efforts to implement his conspiracy symbolized a living threat to all Southerners.[3] For six tense weeks, the question of Brown's insanity—and thus of his legal fate—bedeviled Virginia authorities and slavery apologists everywhere. In both instances, it threatened the political ambitions of Virginia's fiery governor, Henry Alexander Wise.

This essay explores the ways in which some of Brown's contemporaries exploited the insanity issue for partisan ends and shows how the "logic" of the politics of insanity has shaped our understanding of the impact of the Harpers Ferry raid on the sectional crisis. Rooted in persisting, unexamined assumptions about mental illness and its influence in history, a culturally

determined pattern of reasoning has misled historians seeking to understand Brown and the significance of his raid. My purpose, therefore, is to
analyze the politics of Brown's supposed insanity and the underlying logic
that bound Wise and Brown in an uneasy, fateful compact to affirm his
rationality.[4]

An Insistent Question

Predictably, Old Brown refused to plead insanity. As one of his attorneys
read Lewis's telegram in court, the Old Man, still weak from his wounds,
raised himself up from his courtroom cot to condemn the effort to exonerate him on what he insisted were spurious grounds. "I look upon it," he
declared, "as a miserable artifice and pretext of those who ought to take a
different course in regard to me, if they take any at all, and I view it with
contempt more than otherwise." Fearful of being dismissed as a lunatic,
Brown insisted on his own sanity. "Insane persons, so far as my experience
goes, have but very little ability to judge of their own sanity," he said, "and
if I am insane of course I should think I know more than all the rest of the
world; but I do not think so. I am perfectly unconscious of insanity, and I
reject, so far as I am capable, any attempt to interfere in my behalf on that
score."[5] If his insistence that he was "unconscious" of any insanity was
undercut by his premise that the insane cannot assess their sanity, no one
mistook his intent. The trial proceeded.

But Brown's insistence that he was sane did not silence those who sought
clemency for him. During the trial, a cousin, Sylvester H. Thompson, who
had been "intimately acquainted" with Brown and his family for twenty
years, swore before a Cleveland judge that his own mother and maternal
grandmother had both "died insane." Altogether, Thompson swore, three
of John Brown's aunts, five of his cousins, one of his brothers, three of his
sons, and several other relations had been "insane." And although Brown
himself was a man of "pure morals" and "high integrity," his mind had
been "over worked" about slavery, leaving him "an insane man upon that
subject." On November 5, three days after Brown was sentenced to hang,
one of his uncles, the Reverend Edward Brown of La Crosse, Wisconsin, also
appealed for clemency on the grounds that John Brown's "once balanced
mind has been unsettled by wrongs received [in the Kansas border warfare
of 1856] . . . and his mania naturaly [*sic*] looks toward avenging his wrongs
on what he regards as their author." Citing the presumed hereditary insanity in Brown's maternal family, Edward Brown argued that clemency
would produce a "chivalrous disarming of northern prejudice." Underscoring this point, Governor E. D. Campbell of Wisconsin vouchsafed Edward
Brown's honesty and suggested to Wise that "sound policy . . . dictates to

commutation of Brown's punishment," a view which "doubtless will be the 'sober second thought' of all."[6]

Contrary to Brown's wishes and instructions to his initial counsel, however, a new team of Northern-supported attorneys undertook to win clemency after Brown's conviction. After a final visit to the Old Man, attorney Hiram Griswold forwarded Sylvester Thompson's petition and affidavit of insanity to Wise, respectfully informing him that "on questions connected with Slavery and the liberation of the Slave [Brown] is insane." At the suggestion of Montgomery Blair, a prominent Maryland Republican who wanted to avoid public identification with Brown, George H. Hoyt, a young attorney and confidant of Brown's Boston antislavery supporters, rushed to Ohio to gather proof of Brown's "insanity." On November 23 Hoyt gave Wise nineteen affidavits, signed by acquaintances and relations of Brown, attesting to Brown's good character but asserting that he had been partially or wholly insane, at least since one of his sons had been killed in Kansas.[7] Blair himself wrote the petition accompanying the affidavits.[8]

Appeals came from all quarters. Prominent Democratic newspapers in the North urged clemency; even Tammany Hall sent a delegation to Richmond to plead for Brown's life.[9] Twenty-two Philadelphia petitioners deplored Brown's "deluded" attitudes about "negro emancipation," but argued that Virginia's honor and the nation's unity would best be served by sentencing the "crazy" man to prison. Several of Brown's business acquaintances similarly questioned his mental stability.[10] The prominent manufacturer, Amos A. Lawrence, who had assisted Brown financially, protested that Brown had confided plans for his "quixotic expedition" to none of his supporters and suggested that hardship, illness, and advancing age had made Brown's mind erratic. "We have a regular Puritan to deal with," Lawrence cautioned, "a man formed to be a martyr—pious, honest & brave"; and from his blood "would spring an army of martyrs." Unlike most petitioners, Lawrence asked only that Virginia provide "the fullest & fairest trial & conviction" before executing the Old Man.[11]

Were Brown's sympathizers sincere in attesting to his "insanity"? Did Brown indeed exhibit symptoms we today recognize as indicative of mental disorder? In part because the cultural context of antebellum America in which these questions must be addressed has been poorly understood, scholars have assessed Brown's mental state by weighing the evidence contained in petitions and other similar sources. They have assumed either that the affiants attested to a sham "monomania" or that Brown's behavior exhibited a mental disorder they identify as variously as paranoia and obsessive-compulsive neurosis. That approach has failed, however, even to clarify the question; as a basis for responsible assessment, it is inadequate. Using a wider evidentiary base and mapping modern systems of classification onto

Brown's behavior, I have elsewhere argued that, at least in the years after the Kansas border war, Brown experienced pronounced, recurring shifts in mood accompanied by grossly inflated ideas of his prowess as a military leader. Buoyed by his religious faith, Brown frequently asserted that he was God's "instrument" to free the slaves. In these situations, Brown was not "psychotic," but his moods distorted his judgment and may have been symptomatic of the affective disorder that haunted his son Frederick.[12]

In the mid-nineteenth century the term "insanity" was still widely used to indicate any form of madness—whether "mania," "melancholia," "dementia," or "idiocy," according to traditional labels—as well as "lypemania" and "monomania," illnesses recently identified by followers of the French reformer, Philippe Pinel. What we call psychiatry was just emerging as a medical specialty. The few physicians with patients suffering from "diseases of the mind"—alienists or psychiaters, as they were known—were superintendents of the public and private asylums for the insane then spreading across the country. These physicians understood that mental illness might affect the emotions without "any appreciable lesion of the intellect"; but in the courts a narrow interpretation of insanity as profoundly deranged thinking prevailed. Even today, although the term *insanity* has long since lost medical significance, in law it is still synonymous with psychosis: psychiatrists tend to believe that only mental illnesses featuring delusions or hallucinations satisfy the legal requirements of insanity.[13] In short, one can be mentally ill without being legally insane. That was much truer in antebellum America, when insanity was defined in narrowly rationalistic terms.

In the 1850s courts in Great Britain and the United States had begun to cite the 1843 M'Naghten test of insanity. That rule required a jury to assume a defendant sane unless his attorneys could prove that, at the time of committing an indictable offense, he was "labouring under such a defect of reason, from disease of the mind, as not to know the nature and quality of the act he was doing; or if he did know it, that he did not know he was doing what was wrong."[14] In short, an accused person was insane only if he or she failed to grasp the consequences of a wrongful act or did not know that the act was wrong. But how was the word "know" to be construed? In practice, courts held that the M'Naghten rule required only that a defendant answer questions correctly to be considered sane, whatever his or her understanding of the act or emotional state at the time. Then as now, juries tended to assume that insanity meant cognitive impairment. Mental diseases such as schizophrenia and manic-depressive illness (bipolar disorder) were not yet recognized as distinct disorders. The M'Naghten rule did not comprehend either mood disorders or personality disorders, such as psychopathy, as falling under the rubric of "insanity."[15]

In a variety of ways, Brown's petitioners said—and intended to say—that the Old Man was irrational about slavery. He was not merely "excitable" or "furious" when the subject was raised; he was obsessed with attacking slavery itself. His "monomania" thus satisfied the legal definition of insanity, his petitioners averred, not because Brown had violent impulses but because he was incapable of seeing the moral implications of his own violent attacks on slavery. At least two of the petitioners said they had concluded Brown was mad before he launched his "war" against slavery in Virginia, and one affiant—his half brother, Jeremiah—claimed he had told him so to his face. The petitioners may well have fabricated stories in hopes of gaining a commutation of Brown's sentence, but Jeremiah's story is consistent with the tenor of his criticisms of "brother John" in his private correspondence.[16]

These petitions did not, however, shake John Brown's resolve. He understood clearly what was at issue in the clamor over his sanity. If he were adjudged mad, his sacrifices would be for naught, his passion to end slavery would be dismissed as madness. "It is a great comfort to feel assured that I am permitted to die for a cause,—not merely to pay the debt of nature, as all must," he wrote to Tilden four days before his execution and a week after Tilden's affidavits had reached Wise. "My whole life before had not afforded me one half the opportunity to plead for the right. In this, also, I find much to reconcile me to both my present condition and my immediate prospect." Brown added pointedly: "I may be *very insane;* (and I *am* so, if insane at all). But if that be so, *insanity* is like a very pleasant dream to me. I am not in the least degree conscious of my *ravings,* of my fears, or of any terrible visions whatever; but *fancy* myself entirely composed, and that my *sleep, in particular,* is as sweet as that of a healthy, joyous little infant. . . . I have scarce realized that I am in prison, or in irons, at all. I certainly think I was never more cheerful in my life."[17]

Governor Wise's Dilemma

The question of Brown's punishment had political implications in Virginia. Governor Wise had been embarrassed by Brown's success in holding the federal arsenal at Harpers Ferry for thirty hours and by the failure of the Virginia militia there to mount an assault on the small fire-engine house that came to be known as "John Brown's Fort." Had he arrived in time to take personal command, Wise declared, he would "not have parleyed with them a moment, would have ordered the attack, and led it." To Wise, Virginia's honor was at stake: to dismiss Brown as a lunatic, as many Republicans tried to do, made light not only of the "invasion," but of the state's honor.[18] After interrogating Brown and caucusing with political associates,

Wise resolved to have Brown tried in a Virginia court rather than remand him to federal authorities. Politically compromised by Brown's temporary success and barred from seeking a second term as governor, Wise hoped to rescue his floundering political ambitions by converting Harpers Ferry into a springboard for a "Southern rights" candidacy for the presidency. Blaming President Buchanan for failing to guard the arsenal adequately, he portrayed Brown's attack as a logical outcome of the popular sovereignty espoused by his leading rival for the Democratic nomination, Stephen A. Douglas of Illinois.[19]

Picturing Brown's "little band of desperadoes" as agents of a wider conspiracy, Wise for weeks paraded more than a thousand militiamen around Charlestown, where Brown was tried and then hanged on December 2. Wise also demanded that President Buchanan send troops to guard Harpers Ferry against further raids and that Buchanan as well as the governors of Ohio and Pennsylvania issue proclamations warning Northerners to "desist from unlawful schemes" against the South and its peculiar institution. Wise insisted that the North was responsible for Brown's attack. "An entire social and sectional sympathy has incited their crimes and now rises in rebellion and insurrection to the height of sustaining and justifying their enormity," he charged.[20]

Wise was furious about the Northern response to Brown, especially because some Brown sympathizers had even threatened Wise's life if he failed to save Brown. In a confidential letter to former New York Mayor Fernando Wood written on November 6, just four days after Brown's sentencing, Wise rejected all appeals for clemency. "I could reprieve him for 90 days only," he wrote. "I *shall not* reprieve him; for this *sympathy* is an insurrection against us worse than Brown's insurrection in arms. I am challenged to make an issue with it & I shall determinedly do so."[21] In fact, Wise determined to punish everyone he could lay hands on. On November 7 he telegraphed Andrew Hunter, his special prosecutor at Charlestown, urging him to seek indictments against two Brown confidants, former New York Congressman Gerrit Smith and the black abolitionist, Frederick Douglass. As to the young men taken prisoner with Brown, Wise declared: "I wish you to understand confidentially, that I will not reprieve or pardon one man *now* after the letters I have received." Privately, Wise had decided Brown and all his "volunteer-regulars" had to hang.[22]

On November 16 Wise was already preoccupied with the staging of Brown's execution. The problem was to minimize its impact in the North. Fearful of attempts to rescue Brown, Wise planned to have four hundred armed men at the hanging and an additional regiment at the ready nearby. He regretted Judge Parker's failure to order the simultaneous executions: Brown "ought to be hung between two negroes & there oughtn't to be two days of excitement." Wise clearly recognized the political value of the hanging scene for himself in Virginia and the South. "It gives the Legislature the opportunity of uniting with [the] Executive in hanging Brown," he wrote Hunter. "Ought *I to be there?* It might be necessary in order to proc[laim]: M[artial] law." But whether in Brown's presence or not, Wise was determined to have him swing. If the court of appeals did not decide Brown's fate before December 2, Wise vowed, "I'll hang Brown."[23]

Wise's resolve was, however, difficult to sustain. A day after his telegraph to Hunter—November 8—Wise received Griswold's letter transmitting Sylvester Thompson's petition for clemency on the grounds of hereditary madness in Brown's family. Griswold assured Wise that Brown himself had condemned the threats against the governor and had not solicited the appeals on his behalf. On the back of Griswold's letter, Wise noted, "This mode of attesting the fact of insanity, by opinion of a relative at a distance, not accessible to cross-examination, not sustained by an expert, and by counsel, is incompetent to establish the fact."[24] Two days later Wise ordered Dr. Francis T. Stribling, superintendent of the Virginia Western Lunatic Asylum at Staunton, to examine Brown personally, but without disclosing his purpose. Stribling was to determine whether Brown was "sane, in the sense of legal & rational responsibility for crime." If he is insane, Wise said, "he ought to be cured"—the phrase "before he is executed" was struck out here—"and, if not insane, the fact ought to be vouched in the most reliable form, now that it is questioned under oath & by counsel since conviction." This suggests that Wise knew that to ignore the petitions would expose him to charges of evading the question of Brown's mental state and rushing to judgment. Yet he swiftly countermanded his confidential order to Stribling, and no examination was made.[25]

In fact, Wise dared not order a sanity examination or risk a sanity trial. On the one hand, as a lawyer, he must have known that the M'Naghten test required not that a "sane" defendant be emotionally balanced but only that he understand the consequences of his actions and be able to distinguish right from wrong. Brown could certainly persuade a jury that he knew what he was doing. A judgment of insanity was possible only if the defendant showed a "defect of reason." Hence, any juror satisfactory to the prosecution would surely find Brown sane on the basis of his own testimony. On the other hand, affiants on Brown's behalf insisted that he suffered from "monomania" and was wholly irrational about slavery. On that point, Wise could not be so sure of Stribling's opinion in advance. "Monomaniacs" were notoriously clever at concealing their aberrant ideas, as Brown would surely be if his attorneys questioned him in court about slavery. If Wise staged a sanity trial, his prosecutors might therefore have to contend that Brown met the M'Naghten sanity test by showing that "monomania" had not destroyed his reason concerning slavery. But that implied that it was sane—or at least not insane—to despise slavery, even to the point of being willing to die to end it. The narrower test, then, risked further political embarrassment for Wise. Since the day of Brown's capture he had missed no opportunity to condemn the "sum of all villainies."[26] From Wise's standpoint, therefore, any public debate should focus on Brown's violent means rather than on his hatred of slavery—a sentiment widely shared in the North.

In principle, as previously seen, it was perfectly possible to suffer from "monomania," a mental disease producing excitement and irrationality on specific subjects, and still to be considered mentally sound in the narrow sense required by M'Naghten. Thus a sanity trial would be epilogue to Brown's criminal trial and conviction, not only raising hopes among his sympathizers but undue concern in the South as well. Leading alienists like Isaac Ray, whose prestigious treatise on the medical jurisprudence of insanity distinguished more forms of insanity than did M'Naghten, argued that courts ought to free defendants whose "mania" or "monomania" originated in the emotions. The issue had been widely enough discussed in popular magazines for Wise to fear that his political enemies might accuse him of cruelty should Stribling or another alienist called by the defense conclude that Brown suffered from "partial moral mania"—monomania affecting the emotions.[27]

In drawing up his order for an examination, Wise asked Stribling to determine whether Brown was sane only in the sense of "legal & rational responsibility." In choosing that language, Wise revealed an awareness of legal controversies over the M'Naghten test, as well as his own concern to keep the question of the Old Man's sanity on narrow, substantive grounds. In rescinding his order, Wise was prudent on two counts: First, he avoided the risk of an examination or a public hearing that might *not* confirm Brown's sanity in every respect. Second, he avoided the delay in Brown's execution that a sanity trial would entail. Such a trial would inevitably postpone the execution until Wise's successor was in office, with the result that he, not Wise, would get the political credit for stretching the neck of Virginia's enemy.

Besides, Wise had convinced himself of the Old Man's sanity. Shortly after the raid, he rejected the "Republican" idea that Brown was unstable. He had reached this conclusion on the basis of an interview with Brown that he and other officials had conducted at intervals over two or three hours on the afternoon the raid ended. In addition, Wise had the testimony of Colonel Lewis Washington, his military aide, who had been one of Brown's hostages during the raid.[28] In an impromptu speech after his return from Harpers Ferry, Wise declared: "They are themselves mistaken who take

[Brown] to be a madman. He is a bundle of the best nerves I ever saw cut and thrust and bleeding and in bonds. He is cool, collected, and indomitable." Wise cited Washington's testimony that the Old Man had been "humane" to his hostages and Washington's endorsement of the veracity of Brown's statements in the interview. "He inspired me with great trust in his integrity as a man of truth," Wise said of Brown. "He is a fanatic, vain and garrulous; but firm, truthful, and intelligent."[29]

Nor did Wise ever publicly waver from this assessment. Justifying his failure to ask for a professional evaluation of the condemned man, Wise later said he had rejected such advice because Brown was unquestionably sane. "I know that he was sane, and remarkably sane," Wise told the Virginia General Assembly on December 5, "if quick and clear perception, if assumed rational premises and consecutive reasoning from them, if cautious tact in avoiding disclosures and in conveying conclusions and inferences, if memory and conception and practical common sense, and if composure and self-possession are evidence of a sound state of mind." He then praised Brown for having "spurned this mawkish plea of monomania."[30]

But as usual Wise's praise of Brown's fortitude was coupled with contempt for those who first financed and armed Brown and then pleaded his insanity. "Before his failure and defeat in what, in their correspondence with him, they called a 'glorious cause,'" Wise remarked of Brown's abolitionist friends, their sympathy "was all with his desperate daring and success; and now it is with his insanity for a plea against the legal penalties of his crimes, which had their origin in this very sympathy." The "sympathy" of these "reformers" had acknowledged Brown's "insanity too late to snatch from his hands the weapons it had placed there; too late to save the lives taken by its own incitement; and too late to save him from a felon's fate." The dialectic of insanity implied that if Brown had been mad, his Northern supporters were accountable only for initially failing to recognize his madness. But in truth, Wise was convinced, the issue was not Brown's madness, nor even his criminality. Rather, it was the intent of the people who had "sent" Brown to wreak havoc on Virginia and the South.[31]

As Wise's critics charged, his attempt to blame the North for Brown's "invasion" had made things more difficult for him in Virginia.[32] Fueling Virginians' anger and fear, Wise published in the Richmond *Enquirer* a number of inflammatory antislavery statements by Northerners, including some from letters he had received demanding clemency for Brown. The *Enquirer's* editor, the governor's fire-eating son, Jennings Wise, responded indignantly to charges that his father was a "reckless aspirant for political power" who was magnifying the Harpers Ferry "affair" to the point of jeopardizing the Union.[33] The younger Wise insisted that the Union had "virtually ceased to exist," because Northern state governments were failing to assure protection of the slave states against antislavery filibusters and to extradite fugitives from the raid. When Republican newspapers pictured Wise as a Don Quixote tilting with imaginary abolitionist armies, the *Enquirer* published rumors of impending abolitionist plots to rescue the prisoners at Charlestown. In January, after Henry Wise's term as governor had ended, a committee of the Virginia legislature endorsed his decision to order the buildup of the military force at Charlestown to prevent attempts to rescue the prisoners; the committee also endorsed his belief that Brown's raid was evidence of "a widespread conspiracy . . . against the peace and security of all the Southern States." Even so, some legislators thought it would have been better, "as an act of policy, to have had [Brown] adjudged insane."[34]

Wise apparently believed the rumors that abolitionists would attempt to rescue Brown and his men—but it is essential to appreciate the political context of that belief in the weeks immediately following Brown's raid. Throughout the South, Brown quickly became a symbol of Northern hostility to the "peculiar institution" and the Southern way of life. During the trial, Wise's personal representative on the prosecutorial staff, Andrew Hunter, an attorney for the Baltimore & Ohio Railroad, painted alarming pictures of the slave uprising Brown had allegedly hoped to inspire. Brown's plea that he "never did intend murder or treason, or the destruction of property, or to excite or incite the slaves to rebellion, or to make insurrection" failed to convince Virginians. As Edmund Ruffin noted in his diary, Brown could have succeeded only "through blood-shed & horrors beyond example." Persistent rumors that agents of Brown were at large in the state alarmed Virginians, who applauded the arrests of suspected abolitionists as far away as Texas. Wise received scores of letters from officials across the South telling of arrests of supposed Brown coconspirators.[35]

In Richmond the hostility to Brown and his raiders was palpable, and in Charlestown the court received repeated warnings that Brown would be lynched.[36] Escorting Brown by train from Harpers Ferry to Charlestown, Wise managed to calm a would-be lynch mob in the latter city by pointing out that it would dishonor Virginia to hang Brown before his trial. At least one Northern observer who saw fresh troops marching into Charlestown thought Wise might be anticipating mob violence if he decided to postpone the December 2 execution. Be that as it may, just after the raid, Andrew Hunter pledged that Brown would be "arraigned, tried, found guilty, sentenced and hung, all within ten days."[37] Such haste was not possible under Virginia law, but most Virginians would not be satisfied with lesser punishment or unnecessary delays.

Thus Wise could hang Brown to satisfy Virginians whose outrage over

Harpers Ferry he shared or he could spare the Old Man to placate his own political friends in the North. To be sure, conservative Northern Democrats sympathized with Virginia's sense of grievance over Brown's raid. They supported slavery, but they also feared disruption of the Union. Anxious not to give "Black Republicans" a martyr, they urged Wise to yield to the pleas to save the Old Man. To remain a credible national candidate outside the South, Wise therefore undertook an effort to placate Northern Democrats by shifting responsibility for Brown's fate onto circumstances beyond his control.

Accordingly, he suggested through the *Enquirer* that responsibility to save Brown lay with others. On November 8, Jennings Wise published an editorial, "The Law of Virginia Forbids the Pardon of Brown," to the effect that Henry Wise could not save Brown on his own initiative but could only recommend a sanity trial at the formal request of others. Under the laws of Virginia "an insane man cannot be tried," Jennings Wise noted. Once the question was raised in court, a jury had to determine the defendant's sanity, and only if he or she were judged sane could guilt and punishment be decided. Should a defendant's insanity remain undiscovered until after conviction and sentencing, as was the case with Brown, the executive might order "a postponement . . . until the question of sanity is definitely ascertained." The *Enquirer* thus urged "any persons" who believed Brown to be insane "to institute proceedings for the trial of the fact of sanity." In the absence of such proceedings, the editorial concluded, "*All hopes of Executive clemency should be abandoned*, for, as we have shown, the Executive, if he had the disposition, *has not the power.*"[38]

The editorial appeared two days after Governor Wise had determined privately that he would pardon none of the "invaders." He therefore had ample time to withdraw it had he thought it sent false signals about his intentions toward Brown. Perhaps Wise expected no response to the editorial, but if so, he seriously miscalculated. In the North, men like Montgomery Blair interpreted the editorial as an "invitation to make a demonstration" of Brown's monomania. Blair promptly sent George Hoyt to Ohio to gather the affidavits that the young attorney presented to Wise in Washington on November 23.[39] By failing to postpone the execution or to seek a professional opinion on the issues raised by these affidavits, however, Wise seriously jeopardized his political support in the North. Having encouraged Brown's sympathizers to petition for clemency on the basis of insanity, Wise then failed to act upon the substance of the petitions. Since he was committed to hanging Brown, moreover, Wise's only recourse was to dismiss out of hand the evidence in the affidavits. Had he been sure that Stribling would find Brown sane, Wise might well have attempted to strengthen his position by ordering an examination. Instead, he based his

refusal to intervene solely on his own judgment. "Did I believe him insane," the governor insisted shortly before the execution, "if I could even
entertain a rational doubt of his sanity, I would stay his execution even at
this hour. All Virginia should not prevent me. I would sooner sever this arm
at the shoulder than permit his execution. But I have no such belief, no
such doubt."[40]

Wise's denial that he could save Brown suffered from an obvious flaw.
Under the state constitution of 1852, the governor had broad powers to
"grant reprieves and pardons after conviction, and to commute capital
punishment." He had only to communicate his "reasons" for so doing to
the General Assembly. To be sure, the constitution also provided that this
power could be qualified, and opponents of executive authority in the legislature subsequently narrowed the governor's power to reprieve persons
convicted of treason and denied his power to pardon unless "with the
consent of the General Assembly, declared by joint resolution." But the law
placed no similar constraint on the governor's power to commute sentences.[41] In short, the General Assembly would have had to concur in a
pardon for Brown but not in a *commutation* of his sentence to life imprisonment. Wise's public stance was therefore duplicitous. It was not true that
"all hopes of Executive clemency" had to be "abandoned." If Wise had had
the "disposition," he did indeed have the power to save Brown's life.[42]
Furthermore, Wise's assertion to Fernando Wood on November 6—"If the
executive interposes at all, it is to pardon"—was misleading, if not disin-
genuous. It placed the burden of action on the General Assembly and failed
to mention the governor's authority to commute sentences.

Indeed, just two days before, Wise had acknowledged Wood's warning
that hanging would make Brown a martyr. Wood had asked whether Wise
had "nerve enough" to send Brown to prison for life instead of hanging
him, to which Wise responded: "Yes if I didn't think he ought to be hung,
and that I would be inexcusable for mitigating his punishment. I could do it
without flinching, without a quiver of muscle against a universal clamor for
his life." But Wise chose to dismiss Wood's proposal to commute Brown's
sentence, characteristically representing the matter as one of honor. Had
anyone ever argued, he asked Wood, that a state ought to "spare a murderer
. . . because public sentiment elsewhere will glorify an *insurrectionist* with
martyrdom?" "I have precisely nerve enough," he added, "to let him be
executed with the certainty of [its] condemnation." After all, a Brown in
prison would be no less a martyr than a Brown dead.[43]

Wise's friend and political ally, former President John Tyler, disagreed
with the governor's stance. He knew perfectly well that Wise could save
Brown. Writing to Wise in early November, he suggested that by commuting Brown's sentence to life in prison, "the magnanimity of Virginia will be

commended, the wisdom of her Governor extolled, the enemy disarmed, and the triumph of the Democracy secured." Tyler sweetened this advice by pledging, *"I still look to you as the Southern leader."* When Wise took offense at the advice, Tyler replied: "Do not misinterpret my last note. I merely suggested a point of political policy as cold as marble. Brown deserves to die a thousand deaths upon the Rack to end in fire & terminate in Hell. But still policy should be consulted—the profoundest policy."[44]

Of course, Wise knew what "policy" required. To retain the support of Southerners, he had to hang Brown; to win favor with northern Democrats, he had to spare him. His attempt to deflect responsibility onto the legislature, intended to placate the latter, did nothing for his popularity with Virginians. Rather, policy at home required him to champion Southern rights and defend Virginia's "sovereignty." Without the support of Southerners at the upcoming Democratic convention, moreover, his presidential hopes would certainly be dashed. Thus, whether he believed Brown sane or not, Wise had too much to lose to interfere with the hanging.

Wise's firmness did in fact help recoup his popularity in Virginia. Political friends of Robert M. T. Hunter, Wise's chief rival for presidential support within Virginia, found the climate of opinion so changed after Brown's execution that Hunter's own supporters were "very lukewarm throughout the state. . . . The vote of this state" at the Democratic convention, reported William Old, Jr., the editor of the *Richmond Examiner,* on December 16, "will be cast for the man, who is more distinctly with the popular sentiment on the slavery question."[45] But he reassured Hunter that Wise would "certainly be looking Northward, and eulogizing the Union in a month or two. If he does," Old continued, the nomination "is lost to him." Indeed, Wise's popularity in Virginia had become so intimidating that one influential Democrat cautioned Hunter's friends "not [to] oppose the Governor with too much bitterness." The happenstance of Brown's attack on Harpers Ferry had given Wise a "transcient" popularity so great that Hunter's friends arranged to delay the state Democratic convention until February 13, 1860. "It was important for your interests that it should take place at as late a day as possible, as the Gov[ernor] had made no small capital out of the Harpers ferry affair, and time was needed to let its effect die away," one of his advisors wrote to Hunter on December 21. "Your friends, accordingly, went for the latest time in Caucus."[46] Even Edmund Ruffin, who despised Wise, conceded, "Before the Harper's Ferry affair, he had but little support in Virginia (& none elsewhere) for the presidency which he was seeking so boldly and so shamelessly. But his conduct in and since that affair, though very blameable for indiscretion," had gained him "more popularity than all he ever had acquired for real worth and ability."[47]

To derail Stephen A. Douglas's nomination at the Charleston convention in April, Wise needed Brown not only to symbolize the danger of abolitionism for the South but to evidence the failure of Douglas' doctrine of "popular sovereignty" for the North. Brown was the agent of "Ossawatomite Republicans," Wise said. Popular sovereignty had not made the question of slavery in the territories a "barren abstraction," as moderate Democrats claimed; instead it had made Osawatomie Brown a "border ruffian" in Virginia. Wise therefore denounced "squatter sovereignty" and demanded federal intervention to protect the rights of slaveholders everywhere from Brown and his followers.[48] A sane Brown personified Northern hostility to slavery, whereas, in the dialectic of insanity, a "crazed fanatic" was accountable to no one and symbolic of nothing. For many reasons, then, Wise could not seriously entertain the possibility of Brown's insanity. But Wise's affirmation that Brown was sane, even "remarkably sane," would have been more convincing to his critics had he renounced his bid for the Democratic nomination for president.[49]

Wise's response to his political dilemma was thus twofold. He denied that he had the power to save Brown, and, rejecting the charge that he was intimidated by the demands of Virginians' for "vengeance," he blamed the public demands of "fanatical abolitionists" and "Black Republicans" for his refusal to order a sanity trial or otherwise seek clemency for Brown. Brown was sane, Wise insisted, but that was not the issue. Rather, the issue was the growth of inflammatory abolitionist sentiment in the North, which countenanced, even applauded, Brown's lawlessness. "The very sympathy with John Brown, so general, so fanatical, so regardless of social safety, and so irreverent of the reign of law," Wise wrote a Massachusetts minister who had appealed for Brown's life, "demands his execution, if sentenced by the courts." Yet, Wise added, the same Virginia laws that Brown had "insulted and outraged are now protecting all his rights of defence and all his claims to mercy."[50]

The political cost of this hard line for Wise was disfavor in the North. Supporters like Wood, who had long championed Wise for the Democratic presidential nomination, were especially disappointed. Wood had urged Wise repeatedly to avoid taking public positions on issues that might divide his support within the party.[51] The two men had also discussed political strategy frequently and candidly. In March 1859, pledging to "volunteer no opinion" against the Buchanan administration's controversial policies, Wise told Wood that his son Jennings would consult with him a week hence in New York about "our politics." "You can't offend me by friendly counsel," Wise chided in September, "but I am very apt to follow my own after all— That infirmity I cant [sic] help."[52]

Brown's raid the following month put the alliance between Wise and Wood to the test. When Brown seized Harpers Ferry, Wood was in the midst of a tough, but ultimately successful, campaign to regain the mayor's office in New York. Running as a pro-Southern candidate, he tarred his Republican opponent with Brown, the "bastard" of the "demagogue," William Seward. Wood feared Wise would execute Brown and thus create a martyr, even for the most "ultra" Northern friends of the South—which would, of course, jeopardize Wood's own election effort.[53] Hence, Wise's rejection of his advice to spare Brown convinced Wood that Wise was finished as a national figure. But in January, six weeks after Brown's execution, Wise was still "more than ever hopeful" that the Southern states would join Virginia in supporting his nomination.[54]

The Politics of Pardons

On December 5, three days after Brown's death, Wise attempted once more to straddle the clemency issue. First, he asserted his readiness to intervene, if so directed, to save the lives of Brown's loyal volunteers. In his last regular address to the Virginia Legislature, he stated: "By our laws, the plea of insanity could avail at any time, in any stage of trial, and after conviction, before sentence of the court." Even after convicts were "turned over to the executioner, the executive authority could forefend the law's sentence upon the insane." Wise insisted that if any of Brown's men then awaiting execution could "show or prove insanity . . . he could not be executed as long as I am the Governor of the Commonwealth, until cured in an asylum; and, if insane at the time of committing the offence, he could not be executed, cured or not cured, at all." Once again, Wise claimed to be ready to battle the spirit of vengeance.

At the same time, he expressed contempt for the "hypocritical cant" of those who recommended the insanity plea that Brown himself had spurned. Brown's men were not insane either. "It is a mockery to call them monomaniacs," Wise said of Brown's young followers, four of whom were to be hanged on December 16. "These men needed no mental cure," he declared—as if they were already dead. "Theirs was a malady of devils, which no power but divine could cast out." They therefore deserved no sympathy. "They were deliberate, cunning, malignant malefactors, desperately bent on mischief, with malice aforethought, gangrened by sectional and social habitual hatred to us and ours." And as usual Wise had harsh words for abolitionists: "Many of those who now plead their insanity for them put Sharpe's rifles in their hands . . . and trusted their wits for war in Kansas." He nonetheless reminded legislators they could yet intervene, telling them that his own actions "in respect to reprieve, pardon, or commutation of punishment" would be guided "by your resolves."[55] Thus, if Wise himself had any intention to pardon or commute the sentences of any of

Brown's men, it was not evident in anything he said at the time. Like their leader, none of the six raiders in the Charlestown jail in fact sought clemency on grounds of insanity. All the same, the question of pardoning one or another of them plagued Wise in his last weeks in office.

For reasons of expediency, Wise had twice considered turning one of Brown's men, Aaron Dwight Stevens, over to the federal courts. A handsome, athletic veteran of the Mexican War who had been court martialed and convicted of mutiny in 1855 for "engaging in drunken riot" and assaulting an officer, Stevens had escaped from Fort Leavenworth and later joined free-state forces in Kansas, where he met Brown. At Harpers Ferry, Stevens had been gravely wounded in the neck and head while carrying what Brown later insisted was a flag of truce. On October 22 Wise's personal representative on the prosecutorial staff, Andrew Hunter, warned Wise that Stevens "will probably die of his wounds if we don't hang him promptly." On November 6 Wise had wired Hunter: "As it may seem too severe for fair trial to put Stevens at bar let him be turned over" to federal authorities, and a day later he again telegraphed Hunter: "You had better try [John E.] Cook and turn Stevens over to U.S. Court— Do that definitively." The next day Hunter startled his fellow prosecutor, Charles B. Harding, as well as the court, then impaneling jurors for Stevens's trial, by announcing Wise's decision. Trying Stevens in federal court, Hunter explained, would enable the government to subpoena "the prominent abolition fanatics in the North" who were behind Brown's movement. Over the protests of Harding, who insisted he was not "in league with Gov. Wise or any one else," and with the consent of the astonished prisoner and his counsel, the jury was dismissed and Stevens sent back to his cell.[56]

A month later, however, Wise switched course again. By then Stevens had recovered, but he had also become a "cause"—especially, it was said, among women. A romantic figure who entertained visitors with his "much admired" singing voice, Stevens was still in the Charlestown jail. With the circuit court of Jefferson County then in recess, Wise had a resolution introduced in the lower house of the state legislature directing the Committee on Courts of Justice to authorize the court to try in "a special term, any prisoner charged with felony, who may have had a previous examination." The delegate from Spottsylvania County explained that the purpose of the resolution was to ensure the trial of Stevens in a Virginia court. The expressed reason for a federal trial had been to establish the complicity of "prominent men" in the Northern states in the Harpers Ferry "affair"; but that end would now be satisfied by an investigation by the United States Senate that had been authorized on December 14 and was to be chaired by Wise's political ally, Senator James M. Mason of Virginia. Privately, though, Wise had given a different reason for trying Stevens in a state court. "I say definitively," he wrote Hunter, "that Stevens ought *not* to be handed over to the Federal authorities for trial. He is the deepest felon in guilt of all. I hope you informed the President exactly of the status of his case before the court. I am convinced that there is a political design in trying now to have him tried before the federal courts. He will not be delivered up with my consent."[57]

Wise was equally unmoved by the pleas that he or his office endorse clemency for any of the prisoners before legislative committees looking into the matter. John E. Cook, a twenty-nine-year-old man from a well-to-do Connecticut family, seemed as likely a candidate for clemency as any of the captives. Brown had dispatched Cook to Harpers Ferry more than a year before to lay the groundwork for the raid, and the young man had found work there as a lock tender on the Chesapeake & Ohio Canal, then as a schoolteacher, and finally as a bookseller. He even married a local woman. When Andrew Hunter agreed, despite his cocounsel's outspoken objection, to drop the treason count from Cook's indictment and to permit testimony that "the romance in his nature" had led him astray, some observers thought that Wise was preparing to pardon Cook.[58] But Hunter's concession was a false signal. Neither the tears of Cook's sisters nor the eloquence of his attorneys moved Wise: Cook's contrition and his "confession" notwithstanding, his indictment remained in effect.

Indeed, Wise, ever the chivalrous Virginian, was offended that Cook had given the authorities descriptions of the raiders who had escaped and had identified Albert Hazlett, who had been using an assumed name when he had been extradited to Virginia from Pennsylvania. Such betrayal was neither honorable nor manly. The *Richmond Enquirer* complained of a campaign in Northern newspapers to save Cook that was greater even than the efforts made for Brown. But Wise's pardon could not be "bought" by political favors or "extorted by personal threats." Wise would act if a pardon were deserved, the *Enquirer* insisted, "though opposed by every paper in the broad limits of our country." Although Wise had privately held Stevens to be the "deepest felon," Cook was now *"the most guilty of all the Charlestown prisoners."* He was far from being a mere dupe of Old Brown, the *Enquirer* claimed; indeed, matters were quite the reverse: "Ossawattomie is the victim of John E. Cook." Had Cook not deceived Brown into thinking the slaves were thirsting for revolt, the shrewd old warrior would have "abandoned the undertaking." Thus Cook, not Brown, was the greater villain.[59]

In the case of Edwin Coppoc, the adopted son of Quaker parents residing in Springdale, Iowa, Wise took a different stance. Coppoc had not fought in Kansas and had been an exemplary prisoner, daily poring over his Bible and saying little to visitors. A letter to his parents, published initially in the Davenport, Iowa, *Gazette*, drew attention to his plight. "I have seen my folly too late," he wrote. "I am condemned and must die a dishonorable death among my enemies, and hundreds of miles away from my home." He insisted that "we were compelled to fight to save our own lives," but "no one fell by my hand." Indeed, Coppoc told his mother, a nonresistant abolitionist, he was "sorry to say that I was ever induced to raise a gun." He beseeched a family friend to come to Charlestown to see him before his execution, promising to pay the friend's travel expenses from the sale of property Coppoc owned in Iowa.[60] After Brown's execution, Coppoc sent his condolences to Mary Brown and his "sisters" Annie Brown and Martha Brewster Brown, who had kept house for the raiders at the Kennedy farmhouse in Maryland. As Watson Brown had lain dying, Coppoc wrote Mary consolingly, "I . . . held his head in my lap." Unhappily, in both letters Coppoc referred to the residents of Harpers Ferry as the "enemy," a choice of words widely noticed in Virginia.[61]

On Monday, December 12, a delegation of three Quakers from Iowa, responding to Coppoc's appeal, filed a petition in the Virginia State Senate asking that his sentence be commuted to "confinement in the Penitentiary." They held a vigil in the Senate lobby. A senator called upon Governor Wise, thus forcing him to take a public position on Coppoc. Wise was sympathetic. He said that mitigating circumstances entitled the Quaker memorial to "the serious consideration of the General Assembly," noting that Coppoc had been orphaned at age six and that, as his guardians had testified, he had been a praiseworthy youth before leaving home the previous August. The three Quakers visited with the condemned man on Wednesday, two days before the executions, and spoke of him as a "quiet and inoffensive youth." But their appeals, which were roundly rejected by the Virginia Legislature, failed to save Coppoc, and he died with "manly firmness" beside his comrades as scheduled. Although Wise's appearance before the Committee on Courts of Justice won praise from Northern newspapers, Virginia politicians counted it a mistake.[62] Wise's favorable comments about Coppoc also prompted three black petitioners to ask the governor to "commute the sentence" of the two black prisoners, Shields Green and John A. Copeland. The petitioners received no reply, and despite their request for the bodies of the two men, together with a plea from Copeland's father, the bodies of the black raiders became the property of Winchester Medical College.[63]

In the end, then, Wise saved none of the prisoners. In his final address to the Legislature on December 5, he once again coupled an assertion of his theoretical willingness to act with reasons why he would or could not. In fact, his damning remarks about Brown's young followers had scarcely invited legislative intervention: his appeal for Edwin Coppoc was the single concession he made to conservatives in the North. Since he had refused to consider the affidavits attesting to Brown's insanity or to consult Stribling about Brown, and had privately pledged to Hunter that he would hang all the prisoners, why had he raised the hopes of the prisoners' friends? Why acknowledge his power, albeit qualified, to reprieve, pardon, or commute sentence, thereby deepening the resentment of those who urged clemency for the Old Man or were still trying to save Brown's volunteers?

A Populist Salvation

Wise's actions in the Harpers Ferry crisis have long puzzled scholars. Eminent Civil War historians like Allan Nevins, echoing Wise's contemporary critics, have deplored his attitude, charging that he unwisely inflamed public fears and fostered extremism both North and South. Above all, Nevins insisted, Wise should have pardoned Brown and thus denied him martyrdom. While acknowledging Wise to be brilliant and scholarly, Nevins dismissed him as an unprincipled political opportunist. Even sympathetic biographers have labeled him "wilful," "imperious" and moody, an "impulsive" and "erratic" politician, and a vain man who "rioted in the eccentricity of his genius."[64] But these assessments omit to credit his political instincts. He fits no familiar mold. Born into the gentry, he was a planter who disdained the conventions of aristocratic life. A "progressive" in his early support of public education and universal white male suffrage, he nonetheless identified himself as a conservative. A political maverick who had switched parties twice, he derailed the Know-Nothing movement in Virginia with his election as governor in 1855. Despite his opposition to the proslavery Lecompton Constitution for Kansas and his earlier support for Whiggish internal improvements, he was a "good Southerner," who eventually endorsed secession and fought for the Confederacy.[65]

Wise's critics have failed to grasp his political dilemma after Harpers Ferry and to factor the politics of insanity into his conduct during his last months in office. The hysteria created by John Brown's raid challenged Wise's skills as a popular leader. In fact, Wise was a new kind of politician in Virginia, obeying the imperatives of a democratic politics, voicing the feelings of a new majority. The revised constitution of 1852 not only provided for the popular election of the executive, hitherto chosen by the legislature, but greatly broadened the franchise, creating new voters especially in the underrepresented western counties. Wise himself had fought for these reforms at the convention of 1850–51, thus expanding his own following in the western counties of the Old Dominion. His casual dress and careless conversation, which was peppered with expletives, won favor among these new voters, and his flamboyant and emotional speaking style, despised by some traditional politicians, enthralled popular audiences. He had long predicted a Northern assault upon the Old Dominion and promised to repel it.[66] Vindicated at last by Brown's "invasion," he could not ignore that "challenge" or the opportunity to demonstrate his leadership. Even if he had abandoned his quest for the presidency and acted with the "magnanimity" that many petitioners pleaded for, Wise would have had to renounce as well his effort to represent the wishes of common Virginians if he championed Brown's case in the Legislature. In defending Virginia's honor, he was articulating values he shared not only with Virginians but with self-respecting whites throughout the South.[67]

But even after Brown's execution, Wise could not escape the dilemma created by his ambition for the presidency. He could not ignore the impending executions of Brown's youthful followers and the clamor in the North for clemency. Nor could he afford to deny responsibility for their fate. In the struggle for control of the Virginia delegation to the Democratic National Convention in Charlestown, Wise's leading opponent, Robert Hunter, enjoyed strong support within the party.[68] Wise was counting on his popularity among the common people to gain the party's endorsement—but to salvage that popularity and secure his delegation's support, he had to be in charge. Indeed, if he were to represent the interests of the South in the larger contest with Stephen A. Douglas for the nomination, he had to be heroic—to champion Southern rights. This had been his posture from the outset. When federal authorities sought custody of Brown and his men, Wise had boasted that the federal government could have "what was left of them" after Virginia finished with them. His extravagant military displays, so widely ridiculed in the North, were appeals to Virginians' shared admiration for martial virtues. When Brown's correspondence with public men like Ohio Congressman Joshua Giddings and former New York Congressman Gerrit Smith fell into Wise's hands, he and his confidants quickly decided to link the so-called invasion to the Republican opposition and to picture "Osawatomie Brown" as the inevitable consequence of "popular sovereignty."[69] The governor's crony, Senator James M. Mason, who had huddled with Wise at Harpers Ferry, promptly introduced a resolution in the Senate that launched his six-month investigation of the "invasion" and its supporters. In short, every effort of the Republicans to dismiss Brown as a madman or the raid as a witless or merely criminal act had to be refuted.

Thus, to the end the governor affirmed Brown's sanity in part because his case against the abolitionists and Democratic moderates required a sane and formidable abolitionist enemy. In a sense, Wise had entered into a tacit collaboration with his adversary. Together, but for different reasons, they maintained the fictions of Brown's importance as a military threat to the South and as the agent of a widespread conspiracy at the North. What Wise failed to acknowledge was that his own testimony to Brown's good character would greatly enhance the martyr's significance as a moral symbol in the North.

A Troubled Alliance

The lynchpin of the politics of insanity was thus the curious relationship between Wise and Brown. Some writers have argued that Wise's endorsement of Brown's truthfulness and sincerity was based on an affinity between the two men. Although this presumed relationship had to be based on very limited contacts between the two, it contains an element of truth. Wise apparently respected Brown's word as a gentleman and stood in awe of his audacity. Both men, moreover, honored the code of the warrior and respected the traditions of chivalry in the treatment of a fallen adversary.[70] As Andrew Hunter put it in his testimony to the Mason Committee: "I was struck with the respect and courtesy they mutually had for each other. Brown was impressed with a high regard for Governor Wise, and the governor with an estimate of him, in which I at first participated."[71] In a thoughtful study of the relationship between Wise and Brown, Craig Simpson has suggested that Wise may have seen qualities in Brown that he "desired to emulate" and that Brown shook the Virginian's troubled convictions about the morality of slavery. Simpson speculates that Wise respected Brown's wisdom in planning to place white officers over the liberated slaves in his army and in providing the latter with pikes rather than firearms. Wise recognized the dangers of disaffection among nonslaveholding whites in the area from whom Brown expected support. In short, the governor could respect his adversary's shrewdness and commitment.[72]

But in the end, of course, the two could not be friends. Wise himself sharply qualified his praise for Brown when he referred to the Old Man and his men as "murderers, traitors, robbers, insurrectionists" and "wanton, malicious, unprovoked felons."[73] In fact, during the weeks after the raid Wise saw Brown only once, and his purpose in that visit was to ask the prisoner to repudiate statements he had made in court. Although the two used each other to reach wider audiences, their perceptions of a just society and the dictates of conscience were fundamentally opposed. Brown condemned slavery as the "mother of all evils" and the slave codes as "wicked enactments" that denied the slaves' humanity; Wise despised Brown's fanaticism and lawlessness. He was going to hang Brown, and the Old Man knew it.

As we have seen, both men wished to picture the raid as a formidable assault upon the peculiar institution. But their reasons for doing so differed. Each had a stake in how the Harpers Ferry "affair" was perceived beyond the courtroom, where Brown played his role and received his sentence. Brown strove to be seen as a man of faith and pure motives, and he wanted a pulpit from which to condemn slavery. Wise desired Brown to be a convincing insurrectionist and to picture the Old Man's attack as the inevitable consequence of failed policies of moderation. So long as Brown remained faithful to the testimony he had given to Wise and Hunter at Harpers Ferry, Wise was prepared to endorse Brown's sanity and truthfulness. In other words, whether or not the governor felt genuine respect for his adversary, his public affirmation of Brown's veracity was essentially expedient. As Simpson himself has observed, Wise's "eulogies" of Brown "were always made in the context of denying his insanity."[74]

In two important respects, the relationship between Wise and Brown has been misunderstood. First, it was, as I have suggested, contractual and opportunistic, a response in part to the prompt declaration of many Northern newspapers and public figures that Old Brown was mad. Second, it was predicated on a selective perception of what Brown said to Wise at Harpers Ferry. In fact, the two men talked past each other: neither was capable of bridging the cultural gap that had brought them into conflict. Thus, at the heart of the politics of insanity was a curious denial—a blindness to reality— that the two antagonists shared. For in their lengthy meeting after the raid, Brown betrayed what Wise might in other circumstances have seen as signs of mental disorder. Had Wise not been seeking the presidency, he might have chosen to quiet public fears by writing Brown off as a madman and minimizing his threat to civil order. But Virginians were calling for retribution, and Wise therefore needed a man to hang, however strange Brown may have seemed.

If after the raid the prisoner's mind was "clear," "quick," and "remarkably sane," as Wise claimed, Brown must have had extraordinary stamina. He had begun his attack late Sunday evening and was engaged in fighting all Monday afternoon. Robert E. Lee's storming party of marines didn't overwhelm Brown's position in the fire-engine house until about 7:30 A.M. Tuesday. Failing to dispatch the Old Man with a powerful thrust of his light dress sword to the abdomen, the leader of the assault team, Marine Lieutenant Israel Green, had knocked his adversary unconscious by repeated blows with the haft or hilt of his weapon. Brown lost considerable blood before his wounds were dressed, but he regained consciousness soon after he was dragged from the engine house and stretched out upon the grass. There despite a menacing mob of angry and undisciplined volunteers eager t avenge the deaths of the five citizens shot by the raiders and to puni "insurrectionists," Brown promptly began to talk to newsmen. Five ho later, Wise reached the scene to find the Old Man still alert and talkative then Brown had not slept or eaten for more than forty-eight hours. A fifty-nine, Brown exhibited an energy that both contemporaries and historians have acknowledged to be remarkable.[75]

Wise was more impressed with Brown than were others present at the October 18 interview following the raid. Robert E. Lee dismissed Brown as a "fanatic or madman," and J. E. B. Stuart thought Brown was shamming serious injuries to gain sympathy.[76] Even Wise's confidant, Andrew Hunter, soon viewed Brown with skepticism. During the interrogation, ample grounds for such doubts appeared. Brown admitted at times that he was confused or that he could not remember things. His "clever evasions" actually implicated others. For a man habitually deliberate of speech and by his own assessment awkward in expressing himself, he spoke "freely, fluently, and cheerfully, without the slightest manifestation of fear or uneasiness," according to a reporter from the conservative *New York Herald*.[77]

Although one of his sons and eight other young comrades lay dead outside the paymaster's office, and another son was dying, Brown seemed elated and evinced undisguised pride in his failed expedition. He responded to questions about whether he had more men under his command than those captured or killed at the Ferry by stating that he expected reinforcements (black and white) from a number of neighboring Southern states, as well as Canada.[78] As Hunter testified on January 13 before the Mason Committee, Brown had been alert and talkative throughout the rambling interview. "I can hardly describe his manner," Hunter told the committee. "It struck me at the time as very singular that he should so freely enter into his plans immediately. He seemed very fond of talking." Even Wise admitted that Brown was "vain and garrulous." Brown had proudly asked the governor to read the lengthy articles of his constitution for a "Provisional Government," the terms of which, from Hunter's perspective, implicated Brown irrevocably in treason. Even though he declined to answer some questions, Brown had literally handed his captors a case against himself. Wise soon asked Hunter to make notes of Brown's responses. When the prisoner was asked how many supporters he had expected to aid him in freeing the slaves, Hunter told Chairman Mason, the Old Man "quite as promptly, and clearly, and distinctly replied . . . three thousand or five thousand, if he wanted them. There was a pause there. I was struck by the reply, and I thought it was about to lead to some very important developments." At this point, Brown's loyal young officer, Aaron Stevens, who was lying wounded beside Brown, "interposed and remarked he [Brown] was not sure of any aid, but he only expected it; 'you do not understand him.'" Brown then amended his remarks. "Yes, I merely expected it; I was not certain of any support," he admitted but went on to explain that he was anticipating assistance from "all quarters."[79]

Wise might have been given pause by such remarks. His own newspaper reported similar boasts. Brown told reporters, for example, that had he succeeded at Harpers Ferry, he "contemplated the capture of Washington, the seizure of the Federal Government, and the imprisonment of the President and his Cabinet." During the raid, Brown claimed: "I can have five thousand men here in less than twenty four hours at my call."[80] Such reports might be considered hearsay, of course. But the testimony of the Ohio affiants contained evidence of the same kind of grandiose claims that Brown made at his October 18 interrogation. Affiant James W. Weld swore Brown had stated to him that he "wanted a hundred men to march to Kansas . . . that the men were ready; he only wanted money to equip them and support them." When Weld expressed doubts about taking military action against slavery, Brown "replied that with a hundred men he could free Kansas and Missouri too, and could then march to Washington and turn the President and his Cabinet out of doors." In this long conversation, Weld reported, Brown had "seemed unable to think of anything else."[81]

We know today that such inflated claims were not plausible. Not only had it taken Brown two years to assemble a force of twenty-one men, but only a handful of others were ready to join his band, even if he had waited longer to commence actions. To be sure, many whites in the western part of Virginia disliked slavery, and enclaves of Northern settlers lived near Harpers Ferry. But in all the time that his spy, John Cook, had lived at Harpers Ferry, the youth had found no recruits, black or white. Brown himself, moreover, had told Cook not to alert the slaves generally for fear of betraying the movement before Brown could strike. The Old Man thus had no rational grounds for such extravagant claims of support. Of course, Wise did not know that on October 18. Perhaps he suspected that Brown's armies of abolitionists were mere phantoms, conjured up by bravado. But it served his political purpose to give credence to such stories and to the wild rumors of plots and rescue attempts that justified his display of force.

Both he and Hunter, however, soon realized that Brown was confused about the fundamental purpose of his raid. Brown could not say precisely what he would have done if slaves had flocked to his standard. He gave incomplete and conflicting statements about his plan. At the interrogation after his capture, he said he had intended to arm "liberated" slaves to allow them to defend themselves. That was what Wise and other officials expected to hear—and that was all they heard. But the Old Man said something more. When Ohio Congressman Clement Vallandigham asked Brown whether he expected a general rising of the slaves on his account, Brown replied vaguely: "No, sir; nor did I wish it; I expected to gather them up from time to time and set them free."[82] That point is crucial, because the Virginia authorities convicted Brown of inciting slaves to insurrection. Had he hoped merely to send them North, the Virginians' case for "servile war" would have been shaken.

They saw no middle ground between "running slaves off" and a bloody uprising. To Brown, though, it seemed perfectly consistent to suggest that he did not intend large-scale violence, despite the hundreds of rifles and revolvers he stole from the arsenal or brought from Kansas and the thousand pikes he had specially manufactured for the slaves. If he remained in the field for a long campaign, as he had in Kansas, the weapons might presumably have been doled out in small numbers over time.

Ironically, he dramatized this problem of conflicting perceptions and captured sympathetic Northern audiences in a moving courtroom speech, heralded by abolitionists as a classic statement of the antislavery creed. Asked by Judge Parker on November 2 if he wished to speak before his sentence was pronounced, Brown responded by denying that he was guilty of the crimes of which he had been convicted—treason, murder, and conspiracy to incite an insurrection—avowing that his only purpose was to free the slaves. "I intended certainly to have made a clean thing of that matter, as I did last winter when I went into Missouri, and there took slaves without the snapping of a gun on either side, moving them through the country, and finally leaving them in Canada. I designed to have done the same thing again on a larger scale," he told the court. "That was all I intended to do."[83]

Scholarly apologists of Wise have long pronounced the speech deceitful and dishonorable. Brown's statement was not an outright lie, as Robert Penn Warren later charged.[84] The speech, moreover, did not in Brown's view contradict his earlier statements. The key words of the testimony he gave during his initial interrogation were "from time to time." Brown supposed all along he would be conducting operations in Virginia for an extended period. At one time he had called the Virginia scheme a "subterranean pass way."[85] Just months before the raid, John Brown, Jr., acting on his father's instructions, had scouted out the region near the Virginia/Maryland border with Pennsylvania for loyal abolitionist conductors and safe houses in which to conceal slaves the raiders would be sending to freedom. Brown's men assumed that all they would be doing was raiding plantations and running slaves up North: they were shocked when Brown announced that he intended to attack Harpers Ferry and seize the arsenal and armory.[86] That was a substantial change in plans, although it did not preclude the sort of further action the men expected. Moving swiftly to evade pursuers, the Provisional Army would harass plantations and perhaps skirmish with patrols but avoid a general engagement.[87]

For their part, Virginians were scandalized at Brown's speech. Andrew Hunter told the Mason Committee he was "greatly surprised" at Brown's claim that "his sole purpose in coming to Virginia was to run off slaves. . . . I was immediately struck by the palpable inconsistency between that statement and what he had communicated to Governor Wise and myself at

Harper's Ferry, just after his capture." At the interrogation, Hunter said, Brown had "promptly and distinctly" declared that he did not intend to "stampede slaves off." On the contrary, "he designed to put arms in their hands to defend themselves against their masters, and to maintain their position in Virginia and the South," Hunter said. "As soon as he got a footing there, at Harper's Ferry, and as his strength increased, he would gradually enlarge the area under his control, furnishing a refuge for the slaves, and a rendezvous for all the whites . . . disposed to aid him, until eventually he overrun [*sic*] the whole South."[88] Clearly, Hunter had inferred much from Brown's brief responses: his imagination had supplied the pattern of events that Brown had neglected to detail in his long October 18 interview with Wise and other officials.

If believed by the public, Brown's apparent repudiation of any intent to inspire insurrection and his claim that he meant only to "run off" slaves threatened to cut the ground out from under Wise's public position. Since the governor had pictured Brown as a menacing yet truthful adversary, his own credibility might be damaged if Brown renounced his earlier statements convincingly—or so Wise feared. Thus in a sense Wise was hostage to the man he would hang. Tacitly, the quid pro quo for Wise's public praise of Brown was Brown's standing by his boast that he would have armed the slaves to defend themselves. To Virginians this was equivalent to an admission that Brown had planned an insurrection. In political terms, the most fundamental crime for which Wise and Hunter tried Brown was conspiracy to incite the slaves to rebel. When Brown seemed to repudiate that charge in his courtroom speech, the implicit contract between Wise and Brown was broken.

Hunter pointed out the "contradiction" to Wise. From the perspective of Wise and Hunter, Brown had renounced his earlier out-of-court position, and Wise accordingly went to see Brown in the Charlestown jail to demand an explanation of the contradiction between his statements. Brown assured the governor that he had not changed his view. After this brief interview, Brown sent Hunter a short letter explaining the apparent "confliction" between his statements. Although this satisfied Hunter that the Old Man had returned to "the ground he occupied originally," Brown later sent his jailor to bring Hunter to his cell so that he could explain the seeming inconsistency further. He also urged Hunter to "vindicate his memory" by publishing the statement.[89]

What Brown actually said in his letter was that his statements "respecting the slaves we took *about the Ferry*" were not really in conflict. Brown "had given Governor Wise a *full and particular* account" after the raid, but in court, surprised to receive sentence before the other defendants, he had forgotten much that he had intended to say and did not weigh his words carefully. "It was my object to place the slaves in a condition to defend their liberties, if they would *without any bloodshed, but not* that I intended *to run them out of the slaves States,*" he wrote. According to Brown, he had not been aware of any inconsistency in his statements until Wise came to see him. Now he pleaded that "a man in my then circumstances should not be expected to be *superhuman* in respect to the *exact purport* of every word he might utter." He was eager to salvage Wise's high opinion of him; his veracity must therefore not be questioned. "What I said to Governor Wise was spoken with all the deliberation I was master of, *and was intended for truth;* and what I said in court was *equally intended for truth,* but required a more full explanation *than I then gave,*" he explained.[90] Wise and Hunter were satisfied: Brown had restored the contract. But his letter to Hunter was not his last word on the subject.

Brown had given the Virginians what they required. In return, he wanted Wise to reaffirm his earlier praise of his prisoner. In a letter written just three days after his note to Hunter and obviously intended for publication, Brown tried to put pressure on Wise to meet his end of their unstated bargain. Writing to his cousin, the Reverend Heman Humphrey, a former president of Amherst College, Brown declared that he wished to correct mistaken newspaper reports "that I told Governor Wise that I came here to seek revenge for the wrongs of either myself or my family." The statement was "utterly false." "I never intended to convey such an idea, and I bless God that I am able even now to say that I have never yet harbored such a feeling." He urged Humphrey to examine the testimony of witnesses at his trial "who were with me while I had one son lying dead by my side, and another mortally wounded and lying on my other side." He had not taken revenge on his helpless hostages. "I do not believe that Governor Wise so understood," Brown said pointedly, "and I think he ought to correct that impression." Then he added: "The impression that we intended a general insurrection is equally untrue."[91]

In the context of this dialogue-at-a-distance, Brown's well-known final "prophecy" takes on a new meaning. On December 2, as the Old Man stood on the porch of the Charlestown jail observing hundreds of marching soldiers in the streets, his only escort to the scaffold, he remarked: "I had no idea that Governor Wise considered my execution so important." Then he gave a handwritten, two-line statement to a bystander. The first line read: "I John Brown am now quite *certain* that the crimes of this *guilty, land: will* never be purged *away;* but with Blood." But for whom were these remorseless words intended? Oswald Garrison Villard, Brown's first scholarly biographer, implicitly assumed that Brown spoke to the North. He concluded that this embryonic jeremiad was a "final, wonderfully prophetic and imperishable message to the 'million hearts' of his countrymen which, as

Wendell Phillips said, 'had been melted by that old Puritan soul.'" In this interpretation Villard betrayed both his admiration for Brown and his kinship to his abolitionist grandfather, William Lloyd Garrison. But the prophecy may also be read as a reassertion of the warning regarding slavery's impending destruction that Brown had given Wise on October 18.

The second line read: "I had *as I now think: vainly* flattered myself without *very much* bloodshed; it might be done."[92] That sentence dampened the force of the prophecy: it seemed anticlimactic, an afterthought. Yet it is equally important, for it captured the ambiguity of Brown's case against his captors. It may even have been a final effort to explain that he had not intended insurrection but something less terrifying. Arguably, that second sentence conveyed Brown's claim to be innocent of insurrection and his paradoxical belief that the blood of whites had to be spent for the suffering of blacks.[93] It appealed to his still unexplained contention that the violence he unleashed in Virginia might somehow have been limited, discriminating, just. In suggesting that he had "vainly flattered" himself in so thinking, Brown echoed the style of Protestant piety so conspicuous in his prison letters to friends in the North. Yet his prophecy also reflected a mood different from the expansiveness and braggadocio of October. It implied regret that Brown had been mistaken about his own powers. But it was not an admission that he erred morally in what he set out to do. He had claimed to be God's agent to free the slaves and to save his "guilty land" from the punishment it would receive in full measure. If he had not freed the slaves, he suggested that their emancipation was nonetheless inevitable.

Thus Brown's collaboration with Wise had its limits. Neither man repudiated his early assessment of the other, but their tacit collaboration was based on false understandings. On some level of imagination, Brown was unable to think through his purpose at Harpers Ferry. More important, perhaps, Wise had failed to see Brown's grandiosity—either because Brown's wild claims that thousands of men might follow him to Virginia fed Wise's own sense of peril and were congruent with his expectations or simply because he was determined to find vindication for his own warnings about the dangers of Northern abolitionism and Douglas's "popular sovereignty." Brown may have suffered from a mood disorder that nourished his belief in impending calamity, as I have suggested. But Wise's vision was also apocalyptic. To him the Southern nightmare played out at Harpers Ferry confirmed the South's darkest fantasies about militant abolitionists and about the foreshadowing in Kansas of direct attacks upon the South. If Brown prophesied civil war, Wise offered only the slimmest hope of saving the Union. Ultimately, the deepest affinity between Brown and Wise was not their prideful sense of honor. It was their common appeal to images of destruction.

A False Logic

The question of Brown's mental state still bedevils us. Echoes of the politics of insanity resonate in the literature of the coming of the Civil War. As Oswald Garrison Villard observed: "If it could be roundly declared that he was partially or wholly deranged, it would be easy to explain away those of his acts which at times baffle an interpreter of this remarkable personality." But historians of the "needless war" school, who argue that the war was the result of chance, political bungling, and hysteria whipped up by abolitionists and fire-eaters, have done just that. "John Brown's raid, so malign in its effect on opinion, North and South, might justly be termed an accident," wrote Allan Nevins in 1953. "Nothing in the logic of forces or events required so crazy an act." Even scholars more friendly to Brown accept the same implicit logic. If John Brown's assault on Harpers Ferry was "the private product of his own disordered mind," Richard O. Boyer has noted, then it had "no political context, no social background. . . . If Brown was insane, he was not representative of anyone but himself." In denying Brown's insanity, Boyer restores his hero to the logic of forces from which Nevins would banish him. To "deprive" him of that "poetic drive which turned his days into significant drama is to rob him . . . of that deep dynamic communion where he conversed with himself and eternity and united . . . with all men and all history."[94] Only a sane Brown belonged in history.

An implicit premise of this dialectic seems to be that the madman stands outside the pattern of events. The sources of his conduct lie primarily within his own tormented mind—in the microstructure of cognition, perhaps, where some organic impairment or biochemical imbalance dictates the course of his aberrant behavior. Perhaps this sense of his isolation reflects the actual social segregation of the insane that Western society has imposed in varying ways for centuries, as well as the fear, revulsion, and shame of finding madness in one's own family.[95]

But the politics of insanity reflected in recent historical writing neglects a subtle nexus between society and the mentally ill. Although the idea of mental illness is evidently common in every society, popular responses to the "insane" vary widely. The forms of mental illness are at least in part socially defined, and the content of the delusions of mental patients is culturally determined. If Brown's contemporaries could not agree whether he was mad, many recognized in him the social type of the "Puritan warrior." Among those who thought him insane, some nonetheless believed him morally right about slavery. They had no difficulty in identifying him as only a "monomaniac"—a person crazy on one subject—because his basic values were recognizably their own. In his war against slavery, he simply went too far for them. As Lincoln said, although Brown "agreed with us in thinking slavery wrong, that cannot excuse violence, bloodshed and treason."[96] We know today that people suffering from mood disorders may, when "high," accomplish creative work and even win acclaim as leaders.[97] As Melville said of his fictional monomaniac, "Ahab, to that one end, did now possess a thousand fold more potency than ever he had sanely brought to bear upon any one reasonable object."[98] If the mercurial moodswings of Old Osawatomie Brown helped to bring him to Harpers Ferry, to his contemporaries his alleged monomania did not, in the end, invalidate his commitment to his cause or trivialize his personal struggle. In part because Governor Wise pictured Brown as an agent of Northern hostility to slavery, in part because of his own genius with words, Brown on the gallows was a potent symbol, North and South.

In the nineteenth century madness was shrouded in mystery. Some common mental disorders had not yet even found a name. John Brown personified a new, controversial kind of "moral insanity," which gave to the debate over his sanity implications beyond its immediate political fallout and its impact on the sectional crisis. In the final analysis, the politics of insanity was part of a process of cultural transformation, blurring older distinctions between madness and reason and domesticating political violence in the republic. In so doing, it helped to shift the streambed of Anglo-American culture toward a new consciousness of the limits of rationality.

Notes

The author wishes to thank Howard Feinstein, who commented on an early version of this paper, and Byrgen and Paul Finkelman, Pamela Holway, Idus Newby, and Rita Roberts for valuable clarifications and suggestions.

1. Asahel H. Lewis, telegram, Oct. 26, 1859, cited in the *Cincinnati Daily Gazette,* Oct. 28, 1859. A useful collection of wire dispatches and stories—without attribution or comment—published within weeks of Brown's execution by Robert M. De Witt of New York City is *The Life, Trial, and Execution of Captain John Brown, Known as Old Brown of "Ossawatomie"* (1859; repr. New York, 1969), pp. 64–65. (Lewis's telegram appears on p. 64.) Lewis was the editor of the *Akron Summit Beacon:* see the article by Howard Wolf in the *Akron Beacon Journal,* May 9, 1930, copy in the Boyd B. Stutler Collection, West Virginia Department of Culture and History, Charleston (hereafter Stutler Collection). Oswald Garrison Villard was mistaken in saying that attorney Lawson Botts surprised his client by reading Lewis's telegram to the court but correct that Brown's attorneys read it to him before the session opened. Hence, Brown had a brief opportunity to consider his reply in court (Villard, *Biography,* pp. 489 and 506–7).

2. The writer, Lewis E. Harvie, was a longtime supporter of Wise's current rival for the Virginia Democracy's endorsement for the Democratic nomination for president in 1860, Senator Robert M. T. Hunter: see Lewis E. Harvie to Robert Mercer Taliaferro Hunter, Oct. 18, 1869, in Charles Henry Ambler, ed., *Correspondence of*

Robert M. T. Hunter, 1826–1876, Twelfth Report of the Historical Manuscripts Commission, in *Annual Report of the American Historical Association for the Year 1916,* 2 vols. (Washington, D.C., 1918), 2:272–73.

3. In his classic analysis of the response to Harpers Ferry, C. Vann Woodward urges scholars "not to blink" at Brown's "close association with insanity." But his own assessment stops short of making a judgment: see Woodward, "Private War," esp. pp. 46–48 and 57–60.

4. Governor Wise's biographer, Craig Simpson, claims that Brown "inspired" Wise to "assist in the creation of his legend" by convincing Wise of his sanity. Simpson explains Wise's qualified public tributes to his enemy as in part a measure of respect, empathy, and ambivalence about his own values. See Simpson, *Wise,* pp. 203–14, and "John Brown and Governor Wise: A New Perspective on Harpers Ferry," *Biography* 1 (Fall 1977): 15–38, esp. pp. 17 and 31. Even writers aware of Wise's presidential hopes have failed to take account of the politics of the insanity issue. Allan Nevins, for example, agreed that Wise had quite properly concluded that Brown understood the nature of his acts and thus legally should be hanged. But Nevins, who believed Brown a "paranoiac," said that Wise should nonetheless have acted on expedient grounds and "seized the opportunity of depriving the antislavery fanatic of the martyrdom for which he longed": (Nevins, *Emergence*), 2:93. Simpson notes correctly, however, that had Wise managed to reprieve Brown, he "would still have been uncertain of Yankee support, besides risking the complete collapse of his hopes in the South" (Simpson, *Wise,* p. 26). Clement Eaton criticized Wise for insisting that Brown be tried in a state rather than a federal court, yet Eaton also quotes evidence that Wise's popularity in Virginia rose because of his "dramatic and resolute handling of the John Brown raid." See Clement Eaton, *The Mind of the Old South* (New Orleans, 1967), pp. 100–101.

5. Although Virginia authorities accused the correspondents of some Northern newspapers of sending false reports, wire service reports were generally reliable and were reprinted verbatim in the major papers. Compare the account here, for example, as cited in the Republican Cincinnati *Daily Gazette,* Friday, Oct. 28, 1859, with the text in the conservative *New York Journal of Commerce,* Oct. 28. See also *The Life, Trial and Execution of Captain John Brown,* pp. 64–65.

6. Sylvester H. Thompson to Henry A. Wise, Oct. 31, 1859, Henry A. Wise and Family Papers, Library of Congress; the Reverend Edward Brown to Henry A. Wise, Nov. 5, 1859, in ibid.; E. D. Campbell to Henry A. Wise, Nov. 7, 1859 in ibid. (hereafter Wise and Family Papers).

7. Hiram Griswold to Henry A. Wise, Nov. 7, 1859, quoted in Villard, *Biography,* pp. 507–8. Brown's old friend, Judge Daniel R. Tilden, personally engaged Griswold as Brown's attorney, and, with Brown's half brother, Jeremiah Root Brown, assisted in preparing the affidavits. "Gigantic efforts will be made to show the Virginians that Old Brown is out of his head," a Cleveland newspaper reported (*Cleveland Plain Dealer,* Nov. 23, 1859, copy by Katherine Mayo, Oswald Garrison Villard Collection, Rare Book and Manuscript Library, Butler Library, Columbia University). The nineteen affidavits, together with Chilton's Nov. 21, 1859, letter of transmittal, are in the Wise and Family Papers. For an analysis, see Robert E. McGlone, "The 'Madness' of Old John Brown: The Problem of Psychiatric Diagnosis in History," paper presented at the annual meeting of the American Studies Association, Miami Beach, October 1988.

8. Hoyt copied the petition over, Blair told Governor John A. Andrew, "because Hoyt's hand writing was more legible than mine." As Blair explained to Samuel Chilton of Washington, who served as Brown's cocounsel, he had not appeared in the case himself because "I did not wish to connect the Republican party with

Brown's defense" (Montgomery Blair to John A. Andrew, n.d. [c. Dec. 15, 1859], John Brown Collection, Massachusetts Historical Society, Boston).

9. See the *New York Weekly Tribune*, Nov. 12, 1859. Border-state Republicans, by contrast, condemned Brown's "mad" seizure of the federal armory at Harpers Ferry and denied complicity in the raid: see also the *Cincinnati Daily Gazette*, Friday, Oct. 28, 1859. The Republican *St. Louis Democrat* demanded that Brown and his followers "die the ignominious death of traitors and murderers. And here we would protest against any plea of abatement, on the grounds that 'Old Brown' is not in his right mind. The madness engendered as the spirit of unholy vengeance, is not a mood on which the Spirit of Mercy can look with a benignant eye. Like the drunkenness which culminates in crime, it has but a preliminary stage of that instigation by the devil, which the law itself makes emphatic mention of" (cited in the *New York Journal of Commerce*, Oct. 24, 1859).

10. See the petition addressed to Henry A. Wise, Philadelphia, Nov. 30, 1859, Ferdinand J. Dreer Collection, Historical Society of Pennsylvania, Philadelphia. Writing from a "sense of duty," one old business acquaintance asserted that he had long been "thoroughly convinced" that Brown's "fanciful theory" about the price of wool he had been selling in the East for Ohio growers was evidence enough that Old Brown "was of unsound mind" (Aaron Erickson to Henry A. Wise, Nov. 8, 1859, Wise and Family Papers).

11. Amos A. Lawrence to Henry A. Wise, Oct. 25, 1859, Wise and Family Papers. In recognition of Lawrence's contributions to the free-state cause in Kansas, settlers there named the seat of their government after him—whereas to Wise, Lawrence's appeal might as well have come from Satan himself.

12. See McGlone, "The 'Madness' of Old John Brown." Although many scholars have given weight to Brown's religious convictions, few have recognized how fundamentally he came to believe himself a soldier and that war was his vocation. Brown's most astute modern biographer, Stephen B. Oates, notes Brown's belligerence in Kansas but follows Villard in emphasizing Brown's Calvinist piety (Oates, *Purge*, esp. p. 333).

13. See Isaac Ray, *A Treatise on the Medical Jurisprudence of Insanity*, 3d ed. (Boston, 1853), ch. 1. For the modern period, see Abraham S. Goldstein, *The Insanity Defense* (New Haven, 1967), pp. 59–66.

14. See the M'Naghten case, 10 Clark and Finnelly's Reports, House of Lords, 12 vols., 1831–46 (Great Britain) 200 (1843). A collection of significant cases can be found in John L. Moore, Jr., "M'Naghten Is Dead—Or Is It?" *Houston Law Review* 3 (Spring/Summer 1965): 58–83.

15. Goldstein, *Insanity Defense*, pp. 59–66. Charles Rosenberg observes that the M'Naghten rule was "a purely cognitive test." By 1880 leaders in British and American psychiatry were already arguing that the M'Naghten test was "essentially irrelevant": control, not understanding, was the real issue. See Charles Rosenberg, *The Trial of the Assassin Guiteau: Psychiatry and Law in the Gilded Age* (Chicago, 1968), pp. 54–55. In recent years the "irresistible impulse" rule, acknowledging that mental diseases may impair self-control, has become a supplement to M'Naghten in many states (Goldstein, *Insanity Defense*, pp. 45 and 65–68).

16. On the credibility of the affiants, see McGlone, "The 'Madness' of Old John Brown," pp. 39–44; on the family's illness, pp. 19–38. On Jeremiah's opposition to his half brother's "war," see Florilla Brown Adair to Jeremiah and Abigail Brown, Nov. 8, [1856,] typed copy, Brown-Clark Collection, Hudson Library and Historical Society, Hudson, Ohio; Samuel Lyle Adair to "Dear Brother Jeremiah," March 12, 1857, typed copy, ibid.; Jeremiah Root Brown to "Brother Adair" [the Reverend Samuel Lyle Adair], Aug. 18, 1856, Adair Family Collection, Box 3, Folder 9, Kansas

State Historical Society, Topeka; and McGlone, "The 'Madness' of Old John Brown," pp. 42–44.

17. Quoted in Ruchames, ed., *Reader,* pp. 154–55. A slightly altered version occurs in Sanborn, ed., *Life,* pp. 609–10.

18. "Speech of Governor Wise," *Richmond Enquirer,* Oct. 25, 1859. Three days after Brown's capture, the *Chicago Press and Tribune* claimed that "there is not a public journal of any party, or public man of any shade of opinion found to approve their [the conspirators'] means or justify their ends." Brown was "mad as a March hare." All that mattered was that "the stark mad enterprise was the work of addled brains; that in itself is incontestible evidence of the insanity of its originator; . . . that the purposes of the *emeute* are foreign to Republican policy; that the means chosen . . . are utterly repugnant to Republican sense of right and wrong": *Chicago Press and Tribune,* Oct. 21, 1859, quoted in Richard Warch and Jonathan F. Fanton, eds., *John Brown* (Englewood Cliffs, N.J., 1973), pp. 120–21. See also the December 6 speech of Senator Henry Wilson of Massachusetts, who had publicly clashed with Brown over his raid into Missouri months before Harpers Ferry (quoted in ibid., pp. 128–29). On Wilson's earlier criticism of Brown, see Rossbach, *Conspirators,* p. 205.

19. Under the editorship of Jennings Wise, the *Enquirer* promoted Wise's candidacy assiduously. See, for example, "Shall the Charleston Convention Nominate Henry A. Wise?" *Richmond Enquirer,* Nov. 11, 1859. For a candid public admission of his ambition, see "Speech to Virginia Medical Students at Richmond," ibid., Dec. 26, 1859. On Wise's plan to win the presidency, see Clement Eaton, *The Mind of the Old South,* rev. ed. (Baton Rouge, 1967), pp. 98–99. For Wise's comments on Douglas, see "Governor's Message to the Legislature of Virginia," *Richmond Enquirer,* Dec. 6, 1859.

20. See "Speech of Governor Wise," *Richmond Enquirer,* Oct. 25, 1859; "Governor's Message to the Legislature of Virginia," ibid., Dec. 6, 1859; "Governor's Message to the Legislature of Virginia," ibid., Dec. 6, 1859.

21. Henry A. Wise to Fernando Wood, Nov. 6, 1859, copy in Frank G. Logan Collection, Chicago Historical Society (original in Wise and Family Papers). Copies of numerous threatening letters may be found in the Wise and Family Papers; for a sample, see "Demoniac Letters," *Richmond Enquirer,* Dec. 6, 1859.

22. Henry A. Wise to Andrew Hunter, telegram, Nov. 7, 1859, Josiah P. Quincy Papers, Massachusetts Historical Society, Boston.

23. Henry A. Wise to Andrew Hunter, Esq., Nov. 16, 1859, Massachusetts Historical Society, *Proceedings,* 3d ser., 1 (1907–8), pp. 93–94.

24. Hiram Griswold to Henry A. Wise, Nov. 7, 1859, Wise and Family Papers.

25. Henry A. Wise to Francis T. Stribling, Nov. 10, 1859, typed copy, Stutler Collection.

26. John Brown to "My Dearly beloved Wife, Sons: & Daughters *every one,*" Nov. 30, 1859, quoted in Ruchames, ed. *Reader,* p. 158. For contemporary ideas regarding monomania, see Ray, *Treatise on the Medical Jurisprudence of Insanity,* pp. 162–65.

27. For Ray's argument, see his *Treatise on the Medical Jurisprudence of Insanity,* pp. 170–74. For a discussion of the commonplace uses of the term *monomania,* see McGlone, "The 'Madness' of Old John Brown," pp. 53–59. Law dictionaries still define insanity in terms derived from M'Naghten, as "such a want of reason, memory, and intelligence as prevents a man from comprehending the nature and consequences of his acts and from distinguishing between right and wrong conduct." A host of medically obsolete illnesses such as monomania and lunacy, some embedded in common law, are included with more current diagnostic labels. See, for example, Henry Campbell Black, *Black's Law Dictionary,* 4th ed. (St. Paul, Minn., 1968), pp. 1158 and 929–36.

28. See "The Insurrection in Virginia: Col. John A. [*sic*] Washington's Statement," *New York Herald*, Oct. 24, 1859.

29. "Speech of Governor Wise," *Richmond Enquirer*, Oct. 25, 1859.

30. "Governor's Message to the Legislature," *Richmond Enquirer*, Dec. 6, 1859.

31. Ibid.

32. The *New York Times*, for example, held Wise responsible for the panic in the South: "The mischief which the frantic philippics of Gov. Wise and his organs are daily doing runs far and wide through the national mind." Either through "pusillanimity" or "paltry political cunning," Wise was making Brown a "political martyr" by the "official fury which insists on implicating the whole Northern people in his crime" (*New York Times*, Nov. 14, 1859). As the paper also claimed: "The Southern public has been thrown into a state of irrational and senseless alarm by this paltry invasion at Harper's Ferry. . . . Gov. Wise and his partisans in Virginia seem determined to play upon this panic for the promotion of their political ends, and for his own elevation to the Presidency" (ibid., Nov. 11, 1859).

33. *Richmond Enquirer*, Nov. 25, 1859.

34. Quoted in Barton Haxall Wise, *The Life of Henry A. Wise of Virginia, 1806–1876* (London, 1899), pp. 255–56. James A. Seddon, a Hunter ally, concluded: "The Harper's Ferry affair ought to have been treated and represented either in its best light as the mad folly of a few deluded cranks branded fanatics, or, more truly, as the vulgar crime and outrage of a squad of reckless, desperate Ruffians . . . and they should have been accordingly tried and executed as execrable criminals in the simplest and most summary manner. There should not have been the chance offered of elevating them to *political* offenders or making them representatives and champions of Northern Sentiment. . . . Wise has *exploited* this whole affair . . . to aid his vain hopes for the Presidency." Like many Northern Democrats, Seddon thought Wise had "conjured up a Devil" by "arraying the roused pride and animosities of both sections against each other." Only Douglas could tame that devil by stepping aside in favor of a Southern candidate. See James A. Seddon to Robert M. T. Hunter, Dec. 26, 1859, quoted in Ambler, *Correspondence of Robert M. T. Hunter*, pp. 280–84.

35. Brown quoted in *The Life, Trial, and Execution of Captain John Brown*, p. 94; for Ruffin's comment, see William Kaufmann Scarborough, ed., *The Diary of Edmund Ruffin*, 3 vols. (Baton Rouge, 1972–89), 1:350–51. On the arrests, see Woodward, "Private War," pp. 61–68, esp. p. 64.

36. *St. Louis Globe Democrat*, quoting an interview with Parker dated March 28, Apr. 8, 1888, Stutler Collection. Parker, who sat as the trial judge, also insisted later that Brown was sane and "in no sense a fanatic" (Richard Parker, "The Trial of John Brown," unpublished MS., n.d., Miscellaneous Manuscripts Collection, Library of Congress, pp. 17–18).

37. Quoted in Harold Holzer, "Raid on Harpers Ferry," *American History Illustrated* 19 (Mar. 1984), p. 15. Andrew Hunter was not then aware of the mandatory thirty-day waiting period after sentencing.

38. *Richmond Enquirer*, Nov. 8, 1859.

39. George H. Hoyt to "My Dear LeBarnes," Nov. 16, 1859, Richard J. Hinton Collection, Kansas State Historical Society, Topeka.

40. Quoted in Nevins, *Emergence*, 2:93.

41. See Article I, Section 5, *New Constitution of the Commonwealth of Virginia adopted by the State Convention sitting in the City of Richmond, on the 31st day of July, 1851* (Richmond, 1851), p. 25. In 1852 the Legislature specifically acknowledged that power, providing that the governor might order the superintendent of the penitentiary to "receive and confine" anyone whose death sentence was commuted to life imprisonment. See ch. 24, *Acts of the General Assembly of Virginia Passed in*

1852 (Richmond, 1852), pp. 83–84. Ironically, at the constitutional convention of 1850–51, it had been Wise and his allies who succeeded in defeating a motion to eliminate the governor's power "to commute capital punishment." For the legislation limiting the governor's power to pardon or reprieve a person convicted of treason against the Commonwealth of Virginia, see the *Digest of the Laws of Virginia, of a Civil Nature, and of a Permanent Character and General Operation,* comp. James M. Matthews, 2 vols. (Richmond, 1857), 2:501.

42. When Wise's biographer, Craig Simpson, quoting the Nov. 12, 1859, *Shepherdstown Register,* states that Wise "might have *recommended* a commutation of sentence," he misses a key point (Simpson, *Wise,* p. 370; my emphasis). For a commutation, Wise did not require a joint resolution of the legislature. He could effect a commutation, not merely recommend one, simply by presenting his reasons to the General Assembly—but that, of course, would have been political suicide in Virginia at the time.

43. Henry A. Wise to Fernando Wood, Nov. 6, 1859, Wise and Family Papers (copy in Frank G. Logan Collection, Chicago Historical Society); Wise to Wood, Nov. 4, 1859, Ferdinand J. Dreer Collection, Historical Society of Pennsylvania, Philadelphia.

44. John Tyler to Henry Wise, Nov. 2 and Nov. 9, 1859, Ferdinand J. Dreer Collection, Historical Society of Pennsylvania, Philadelphia.

45. "The feeling in Virginia is so strong on the sectional question, and Wise so prominent in connections with it, that, I am unable to form a guess just now, at the complexion even of the legislature. Before this he was excessively [unpopular]": William Old, Jr., to Robert M. T. Hunter, Dec. 16, 1859, in Ambler, *Correspondence of Robert M. T. Hunter,* pp. 278–79.

46. Wise's popularity would, however, fade quickly, Hunter's friend assured him. "It has even now been much impaired by his proposition to commute the punishment of Copper [*sic:* Coppoc]": Frederick W. Coleman to Robert M. T. Hunter, Dec. 21, 1859, in ibid., p. 280.

47. Quoted in Eaton, *The Mind of the Old South,* pp. 100–101.

48. "Speech of Governor Wise," *Richmond Enquirer,* Oct. 25, 1859; "Governor's Message to the Legislature," ibid., Dec. 6, 1859. Wise's reference to a "barren abstraction" was a slap at the *Examiner,* which had opposed including the demand for federal protection in the territories in the Democratic platform. See the discussion of the issue in the Whig opposition paper: "Presidential Intrigues—Wise and Hunter," *Richmond Whig,* July 8, 1859. For Wise's position, see the editorial in the *Richmond Enquirer,* Oct. 20, 1859.

49. See the *Richmond Enquirer,* Oct. 28 and Nov. 11, 1859. The *Enquirer* claimed that "the Union can *only* be preserved by his *election*" (Dec. 2, 1859).

50. Henry A. Wise to the Reverend William C. Whitcomb, Nov. 17, 1859, quoted in the *Baltimore American,* Nov. 26, 1859.

51. See Fernando Wood to Henry A. Wise, Mar. 13, 1859, Wise Collection, University of Virginia, Charlottesville.

52. Henry A. Wise to Fernando Wood, Mar. 16, 1859, Henry A. Wise Letters, Archives Division, Virginia State Library, Richmond; Wise to Wood, Sept. 10, 1859, ibid. (hereafter Wise Letters).

53. Wise's failure to intervene on Brown's behalf demonstrated to Wood his own impotence in shaping Southern policy. He was, Jerome Mushkat says, the South's candidate, but also its captive: see Jerome Mushkat, *Fernando Wood: A Political Biography* (Kent, Ohio, 1990), pp. 94–95.

54. Henry A. Wise to Fernando Wood, Jan. 20, 1860, Wise Letters. Wise was deceived. In the end, Hunter's friends secured an uninstructed Virginia delegation

that cast its vote for Hunter on all forty-five ballots at the Charleston convention, where the sectional divisions widened by the John Brown raid helped shatter the Democracy. Roy F. Nichols concludes that Hunter's friends inadvertently hurt his chances with Southern delegates by evidencing a "national" character at the convention. Ironically, Hunter's plan to "destroy" Wise in the 1857 senatorial campaign had centered on the idea of creating the impression that Wise was "resolved to unite Virginia to the Northern States and sever her connection with the South": see William Old, Jr., to Robert M. T. Hunter, Aug. 15, 1857, in Ambler, *Correspondence of Robert M. T. Hunter,* pp. 217–19.

55. Quoted in the *Richmond Enquirer,* Dec. 6, 1859.

56. The federal claim to jurisdiction arose from Brown's seizure of federal property and the fact that much of the fighting had occurred on the grounds of the federal armory: see Andrew Hunter to Henry A. Wise, telegram, Oct. 22, 1859, quoted in Villard, *Biography,* p. 485; Wise to Hunter, telegram, Nov. 6, 1859, Josiah P. Quincy Papers, Massachusetts Historical Society, Boston; *New York Journal of Commerce,* Nov. 9, 1859.

57. Wise's resolution and the delegate from Spottsylvania County both quoted in the *New York Daily Tribune,* Dec. 12, 1859; Wise to Hunter, Dec. 18, 1859, copy in Josiah P. Quincy Papers, Massachusetts Historical Society, Boston. When George Sennott, the Boston attorney representing Stevens and Hazlett, spoke to Buchanan, the president expressed sympathy for the young men "but did not promise to take action": report from the *New York Herald,* quoted in the *Chatham [West Canada] Tri-Weekly Planet,* Mar. 3, 1860. Political designs notwithstanding, Stevens would finally go to trial after Wise's term expired. He and his comrade-in-arms, Albert Hazlett, were hanged March 16, and their bodies delivered to Marcus Spring of Perth Amboy, New Jersey, whose wife, Rebecca, had championed their case. The last of Brown's party to be executed, Stevens and Hazlett were buried on the grounds of Theodore Dwight Weld's school at Newark, New Jersey: see the *Chatham Tri-Weekly Planet,* Mar. 17 and Mar. 19, 1860; Woodward, "Private War," p. 55.

58. Since the governor could not pardon treason without legislative approval, Hunter's willingness to drop the treason count was seen as a signal that Wise would pardon Cook. But the charge remained in the indictment. When Cook was acquitted of treason but convicted on the remaining counts, Wise did not attempt to pardon the young man: see "Why Cook Was Acquitted of Treason," *Cincinnati Daily Gazette,* Nov. 16, 1859. The trials of Cook and the other "insurgents" may be followed in the *Richmond Enquirer:* see esp. Nov. 1 and Nov. 15, 1859. Oddly, as a Virginia resident Cook was the only one of the raiders who could legally have committed treason against Virginia.

59. *Richmond Enquirer,* Nov. 25, 1859. On December 9 Cook had sent a letter to the *Cleveland Leader* denying false stories about his last interview with Old Brown. But he related one point almost precisely as it had appeared in the wire service dispatches. Brown had reproved Cook for claiming that the Old Man had sent him ahead to Harpers Ferry more than a year before the raid as a spy, saying, Cook reported, that Brown "rem[e]mbered distinctly telling me not to go there" (quoted in the *New York Daily Tribune,* Dec. 16, 1859). In this, Brown's memory failed him.

60. Quoted in the *New York Daily Tribune,* Dec. 16, 1859.

61. Quoted in ibid., Dec. 12, 1859.

62. Quoted in ibid., Dec. 16, 1859. On the Northern response, see Villard, *Biography,* p. 570. On Virginians' opinion about sparing Coppoc, see Frederick W. Coleman to Robert M. T. Hunter, Dec. 21, 1859, in Ambler, *Correspondence of Robert M. T. Hunter,* p. 280; see also the *Richmond Whig,* Dec. 16, 1859.

63. *New York Daily Tribune,* Dec. 17, 1859. Wise had responded to the request of

John Copeland, Sr., for his son's body with a telegram and noted: "Ansd.— Yes: to your order to some white citizen— You cant [*sic*] come to this state yourself. H. A. Wise, Decr. 12th about 5½ p.m. 1859." In response to a telegram from the mayor of Oberlin requesting the body, Wise noted: "No answer to this as I telegraphed the father of the prisoner that his body would be requested of the sh[eri]ff to be handed over to a white citizen agent" (written on the reverse side of the telegram from A. N. Beecher, Dec. 17, 1859, Wise and Family Papers. The elder Copeland's agent apparently did not show up for the body.

64. See the discussion of Wise's temperament in Simpson, *Wise,* pp. 6–7. Wise's grandson, Barton Haxall Wise, saw the governor as "a creature of impulse," with an "erratic," "excitable," combative temper (Barton Wise, *Life of Henry A. Wise,* pp. 404–5).

65. Nevins, *Emergence,* 2:42, 92–93; Simpson, "John Brown and Governor Wise," p. 16.

66. Scarborough, ed., *Diary of Edmund Ruffin,* 1:118–19. James A. Seddon loathed what he perceived as Wise's "favorite policy of swaggering and bullying" (Seddon to Robert M. T. Hunter, Dec. 26, 1859, in Ambler, *Correspondence of Robert M. T. Hunter,* p. 281). On Wise's prediction of a Northern assault, see Simpson, "John Brown and Governor Wise," p. 18.

67. See Potter, *Impending,* pp. 382–83. A perceptive analysis of the pervasive cult of chivalry and honor in the South is Bertram Wyatt-Brown, *Southern Honor: Ethics and Behavior in the Old South* (New York, 1982).

68. On the political struggle, see, for example, "An Appeal for Popular Expression," *Richmond Enquirer,* Dec. 23, 1859.

69. Wise quoted in the *New York Journal of Commerce,* Oct. 20, 1859. On February 21, 1860, Wise went to Charlestown ostensibly to preside at one such martial display. "Yesterday was spent in a grand military parade and review by the Governor. During the afternoon Governor Wise and staff had a long interview with the prisoners, urging them to prepare for death, as the sentence of the Court would be carried into effect without any interference on his part. . . . Governor Wise said that Coppee [*sic*] was the only one he ever thought of commuting, but now he had determined to hang them all." Clearly, when speaking to a local audience, Wise's disclaimers about having the authority to intervene were forgotten! See the *Richmond Enquirer,* Nov. 25, 1859. Touting Wise for the presidency, the *Richmond Enquirer* also openly attacked Douglas as the "great representative man of the dogma that the Territorial Legislatures have the right to abolish slavery" (Nov. 22, 1859).

70. David Potter thought Wise a man "far gone in chivalry," who was "smitten" by Brown's courage (Potter, *Impending,* p. 375); Craig Simpson believes Wise empathized with Brown so far that he hanged the Old Man because "such a valorous and devoted man deserved the death he earned and for which he so obviously pined" (Simpson, *Wise,* p. 27). See also Brown's speech at the opening of his trial, insisting that he be treated as a captured warrior. A perceptive study of Brown as a "violent antinomian" can be found in Wyatt-Brown, "Antinomian," pp. 97–127. On Brown's embrace of martial virtues, see Robert E. McGlone, "Forgotten Surrender: John Brown's Raid and the Cult of Martial Virtues," *Civil War History* 40 (September 1994): 185–201.

71. Quoted in the *Mason Report* (report of the Senate Select Committee appointed to inquire into the late invasion and seizure of the public property at Harper's Ferry), *U.S. Senate Committee Reports,* no. 278, 2 vols. (36th Cong., 1st Sess., 1859–60), 2:62.

72. Simpson, "John Brown and Governor Wise," p. 20; Simpson, *Wise,* ch. 11, esp. pp. 203–5.

73. Speech of Dec. 5, 1859, reported in the *Richmond Enquirer,* Dec. 6, 1859.

74. Simpson, "John Brown and Governor Wise," pp. 25–26.

75. See, for example, Villard, *Biography,* pp. 449 and 455–56.

76. Robert E. Lee to Col. S. Cooper, Adjutant General U.S. Army, Oct. 19, 1859, quoted in the *Mason Report,* pp. 40–43; J. E. B. Stuart to "Dear Mama" [Mrs. Elizabeth Stuart], Jan. 31, 1860, Stutler Collection.

77. Quoted in Villard, *Biography,* p. 456. Wise's friend, Congressman Clement L. Vallandigham of Ohio, tried to get Brown to implicate Vallandigham's Republican rival, Congressman Joshua Giddings, in Brown's movement. Brown acknowledged that Giddings had justified the Oberlin slave rescuers but added, "I do not compromise him certainly in saying that." When Vallandigham asked whether Brown had told Giddings about his plan to attack Harpers Ferry, Brown replied: "No, sir! I won't answer that, because a denial of it I could not make—and to make an affidavit [affirmation?] of it I would be a great dunce." This was hardly a "clever evasion." This version is the report of C. W. Tayleure in the *Baltimore American,* Oct. 21, 1859. Other reports vary slightly: "No, I won't answer that because denial of it I would not make, and to make any affirmation of it I should be a great dunce" (*New York Herald,* Oct. 21, 1859). But either wording is puzzling: a simple "no" might have removed Giddings from suspicion.

78. Quoted in the *Baltimore American & Commercial Advertiser,* Oct. 19, 1859, p. 1.

79. Quoted in the *Mason Report,* pp. 60–61. At the interview following the raid, Wise had asked how much assistance Brown expected from the Harpers Ferry area. At first Brown declined to answer. But "upon reflection," he stated: "From my visits and associations and enquiries about here, I have a right to expect the aid of from three to five thousand men," adding that he looked for aid from "*every state*" (*Richmond Enquirer,* Oct. 21, 1859).

80. Brown quoted in the *Richmond Enquirer,* Oct. 25, 1859, and in the testimony of W. W. Throckmorton, cited in the *New York Herald,* Oct. 24, 1859.

81. Affidavit of James W. Weld, n.d., Wise and Family Papers.

82. Quoted in the *New York Herald,* Oct. 21, 1859, and in the *Baltimore American,* Oct. 21, 1859.

83. Brown's speech has been widely reprinted, but see the *Richmond Enquirer,* Nov. 4, 1859.

84. See Robert Penn Warren, *John Brown: The Making of a Martyr* (New York, 1929), pp. 226–27 and 412.

85. On Brown's early plan, see Oates, *Purge,* pp. 61–64 and 86.

86. See John Brown to "Dear Wife & Children All," Oct. 1, 1859, James W. Eldridge Collection, Huntington Library, San Marino, California; Brown to "Dear Wife & Children *All,*" Oct. 8, 1859, Stutler Collection. On John Brown, Jr.'s role in the conspiracy, see McGlone, "Rescripting a Troubled Past: John Brown's Family and the Harpers Ferry Conspiracy," *JAH* 75 (March 1989): 1179–1200, esp. p. 1191. Indeed, a brief "mutiny" followed Brown's disclosure of his plan to take the Ferry. The only contemporary account is Charles Plummer Tidd's neglected letter of February 10, 1860, to Thomas Wentworth Higginson, now in the Higginson Papers, Boston Public Library. Brown's daughter, Annie, acknowledged in an 1886 statement to Franklin B. Sanborn that a version of the mutiny she had reported was in error (statement of Annie Brown Adams [1886], John Brown Collection, Chicago Historical Society). Owen Brown's reminiscent account appeared in Sanborn, ed., *Life,* p. 541.

87. Stephen B. Oates in fact argues that Brown intended to gather a force of "thousands" of slaves at Harpers Ferry, then move southward, sending out parties to liberate slaves, seize arms and provisions, take hostages, and spread terror and revolution through Virginia, Tennessee, Alabama, and eventually the whole South (Oates, *Purge,* pp. 278–79).

88. Quoted in the *Mason Report,* pp. 62–63.

89. Hunter claimed that he viewed Brown's letter of explanation "as of very little importance" and gave it to Charlestown's *Spirit of Jefferson,* a village newspaper. Although Hunter made light of Brown's letter before the Mason Committee, he took an oath on January 17 before the mayor of Charlestown that Brown's letter was authentic so that he might enter it in evidence (*Mason Report,* p. 63).

90. The statement is appended to Hunter's testimony in the *Mason Report,* pp. 67–68. What is noteworthy about Brown's "clarification" is that it did not confirm his own courtroom disclaimer of any intent to incite an insurrection. Rather, it gave credence to the claim of Wise and Hunter that Brown intended to keep the freed slaves in Virginia and arm them as soldiers in his Provisional Army. In his effort to remove any "confliction" between his statements and to retain the confidence of Wise and Hunter in his veracity, he had thus impeached his own courtroom testimony.

91. John Brown to Heman Humphrey, Nov. 25, 1859, quoted in Ruchames, ed., *Reader,* pp. 149–50.

92. Facsimile, John Brown, Jr., Papers, Ohio Historical Society, Columbus.

93. Many still believed in retributive justice. At his Second Inaugural, Lincoln suggested eloquently that a just God might will that "every drop of blood drawn with the lash shall be paid by another drawn with the sword" (quoted in T. Harry Williams, ed., *Selected Writings and Speeches of Abraham Lincoln* [New York, 1943], pp. 259–60).

94. See Villard, *Biography,* p. 509; Allan Nevins, *The Statesmanship of the Civil War* (New York, 1953), pp. 29–30; and Boyer, *Legend,* p. 129.

95. Michael Foucault has raised profound questions about culture and our notions of aberrant behavior. See Foucault, *Madness and Civilization: A History of Insanity in the Age of Reason,* trans. by Richard Howard (Vintage ed.; New York, 1965), and *The Birth of the Clinic: An Archaeology of Medical Perception,* trans. by A. M. Sheridan Smith (Vintage ed.; New York, 1973).

96. Lincoln, speeches at Leavenworth, Kansas, Dec. 3, 1859, and at Cooper Union, Feb. 27, 1860, in Basler, *Works of Lincoln,* 3:502 and 538–42, quoted in Potter, *Impending,* p. 380.

97. Research on the question of mood disorders should begin with Frederick K. Goodwin and Kay Redfield Jamison, *Manic-Depressive Illness* (New York, 1990), ch. 14. Also see the summary in Ruth Richards et al., "Creativity in Manic-Depressives, Cyclothymes, Their Normal Relatives, and Control Subjects," *Journal of Abnormal Psychology* 97 (Aug. 1988): 281–88, especially p. 287. In a popular, impressionistic treatment, Ronald R. Fieve cites a host of prominent people whom he believes to suffer from mood disorders. Of John Brown, Fieve says only that he "was able to attract a large following precisely because of the grandiosity of his ideas." See Ronald R. Fieve, *Moodswing: The Third Revolution in Psychiatry* (Toronto, 1975), p. 137.

98. Herman Melville, *Moby-Dick or, The Whale,* ed. Charles Feidelson, Jr. (Indianapolis, 1964), p. 248.

9

SEYMOUR DRESCHER

Servile Insurrection and John Brown's Body in Europe

THE MOST FAMOUS and graphic European image to appear in the wake of the raid on Harpers Ferry was an engraving, entitled *John Brown* (fig. 9.1). Against a dark landscape and a dull, cloudy sky a small human figure hangs from a gallows. The body's features are almost completely blanketed in shadow. From the heavens alone come shafts of light, breaking through the dreary obscurity to fall upon the gallows and the figure. Beneath this bleak illustration initially appeared the words: *"Pro Christo-Sicut Christus, John Brown,*—Charleston. Designed by Victor Hugo."

The engraving was the frontispiece to the most widely publicized commentary on John Brown to reach America from across the Atlantic. Hugo's letter on John Brown, originally written in early December 1859, was reprinted in newspapers and pamphlets on both sides of the Atlantic and was viewed by American abolitionists as a document that "will be read by millions with thrilling emotions." In it, France's most famous contemporary writer declared in exclamatory prose that the whole civilized world (namely, England, France, and Germany) was witnessing with horror a travesty of justice—"not in Turkey, but in America!" "The champion of Christ . . . slaughtered by the American Republic," "the assassination of Emancipation by Liberty," . . . "something more terrible than Cain slaying Abel . . . Washington slaying Spartacus!" Hugo had written the letter as an impassioned public plea to save Brown from execution. The engraving was appended to later publications of the letter to portray Brown as a crucified Christian martyr and slave emancipator, with the gibbet as his cross.[1]

Hugo's letter became the most prized gem among a number of overseas commentaries on John Brown published in Garrison's *The Liberator* during the winter of 1859–60. The American Anti-Slavery Society gave prominence to "opinions from over Sea" in its annual report of May 1860, entitled *The Anti-Slavery History of the John Brown Year*. The report prayerfully observed that the judgments of a foreign country, "in some sort, fore-

Figure 9.1. Frontispiece from *John Brown par Victor Hugo* (Paris, 1861).
(Courtesy of the Lilly Library, Indiana University, Bloomington, Indiana)

shadow those of future times." To a bitterly divided United States, Hugo's letter was touted as typical of the meaning given John Brown's death in all of the civilized world's opinion.[2]

Actually, the engraving had been completed five years before the Harpers Ferry raid when Hugo, in exile on the island of Guernsey, was campaigning against the execution of a local murderer. When the British government allowed the sentence to proceed, Hugo artistically transformed the death into a plea for the abolition of capital punishment in Britain. But John Brown suited Hugo's cause even better. On the gallows of Charlestown hung not a criminal but a liberator/messiah: Brown foreshadowed the criminal/hero Jean-Valjean in *Les Misérables*. Although less consistently interested in either slavery or America than many of his French contemporaries, Hugo was also moved to attach the engraving to the letter by the coincidence of Brown's execution day, December 2, 1859, with the anniversary of Louis Napoleon's coup d'état against the Second French Republic, eight years earlier. The first printing of the engraving in Paris was actually seized by the police because it bore the date "December 2."[3]

Historians of the Civil War era have approached the John Brown affair almost exclusively as a domestic conflict with domestic impacts. Any venturing beyond North America has been limited to identifying a few European celebrities who took note of him in their writings or private correspondence. Yet a wider range of overseas observers were stirred by John Brown's fate, at least long enough to link it momentarily with major themes of nineteenth-century Western culture: civilization and barbarism, Europeans and non-Europeans, slavery and human progress, and, above all, the role of violence in the pursuit of, and resistance to, social change.

The Structure of Communication

If the aftershocks of the attack on Harpers Ferry reverberated across the Atlantic, the fate of John Brown was not of uniform interest throughout Europe. Nor did the turmoil in America generally stimulate the impassioned intervention of Europe's intellectuals: in all likelihood American abolitionists seized so eagerly upon Hugo's letter because he was the only eminent European intellectual to proclaim, and with maximum publicity, his unreserved support of Brown's act. Indeed, in American reprints of European reactions it is the comparative silence rather than the outspokenness of Europe's intellectuals that is striking. Hugo was the sole individual whose words were directly quoted in *The Liberator* or the annual report of the American Anti-slavery Society. For the most part, Brown intruded upon European consciousness only in the anonymity of press reports and editorials. The Harpers Ferry affair and its aftermath was thus almost exclusively journalistic.

There was also a clear geographical pattern to transatlantic attention. Interest in the various phases of the affair was far more evident in the newspapers of Britain than in those of the Continent, and far more intense in northern England and southern Scotland than in other areas of Britain. On the Continent published discussion of John Brown seems to have been most extensive in France, but still far less abundant than the British commentary. In most Continental newspapers, John Brown's fate did not elicit more than an isolated editorial comment. Even the affair's most dramatic moment, the execution, usually appeared as no more than a brief news item.

Newspapers in Europe's maritime nations with well-developed Atlantic trading networks often had private correspondents reporting on events in America. But as one moved into the interior regions of Europe, there was a clear diminution of interest in and coverage of American affairs. Europe's communications were, moreover, with the commercial centers of the United States, especially New York, which meant that news summaries were usually filtered through Northern correspondents or excerpted from Northern newspapers. Even in European cities that had powerful economic links with the interests of the Southern states, leading newspapers generally relied on Northern-based American correspondents to supply them with accounts of events. Thus, as one historian of the period has noted, "By the end of the antebellum period . . . the cultural and intellectual blockade which the slave South had erected to protect itself against the North had become equally effective as a barrier against intrusion from across the Atlantic."[4] It was only around 1860 that the South began serious collective efforts to bypass the Northern network, and this was undertaken more with an eye to political economy than with the intention of influencing public opinion about the South.[5]

The communications network, however, was not the principal factor influencing European reaction to the John Brown crisis in America. Garrison's *Liberator* was typical in emphasizing the European response as an overwhelmingly British phenomenon. By the 1850s Anglo-American trade, immigration, tourism, cultural exchange, and political interaction were all far better developed than links between any other European nation and the United States. In addition to the steady flow of people from the British Isles to this country, forty thousand American tourists a year visited England, and the lion's share of American overseas exports went to Great Britain.[6]

As regards interest in John Brown, the most significant factor was the political and cultural network linking the American and British antislavery movements. By 1859 this Anglo-American network had been in place for more than a generation. During this period, ideas, money, convention dele-gates, petitions, addresses, abolitionist lecturers, and runaway slaves criss-crossed the Atlantic, creating a pattern of continuous communication, punctuated by periodic mass mobilizations. Since the British abolitionists had long since succeeded in dismantling the legal apparatus supporting British colonial slavery (this was accomplished between 1833 and 1838), the persistence of slavery in the United States, where it was both vigorously expanding and dominated by an English-speaking planter class, was of prime concern to British abolitionists.[7]

But if the Anglo-American antislavery connection was a generation old, its British component was in serious decline by the late 1850s. British aboli-tionism was fragmented, highly localized, and greatly reduced in numbers and local chapters. Its leadership aging, sustained by a narrowing social base, it had, except on rare occasions, become marginal to British political life. Its heyday as a viable pressure group within the arena of domestic and imperial policy, its status as a movement that could shore up or undermine governments, was over. The reduction of the number of areas in the Amer-icas that still imported slaves from across the Atlantic, combined with some dismal failures of abolitionist-inspired experiments in Africa, had reduced mass support for the movement. By the time of the John Brown affair, the last serious manifestation of mass British abolitionist sentiment had oc-curred more than half a decade before, with the enthusiastic reception given to Harriet Beecher Stowe, the author of *Uncle Tom's Cabin*.[8]

Nevertheless, the antislavery movement retained a powerful residual constituency in Britain compared with the rest of contemporary Europe. Interest in John Brown was thus greater in Britain than on the Continent, and greatest in what had been the traditional heartland British abolition-ism—the industrial regions of northern England and southern Scotland. Antislavery embers still glowed in the old abolitionist "petition" towns—such as Halifax, Bolton, Leeds, Sheffield, Newcastle-upon-Tyne, Glasgow, and Edinburgh—where masses had readily gathered to petition against slav-ery in the preceding decades. Only in such places were meetings called so that the public could hear lectures about John Brown and American slavery in the winter of 1859–60.[9]

The Structure of Interpretation

If the intensity of interest in John Brown was affected by the previously existing networks of information and political interaction, European judg-ments on the John Brown affair were shaped even more by the mentality of the mid-nineteenth century, which exalted Europe's civilizing mission. Brown's story thus unfolded within a larger conceptual world that evaluated both the meaning and the significance of his actions and those of his fellow citizens. European culture and its extensions formed a core world of standards and behaviors connoted by the term *civilization*.[10] "Outrages to civilization" might be identified within Europe, for example when the papal government refused to return a Jewish child who had secretly been taken from his family and baptized. The charge of an outrage or affront to civilization was equally applicable to an abuse by one's own group perpetrated against those under the domination of a "civilized" power—British colonial "outrages" against native Australians, for example. Revolutionaries used the binary formula of civilization/barbarism or civilization/savagery as readily did conservatives. In a hagiographical book about John Brown, a French revolutionary expressed special disgust for American "Red Indian" slaveholders, implying that the slaves of "savages" were forced to endure a level of human degradation even worse than that experienced by slaves of civilized white masters.[11] Hugo's reference to the whole "civilized world," in his own letter on Brown, casually located that world in Western Europe and the United States, whereas barbarity or savagery was generally characteristic of those non-European areas, cultures, peoples, or customs that contradicted the patterns or aspirations of the civilized core. The people of the United States (or at least its cultivated classes) were generally not only accorded full membership in the "civilized world" but was often placed at its forefront by European observers. Hence the invective which Hugo brought to bear on the "corruption" of one of the world's leading civilized sectors.[12]

In this conceptual world, civilization was not only a condition but also a process, comprising both an internal transformation of the North Atlantic core and that core's gradual incorporation of the uncivilized periphery. One could choose to emphasize material, intellectual, or moral dimensions of that transformation, but even traditionalists within Europe acknowledged a process of dynamic alteration of the non-European world. Even those who rejected some aspects of such "progress" understood that the rest of the world was becoming increasingly synchronized with the European core, and the United States was recognized as a prime agent of this transformation. Most of the media that took note of John Brown thus generally qualified the United States as a progressive member of the "civilized world."

Those Europeans describing world trends around 1860 tended to regard the civilizing process as dependent on the expansion of European settlement overseas. In the various overlapping taxonomies that Europeans used to subdivide the world, the United States was usually joined with Great Britain and its imperial white settler colonies. Britons and Americans were united by ties of language, culture, religion, law, and economy; by a shared heritage of representative institutions; and by relative immunity to both mid-century Continental revolutions and royal authoritarianism. There was an increasing tendency to conflate these similarities as shared characteristics of the "Anglo-Saxon race." The rhetorical emphasis on Anglo-Saxonism as an indelible and distinctive biological inheritance was far more popular by the end of the 1850s than it had been even a generation before.[13]

By the mid-nineteenth century the older linkage of the Anglo-Saxon myth with individual liberty and political freedom solely within England had, moreover, undergone a profound change. The myth was now casually associated with the idea that the people of the entire planet were gradually being molded so as to share in the qualities of a superior Anglo-Saxon physical stock. The moral, political, and economic progress of humanity was dependent upon, and evidenced by, the geographical expansion and dominance of that dynamic race, the one most capable of transforming the less endowed. Newspapers encountered little criticism in Britain when they spoke with pride of Anglo-Saxon energy in peopling the world, or even when they described, with philosophical resignation, the southward expansion of the United States toward Central America as the great leavening agent of the Americas. Continental Europeans also readily accepted the language of race, and more than occasionally wondered whether they, too, could replicate the energy of the Anglo-Saxon race in seizing the opportunities afforded by the unfolding capitalist and demographic transformation of the world.[14]

Since attachment to liberty was a putative characteristic of Anglo-Saxons, antislavery could be incorporated into the racial mythos, and the emancipation of slaves in the British Empire used as prima facie evidence of Anglo-Saxon superiority. Mid-century British journalists never tired of citing Britain's leading role against the African slave trade and colonial slavery. Even radical American abolitionists (including Theodore Parker, one of John Brown's early supporters) could combine Anglo-Saxonism with vigorous opposition to the extension of slavery.[15]

If Europeans generally included the United States within the ambit of civilization, the existence and especially the dynamic expansion of the slave system there posed a conundrum for the conceptualizers of progress, for by 1859 the ending of personal bondage was viewed as a key indicator of the civilizing process. In the century before the Harpers Ferry Raid the absence or removal of personal bondage had become a distinguishing feature of Europe's high state of civilization. Serfdom had been abolished in central Europe, and the Russian government was drawing up plans for the ending of serfdom in its last European stronghold.[16] Slavery had also beaten a retreat, if an uneven one, in larger parts of the Americas. The institution had been abolished in the British, French, Danish, and Swedish overseas colonies, and the Dutch were formulating plans to end their Caribbean slave system. Brazil having ceased to import African slaves at the beginning of the 1850s, Cuba remained the sole major importer of transatlantic slaves into the Western Hemisphere. Only the United States seemed to be moving massively against the thrust of history: its slave system was vigorously expanding—economically, demographically, and politically. Far from bending to the prevailing doctrine of progress, Southern slaveholders were in fact increasingly vocal about preserving and extending their dynamic institution.[17]

Nevertheless, until the late 1850s the weight of planetary evidence for emancipation allowed Europeans to explain away American slaveholders' victories as a distressing exception, and to search the horizon for countervailing signs. If the end of American slavery was "but a question of time," Europe was relieved of responsibility for encouraging immediate, and risking violent, emancipation. Commenting on the Dred Scott Decision early in 1857, the London *Times* managed to transform the apparent setback into a signal of "progress" by dispensing an array of historical tranquilizers. If the British had slain "the monster," if even the unstable French Republic of 1848 had redeemed itself by slave emancipation, if American abolitionists continued to agitate, if Mrs. Stowe's book could circle "the world in a few months . . . pleading for human rights," if the idea of "the natural inferiority of the black race" and biblical arguments for enslavement had been "given up" (except in planter hearts hardened by abolitionist "violence or indiscretion"), then the advancing tide of human freedom and the superiority of free labor, would, somehow or other in the Anglo-Saxon manner, peacefully prevail in the long run.[18]

The ideology of civilization, peaceful progress, and racial superiority therefore jostled uncomfortably alongside portents of disruptive and violent threats to that ideology. In mid-November 1859, in the same issue that reported the news of "Old Brown's" trial, the London *Times'* principal editorial anxiety regarding America was the possibility of a war over the San Juan Islands in connection with the disputed maritime border between the United States and British Columbia. The *Times* drew a fearful picture of the potential reversal of Anglo-Saxon progress:

> Europe and Asia would look on with surprise and exultation, watching paroxysms of frenzy among that terrible Anglo-Saxon race which had seemed to monopolize the ALMIGHTY's permission to go forth and people the earth; wondering to see that vast family whose expansion they had envied, whose industrial energy they had found it vain to emulate, and whose free thoughts, wafted over the world, were ever sowing themselves in uncongenial soils, now engaged in the mad enterprise of destroying their common property and shedding their own blood.

Still, the race's ability to resolve its problems without recourse to violence would no doubt triumph once again. Whatever the unsavory qualities of Britain's "American cousins," "the respectable portion of the great American people . . . has sentiments as civilized as those of the same classes in Europe."[19] It was within this rather rosy frame of reference that the events of John Brown's raid were reported to Europe.

The Salience of the John Brown Affair

Although the news of the seizure of Harpers Ferry reached Europe at the end of October, discussion of Brown's fate peaked toward the end of December, after the arrival of news of his execution and its aftermath. There was a final surge of discussion early in January, following the publication of Buchanan's State of the Union address. Thereafter, except in the British antislavery circles, discussion of Brown virtually ceased. Even during the height of interest, the British newspapers that offered the fullest coverage issued reports or editorials on an average of every three or four days, while periodicals, if they took note of John Brown at all, mentioned him only once.[20]

Therefore one must take due note of the limits of European concern, even at the peak of concern. Most Continental and many British newspapers carried only brief notices of the trial and execution. After the initial scare, there was a tendency to dismiss the political significance of Harpers Ferry altogether by describing it simply as a riot. The correspondent of *L'Indépendance Belge*, published in Brussels, observed that, in terms of its size, Brown's attempt qualified as no more than a minor European *émeute*. The most eloquent evidence of the limited salience in Europe of the John Brown affair, however, was its almost total omission from the year's end editorial retrospectives. Reviewing the year 1859, and sometimes the whole decade, editors failed to perceive that the raid had any major implications for the future. Harpers Ferry did not even make the list of significant incidents in the *Annual Register of World Events* for 1859.[21]

The proceedings in northern Virginia and their impact throughout the United States were overshadowed by the events unfolding in the Italian peninsula. Europe's attention was focused on the reverberations of the French Emperor's victory over the Habsburg monarchy in Lombardy, the continuing process of Italian unification, the fate of the papal territories in central Italy, the shifting balance of power in western Europe, and the possibilities of an Anglo-French conflict. If any revolutionary possessed true celebrity status in Europe it was Giuseppe Garibaldi: during the winter of 1859–60 his past and potential role in Italian unification was a source of endless speculation. Even in the British radical and abolitionist press the focus was not on "Captain Brown" but on "General Garibaldi," whose moves and words were monitored to gauge the immediate danger of future violence in the Italian peninsula. The London *Daily News,* for example, which was quite sympathetic to John Brown's motives and generally hostile to Southern initiatives, prominently featured Garibaldi's appeal for funds to the "Ladies of Italy" on the same day that it published the news of Brown's execution.[22]

One could easily catalogue a number of issues that outweighed the events in Virginia in terms of news—or editorial worthiness—from November through January. The imminent emancipation of the serfs in tsarist Russia and the emancipation of the Jews in the Habsburg realms were frequent topics of discussion. Even with regard to the United States, John Brown's Raid had to compete for attention with William Walker's renewed attempt to conquer Nicaragua, and with U.S. General William S. Harney's invasion of the disputed San Juan Islands. In some newspapers the violent death of John Brown was accorded less editorial space than the almost simultaneously reported demise of Washington Irving, nor did Brown make any of the annual lists of the illustrious dead with which many newspapers closed their books on the past year's events.[23]

The Core Tension:
Servile Insurrection and Human Fortitude

If the news emanating from the distant hills of Virginia could hardly compete with the intrigue and anticipation generated by political and diplomatic maneuvers on both sides of the Alps, John Brown did, nevertheless, make Europeans aware, in more personalized terms than ever before, of the depth of the crisis looming across the Atlantic. The traditional image of a prosperous, philistine, invincible United States was transformed. The first news of Harpers Ferry conjured up one of the most shocking phrases of nineteenth-century political rhetoric. Newspapers reiterated the same sketchy details in almost identical words: some five to seven hundred slaves had risen in "servile" or "Negro" insurrection somewhere in Virginia and seized an arsenal, with some destruction of life and lines of communication.[24]

The term *servile insurrection* resonated with historically loaded meanings emanating from two sources. The first was ancient Roman history. From classical antiquity Europe derived stories of desperate slave revolts followed by ruthless suppressions in which no quarter was given and no bounds were set on vengeance. In its earliest editorial accounts of the Harpers Ferry uprising the London *Times* in fact referred, with Victorian propriety, to history's averting its face from the unspeakable cruelties of this aspect of the ancient world. The second source of Europe's image of servile insurrection was drawn from a more recent event. The St. Domingue uprising of 1791 and the subsequent Haitian war of independence of 1803 against the first Napoleon furnished the ultimate image of servile insurrection—a war of scorched earth, and of mutual mutilation and extermination. The combatants did not respect the civilized taboos regarding innocence, age, sex, or helplessness. Imprinted on European memory was the image of the brutal climax to that insurrection, the massacre of whites by Jean Jacques Dessalines, the leader of the Haitian army of independence, after his moment of victory.[25]

By the mid-nineteenth century, then, there were two sharply bifurcated images of black slaves in particular and Africans in general. One presented blacks as fundamentally passive, either docile and gentle by nature or dulled into a state of permanent submissiveness by the dehumanizing experience of slavery. The basis for the other image was rage: blacks as creatures of suppression and brutalization, who, when offered the opportunity, would retaliate with blind vengeance. Both images could be ascribed to people in a state of primitiveness, savagery, or barbarism—a condition indigenous to sub-Saharan Africa and intensified in the plantation societies of the New World. The transition from slavery to freedom could well be accomplished without unfettered violence, as the slave emancipations of the 1830s and 1840s in the British, French, and Scandinavian Caribbean colonies demonstrated. But a sudden collapse of authority could also lead to bloody chaos.[26]

Most initial news reports on Harpers Ferry referred to a "servile" or "negro" insurrection in their headlines. In addition, almost all used adjectives like "horrible" or "fearful" to describe the envisioned consequences of unleashing the "hell hounds" of such an uprising. Sketchy news also allowed editorialists to invoke the "naturally rebelliousness" image of black slaves. Some reports indicated that both whites and blacks were involved, leading to speculation about the violent propensities of three volatile, suppressed Southern groups: enslaved blacks, free blacks, and impoverished whites. Throughout the later infusions of more information the label *servile insurrection*, with its connotations of pillage, mutilation, torture, rape, and brutality, clung to the affair.[27]

After about a week, though, the failure of the slaves to rise and the relatively easy confinement of the raiders became clear. Newspapers that pursued the story now began to offer, again in bare outline, the second major image of the affair—the mad or audacious leader of the raid who had survived the ordeal and was being indicted for murder and treason. All the reports eventually included a number of points. To his followers the leader of the abortive uprising was a truly patriarchal figure ("Old Brown") and a warrior ("Captain Brown"). Brown's New England heritage, his participation in the Kansas guerrilla wars, his stoic resignation to his fate, the impressive courage with which he bore his physical wounds, and, above all, his calm and defiant appeal to an authority higher than his Virginia judges gradually fleshed out the central character of the story.[28]

Literally by his presence, Brown thus shifted the focus away from the imagined bodies of helpless innocents sacrificed to savage insurrection. Even reporters who claimed to be abolitionists peppered their early accounts with disapproving nouns like *madman* or *fanatic,* although these were later accompanied by less clearly negative historical symbols: Puritan, Cromwell, Ironside, Spartacus. "Old" Brown was a man weathered but not bent by bitter struggles that had cost him two sons. Almost all reports remarked upon the hasty proceedings, which brought Brown into court bedridden with his wounds.[29] Accordingly, to the initial descriptions of the leader as insane or fanatic were added terms of understanding and even justification. The Kansas battleground had produced a wild old man, "maddened" by fate, or even the "injured soul" of a hero. Other commentators harked back to the distant past, the "enthusiasm" of Puritanism, the "lofty" fanaticism of the Reformation, or to the noble tragedy of an Othello, "who loved his fellow man not wisely but too well." Even those who remained steadfast in refusing to exempt the raid from its original overtones of madness wrote with begrudging nuance of Brown's "insanity of fanaticism rather than the insanity of ambition or crime."[30] It was recognized that John Brown was fabricating his final self, controlling first his wounded and then his condemned body. A "Carlylesque" hero was in the making. Almost every report of some length spoke either of his sincerity, or courage, or clarity, or bravery, or religious energy, or firmness.

As Brown's composure in the midst of overwhelming hostility and power helped to displace, or at least to dilute, the all-pervasive obsession with servile insurrection, the waters of the Potomac at Harpers Ferry were metaphorically mixed with the waters of the Nile. In his apologia Brown spoke of having merely wished to liberate and to draw off the slaves, rather than to stir up an uncontrollable servile or racial conflict. Few European newspaper reporters discussed the evidence that might have clashed with the image of a flight into freedom. Instead, Brown's invocation of divine law received the broadest coverage, making him both victim and judge of an all-too-inhumane institution.

Precisely because a black servile insurrection had utterly failed to occur, attention had shifted to the free white prisoner, and Hugo's exclamatory dichotomies captured this decisive shift. Brown "sounded to these men, these oppressed brothers, the rallying cry of Freedom. The slaves, enervated by servitude, made no response to the appeal. Slavery afflicts the soul with

Weakness!" Brown's own strength of soul was correspondingly magnified.[31] Brown's spare responses caused one British editorial to contrast the taciturn superiority of the Harpers Ferry leader to the loquacious, self-advertising, and inferior rhetoric of European revolutionaries. While a great many European newspapers conceded the criminality of the act and the state's right (if not its obligation) to punish the captive survivors, there was an exceptionally broad consensus that, for a man of violence, Brown was an extraordinary individual. The dramatic appeal of his courtroom behavior induced *Le Monde Illustré* of Paris to feature the affair in its issue of December 17, 1859.[32]

The execution was the most heavily reported moment of the affair. Again the reports all emphasized Brown's "firmness" and "courage." Some accounts described the final interview with his wife as unemotional, others emphasizing its congruence with the stoic character Brown had already manifested during the trial. He had chosen the quintessentially nineteenth-century male role at Harpers Ferry. Moreover, the one insertion of the feminine—Mary Brown—into the drama conformed, in exquisite detail, to the proprieties of the nineteenth century and to its vision of antiquity. Mrs. Brown was, at least in the relatively sympathetic European accounts such as that of London's *Morning Star*, "courageous without insensibility, tender without weakness, and her bearing in the last interview was worthy of a Roman wife." The more attention reports allotted to the details of Brown's personal behavior, the more the real captive superseded the hypothetical servile war. Of all the European reports *The Liberator* chose for its first reprint the comments of the *Morning Star* under the headline "THERE WAS NO 'BUNKUM' IN BROWN." The *Star* emphasized the general admiration for the raw courage of "OSSOWATOMIE BROWN," his "true grit," with "no fine sand." He was an "angular bit of granite," an "unbending gnarled oak," "a square man" with "a backbone," undeviating from the perpendicular. His refusal of slave-tainted clerical comfort, his preference for the company of an enslaved mother and her children, were congruent with his "higher-law" view of Virginia's secular arm. Finally, the report took note of his unwavering body, standing with the rope around its neck for several minutes. On the threshold of eternity, "he neither blenched nor wearied."[33]

Closely linked with the language used to describe the execution was the meaning assigned to Brown's death. Just as the initial reports had employed the language of unfiltered violence, so the language of martyrdom was immediately embedded in sympathetic reflections on the execution. Although very few editorials offered Brown to their readers as an unqualified martyr, most referred to the use of that term by many Americans.[34] There was much more agreement in the European press on the personal courage and sincerity of John Brown than on whether he had correctly interpreted the injunctions of the Gospels or had actually convinced the majority of American Northerners of his place among the truly martyred.[35]

Servile Insurrection and the South

If the images of mass insurrection and of Brown's indomitable individual fortitude dominated portrayals of the Harpers Ferry affair, images of fear and terror quickly became affixed to John Brown's captors and indeed to the whole South. Since most of Europe's correspondents and American newspaper sources were situated in the North, few accounts interpreted the events from a Southern perspective.

A central judgment of the South emerged from the very first news of Harpers Ferry, which would be elaborated through the later stages of the affair. The South became a region, a society, under the grip of a single, overwhelming emotion: panic. Southern panic and its consequences informed almost every European report on the incident, and, as events continued to unfold, an initial acceptance of Virginia's mobilization as necessary against a massive and unfathomable threat gave way to widespread disparagement of the South's overreaction. This sense of emotional disproportion made itself felt in most aspects of reporting. One correspondent bewailed the difficulty of explaining the massive mobilization of whites in Virginia and throughout the South in response to what his readers would properly regard as no more than a routine disturbance in Europe. Another speculated on how far the Virginian race, descendants of Washington and Jefferson, had degenerated into a group of trembling cowards, as fearful of the blacks whom they enslaved, and of the Northerners with whom they traded, as of the ideas of progress that they inevitably encountered in the world beyond their region. Even sympathetic newspapers allowed unmistakable notes of pity or contempt into their comments on the "sad picture of panic" among the Southerners. The contrast between the South's self-proclaimed chivalric virtues also invited occasional sneers about Southern manliness by reference to its fear in feminine terms.[36]

Most significant, it was not simply those who most closely identified or sympathized with the abolitionists who condemned the South's panic. Some of the most conservative European newspapers were contemptuous of the hasty trial and execution. The rush to indictment, judgment, and execution increased European journalistic unease, leading in turn to a very general conclusion that the South, by its overreaction, had helped transform a senseless adventure into an act of heroism and a political crisis.[37] Granted, the more conservative European newspapers acknowledged the existence of grievances that justified some action on the part of the South, pointedly balancing accounts of Southern fear by references to provocative

Northern "fanaticism." Even such reports, however, emphasized fanaticism as only one tendency within the North, whereas the more virulent manifestations of Southern behavior were taken to illustrate the tenor typical of the region. While some of the Southern reactions to John Brown's raid were ascribed to fears of a rescue operation and to the Northern abolitionist meetings in support of Brown, potential sympathy for the Southern action as a case of constrained self-defense was constantly subverted by fresh reports of Southern escalations.

Because of the differences between social conditions in Europe and the American South, many Southern acts appeared both excessive and irrational. Especially baffling were the intimidation campaigns launched against people of color and white outsiders. Even those who sympathized with the execution of Brown himself found the "colorophobia" reported in various states to be incomprehensible in light of the failure of the uprising. Motions introduced in Southern state legislatures to expel or enslave resident free blacks, for example, were seen as signs of a society gone out of control. The legislative agitation was rendered even more "outrageous" by news of Southern threats and mob violence against Northern tradesmen and European workers suspected of being sources of disaffection. There was a steady progression of discomfort from comments upon the "barbarous" haste evident in the trial of "Old Brown" to reports about incidents of extralegal popular behavior from Virginia to Texas.[38]

European newspapers soon began to use the rhetoric of insurrection and revolution against the planters. They affixed to the South terms drawn from the French Revolution: the "Great Fear" and the "Reign of Terror." The South's cultivated self-image as a traditional society, paternally ruled by its rural gentry, was now shattered by journalistic analogies to the angry peasant crowds of provincial France in 1789, or to the revolutionary terrorists of Paris in 1794. For Europeans, then, the story that began in late October 1859 with the evocation of a savage servile insurrection shifted toward recounting lawless coercion in the South during the winter of 1860.[39] Southerners, moreover, made sympathy difficult even for conservative Anglo-Saxonists in Great Britain. The South generally identified British official policy as actively and subversively abolitionist, citing everything from its Canadian refuge for runaway slaves in the North, to British opposition to American southward expansion into Cuba and Central America, to British abolitionist hegemony on the high seas. Virginia's Governor Wise also managed to offend all British journalists with a speech against Northern aggression that included a call for the seizure of British vessels transporting a fugitive to Britain. Brown's "fanaticism" was thereby transferred to Virginia's chief executive.[40]

If the John Brown affair undermined sympathy for the slaveholder-dominated South among conservatives, it also diminished sympathy with a slaveholder-dominated America among both traditionalists and radicals. Hugo was not alone in identifying the action of Virginia as that of the United States. Especially on the Continent, the United States as a whole was held responsible for the execution of John Brown and his followers. For traditionalists and monarchists, Virginia's behavior was but the latest illustration of a fundamental affinity between republics and slavery extending back to the pagan Mediterranean world.

In Paris, one commentary on Harpers Ferry quickly escalated into a debate between traditionalists and secularizers on the papacy, whose temporal claims in Italy were in peril. How could one expect real progress toward the termination of slavery, declared the Catholic and monarchist *L'Union*, until the world was converted to the one true apostolic faith? The secular Parisian press immediately countered with the observation that nineteen hundred years of traditional Catholicism had not ended slavery. The papacy still made no effort to excommunicate or otherwise discipline slaveholders in the vast territories of plantation Americas served by its clergy and within societies swearing allegiance to Rome. In this discussion reflections on the fate of John Brown were immediately translated into a debate over the merits or evils of various European regimes.[41]

Extending guilt for Brown's execution to the entire American polity suited some radical perspectives as well. In Hugo's own plea it was not the state of Virginia but the American Union that was sending a martyr to the gallows/Crucifix, not slavery but "liberty" that was murdering "emancipation," not Governor Wise but Washington who was slaying Spartacus. The Union, not the South, would be rent asunder by the execution. Hugo philosophically looked forward to disunion as the ultimate price to be paid for the ultimate sacrilege of *lèse-humanité*. For some Continentals, the outcome of the Harpers Ferry affair proved that the United States had betrayed its revolutionary heritage, that it was sinking even below the level of a Russia now clearly committed to ending serfdom. Europe's submerged nations and classes had little to hope for from such an America. If Brown was recognized as a revolutionary comrade, his society was denied its status at the forefront of progress. Such revolutionary exiles as Karl Marx paid little attention to the personal fate of Brown but wondered instead whether the raid, like the imminent Russian emancipation, might not signal the spread of great social upheavals beyond the boundaries of revolutionary Europe in 1848.[42]

In Britain, though, there was a less unidimensional understanding of the United States. The distinction between South and North, and even between regions within these two geographical areas, was axiomatic. The discussion of the meaning of the John Brown affair revolved around the significance accorded to three major concepts: slavery, violence, and race. Arguing from the South's mood after Harpers Ferry, or (less frequently) from the potential of slave rebellion, Britons reached a general consensus on the long-term social fragility of the South. The political power of the South in the federal system and the economic power produced by the Southern domination of world cotton production were short-term advantages that would ulti- mately yield to the general pattern of European development. There was little echo in Britain of the Southern argument that it could diverge from, much less reverse, the thrust of history toward civil liberty as exemplified by Western European history. Even commentaries that presumed the Har- pers Ferry affair would likely cause a backlash of fear did not alter their "European" consensus. There remained only two solutions to the problem crystallized by John Brown: emancipation by violence and blood, or a grad- ual elimination of the slave-labor system. Even if the pathway to gradual emancipation was unclear, the successive European emancipations had shown that, one way or another, America was destined to end slavery. Harpers Ferry might be interpreted as a momentary setback for emancipa- tion, but it could not alter the ultimate course of history.[43]

"The Thunderer":
Servile Insurrection versus Anglo Saxonism

If the long-term course of world history remained clear, John Brown's raid did not convince all European commentators that he had actually fur- thered the cause of emancipation. Yet even periodicals that had denounced the raid from beginning to end did not show a lasting sympathy with Brown's captors. The *Times* of London offers the outstanding European example of how an articulated intention to offer a balanced, detached in- terpretation, including even an attempt at a sympathetic view of the South- ern reaction, was undermined by the flow of events and the escalating passions over John Brown. In the mid-nineteenth century the *Times,* nick- named "the Thunderer," was widely regarded as the most authoritative single organ of British public opinion, and the *Times* regarded British slave emancipation as one of the glories of British history, irrefutable evidence of human progress. Britain's legal and peaceful implementation of emancipa- tion, which recognized both human and property rights, was the very model for social change in the civilized world. The *Times* thus confidently foresaw a nonviolent transformation of the peculiar institution in the United States.

By the late 1850s, however, the *Times* had also been engaged in a generation-old campaign against the philanthropic politics of the British abolitionist movement. For decades "the Thunderer" stormed against the inflated rhetoric and grand plans of the enthusiasts of "Exeter Hall," with their policies of protecting black labor in the West Indies or of limiting the flow of alternative "coolie" labor from Africa or Asia, and against their vast projects for the publicly funded development of free labor in Africa. While speaking casually of the "exploded theories" of Negro racial inferiority, the *Times* readily opened its pages to the most demeaning portrayals of Africans and Afro-Caribbeans. At the very moment that its views on John Brown were being elaborated on its editorial pages, for example, it featured exten-sive excerpts of Anthony Trollope's disparaging portrait of West Indian blacks' character and culture.[44]

Refusing to regard slavery as the exclusive, or even the central, issue of the John Brown affair, the *Times* insisted that Brown's fate be viewed in the context of the economics of cotton, of the political prospects for American self-government and federalism, and of the racial relationship between Anglo-Saxons and Africans. After weighing these factors, the *Times* de-nounced the Northern fanatics who endangered Anglo-Saxon destiny, eco-nomically, politically and racially. If the Virginians had hanged a "poor old man," he remained simply a malefactor, not a martyr. Personal courage could not exonerate a movement that threatened to wipe out the gains of two hundred years of Anglo-Saxon economic and moral progress in North America, or to reduce its Southern states, which were of the "purest English blood," to "the level of Haiti or Costa Rica." The *Times* returned again and again to the ultimate talisman of servile insurrection and Haitian-style scenes of murdered planters and ravished white women. In this spirit the *Times* welcomed the manifestations of anti-Brown sentiments in the North, even quoting (without denunciation) a proslavery rally in New York that promulgated both racist and biblical arguments for slavery. This, concluded the *Times*, was evidence of the trend of public opinion in the United States produced by John Brown's raid.[45]

The stance taken by the *Times* provoked rejoinders from other British publications. For abolitionists the most useful of the many British re-sponses were those that appeared in periodicals not previously implicated in abolitionist initiatives. *The Economist,* a free-trade periodical that usually steered clear of abolitionist causes, was sufficiently alarmed to intervene directly against the *Times*. Karl Marx and Friedrich Engels were impressed enough with *The Economist*'s editorial that they dispatched it to the United States for reprinting in the pro-Republican *New York Tribune*.[46] In its rebuttal *The Economist* pointedly contrasted the alarmist view of the raid promul-gated by the *Times* with the paper's passivity toward pro-Slavery argu-ments. Yes, the Harpers Ferry attempt was "gross folly," "a gross wrong" perpetrated by a "noble-minded" "fanatic." But when the *Times* treated Southern planters as innocent sufferers rather than the "headstrong, domineering, insolent, cruel, offensive, irritating and bullying party," after half a century of fruitless nonviolent abolitionist preaching, the *Times* betrayed the English antislavery tradition. The sin of civil strife was now almost wholly on the heads of the slave states. *The Economist* was not surprised by the "insolent doctrines" of Anglo-Saxon race superiority that were often "half-echoed" by the most popular organ of English opinion. The true surprise had been the equivocation of the *Times* on the issue of slavery itself. *The Economist* refused to allow such thoughts to "go forth to the world with that *imprimatur* of English public opinion on them which their mere insertion in *The Times* gives."

The London *Daily News,* another opponent of the *Times* whose comments were recirculated in America, was far readier than *The Economist* to sympathize with Brown's motives. Nevertheless, his calamitous mistakes were regretted "by the true friends of the negro throughout the North." That his success would have been "the commencement of anarchy" was the "prevalent opinion and feeling of the North." But Brown, the North, the *News,* and most Englishmen would all agree that "no power in human society could make it wrong to strike down a slaveholder." So why should the North make itself an accomplice in the perpetuation of slavery? Above all, why should *Englishmen* declare "that *our* credit or interest" lay in the maintenance of a hateful domination? "Our religion, laws, and manners forbid and annihilate Slavery." Even British racial ideology was sent into the field in favor of emancipation: "The Anglo-Saxon race, of all races of mankind, can assert it superiority without invading the rights of other races less favored in their development." As with *The Economist,* slavery, not race, was the central issue for British public opinion. In the British version of history and political science the South would find demonstrated the ultimate foundering of its peculiar institution. Nor would it find in British history that path to emancipation strewn with "insurrection and extirpation," the South's most legitimizing images. Instead it would find, if it did not change course, "protracted, wearisome and certain ruin." Seeing neither the likelihood of further insurrection nor the dissolution of the Union as the result of Harpers Ferry, the *Daily News* saw no reason whatever to sanction the *Times* equivocation on slavery.[47]

For a few weeks the *Times* continued to blame New England and abolitionist agitation for the growing Northern acceptance of proslavery arguments and for turning the Upper South against gradual emancipation. But as it chronicled the spate of antiblack initiatives in the South, the *Times* also began to distance itself from proslavery arguments. At first it did so only negatively. It could not "congratulate the abolitionists on the success of their exertions, which have plunged the race they favor into deeper darkness, and have made the subjection of man to man the belief of a Christian people." But it emphatically deplored new marks of "political reprobation" toward the African race, "which may well make the philanthropist despair." The *Times* ridiculed the American embassy's denial, on grounds of race, of a travel visa to Sarah Remond, an American black abolitionist traveling in Britain. It quoted with disdain President Buchanan's State of the Union address, which reaffirmed that property in persons could be carried into any United States territory. It described, in tones of civilized outrage, atrocities committed "against coloured seamen" on an American vessel on the high seas and indicted in a British court. Its editorial page concentrated on Southern legislative attempts to re-enslave or degrade free people of color. It contemptuously dismissed the statement by Henry Wise, the governor of Virginia, that equated British aid to runaway Negroes with the invasion of Harpers Ferry. For such Southern vitriol the *Times* reserved the deepest of its ethnic slurs: Governor Wise's "climax of Southern extravagance," it editorialized, "reminds one more of Irish 'patriotic' oratory than of anything coming from a reasonable part of the world."[48]

With this raciocultural demotion of Virginia's chief executive, the rhetoric of Anglo-Saxon unity had vanished. Even the *Times*'s usually careful distinctions between and within North and South were dismissed in a cascade of disgust. If Britain could not yet afford to turn its back on American cotton, its leading newspaper would waste no sympathy on the fanatics of either section. "Neither England nor our American colonies have anything to envy in the social state of the Slave-holding Republic." Whether insurrectionary or not, the United States, with its clouded future, was decoupled from the brighter horizons of the British empire. By the end of January 1860 the *Times* was concentrating on counting the successive monuments "to the social convulsion of 1859." It only lamented the fact that "free cotton" raised in Africa, India, or China could not in "any reasonable time drive out of culture the slave-grown cotton of America." In its rapid editorial spin away from the South, the *Times* revealed the antebellum limits to British conservative sympathy.[49]

The British Abolitionist Response

Insurrection, not race, was the spectre haunting John Brown's sympathizers as the news of his trial, execution, and subsequent sanctification made its way across the Atlantic. Wendell Phillips might tell the abolitionist faithful in Massachusetts that "the lesson of the hour is insurrection," but this was neither the lesson of the hour nor of the affair for most British abolitionists.[50] Rather, Harpers Ferry intruded upon British political discourse at a peak of Britain's self-confidence in nonrevolutionary change. Charles Dickens had just published *A Tale of Two Cities*, emphasizing the retrospective world of difference between Paris and London during the Great French Revolution. Loftily surveying the world at the close of 1859, the press reflected with complacency and pride on Britain's immunity to revolution during the previous half century of European upheaval. Of all the world's major powers Britain was the only one that did not either look uneasily backward on recent revolutionary violence and postrevolutionary bureaucratic despotism, or gaze vertiginously forward into the abyss of civil conflict or social transformation.

The stately path to legal change appeared to be most successfully embodied in the annals of the British imperial parliament. Within the British Isles, "party spirit" was "only sufficiently active to give healthy exercise to the body politic." The fires of class hostility were banked. Many newspapers that claimed to give voice to the working classes were not speaking in a revolutionary idiom. After all, east of the Channel lay despotism, from Napoleon III's bureaucratic French empire to tsarist Russia. Westward lay the unstable polities of Latin America and the lamentable spectacle of a fragmenting United States of America.[51] The Pax Britannica of the world's oceans was unchallenged. The lion's share of the world's manufacturing exports departed from British ports. If Irish nationalists kept up a steady drumfire of hostility, neither Ireland nor India, the two troublespots of the decade before Harpers Ferry, were particularly threatening. At most, limited parliamentary reform, not social or national revolution, was at issue. Moreover, the prevailing self-satisfaction with the present was projected upon the past. When news arrived of John Brown's body making its troubled way back from Virginia to New York, the British were quietly interring Thomas Babington Macaulay, the historian-laureate of Whiggish gradualism, in Westminster Abbey.

Given the previous decade's torrent of rhetoric on the Anglo-Saxon knack for compromise, it was clear that the attempted insurrection at Harpers Ferry, even without overtones of slave or racial violence, would pose difficulties for a nation so assiduously cultivating a nonrevolutionary ideology. When the *Times* wished to subvert the positive spin of Brown's religious convictions, it called attention to his provisional constitution (sanctioning the seizure of property) and linked his religious pedigree to the Anabaptists, Puritans, Fifth Monarchy men, and French Republicans of the July Monarchy.[52]

If the revolutionary element in Brown's raid was thus a challenge to British public ideology at the end of the 1850s, it was a source of particular embarrassment to those Britons who took the most active interest in John Brown. The central historical tenet of the British abolitionist movement was that it had succeeded (in true British fashion) by the peaceful conquest of public opinion. Whatever the factional differences within British and

American antislavery during the three decades before Harpers Ferry there had been general agreement on nonviolence as the only moral and practicable way to slave emancipation.[53]

The initial impulse of abolitionists in Britain was consequently to distance their movement from the dreaded image of violent insurrection. The first English reaction to be republished in Garrison's *Liberator* (excerpted from the sympathetic London *Examiner*) began with the observation that slave risings in the South had become much *less* frequent after the formation of the American abolitionist movement. Antislavery's "wisest leaders" knew that "fruitless risings" only worsened the conditions of slavery. Harpers Ferry was "but an insignificant incident in the history of the great social struggle." The *Examiner* was not prepared, however, to discount entirely the justice of those who "manfully rose against their chains." The *Antislavery Reporter,* the organ of the British and Foreign Antislavery Society, was even more circumspect in its first comment on Harpers Ferry. It noted that Brown would have many sympathizers, especially among "those who justify employment of arms." Even among "those who took the opposite position"—namely, the Antislavery Society itself—there were "few who would not heartily commiserate with him, while they disapprove of his rash attempt." The *Reporter* pointedly echoed the Quaker *Friends Review* for its final comment: "The principal actors must have been labouring under a species of insanity, or the blindest fanaticism." Considering the means "inconsistent with Christianity and totally indefensible on religious grounds," they profoundly deplored the raid.[54]

Abolitionists in Britain did not remain as defensive and anxious to bury the event as did the *Antislavery Reporter.* As John Brown's performance altered his image, Harriet Martineau, writing to the *National Anti-Slavery Standard,* resoundingly denied the least possibility of insanity, leaving it to better informed Americans whether or not his "scheme" was wild or hopeless. But Martineau quickly shifted the focus from the actual or revolutionary potential of Brown to his more Christian virtues. He was no mere European (above all no *Irish*) revolutionary. He had none of "the passion, frenzy and selfish vanity" of the political agitators on Martineau's side of the Atlantic. If his act remained "a mystery, and a painful one," the moral greatness of the actor was clear. His conduct and speech placed him not among the failed revolutionaries of the previous decades but alongside the persecuted victims and martyrs of Christianity's early heroic period. At the end, only the figure of the solitary, upright victim-hero on the gallows remains in Martineau's letter. The uncomfortable havoc of revolutionary violence disappears as completely as in the impenetrable horizon of Hugo's engraving.[55]

Brown's standing within British antislavery can best be observed in a series of explanatory lectures offered on his career during the winter of 1859–60. One of the two principal speakers was Frederick Douglass, a veteran spokesman of American black abolitionism. Douglass reached Liverpool late in November 1859. Although he had been planning the trip before Harpers Ferry, news of the raid sent him fleeing northward to Canada, in anticipation of a warrant for his arrest: Douglass was implicated by foreknowledge of, if not actual participation, in the raid. When Douglass left the United States he was probably deeply uncertain as to what connection he wanted to admit to Brown's action, or what to say about it. The day the raid was announced in Philadelphia, Douglass gave a routine lecture there without mentioning the raid, "as if he did not want to acknowledge the fact that Brown had committed himself, and as if Douglass himself were innocent of any knowledge of it."[56]

Douglass's flight to avoid arrest and the published rumors of his serious implication in the affair preceded him to England. He avoided broaching the subject during his first lecture in the abolitionist-friendly town of Halifax. No doubt Douglass was considering the impact of any discussion of Brown's raid on his audience, in addition to the use that might be made of his words in the event of his return to America. First, there was a published accusation from America to be dealt with—that Douglass had been a coward, running rather than standing firm and sharing martyrdom with his old friend. Douglass's first published remarks in connection with Brown were designed to dispose of that implicit question humorously. Alluding to his initial visit to England as a runaway slave, he quipped, "I've always been more distinguished for running than for fighting." Now he was a runaway again, returning "to the home of all oppressed nations." In coming to England he had simply stuck to his original plans and repeated his previous flight.[57]

But neither Douglass's personal relationship with John Brown nor his "manliness" in staying or running was important in British abolitionist circles. In fact, he was continually greeted by and sent off to cheers and enthusiasm during his tour. The principal problem he faced with a British abolitionist audience was to address their concern about Brown's own appeal to arms. Douglass had himself long since drawn the Whiggish distinction between the French and the English paths to emancipation. In the wake of the second French slave emancipation in 1848, he had told an audience at Rochester, New York: "What is bloody Revolution in France is peaceful reformation in England. The friends and enemies of Freedom meet not at the barricades thrown up in the streets of London; but on the broad platforms of Exeter Hall. Their weapons are not pointed bayonets, but arguments. Friends of freedom rely not upon brute force but moral power. Their courage is not that of the tiger but that of the Christian." That dichotomy was no less strongly embraced by his British audiences in 1859. Douglass had to acknowledge this nonviolent point of departure.[58]

As news of Brown's impressive posture in captivity increased the possibilities of throwing a more sympathetic light on the entire affair, however, Douglass embarked on a strategy of breaking down the dichotomy between Christianity and violence, and of making the courageous "tiger" show his teeth in the most benign manner. Douglass introduced his later discussions of Brown by explicitly acknowledging that even the most sympathetic British audiences might find it difficult to condone John Brown's project. People had heard with astonishment that a small band of "madmen" had invaded Harpers Ferry and committed criminal acts. Many who were otherwise "well-disposed" thus understandably regretted and even condemned Brown's action. Douglass refused to ask them to advocate anything like "insurrection," or to support armed intervention or even British diplomatic action.

But at that point he would begin to use the abolitionists' consensual hostility to violence in order to invert the meaning of Brown's raid. Was it not the South that was in a state of continuous "insurrection," of class warfare, and of violence against the family?[59] Resurrecting one of Brown's earlier schemes, he pictured him not as a revolutionary launching a new constitution but as a Moses. Brown had simply intended to unleash a great exodus of the enslaved up the "corridor" of the Appalachian Mountains to freedom, leading the freed masses to the promised (and gloriously British) land (Canada/Canaan). Brown had not intended to shed blood; like Moses he had intervened between the death-dealing master and the slave. Perhaps with a bit of good fortune Brown would have been another Washington, but ill fortune intervened and he became instead an apostle and martyr. Step by step the audience witnessed a rhetorical metamorphosis. From a seemingly wild and hopeless venture, whose success would have produced immeasurable bloodshed, Brown's raid was recast in British meeting halls as a bloodless representative of British-style patriotism and biblical salvation. Harpers Ferry was transferred to the banks of the Nile.[60]

In four months of well-attended meetings Douglass's translation of Brown was always received with cheers and resolutions of thanks. He was quickly joined on the John Brown circuit by Britain's own premier veteran antislavery lecturer, George Thompson. As the American and the Briton separately toured a dozen towns in northern England and southern Scotland, Thompson's message on Brown (despite his pro-Garrisonian differences from Douglass on the nature of the American polity) dovetailed with that of Douglass. Thompson's Brown was a leader whose aim was to break the greatest number of chains with the least effusion of blood, whose defense of Kansas had increased his impatience, who had watched two sons die before his eyes, who had comforted his grieving wife, who had gone to the gallows with greatness. Therefore "one of whom the world was not worthy went to join the glorious army (thus it has ever been) of beatified martyrs and confessors." As with Douglass, the audiences always passed votes of thanks and support for American antislavery by acclamation.[61]

Yet the continuous cheers should not obscure the limitations of Brown's seemingly effortless sanctification. Douglass always began his discussions of Brown with the acknowledgment of the peculiar unease his name produced in an audience. Douglass always felt equally constrained to emphasize that what was wanted from Britons was neither funds nor support for similar martyrs. He issued no call for British volunteers to flock to Canada, in the way Garibaldi would request (and get) British volunteers to land in Italy a few months later. Not a single meeting featured an address calling for a thousand new Browns for every raider who was killed or hanged in Virginia. Rather, Douglass requested, and received, the traditional moral condemnation of slavery.[62]

Thompson's lectures were equally revealing. Following the enrollment of Brown among the glorious (and safely) dead, he "supplemented his discourse with a few observations on the offense for which Brown suffered." He condemned "the instrumentality" that Brown had "employed for the accomplishment of a humane, good and Christian object." Thompson concluded that Brown had served the cause better by failing and dying than he ever could have by succeeding. In other words, the promulgation of truth, the renovation of public opinion, and legal change (the tripartite tradition of abolitionism) should continue. Harpers Ferry had jolted the public mind, but it was an event, a leader, and a model of action that no one should follow.[63]

Sharing the platform with Douglass at Wakefield in January 1860, Sarah Remond, after praising Brown's motives, also placed herself "decidedly against such attempts as the one he had undertaken, the power of moral suasion being of itself sufficient to effect the object they had in view." Douglass had the same message for his audiences, as soon as his speech shifted from the glorious sacrifice of 1859 to what was now to be done. Peaceful agitation remained not only the proper policy for British supporters of American emancipation but for American abolitionists as well. The message both delivered to and echoed by British abolitionists seems clear: granted Brown's beatification, and the abolitionists' splendid attempt to snatch martyrdom from madness, one such victory was more than enough.[64]

One can also measure the behavioral limits of British abolitionist sympathy with John Brown in comparative terms. There was no collective mobilization in Britain before, or in response to, Hugo's desperate appeal. Yet British abolitionists had mounted just such a mass appeal fifteen years before to stay the execution of another John Brown, under sentence of death for aiding the flight of a fugitive slave. In 1844 a South Carolina judge had condemned one John L. Brown, a native of Maine, "to hang by the neck until your body be dead." News of the sentence reached Great Britain in March 1844, where it ignited widespread media discussion. Resolutions were passed at public meetings in Liverpool, Edinburgh, Glasgow, and Dublin, warning that if Brown were executed the ghost of the murdered man "would shame American travellers whenever they set foot on the shores of England."[65] However, the most imposing British activity on behalf of John L. Brown was the nationwide circulation of a collective clerical address directed to the governor of South Carolina. It originated in Lancashire, the English county in which mass abolitionist petitioning had first begun, in 1787. The clerical memorial quickly obtained thirteen hundred signatures of ministers and other notables, whereupon it was dispatched, along with accounts of the proceedings in Glasgow, Edinburgh, and Liverpool, to the United States via the American ambassador in London. The cause of John L. Brown was even raised in Parliament, skirting the proprieties of noninterference in foreign legal proceedings. For *The Liberator,* in 1844, no single event in the United States since the beginning of antislavery agitation had ever "so powerfully affected the public mind in Great Britain." The commutation of John L. Brown's sentence was attributed to a surge of public sentiment that overawed even the South.[66]

Not that the British mobilization of 1844 had been entirely forgotten fifteen years later. Responding to the publication of Hugo's appeal in the London *Daily News,* a correspondent reminded readers that John L. Brown's sentence of execution had kicked up an antislavery storm in Britain and that his life had consequently been saved. British religious and benevolent feeling was "surely as strong and vigorous as it was in 1844."[67] Victor Hugo had led the way; the newspapers and churches of Britain could follow. But the appeal was not taken up by the press, nor by the churches, nor even by the abolitionist societies of northern England and southern Scotland. Indeed, none of these bodies had needed Hugo's letter to remind them of past mobilizations. Nor was the correspondent wrong in assuming that significant religious, benevolent, and even antislavery sentiment remained alive in Britain. Four years after Harpers Ferry there was a considerable mobilization in favor of the North. British antislavery still had a usable past. One may therefore surmise that the difference between the "young" John Brown of 1844 and the "old" John Brown of 1859 lay less in the state of British feelings about antislavery than in a critical distinction between the two cases. However much Frederick Douglass might urge that old Brown had come to liberate, and not to annihilate or to confiscate, even the warmest crowds drew a thin red line between the bloodless crime of 1844 and the seizure of an arsenal and hostages amidst deadly gunfire.

Another mobilization closer in time to Harpers Ferry than the John L. Brown affair reveals how the abolitionist core could expand to impressive proportions around the right symbol. The greatest mobilization of British antislavery in the 1850s was centered on a group of completely invented heroes: the characters of *Uncle Tom's Cabin.* Harriet Beecher Stowe had more readers and certainly was the recipient of more adulation and public acclaim in Britain than in America. Her visit to Britain in 1852 resembled a triumphal procession. In honor of the occasion, antislavery factions managed to mute their differences. A popular antislavery "Address" from the "Women of England to their Sisters, the Women of the United States of America" accumulated half a million signatures. An "Uncle Tom Penny Offering" campaign netted the author $20,000 (in lieu of foregone royalties) before her departure. Historians of British abolition rightly treat Stowe's visit as *the* abolitionist event of the decade.[68]

By contrast, the series of Douglass-Thompson lectures, the outstanding public event of the John Brown affair, was a regional not a national phenomenon. Brown received neither the benefit of a collective appeal for his life nor a mass outpouring of condolence afterwards. As far as I have been able to determine there was no "John Brown's Penny" (or even farthing) subscription launched in his memory or collected for his widow. All in all, the abolitionists' response mirrored the general attitude of Britons toward the John Brown affair. No part of the British political spectrum welcomed, or even sanctioned, an escalation of violence as the best or most likely way of eradicating America's peculiar institution. In this respect a common political culture seems to have overridden the fault lines in British society.

Eclipse and Revival

The British and Foreign Antislavery Society, in its annual report of July 1860, characterized Brown's raid, trial, and execution as "matters of history."[69] It was now more interested in the ongoing process of Southern "proscription." The proabolitionist *Edinburgh Review,* in October 1860, described the Harpers Ferry insurrection as an "aggression of so utterly unjustifiable and absurd a character (notwithstanding the lofty qualities of John Brown who led it)" that it might have given a real triumph to Virginia and to the Federal government, had they acted with restraint. Instead a "Reign of Terror" had unfolded in the South, marking the period since Harpers Ferry as "revolutionary." Moreover, some Northerners, if less directly violent than the Southerners, fed the fires of revolution. Long "trains of pilgrims were seeking the graves of John Brown and his sons." Escapes of accomplices of Brown from Federal agents proliferated. Public meetings quickened "the blood of old men, in memory of revolutionary days."[70]

By the winter of 1860 British newspapers had all too many occasions to compare the smooth functioning of British institutions with the vindictiveness and violence engulfing the North American republic. John Brown became only one incident among the rush of larger events. The first anniversary of Brown's death in the United States was apparently passed over in silence in Europe. In London or Edinburgh, for example, where a commemoration of the anniversary would not have triggered a counterdemonstration such as occurred in Boston, none was called. The *Annual Register* of 1860 again failed to mention John Brown in its survey of the events of the past year.

For three years after his execution, John Brown's attempted insurrection was no more than one small item on the lengthy checklist of events leading up to Southern secession. The relationship of the North to slavery remained deeply ambiguous until the middle of the Civil War. It was the Emancipation Proclamation, formally enacted on January 1, 1863, that brought John Brown modestly back into European public discourse. The London Emancipation Committee had been founded in 1859 to sustain a Garrisonian organization in the metropolis, but it did not hold a public meeting until three years after the Harpers Ferry affair. Only in 1863, changing its name to the London Emancipation Society, was it finally able to attract a large membership, including intellectual and political support from John Stuart Mill, John Bright, and Richard Cobden.[71]

On December 2, 1863, the society organized its first public meeting in commemoration of John Brown's execution. After three years of bloody conflict and the prospect of settling the emancipation issue by the sword, the abolitionist speeches at the crowded Whittington Club were stocked like an arsenal. With French troops ensconced in Mexico, the chairman felt free to draw upon the parallels of December 2, 1851 (when liberty was "garroted" in France), and of 1859, when a liberator's death heralded the emancipation of a race. Brown was no longer a solitary victim on the scaffold/cross but the might-have-been Garibaldi of America, whose song of resurrection became the American "Marseillaise." Warrior analogies abounded. Cromwell, Washington, Mazzini, Garibaldi, and Kossuth were all John Browns. In language that might have come from Prussia's new minister-president, Otto von Bismarck, speakers proclaimed that the issue would now be settled, not by soft voices, but by the cannon's iron lips, the sabre's tongue, and the artillery's thunder. The martyr whose soul was marching southward would soon be advancing against the legions of the French Emperor in Mexico. John Brown was also marched briskly through an honor roll of national liberation warriors from Washington to Garibaldi in whose company no Englishman at the Whittington Club could feel ill at ease. General Dessalines was duly absent from the list: in December 1863 the soul of John Brown led a Union army, not a slave revolution.[72]

Brown underwent an even more militant metamorphosis on the Continent during the closing stages of the American Civil War. In 1859 some of Europe's revolutionaries had viewed Brown's execution as simply one more grim benchmark in the backlash to the victories of 1848. The execution at Charlestown marked the United States as belonging to the same implacable system as Europe's bourgeois and feudal regimes.[73] The Emancipation Proclamation, however, allowed revolutionaries to incorporate the conflict into a broader scenario, that of world liberation. In 1864, from revolutionary exile in Belgium, Pierre Vesnier published Europe's longest work on Brown, *Le Martyr de la liberté des nègres, ou John Brown, Le Christ des noirs*. Vesnier, a French journalist, had fled first to Geneva and then to Brussels after Louis Napoleon's coup of December 2, 1851. A member of the International, he was elected to the General Council of the Paris Commune in 1871 and was regarded as an ultrarevolutionary even by other members. Vesnier dedicated his book to all the suffering and degraded of the earth, to the immense mass of black, brown, and yellow servitude that covered Africa, Asia, and much of America, and to the proletarians of Europe, still slaving in the galleys of barbarous civilization. The book was structured according to the "passion" of John Brown—in thirteen stations, or days of suffering, from his capture at Harpers Ferry to his execution/crucifixion.[74]

Brown's life was the eternal story of good versus evil, attuned to a Continental timetable. He was born in the energized generation of the Great Revolution, along with a list of heroes somewhat different from that offered in London's Whittington Club. Etienne Cabet, Auguste Blanqui, Louis de Saint-Just, Vincent Ogé, the Marquis de Lafayette, and Robert Blum joined Kossuth and Garibaldi. Brown's inquisitors also joined the Duke of Alba, the "Catholic Pharisees" of Belgium, Pontius Pilate, Marshall Radetsky, and all despots from the pharaohs to the Bourbons. Vesnier accordingly embraced, with exaltation, the primordial taboo of "servile insurrection." The Saint Domingue revolution, the last resort of Brown's detractors in 1859, was recounted with zest by Vesnier, who made a point of dilating on Dessalines' racial massacre after the final defeat of Napoleon's troops. Haiti had its "Sicilian Vespers"; "the whites were slaughtered without distinction for age or sex in six months of calculated butchery." The massacre was necessary.[75]

Vesnier made clear the meaning of servile revolution for Southern slaves by drawing on parallels. Revolutionary massacre linked the Haitian past to the American present. If the blacks of the United States South made "their night of August 24" (the date of the Parisian massacres of 1792) "their Sicilian Vespers," their "Saint Bartholomew of the whites, they would fulfill a great obligation, because slavery, that crime of crimes . . . justifies everything, authorizes everything" committed by its victims. Vesnier's formula was the "frightful and yet the only possible and desirable solution to the terrible struggle which desolates the United States." "The Negro race will exterminate the white race, it being necessary that one die so that the other may live." Vesnier invoked both racism and race to justify this massacre of Southerners. Prejudice decreed that the two races could not live together. Whites were not suited to cultivating in the tropics without blacks. In case the reader had missed the iron necessity of his solution Vesnier left no adjectival hiding place: "The only desirable, just, useful, opportune, indispensable, solution is that the black race remain alone, in free possession of the soil, which it alone can cultivate. . . . That, terrible as it is, is the only solution that a sincere friend of humanity and justice can maintain."[76]

Ideas coursed swiftly through four hundred pages of revolutionary martyrology and policy recipes. Brown himself, according to Vesnier, had been innocent of a genocidal solution, having had only the bloodless exodus model in mind. Vesnier was less forbearing. Since Brown had been executed on false charges, Vesnier decreed that each minute of Brown's thirty-odd minute agony on the gallows would have to be repaid with a hundred thousand lives. (He did not mention that his sentence would require a true decimation—the death of one-tenth of the entire United States population in 1860, including those of all races and ages, both North and South.) After hundreds of pages on various revolutions through the millennia—in the course of which Jesus of Nazareth and all of his apostles were condemned as sanctioners of slavery—Vesnier returned to John Brown in a "Coda," with a song entitled "The Soul of John Brown and the Marseillaise of the Blacks." Brown was thus fully incorporated into the European revolutionary tradition.[77]

Seven years after writing his book Vesnier found himself in the maelstrom of the Paris Commune. As the editor-in-chief of its official journal, he denounced all moderates. Later, however, reviewing his own revolutionary moment for posterity, Vesnier entirely dispensed with the language of extermination: no unarmed enemy was ever struck down by the Commune, and John Brown and servile insurrections in the Americas found no place in Vesnier's history. Indeed, during the American Civil War most European supporters of the abolitionist cause were far less enthusiastic than Vesnier about servile insurrection. They were pleased that, for the most part, slaves ran away to join the Union armies rather than recreating Saint Domingue in the South. Four years after Brown's execution, the London *Daily News* contentedly noted that the much-conjured servile massacres had not come to pass, proving that "it is not the negroes' way to rise in violent insurrection, unless driven to despair by the absence of any prospect of redemption by other means."[78]

But the public apotheosis of John Brown as the martyr/liberator of the American slaves lasted only a short time. The commemoration of 1863 in London was not repeated. For most Europeans, in April 1865 a new figure, not associated with slave uprisings, displaced Brown as emancipation's martyr. In Paris, thousands flocked in sympathy to the American embassy on hearing of President Abraham Lincoln's assassination. Politicians signed collective addresses to "Lincoln the glorious martyr of duty." In other European cities, newspapers devoted their front pages to his life and death, and working-class rallies presented their condolences to the American people.[79]

The distance between the reactions to the deaths of Lincoln and Brown may best be gauged in terms of a similar commemorative tribute. Immediately after Lincoln's assassination a provincial French newspaper, supported by the Parisian press, launched a campaign to pay for a gold medal intended for Lincoln's widow. The names of forty thousand subscribers were eventually published.[80] Some organizers of the Lincoln medal made explicit the analogy between the deaths of Brown and Lincoln. But only five years later, in 1870, did they organize to commission a similar gold medal for Brown's widow, and only in 1874 was the medal finally dispatched to the United States.

Although John Brown did not figure in Vesnier's history of the Paris Commune, the memory of that uprising cast its own shadow over Brown. One had to beware of French Republicans, even when bearing gifts. When a picture of the medal and the letter from the French committee that had commissioned it were appended to a book on John Brown in the 1880s, Frank P. Stearns, its editor, felt compelled to argue that although some of the members of the committee were implicated in the Commune, only one was culpable. The French committee members referred to themselves as "French Republicans"; Stearns referred to them as "French Philanthropists." Name by name, the editor exonerated the signatories. Victor Hugo, at the peak of his popularity, presented no problem. Etienne Arago had been mayor of Paris during the siege of 1870, but he was "not a communist." Victor Schoelcher, the emancipator of the slaves in the French colonies in 1848, was a respectable senator of the Third Republic. Other signatories were designated as republicans, either "moderate" or "advanced." Louis Blanc, although a "visionary" socialist and a "prejudiced writer," had not been part of the Commune. Only one, Melvil Bloncourt, condemned to death in 1874, was designated as "unworthy of the rest." The real trouble was that anarchists, socialists, women's rights eccentrics, and teetotalers in America attached themselves to Brown "like barnacles to a whale." After the entire gold medal committee had passed through the nitric acid test of social and political respectability, only one committee member, "whose character was now better known," had failed the test. And, Stearns asked, "Is there not commonly a Judas among every twelve men?" Just as an American abolitionist had metaphorically transformed Spartacus into Moses before the tolerant eyes of British abolitionists, so now the guardian of Brown's memory transmuted a band of French republicans into apostles. Ritually cleansed of its insurrectionary taint, John Brown's gold piece uncomfortably occupied the commemorative niche never filled by John Brown's Penny.[81]

The handsome book to which the illustration of the French gold medal was appended was perhaps symptomatic of a renewed role allotted to Europeans in the discussion of John Brown. As America demobilized from the Civil War and Reconstruction, attacks on the memory of John Brown had begun to mount. This was a danger, not only to that "hero but to all heroes in the future." Editor Stearns had therefore selected the text of an outsider who could formulate the objective and detached judgment of history upon the subject. What was wanted from Europe was no longer the throbbing prose of a Hugo, nor the "rhetorical" history of a Macaulay, nor even the "artistic" histories of a Voltaire or a Carlyle. Stearns sought one of the new "scientific" historians, who could offer plain facts in the simplest way, who was sympathetic but impartial, as well as clear about facts but profound in his respect for virtue and his admiration for greatness.[82]

Where else could such a historian be found in the 1880s but in Germany? For Americans becoming part of the new international "discipline" of history, only Germany then "possessed the sole secret of scholarship," the institutions, the methods, and the aspiration toward cool, unbiased *objektivität*. For Stearns, in particular, the rough-hewn John Brown required "no splendid Italian ideal, but rather a realistic German Woodcut, like those of Dürer." By both origin and scholarly background Hermann von Holst seemed to be the perfect candidate, with an established reputation in American political history. One of the principal actors in the transmission of German historiographical method to America, he was then a professor at Freiburg who supervised the doctoral dissertations of the founders of the new approach to history at Harvard and Columbia and was himself to become the first chairman of the history department at the University of Chicago.[83] Holst therefore possessed all of the qualifications for rendering a verdict for posterity. He would use German science and moral judgment so definitively that, as far as Brown was concerned, "no rude hand will ever again reach high enough to pull down the record of his fame."[84]

Holst's *John Brown* is a narrative of the fatal conjuncture between the two contradictory moral principles of American history. At Harpers Ferry freedom and slavery came face to face. After two centuries of struggle the balance of power threatened to tilt toward the South and slavery, but "the people of the North had not yet lost their manliness in the voluptuous embrace of the strumpet slavery, and under the poisonous breath of her burning kisses." One man enters the fray to engage the enemy in personal combat. He is a blend of the virtues of all ages and sexes; pure and unselfish as a child; "tender and soft as a girl in her mother lap, and yet every inch a man."[85]

Holst's *Brown* cannot even imagine the possibility of servile insurrection. Rather, Holst's narrative incorporates Brown as Samson. From his initial status as warrior-judge Brown is reduced to a helpless, bleeding despised rebel in the hands of his captors, but his power grows with each passing day. The body language of his bearing and the prophetic language of his coming martyrdom transform the context of the narrative. Holst's *Brown,* like Hugo's, ends at the place of execution. Brown, however, does not hang lifeless and passive in the void, observed only by Heaven. Holst leaves Brown standing on the cusp of death, at the decisive moment of American history. Absent are all of Brown's past actions and all those of his enemies and executioners. Absent is all hint of the surging dispute between criminality and martyrdom. Brown's last motion is not one of passive hanging but a historic swing of his mighty body. With his dying kick Brown gives the ship of slavery "a mighty shove away from the shore," sending it over the "Niagara Falls" of its destiny. He seals the irrepressible conflict.[86]

Reduced to that one moment, to that one gesture, John Brown triumphs. Regardless of whether Americans accepted Holst's defining image, however, for all but a few Europeans scholars, aging abolitionists, and revolutionaries, the old twin images of insurrection at Harpers Ferry and the indomitable old man at Charlestown were already distant and fading memories.[87]

Notes

I would like to thank Richard Blackett, Christine Bolt, David Brion Davis, Stanley Engerman, William W. Freehling, Laurence Glasco, and Van Beck Hall for their helpful comments. This essay was brought to completion with the aid of a research fellowship from the University Center for International Studies at the University of Pittsburgh. A shorter version of this essay appears in the *Journal of American History* 80 (Sept. 1993): 499–524.

1. See Victor Hugo, "Letter to the editor of the London *Daily News*," Hauteville House, Guernsey, dated Dec. 2 and printed Dec. 9, 1859, reprinted in *Letters on American Slavery* (Boston, 1860), pp. 3–6. When he wrote the letter, Hugo believed that the execution had been postponed until mid-December.

2. See "Victor Hugo on John Brown," *The Liberator,* Dec. 31, 1859; *John Brown Year,* pp. 157–66. On American reactions to Hugo's letter, see Monique Lebreton-Savigny, *Victor Hugo et les Américains, 1828–1885* (Paris, 1971), pp. 221–64. Hugo's

letter did not, however, encounter universal acclaim. Although Madrid's *El Credito: Revista Samanal Española* of December 18, 1859, described it as *un bellisimo escrito* and for the *Giornali di Roma* the following day it was an *eloquente lettera*, the *Belfast Daily Mercury* of December 28 evaluated Hugo's appeal as "an address which burlesque's enthusiasm and dignity." (See also note 35, below.)

3. See Hubert Juin, *Victor Hugo*, 3 vols. (Paris, 1984), 2:312–16 and 436–39. For a comparison of the designs of 1854 and 1860, see Ministère de la Culture, *La Gloire de Victor Hugo* (exhibition catalogue) (Paris, 1985), p. 482; and Pierre Albouy, *La Création mythologique chez Victor Hugo* (Paris, 1985), pp. 289–90. Hugo was not involved in the French abolitionist movement before the second French slave emancipation in 1848. On that event, see Seymour Drescher, "British Way, French Way: Opinion Building and Revolution in the Second French Slave Emancipation," *AHR* 96 (June 1991): 709–34. For Hugo's position on French slavery and racism, see Victor Hugo, *Journal: 1830–1848*, ed. Henri Quillemin (1954; repr. Westwood, Conn., 1970), p. 225.

4. Martin Crawford, *The Anglo-American Crisis of the Mid-Nineteenth Century: The Times and America, 1850–1862* (Athens, Ga., 1987), p. 14. The location of the American correspondents was usually indicated in the printed dispatches. In some instances direct fears of encouraging imitation may have dictated virtual silence on the subject of servile insurrections: see, for example, *A Illustracao Luso-Brasiliera* (Lisbon). For mainland Europe my selection of newspapers was based on the collections for 1859–60 in the British Library (in Hendon), supplemented by those in the Library of Congress and the New York Public Library. These included one or more papers from major European cities: Amsterdam, Berlin, Brussels, Copenhagen, Leipzig, Lisbon, Madrid, Milan, Naples, Paris, Rome, Stockholm, and Vienna. Since editorial attention was similarly sparse in all of these cities except Paris, I infer that my sample is not likely to underestimate the level of attention given to John Brown in most areas. For Britain I examined daily or weekly coverage in dozens of newspapers, from Aberdeen to Exeter, covering the general spectrum of British politics (conservative, liberal, radical) but concentrated most intensely on the traditional heartland of antislavery over the previous three generations—the cities of northern England and southern Scotland. For a discussion of regional differentiation in abolitionist sentiment, see Seymour Drescher, *Capitalism and Antislavery: British Mobilization in Comparative Perspective* (New York, 1986). The indexes of both the London *Times* and *Le Temps* of Paris for 1861–65 were used as indicators of the frequency of coverage in the mass press after the events of late 1859 and early 1860.

5. See *L'Indépendance Belge* (Brussels), Dec. 31, 1859, and the despatches of the American ambassador to Belgium concerning a delegation of Southerners to Europe and the formation of a committee of Belgian merchants to trade directly with the South. English sources in general, and the *Times* in particular, disproportionately formed the basis for the selection and reporting of events in European newspapers less closely linked with the transatlantic flow of information. See, for example, *Neue Amsterdamsche Courant*, which lists all American items in its "Engelsche Post" section; the *Dagbladet* (Copenhagen), Dec. 22, 1859; and the *Giornale del Regno delle Due Sicilie* (Naples), Nov. 29, 1859, and Jan. 20, 1860.

6. See Jim Potter, "Atlantic Economy, 1815–1860: The U.S.A. and the Industrial Revolution in Britain," in *Studies in the Industrial Revolution*, ed. L. S. Pressnell (London, 1960), pp. 244 and 248–57.

7. See, for example, Betty Fladeland, *Men and Brothers: Anglo-American Antislavery Cooperation* (Urbana, Ill., 1972), esp. ch. 15; Howard Temperley, *British Antislavery, 1833–1870* (London, 1972), chs. 10–12; Christine Bolt, *The Antislavery Movement and Reconstruction: A Study in Anglo-American Cooperation, 1833–77* (London and

New York, 1969), ch. 1; C. Duncan Rice, *The Scots Abolitionists, 1833–1861* (Baton Rouge, 1981), ch. 6; R. J. M. Blackett, *Building an Antislavery Wall: Black Americans in the Atlantic Abolitionist Movement, 1830–1860* (Baton Rouge, 1983); Ripley, ed., *Abolitionist,* vol. 1 (*The British Isles, 1830–1865*); Clare Taylor, ed., *British and American Abolitionists: An Episode in Transatlantic Understanding* (Edinburgh, 1974); and David Turley, *The Culture of English Antislavery, 1780–1860* (London and New York, 1991).

8. On the decline of abolitionism in the 1850s, see Temperley, *British Antislavery,* pp. 221–47; and Rice, *Scots Abolitionists,* pp. 151–54. On the minor Continental European abolitionist movements, see Seymour Drescher, "Two Variants of Anti-slavery: Religious Organization and Social Mobilization in Britain and France, 1780–1870," in *Anti-Slavery, Religion and Reform,* ed. Christine Bolt and Seymour Drescher (Folkestone, Eng., 1980), pp. 43–63.

9. From announcements and reports I have been able to determine that between December 1859 and April 1860 abolitionist lecturers spoke on Brown in Bradford, Halifax, Sheffield, Ulverston, Leeds, Wakefield, Bolton, Edinburgh, Glasgow, Preston, Leigh, Dundee, Perth, and Dublin.

10. See, above all, David Brion Davis, *Slavery and Human Progress* (New York, 1984), esp. pp. 107–68 and 231–58.

11. See Pierre Vesnier, *Le Martyr de la liberté des nègres, ou John Brown, Le Christ des noirs* (Berlin and Brussels, 1864), p. 383. On the "outrages to civilization," see the *Morning Post* (London), Jan. 1, 1860.

12. "Like France, like England, like Germany, she [America] is one of the great agents of civilization; that she sometimes even leaves Europe in the rear by the sublime audacity of some of her progressive movements": Victor Hugo, "Letter to the editor of the London *Daily News.*"

13. See Reginald Horsman, *Race and Manifest Destiny: The Origins of American Racial Anglo-Saxonism* (Cambridge, Mass., 1981); esp. chs. 1–5; Douglas A. Lorimer, *Colour, Class and the Victorians: English Attitudes to the Negro in the Mid-Nineteenth Century* (Leicester, 1978); Christine Bolt, *Victorian Attitudes to Race* (London, 1971); Leon Poliakov, *The Aryan Myth: A History of Racist and Nationalist Ideas in Europe,* trans. Edmund Howard (New York, 1974); and George W. Stocking, Jr., *Victorian Anthropology* (New York, 1987).

14. See the *Times,* November 17, 1859; *L'Indépendance Belge,* Jan. 5, 1860; Horsman, *Race and Manifest Destiny,* pp. 272–97. On the abolitionist recognition of racial expansion as a mark of greatness and pride for both the "Saxon" and "Celtic" races, see *The Liberator,* May 7, 1844. For a similar vision of Great Britain as the "mother of empires" and her children as the seeds of "free communities in all parts of the globe," a country whose population could "safely challenge intellectual comparison with any other race," and so on, see the letter of a "Northumbrian" in the prolabor *Reynolds Newspaper* (London), Nov. 20, 1859. The same issue published John Brown's final speech to the Virginia court. British concern about the racial dilution of Anglo-Saxonism in the United States was directed primarily toward the rising tide of Continental European emigration to American cities (see the *Warwick and Warwickshire Advertiser,* Jan. 14, 1860). Blackett notes that American blacks did not challenge British racism lest they alienate potential support (*Building an Antislavery Wall,* p. 160). But black abolitionists also shared the general propensity to invoke racial typologies, even if they were not identical to those of Anglo-Saxonists. See, for example, the closing remarks of the Reverend Sella Martin in *The Martyrdom of John Brown: The Proceedings of a Public Meeting Held in London on the 2nd of December 1863 to Commemorate the Fourth Anniversary of John Brown's Death* (London, 1864), p. 22. Note also the following invocation of racial pride in the proabolitionist London *Examiner,* republished in Garrison's *Liberator* on December 8, 1859, as one of the first

indications of the European reaction to Brown's trial: "If we have ever entertained any doubts about the capabilities of the negro race, they arise from the very fact that they have so long borne slavery so patiently and submissively. An Anglo-Saxon race we proudly felt could never thus have been held in subjection." In seeking to banish even the threat of "servile insurrection" from relevance, the *Examiner* (and *The Liberator*) conveniently omitted mentioning either the Norman conquest of 1066 or the Saint Domingue revolution of 1791. On the emergence of Anglo-Saxonism as a culturally significant myth in mid-Victorian Britain, see Billie Melman, "Claiming the Nation's Past: The Invention of an Anglo-Saxon Tradition," *Journal of Contemporary History* 26 (Sept. 1991): 575–95.

15. See Horsman, *Race and Manifest Destiny*, pp. 178–80, on Theodore Parker's acceptance of racial doctrines. Parker, who was a member of Brown's inner circle, was dying of tuberculosis in Italy at the time of the raid.

16. See Jerome Blum, *The End of the Old Order in Rural Europe* (Princeton, 1978).

17. See David Brion Davis, *Slavery and Human Progress*, pp. 233–44; Robert William Fogel and Stanley L. Engerman, *Time on the Cross: The Economics of American Negro Slavery*, 2 vols. (Boston, 1974), 1:103–5; Robert William Fogel, *Without Consent or Contract: The Rise and Fall of American Slavery* (New York, 1990), pp. 81–113; Robin Blackburn, *The Overthrow of Colonial Slavery, 1776–1848* (London, 1988); and Drew Gilpin Faust, ed., *The Ideology of Slavery: Proslavery Thought in the Antebellum South, 1830–1860* (Baton Rouge, 1981), pp. 274–99. On Southern slavery's recognized potential for expansion, see the *Belfast Daily Mercury*, Dec. 27, 1859, citing the authority of *The Economist*.

18. The *Times*, April 22, 1857; see also Crawford, *Anglo-American Crisis*, p. 57.

19. The *Times*, Nov. 17, 1859; this editorial was reprinted the following day by the *Manchester Guardian*. See also the *Carlisle Journal*, Jan. 6, 1860; and the *Bradford Observer*, Jan. 12, 1860.

20. These figures are drawn from a sample of British, French, Belgian, German, Portuguese, Spanish, Dutch, Danish, Swedish, Norwegian, and Italian newspapers and periodicals (see note 4, above).

21. See, for example, *L'Indépendance Belge*, Nov. 16, 1859; the *Liverpool Daily Post*, Nov. 7, 1859; and the *Annual Register of World Events: A Review of the Year 1859* (London, 1860). Slavery could also be an ideological weapon. One British weekly referred sarcastically to "the ruffianly conduct of Harney" of San Juan, "the distinguished general who flogged his negro women to death" (*London Illustrated News*, Dec. 31, 1859).

22. See, among others, the *Caledonian Mercury* (Edinburgh), Nov. 18, 1859; the *Daily News* (London), Dec. 18, 1859; and the *Glasgow Times and Western Counties Chronicle*, Nov. 2, 9, 16, 23, and 30, and Dec. 1, 14, and 21, 1859. The radical *Leader* (London) exhibited the same emphasis (see its issues from November 1859 to January 1860). One of Garibaldi's English military comrades in the revolution of 1848 also figured in John Brown's military preparations: see Jasper Ridley, *Garibaldi* (New York, 1974), p. 460.

23. Exceptionally, the *Leader*'s "National Outlook for 1860" noted that, in the "great Anglo-Saxon republic the year will be ever-memorable for the first, we fear not the last, outbreak of a servile insurrection" (Jan. 7, 1860). In central and southern Europe, newspaper accounts were sporadic and editorial attention was extremely terse. See the *Wiener Zeitung;* the *Deutsche Allgemeine Zeitung* (Leipzig); *El Credito* (Madrid); and *Asmodee* (Amsterdam). The *Giornali di Roma*, Dec. 19, 1859, did make a brief allusion to the "terrible drama at the center of liberty," in referring to a report in *La Lombardia* on the impact of Hugo's letter in Paris. The *Gazzetta di Milano* and the

Neue Preussische Zeitung (Berlin), however, offered no editorial comment on the brief items they published on Brown.

24. See, for example, *Le Constitutionnel* (Paris), Oct. 29, 1859; the *Liverpool Daily Post,* Oct. 28, 1859; the *Manchester Daily Examiner,* Oct. 28, 1859; the *Leeds Mercury,* Oct. 29, 1859; the *North Briton* (Edinburgh), Oct. 29, 1859; *Le Nord* (Brussels), Nov. 2, 1859; and the *Giornali di Roma,* Nov. 15, 1859.

25. For the reference to Europe's averted face, see the *Times,* Nov. 5, 1859. So closely connected was the term *Negro insurrection* with the Saint Domingue revolution that the first account in Madrid's *El Credito* (Nov. 6, 1859) began: "In Harper's Ferry (Haity) an insurrection of 800 Negroes has taken place." On the enduring European association of massacres, atrocities, and arson with the Haitian slave revolution, see Danielle Begot, "A L'Origine de l'imaginaire de violence à Saint-Domingue: Insurrection servile et iconographie," in *Mourir pour les Antilles: Indépendance nègre ou esclave, 1802–1804,* ed. Michel L. Martin and Alain Yacou (Paris, 1991), pp. 95–133, quoting A. Moreau de Jonnès, *Aventures de guerre au temps du Consulat et de la République Paris,* 2 vols. (1858; repr. Paris, 1929), p. 125. For the use of St. Domingue in the John Brown affair, see the *Times* (London), Dec. 23, 1859, citing Edward Everett's speech during a public meeting on Brown at Tremont Temple in Boston. See also the *Morning Herald* (London), Jan. 1, 1860.

26. See Lorimer, *Colour, Class and the Victorians,* ch. 4. For an editorial contemporaneous with the discussion of Brown, see the *Times,* Nov. 3, 1859.

27. See the *Saturday Press* (Fife), Nov. 12, 1859; the *Manchester Daily Examiner,* Dec. 20, 1859; the *Caledonian Mercury* (Edinburgh), Nov. 14, 1859; *Le Siècle* (Paris), Dec. 21, 1859; the *Glasgow Sentinel,* Dec. 24, 1859; *Le Constitutionnel* (Paris), Dec. 19, 1859; *Neue Preussische Zeitung* (Berlin), Dec. 20, 1859; *Journal des Débats* (Paris), Dec. 18 and 24, 1859; the *North Briton* (Edinburgh), Nov. 19, 1859; the *Morning Chronicle* (London), Dec. 17, 1859; the *Aberdeen Journal,* Dec. 21, 1859; *Le Monde Illustré* (Paris), Dec. 17, 1859; and the *Leeds Mercury,* Jan. 14, 1860.

28. See, among others, *L'Union* (Paris), Nov. 16, 1859; the *Glasgow Advertiser,* Dec. 24, 1859; the *Birmingham Journal,* Dec. 17, 1859; and the *Wiener Zeitung,* Nov. 18, 1859.

29. See the *Caledonian Mercury,* Dec. 20, 1859.

30. The *Saturday Press* (Fife), Nov. 12, 1859; the *Caledonian Mercury,* Dec. 16, 1859; the *Leeds Mercury,* Dec. 22, 1859.

31. Lebreton-Savigny, *Victor Hugo et les Américains,* p. 240.

32. *Le Monde Illustré,* Dec. 17, 1859. The *London Illustrated News,* by contrast, offered no artistic dramatizations of the trial or execution.

33. From the *Morning Star* (London), reprinted in *The Liberator,* Jan. 20, 1860. See also the *Bristol Times,* Dec. 24, 1859; *Deutsche Allegemeine Zeitung,* Dec. 20, 1859; the *Belfast Daily Mercury,* Dec. 19, 1859. Occasionally an editorial dilated on the treatment of Brown's corpse as a symptom of Southern fear and rage. So fearful of his survival were his executioners, wrote the *Banner of Ulster,* "that a brave and noble captain prescribed a dose of arsenic, and others suggested decapitation" (Dec. 29, 1859).

34. See the *Daily Post* (Liverpool), Dec. 14 and 16, 1859, and Jan. 9, 1860; the *Saturday Press* (Fife), Dec. 24, 1859; the *Manchester Daily Examiner,* Dec. 20, 1859; the *Caledonian Mercury,* Dec. 20, 1859; *L'Union,* Dec. 21, 1859; *L'Indépendance Belge,* Dec. 17; the *Morning Herald* (London), Dec. 20, 1859; *Journal des Débats,* Dec. 24, 1859; the *Western Daily Press* (Bristol), Dec. 17, 1859; *Le Nord,* Dec. 23, 1859; the *North Briton,* Dec. 31, 1859; the *Glasgow Times,* Dec. 21, 1859; and the *London Illustrated News,* Dec. 24, 1859.

35. The *Manchester Guardian* of Dec. 17, 1859, illustrates the more skeptical vein

of commentary: "Washington has slain SPARTACUS, as the fact is expressed in the tawdry rhetoric of M. Victor Hugo." What seemed at first like an outbreak of "reckless fanaticism" became a more serious matter by the impression it created and the character of its "principal hero," a Puritan warring "for the abstract principle of human freedom." However, "we would not be understood as offering any justification or apology for this attempt." Brown's was a "heinous crime"; the justice of the sentence could not be questioned. The *Guardian* hoped that "English opinion will not be joined" with that part of American opinion that heaped "reproaches upon the authorities of Virginia." Nevertheless, concluded the *Guardian*, tacking once more, Brown had none of the "crazy vanity" of rebels in "old European communities," despite the fact that he shared his fate with "vulgar criminals." For a good example of editorial symmetry between the classical heroic/Christian martyr on the one side and fire-and-blood vengeance on the other, see "A Martyr or a Criminal?" *Aberdeen Journal*, Dec. 21, 1859.

36. Almost every account in the European press first referred to news of Harpers Ferry as a "servile" or a "Negro" insurrection or uprising. From 1859, see, among others, the *Leeds Intelligencer*, Oct. 29; the *Leeds and West Riding Express*, Oct. 29; the *Leader*, Oct. 30 and Dec. 3; the *North Britain*, Oct. 29; *L'Union*, Nov. 2 and 3; *Le Constitutionnel*, Oct. 29; *Le Nord*, Nov. 6; the *Daily Post* (Liverpool), Oct. 28; the *Glasgow Advertiser*, Oct. 29; the *Saturday Press* (Fife), Oct. 29; the *Manchester Daily Examiner and Times*, Nov. 1; the *Manchester Guardian*, Oct. 29 and Nov. 1; the *Caledonian Mercury*, Oct. 29; the *Times*, Dec. 6; the *Caledonian Mercury*, Dec. 16 and 20; *L'Indépendance Belge*, Dec. 8; *Deutsche Allegemeine Zeitung*, Dec. 20; the *Glasgow Times*, Dec. 2; *Reynold's Newspaper*, Nov. 6; and *Faedrelandet* (Copenhagen), Nov. 1. The *Giornale del Regno delle Due Sicilie* (Nov. 12, 1859) referred to "*una insurrezione terrible e' scoppiata*'" of Negroes.

37. See the *Dublin Evening Mail*, Dec. 23, 1859. If John Brown was "half crazed," wrote one Birmingham editor, the Southerners' "abject panic" showed that they had blundered into an execution from the profoundest sense of insecurity. What would have become of our Irish troubles, he asked, if "we had hanged our Cuffeys, our Smith, our O'Brien, our Mitchells, and other makers of tempests in a wash-tub?" Virginians lacked the sense of "contemptuous forbearance" and thus lost the opportunity to turn the tables on the abolitionists (*Birmingham Daily Post*, Jan. 2, 1860). See also the *London Illustrated News*, Dec. 24, 1859; *Le Siècle*, Jan. 2 and 3, 1860; *L'Union*, Dec. 10 and 21, 1859; the *Glasgow Sentinel*, Dec. 24, 1859; the *Leader*, Nov. 19, 1859; and the *Morning Post* (London), Jan. 31, 1860. *L'Univers* (Paris), Nov. 25, 1859, underscored "the barbarity with which the people of Virginia have condemned a political prisoner, after having deprived him of the privilege of a free defense." This judgment was singled out by American abolitionists for quotation in the *John Brown Year* (p. 161) because it came from an ultraconservative and pro-papal organ. Some conservative newspapers found the Southern reaction to be more understandable in view of the abolitionists who defended violence.

38. For ascriptions of fanaticism to both sides, see the *Birmingham Daily Post*, Jan. 4, 1860; and the *Giornali di Roma*, Jan. 12, 1860. On reports of Southern behavior as bizarre and incomprehensible, even to generally conservative newspapers, see the *Manchester Guardian*, Dec. 27, 1859: its correspondent found the excitement in Washington and the South beyond "the power of words to express" and "painful to behold." The South was turning itself into a repressive despotism with a censorship as severe as in France or Russia (see ibid., Jan. 5 and 14, 1860; and the *Birmingham Daily Post*, Jan. 9 and 18, 1860). By January 30, the *Guardian* could refer to Southern behavior as "that of men who totter and reel and rave at the prospect of calamities which they see to be inevitable." See also the *Glasgow Advertiser*, Dec. 24,

1859; the *Warwick and Warwickshire Advertiser,* Jan. 14, 1860; and the *Glasgow Sentinel,* Dec. 10, 1859.

39. See, among others, the *Manchester Guardian,* Dec. 27, 1859, and Jan. 5, 9, 14, and 26, and Feb. 6, 1860; the *Leader,* Dec. 24, 1859, and Jan. 7 and 28, 1860; the *Manchester Daily Examiner,* Jan. 24, 1860; the *Leeds Mercury,* Jan. 10, 1860; the *Morning Herald* (London), Jan. 3, 1860; the *Leader,* Jan. 28, 1860; and the *Morning Post* (London), Jan. 2, 11, and 24, 1860. One newspaper wrote that "Hispanic American commonwealths would be constitutional utopias" by comparison with the situation developing in the slave states (*Birmingham Daily Post,* Jan. 2, 1860).

40. See the *Times,* Jan. 14, 1860.

41. See *L'Union,* Dec. 10, 1859. See also *Le Siècle,* Dec. 17, 1859, and Jan. 13, 1860; and the *Manchester Guardian,* Nov. 5, 1859, and Jan. 13, 1860. A number of editorials seized on the turmoil in order to comment upon domestic and European issues. The Liverpool *Daily Post,* for example, compared expressions of Irish pro-papal sympathy in the crisis of Italian unification with the "fanaticism" of both the North and the South in the United States (Jan. 9, 1860).

42. On Hugo's relative indifference to disunion, see Juin, *Victor Hugo,* 2:438. See also *Le Siècle,* Jan. 13, 1860. The Russian radical, Nicholas Chernyshevskii, saw Brown's defeat as the opening battle of a revolutionary struggle in the United States, but he was far more interested than most European commentators in the confiscatory clauses of Brown's model constitution. Alexander Herzen, like Hugo, was more impressed by the execution of Brown as a betrayal of the American democratic dream. See Hans Rogger, "Russia and the Civil War," in *Heard Round the World: The Impact of Abroad of the Civil War,* ed. Harold Hyman (New York, 1969), pp. 196–99. Harriet Martineau made a favorable comparison between Brown and European (particularly Irish) revolutionaries, to the clear advantage of Brown: see her letter to the *National Anti-Slavery Standard,* reprinted as "An English View of John Brown's Attempt" in the *New York Times,* Jan. 5, 1860. Correspondingly, the most sympathetic recognition of the "feelings of the Southerners" exasperated by antislavery agitation came in the pages of the Dublin *Nation,* reporting a series of lectures on America by William Smith O'Brien. O'Brien admonished abolitionists to correct their own race relations and emphasized (to cheers) the serious calamity that might be entailed in the sudden manumission of the South's slaves (see the *Nation,* Nov. 26 and Dec. 3, 1859). On the strains between Anglo-American abolitionists and Irish nationalists, see Gilbert Osofsky, "Abolitionists, Irish Immigrants, and the Dilemmas of Romantic Nationalism," *AHR* 80 (Oct. 1975): 889–912. Karl Marx seems to have been relatively uninterested either in John Brown as a revolutionary figure or in Brown's constitution. However, as he noted to Engels on January 11, 1860: "In my opinion, the biggest things that are happening the world today are on the one hand the movement of the slaves in America started by the death of John Brown, and on the other the movement of the serfs in Russia": Karl Marx and Friedrich Engels, *The Civil War in the United States,* ed. Richard Enmale (New York, 1937), p. 221. Perhaps because Harpers Ferry could be used to undermine the image of the United States as the world's most advanced democracy, a prolabour and proworker's suffrage British newspaper made no attempt to draw editorial attention to the events. Only after the *Times* began to turn the affair into a devaluation of American democracy did the newspaper counterattack. For its changing stance, see *Reynold's Newspaper,* Nov. 6 and Dec. 4 and 18, 1859; Jan. 1 and 8, 1860; and Dec. 25, 1859, and Jan. 8, 1860.

43. See the *Manchester Guardian,* Jan. 14 and Feb. 6, 1860; the *Caledonian Mercury,* Dec. 20, 1859; *L'Union,* Dec. 21, 1859; the *Glasgow Sentinel,* Jan. 4, 1860; the *Leeds Mercury,* Jan. 10, 1860; and the *Leeds and West Riding Express,* Jan. 14, 1860. Some conservative editorials were less definitive about the outcome, but none asserted

that slavery would emerge victorious over the long term. See, for example, *Le Constitutionnel,* Jan. 20, 1860; the *Leeds Intelligencer,* Jan. 14 and 28, 1860; and E. Forcade, "Chronique de la quinzaine, 31 Décembre 1859," *Revue des deux mondes* 35 (Jan. 1860), p. 232.

44. On the commitment of the *Times* to the theory of progressive, gradual abolition, see Crawford, *Anglo-American Crisis,* pp. 56–61. Beginning with the Brown affair, the *Times* wavered but still hoped for a peaceful future (Jan. 14 and 19, 1860). On the *Times's* policy of deflating philanthropic agitation emanating from "Exeter Hall," see Howard Temperley, *White Dreams, Black Africa: The British Antislavery Expedition to the River Niger, 1841–1842* (London, 1991), pp. 60–63. For its detailed and sympathetic summary of Anthony Trollope's *The West Indies and the Spanish Main* (London, 1860), see the *Times,* Jan. 6, 1860, which included a protest against the "pathetic eloquence" of the abolitionists on "Sambo": "The negro is, no doubt, a very amusing and a very amiable fellow, and we ought to wish him well. . . . That he is capable of improvement everybody admits, but in the meantime he is decidedly inferior—he is but very little raised above the animal." No wonder that when the *Times* quoted a New York proslavery speaker to the effect that "nature" gave the Negro a master "to make him a useful servant" in its own editorial (Dec. 23, 1859), there was considerable doubt about how much difference existed between the views of the editors and those of the New York speaker.

45. See the *Times,* editorials of Dec. 19, 23, and 28, 1859. Its evaluation of the affair was quoted by other newspapers, including Ernest Jones's *The Cabinet Newspaper* (Dec. 24, 1859), which indicates that even Jones, who was imprisoned for sedition as a Chartist in 1848, could accept the *Times's* perspective.

46. "English Feeling on the American Slavery Question," in *Karl Marx, Friedrich Engels Gesamtausgabe (MEGA),* 20 vols. (Berlin, 1972), 18:623–27, originally printed in the *New York Daily Tribune,* Jan. 19, 1860, and dated London, Dec. 31, 1859.

47. From the London *Daily News,* reprinted in the *New York Times,* Jan. 18, 1860, and analyzed at length in *Deutsche Allegemeine Zeitung,* Jan. 7, 1860. On the vigorous reaction against the *Times's* position, see also, among others, the *Liverpool Mercury,* Jan. 7, 1860; the *Sheffield Independent,* Jan. 21, 1860; the *Bradford Observer,* Jan. 12, 1860; and the *Morning Star* (London), Jan. 9, 1860.

48. The *Times,* Jan. 3, 11, 14, 17, and 19, 1860. The *Times* (Jan. 14, 1860) was particularly irritated by the reception of Governor Wise's speech, when he regretted (to "tremendous applause") that an American ship had not seized and boarded the British vessel with "that negro [Frederick Douglass] on board." The paper was quite correct, though, in concluding that Wise's words, including his request for a retaliatory invasion of Canada, might please Irish nationalists: see the *Irishman* (Dublin), Jan. 14, 1860.

49. The *Times,* Jan. 30, 1860. The *Birmingham Post* similarly congratulated its nation on their freedom from extremes, the revolutionary madness of France, the deadening despotism of Austria, as well as the mob legislation and "revolver logic" of the United States (Jan. 9, 1860). See also the *Warwick Advertiser,* Jan. 7, 1860. The *Times* editorial was occasioned by a speech of Lord Brougham in Parliament on January 27, 1860. The *Manchester Guardian* also reflected on the economic catastrophe to Lancaster that might result from a civil conflict in the United States (Jan. 30, 1860). The *Times* retained its symmetrical model of abolitionist fanaticism and Southern rage but took pains, after January 1860, to present itself only as the *national* voice of British antislavery. It lamented both Southern senatorial "fury" and the "vindictive harangues" of Charles Sumner just when the "frenzy caused by John Brown's outrage" had begun to subside. See its editorial of June 18, 1860.

50. Phillips quoted in *The Liberator,* Nov. 7, 1859.

51. See Howard Mumford Jones, "1859 and the Idea of Crisis: General Introduction," in *1859: Entering An Age of Crisis,* ed. Philip Appleman et. al. (Bloomington, 1961), p. 14; see also the *Times,* Jan. 14, 1860.

52. The *Times,* Nov. 21, 1859.

53. On nonviolence among British abolitionists, see Temperley, *British Antislavery,* pp. 170–72, 176–83, and 252–54. British abolitionists were taken by surprise at the "unreasoned exaltation" within the North at the beginning of the Civil War, while Exeter Hall fell silent (see ibid., p. 253 and note). See also Fladeland, *Men and Brothers,* pp. 376–81; Rice, *Scots Abolitionists,* p. 188.

54. Excerpt from the London *Examiner* in *The Liberator,* Dec. 9, 1859; *Anti-Slavery Reporter,* Dec. 1, 1859, p. 272.

55. Harriet Martineau to the *National Anti-Slavery Standard,* reprinted in the *New York Times,* Jan. 5, 1860.

56. William S. McFeely, *Frederick Douglass* (New York and London, 1991), pp. 193–200, esp. p. 197.

57. Quoted in ibid., p. 197. See also the *Halifax Courier,* Dec. 3, 1859. Douglass reiterated the asylum theme in his opening speech at the Halifax Mechanics Hall on November 30, 1859 (ibid.). But Douglass's lectures drew almost no notice beyond the traditional British abolitionist towns. The *Times* mentioned his 1859–60 sojourn in England obliquely, in reference to the Virginia governor's remark that Douglass should have been seized on the high seas (Jan. 14, 1860).

58. John W. Blassingame et. al., eds., *The Frederick Douglass Papers,* 3 vols. (New Haven, 1979–   ), 2:141–42.

59. See the *Halifax Courier* and the *Halifax Guardian,* both of Dec. 17, 1859. See also McFeely, *Frederick Douglass,* p. 203: "The Hanging of John Brown made Frederick Douglass more law-abiding than he had ever been." See also Blassingame et al., eds., *Frederick Douglass Papers,* 3:315–16, for Douglass's speech in Edinburgh, Jan. 30, 1860. For Douglass's increasing self-identification with Brown, see ibid., 3:618 (speech of Feb. 14, 1860).

60. On the exodus theme, see Blassingame et al., eds., *Frederick Douglass Papers,* 3:334 and 417; and the *Anti-Slavery Reporter'*s accounts of Douglass's speeches at Leeds and Newcastle-on-Tyne (Jan. 1 and May 1, 1860). See also ibid., Jan. 1, 1860, for a reprint of the same theme from Charles Dickens's *Once a Week.*

61. See the *Bolton Guardian,* March 24, 1860.

62. See the *Halifax Courier,* Dec. 10, 1859.

63. See the *Bolton Guardian,* March 24, 1860; McFeely, *Frederick Douglass,* p. 204; and the *Anti-Slavery Reporter,* Jan. 1, 1860.

64. The proabolitionist *Leeds Mercury* was explicit: "Nothing could be more disastrous to all classes, nothing could be more wicked after the example of Brown's failure, than another attempt of the same kind"; his fate was thus a warning that feeling against slavery had aroused too much intense feeling to be ignored any longer (Jan. 10, 1860). On the Wakefield meeting, see the *Wakefield Express,* Jan. 14, 1860. On the distinction between the actor and the action, see also the remarks of the chair and motions of thanks to Douglass at the Bradford meeting (*Bradford Observer,* Jan. 12, 1860). At the latter meeting, "A working man (an emigrant returned from the United States) expressed an opinion in condemnation of John Brown and his motives, and a warm discussion followed, which resulted in showing the very fallacious position he had taken up, and the all but unanimous sympathy of the meeting with the cause of abolition" (ibid.). This is the only instance of outright challenge I have come across, and the reporter's marginalization of the dissenter ("worker," "emigrant," "unintelligent") indicates that an unequivocal condemnation of Brown was intolerable to abolitionist audiences.

65. *The Liberator,* April 26, 1844. See also Fladeland, *Men and Brothers,* pp. 295–96, according to whom the slave was reputed to be Brown's mistress.

66. *The Liberator,* Apr. 26, 1844; see also Mar. 1 and May 7, 1844. The parliamentary and public intervention demonstrated how quickly the British could mobilize on the basis of the slightest information. Because the news of John L. Brown's sentence first came through New Orleans, both Lord Brougham and Lord Denman spoke in Parliament on behalf of a sentencing in the state of *Louisiana.* See *Hansard's Parliamentary Debates,* 3d ser., vol. 73 (1844), cols. 491–92 and 1156–60 (March 4 and 8, 1844).

67. *Daily News* (London), Dec. 10, 1859.

68. See Fladeland, *Men and Brothers,* pp. 350–58; Temperley, *British Antislavery,* pp. 224–28; Rice, *Scots Abolitionists,* pp. 173–88; and Glasgow Emancipation Society, *Uncle Tom Penny Offering* (n.p., n.d.).

69. See the *Anti-Slavery Reporter,* July 2, 1860, p. 158.

70. *Edinburgh Review* 112 (Oct. 1860): 292–93.

71. See Temperley, *British Antislavery,* pp. 254–55; Bolt, *Anti-Slavery Movement and Reconstruction,* p. 31.

72. See *The Martyrdom of John Brown,* pp. 3–15. For other works inspired by John Brown, see the poem by Jacques Fernand, *John Brown et ses amis* (Paris, 1861); Alphonse Pagès, "John Brown," in *Chroniques judiciaires* (Paris, 1866); and H. Emile Chevalier and Florien Pharaon, *Un Drame esclavagiste* (Paris, n.d.). Before the end of 1862 John Brown's action at Harpers Ferry was at least as useful to the pro-Southern as the pro-Northern press in Britain. See, for example, Joseph Barker, "Slavery and the Civil War; or, John Brown and the Harper's Ferry Insurrection," *Barker's Review,* Sept. 6, 1862, pp. 1–7. (Richard Blackett kindly brought this item to my attention.)

73. On reactions to Brown among prominent European revolutionaries, see Herbert Aptheker, *Abolitionism: A Revolutionary Movement* (Boston, 1989), pp. 137–38; Jerry Zedlicke, "The Image of America in Poland, 1776–1945," *Reviews in American History* 14 (Dec. 1986): 669–686, esp. pp. 673–74.

74. Vesnier, *Le Martyr de la liberté des nègres,* dedication. With the fall of the Commune, Vesnier fled to London, where he joined the "Society of Refugees," although he was soon expelled from it as a police spy. See William Serman, *La Commune de Paris, 1871* (Paris, 1986), pp. 311 and 536.

75. Vesnier, *Le Martyr de la liberté des nègres,* pp. 217–28.

76. Ibid., pp. 217 and 219.

77. Ibid., pp. 292–94, 348–54, and 378.

78. Vesnier, *Comment a peri la Commune* (Paris, 1892), p. x; *Daily News* (London), Dec. 3, 1863. Although the *New York Herald Tribune,* Dec. 5, 1866, described the British working-class demonstrations for suffrage in 1866 under the heading, "John Brown's Soul Is Marching On," the demonstrators preferred to emphasize the nonviolence of New England democracy as their American example. See also the *Times,* Sept. 26 and Oct. 9, 1866.

79. For the massive and sympathetic response to the assassination of Lincoln see, among others, Donaldson Jordan and Edwin J. Pratt, *Europe and the American Civil War* (Boston and New York, 1931), pp. 226–40; E. D. Adams, *Great Britain and the American Civil War,* 2 vols. (New York, 1925), 2:257–64; and Albert A. Waldman, *Lincoln and the Russians* (Cleveland and New York, 1952), pp. 261–62 and 269–76. At least two liberal newspapers in Paris linked the deaths of Brown and Lincoln as joint victims of the battle against slavery. See *Le Siècle* and *La Presse,* both of April 28, 1865, reprinted in the *New York Times,* May 16, 1865. Brown's death was also recalled at the Wakefield public sympathy meeting in England following Lincoln's assassination (Richard Blackett, "Contested Ground: British Working Class Reactions to the As-

sassination of President Lincoln," (unpublished manuscript kindly furnished by the author).

80. Serge Gavronsky, *The French Liberal Opposition, and the American Civil War* (New York, 1968), pp. 241–42.

81. See Hermann von Holst, *John Brown*, ed. Frank Preston Stearns, trans. Philippe Marcou, 2d ed. (Boston, 1888; orig. publ. 1883), appendix, pp. 189–94. The French committee sent the gold medal to Brown's widow on Oct. 21, 1874: see Juin, *Victor Hugo*, 3:198.

82. See Stearns, "Introduction," pp. 1–17 and 35–40, and *post-script*, pp. 204–15, in Holst, *John Brown*.

83. See Stearns' "Introduction," in Holst, *John Brown*, p. 41. Stearns was aware that his scientific arbiter considered the Civil War to have been an apocalyptic struggle between the Lord of Hosts and the forces of evil, with the North, progress, capitalism, manliness, antislavery, and the Republican party as bearers of the Divine Will. See also Clyde N. Wilson, "Herman E. von Holst," in *Dictionary of Literary Biography*, vol. 47, *American Historians 1866–1912* (Detroit, 1986), pp. 145–47; and Peter Novick, *That Noble Dream: The Objectivity Question and the American Historical Profession* (Cambridge, 1988), esp. pp. 21–26.

84. Stearns, "Introduction," in Holst, *John Brown*, p. 17.

85. Ibid., pp. 70–76.

86. Holst, *John Brown*, pp. 120–25 and 146–50. For the editor, Holst's "final judgement" was conveyed through the image of John Brown's living body at the edge of death: "Millions of eyes were fastened upon him . . . to see whether or not he would betray . . . that he was wearing a mask. . . . But after he had stood ten minutes like a statue . . . the millions drew a deep breath,—he was wholly pure, wholly true" (Stearns, "Introduction," in Holst, *John Brown*, pp. 47–48, quoting Holst himself, pp. 166–67).

87. European interest in John Brown did not lapse altogether. For Soviet historiographic concern, see Rogger, "Russia and the Civil War," in *Heard Round the World*, ed. Hyman, p. 199n3. There is another aspect of John Brown's body in Europe that I have not pursued, namely, the durability of "John Brown's Body" as an enormously popular song. In many numerous variations the tune was still part of the groupsinging repertoire of children in the twentieth century (courtesy of the recollections of Walter Laqueur). That, however, is surely another story.

10

CHARLES JOYNER

"Guilty of Holiest Crime"
The Passion of John Brown

But let me not die without a huge effort,
nor let me dishonorably die, but in the
brave doing of some great deed let me go,
that men yet to be may hear of what happened.

—Homer, *The Iliad*

Loved I shall be with him whom I have loved,
Guilty of holiest crime.

—Sophocles, *Antigone*

Thus, in succession, flame awakening flame
Fulfilled the order of the fiery course.

—Aeschylus, *Agamemnon*

IT WAS AN HOUR before noon that Friday morning when they took John Brown from jail. The prisoner neither protested nor acquiesced. His arms were tied down above the elbows, leaving his forearms free. At the door of the jail an open wagon awaited him. Lying on its bed was a large poplar box, within which was a black walnut coffin. Almost deliberate in his movements, without haste or fumbling, he climbed onto the wagon and sat down upon the box. The sheriff and the jailer sat down beside him, and the wagon moved off toward a field southeast of town. A column of soldiers escorted them, and two more columns of riflemen stood shoulder-to-shoulder along their route. The prisoner observed the military display without comment.[1]

It was bleak and chill that morning as the wagon made its way toward the field. At eleven o'clock it was about as warm as it was going to get.

Tension hovered in the quiet, crisp December air. Even the houses appeared huddled close together, watchful and apprehensive. Brown broke the silence. "This is beautiful country," he said pleasantly to his companions on the wagon. "I never had the pleasure of seeing it before." In the distance they could see the company of troops already in possession of the field and, looming over everything, the gallows. They were almost there.[2]

"Old Brown," as he seemed to be universally known, was fifty-nine years old. He wore the same shabby black suit he had worn at Harpers Ferry and at his trial, the black contrasting vividly with his white shirt and socks and his incongruous red slippers. His frame was tall but gaunt now almost to emaciation, and his grizzled beard was shorter than he had worn it in Kansas. The deep saber cut on the back of his neck, received at Harpers Ferry forty-six days before, was now a scar. His unflinching gray eyes, described by a supporter as possessing "great mesmeric power," were serious but wore no expression of melancholy that morning. Whatever his inner feelings, he showed no fear. His demeanor was characterized by an unexpected serenity.[3]

Now they were there. A group of soldiers surrounded the wagon and the scaffold. They allowed no one to come between them and the prisoner. Pickets were posted at various points, and the crowd was held back at bayonet point nearly a quarter of a mile from the gallows. "Why are none but military allowed in the enclosure?" Brown asked in that incongruously soft, pleasant voice. "I am sorry the citizens have been kept out." But if John Brown looked around him for sympathy and support it was in vain. As his pale gray eyes wandered over the stern, haggard faces of the crowd and the soldiers, he could not help but know that his hour had come. The elaborate security precautions were not necessary. The crowd was quite orderly. They had not come to rescue John Brown; they had come to see him die. Could the tranquil figure who stood immobile before them now, gaunt and impotent, be the demon they had been conditioned to hate and fear?[4]

The earth immediately about the scaffold was bare. The prisoner turned, not hurriedly or even quickly, but just easily, and ascended the steps to the gallows. And still with no haste, but no pause either, he shook hands with Sheriff James Campbell and jailer John Avis. "Gentlemen, goodbye," he told them. His quiet voice did not falter in the least. He stood where they told him to stand and held his head to one side so the sheriff could place the noose about his neck. Then Brown turned slowly, standing erect above the held breaths, and looked down upon the crowd with an invincible fatalism. One can only imagine with what sensations the crowd gazed upon this ritual, with its studied ceremony and show of courtesy. Colonel Thomas J. Jackson was there, commanding a detachment of his cadets from the Virginia Military Institute. So was the aging fire-eater Edmund Ruffin, who had borrowed a cadet's uniform so that he could stand nearer the scaffold for a better view of the hanging. The soldiers and the far-off crowd looked up at the prisoner standing there—frail, shabby, insignificant, yet somehow exalted, too, still wearing that expression of serenity, a martyr to the terrible simplicity of his idea, calling blood to the regeneration of human freedom. Before he left his cell that morning, Brown had written a note to his wife in his thin, cramped script, enclosed in which was a statement for public release: "I John Brown am now quite *certain* that the crimes of this *guilty, land: will* never be purged *away,* but with Blood. I had *as I now think: vainly* flattered myself that without *very much* bloodshed; it might be done."[5]

The sheriff asked the prisoner if he would like a handkerchief to drop as a signal. The prisoner replied quietly, "No, I don't care. I don't want you to keep me waiting unnecessarily." No preacher stood beneath the scaffold to pray for the convicted man's soul: Brown had declined the services of any minister who approved of, or even consented to, the enslavement of human beings. Now they put a white cap over his head. Jailer Avis asked him to step forward onto the trapdoor. "You must lead me," Brown responded dispassionately, "for I cannot see." He stood there for nearly ten minutes, erect, unflinching, unable to see the military units march and countermarch into position. Nor could he see the crowd, some standing motionless with bowed heads, others staring alternately at one another and at the distant figure upon the gallows. But Brown was not blind to the fact that his whole life up to this moment was meaningless compared to the incontestable goodness he believed he could bequeath to it now. He stood there upon the trapdoor, which was supported on the north side by hinges and on the south side by a rope.

When the troops had finally wheeled about into formation, their colonel announced to the sheriff, "All ready." The sheriff appeared not to understand the order, and the colonel had to repeat it. Then the sheriff struck the rope a sharp blow with a hatchet, springing the trap. John Brown fell through the trapdoor until his knees were even with the platform. His arms, below the elbows, flew up horizontally, with fists clinched, and gradually, with recurring spasms, fell. Then all was quiet. And in the hush that suddenly enveloped the whole somber assemblage, his body swung to and fro. The crowd stared. They would remember it, watching John Brown's body sway to and fro like that. Thomas J. Jackson, shortly to be likened to a stone wall, sent up a prayer that Brown's soul might be saved. "Awful was the thought," Jackson would write to his wife that night, "that he might in a few minutes receive the sentence, 'Depart, ye wicked, into everlasting fire.' I hope that he was prepared to die, but I am doubtful." Brown's pulse did not stop beating for thirty-five minutes. Then they cut him down and sent him back to his wife in the black walnut coffin.[6]

So they took him home to the hard and sterile acres of his farm at North Elba, New York, and buried him in the shadow of a great rock, among the rugged hills of the Adirondacks, by the quiet waters of Lake Placid. As the frigid day passed overhead, the abolitionist Wendell Phillips addressed the mourners at the graveside. "How our admiration, loving wonder has grown, day by day," Phillips marveled, "as he has unfolded trait after trait of earnest, brave, tender, Christian life!" Phillips's pious and practiced voice rang out over the fields to the hills beyond. "We see him walking with radiant, serene face to the scaffold, and think what an iron heart, what devoted faith!" Then the chief mourner moved beyond eulogy to apotheosis: "Thank God for such a master. Could we have asked a nobler representative of the Christian North putting her foot on the accursed system of slavery?" His rich voice ringing, Phillips challenged those assembled, "How can we stand here without a fresh and utter consecration?"[7]

Freed at last of time and flesh, absolved of mortality, John Brown was a far more palpable presence in death than he had been in life. Had it not been for the symbolic significance of his passion, John Brown might have been little noted nor long remembered. Measured by his grandiose ambitions, his whole life was a pitiful failure. His various bankruptcies had prompted charges of flagrant dishonesty on his part. He was accused of stealing horses and of murdering five unarmed proslavery settlers at Pottawatomie, Kansas. From 1856 on he depended for his livelihood on the donations of sympathizers, but he proved to be an incompetent revolutionary. His raid on the federal arsenal at Harpers Ferry, quickly put down by federal troops, was ill conceived, ill planned, and ill executed. The slave rebellion he anticipated never took place.[8]

But John Brown's significance lies less in the inadequacies of his life than in the manner of his death. "Let no man pray that Brown be spared," proclaimed the Reverend Henry Ward Beecher before the execution. "Let Virginia make him a martyr. Now, he has only blundered. His soul was noble; his work miserable. But a cord and a gibbet would redeem all that," Beecher declared, "and round up Brown's failure with a heroic success."[9] John Brown's execution was a beginning rather than an end. When his body was laid to molder in the grave, his soul was released into the public domain. Speechmakers, pamphleteers, and editorialists in the North and the South lost no time in constructing a mythic John Brown. His historical significance rests upon his passion, and upon the reactions of men and women on both sides of the Mason-Dixon line to what they read into it.

History and folklore converge in John Brown's passion. His wild career of violence in Kansas and at Harpers Ferry had a legendary dimension, larger than life. And his calm acceptance of death had a mythic, fatalistic quality. But how did John Brown come to his unexpected serenity on the gallows?

What was the root of his commitment to the Christian ideal of martyrdom —of emphasizing the ultimate worth of his cause by consciously laying down his life for it? What accounts for the depth of the responses to his execution? These central problems demand deeper analysis than they have yet received. One promising approach to such an analysis is offered by the conceptual tools of cultural anthropology: the passion of John Brown can be analyzed as a "social drama" in much the same fashion that anthropologists have analyzed events in preliterate societies. The situational approach developed by Victor Turner to analyze disputes among central African villagers would seem particularly useful in this regard. The rhetoric and symbolic gestures of the major actors in the John Brown affair were not, in fact, unlike those of preliterate tribesmen.[10]

There is, of course, a major difference between the passion of John Brown and a relatively localized crisis in a small-scale, and possibly preliterate, society. All the tensions of an emerging capitalist nation undergoing rapid social transformation were immanent within the John Brown crisis. At the same time, the form and content of its discourse derived from major, long-standing traditions of Western thought. Such a crisis stood at the nexus of slavery and freedom in its own time but could stand as well at the nexus of structure and conjuncture, of event and process, in ours. John Brown's actions constitute a crucial dramatic link in the chain stretching from the compromises of the Constitutional Convention through the Missouri Compromise and the Compromise of 1850 to the uncompromisable secession crisis, the Civil War, and ultimately Emancipation.

The concept of social drama, as elaborated by Turner, is very useful for analyzing events manifesting social conflict. Turner's four-stage model may be thought of as a drama in four acts. The first act opens with the breach of some crucial social relationship. The second act dramatizes a phase of rapidly expanding crisis, a phase that tends to polarize the social group. During the third act attempts are made to apply legal or ritual means of reconciliation. Depending on the success or failure of such efforts, the final act expresses either social reconciliation or irremediable schism. This four-act structure results not from the historical actors' instincts or improvisation but from basic models and metaphors—cultural paradigms—carried in their heads.[11] Social dramas are structured in time rather than in space, and they develop in phases. At any point in the process social relations are thus likely to be incomplete. But ideas and images, patterned by actual social events, manifest themselves as symbols somewhere between consciousness and the unconscious. Originating in human passion, these vernacular symbols then precipitate social action. In crises of cross-purposes and competing interests, they mediate between ideals and action.[12] Many opposing values clashed in the social drama of John Brown's passion: conflicts over secular and religious sources of authority, honor and conscience as ethical systems, aristocratic and bourgeois notions of liberty, and seigneurial versus market relations, as well as the more obvious slavery issue. All these conflicts, and more, were caught up in the social drama of John Brown—and all these social conflicts were supported by sharply contrasting cultural paradigms.[13]

To study the structure of social drama, then, is to study the vernacular symbols people employ to achieve their goals. To understand social drama is to understand the process of communication among groups and within groups. Actions in a social drama are guided less by rules or customs than by subjective paradigms existing in the heads of the actors. Such root paradigms, moreover, affect the form and style of behavior even when the actors are not consciously aware of them. Allusive, metaphorical, and existential, root paradigms reach toward the fundamental assumptions that undergird society and are thus available to anyone who chooses to act upon them. Inherently bound up with religion, root paradigms often involve self-sacrifice as a symbol of ultimate victory. Bowed down by the painful shadow of death that nothing could make endurable, Brown knew there was no hope for him. He knew that for the rest of his days, frail and racked, he would live in the hazy presence of a purifying terror. Between his capture at Harpers Ferry and his execution at Charlestown, John Brown came under the sway of such a root paradigm.[14]

The passion of John Brown not only marks his passage from the degraded status of condemned prisoner to the exalted status of martyr but also invokes elaborate ritual and serene self-sacrifice in an effort to cure slavery—the nation's leading affliction. Thus the social drama of John Brown may be seen not only as a functional equivalent to the kinds of "rites of passage" that mark changes in social status but also as equivalent to the "rituals of affliction" that are invoked to cure illness or dispel misfortune.[15]

Act I: The Breach

The first phase of a social drama opens with the breach of some crucial relationship within the social system—a dramatic symbol of dissidence. The attack by John Brown and his men on the federal arsenal at Harpers Ferry, Virginia, constituted the "symbolic trigger of confrontation or encounter." Brown acted—or believed he was acting—on behalf of enslaved African Americans, although in fact he had little contact with African Americans. Governor Henry Wise of Virginia contended that Brown had broken the law of the land and thus sought to begin the drama at the redressive stage, with Virginia as judge. Brown countered that it was not so much that he had broken man-made laws but that the slave states had breached God's laws by holding human beings in bondage. For their part, slaveholders held that it was the free states who had breached the constitutional agreement not to meddle in Southern domestic institutions. At stake, however, was not whose breach of what had instigated the crisis, but who could prevail in the test of wills. Virginia sought to provoke an immediate showdown on the sectional issue while the terms of the dispute appeared to be in her favor. Both proslavery forces and antislavery forces sought to muster their resources of wealth, power, and influence. And the breach quickly became a crisis, a deepening crisis so severe that the normal means of redress would soon prove inadequate.[16]

There was a strange calm just before both slaveholders and abolitionists realized the nature and the implications of the social drama toward which they were being impelled. In South Carolina, the South's hotspur state, initial press reaction was deceptively mild. On October 20, the *Charleston Daily Courier* appeared relatively unruffled, remarking that the raid itself "only demonstrates the impregnable safety of the South, when awakened to her own defense." But Southern impregnability hardly mitigated the offense to Southern honor. "Let the law be vindicated," the *Courier* demanded, "and questions of jurisdiction and process be settled afterwards." The *Edgefield Advertiser* used more colorful rhetoric in its denunciation of the raid a few days later, labeling the affair "a hairbrained demonstration by a pack of crazy fanatics and poor deluded slaves." Nevertheless, the incident cried out for vengeance. "Yet while crazy and deluded," the *Advertiser* asserted, "their offense is rank and can only be expiated by the most condign punishment."[17]

There was something vaguely primal in the way the social drama of John Brown unfolded. The major actors performed their roles as though they were participating in a carefully choreographed ritual dance. Nervous Republicans attempted at first to distance themselves from Brown. Mesmerized by fear that their 1860 electoral hopes would be dashed if they came to be considered a party of fanatics, many attempted to minimize the incident. "But for the loss of life attending the foray of the crazy Brown among the Virginians," the *Cleveland Leader* editorialized, "the whole thing would be positively ridiculous." Another strategy was to express outrage. Horace Greeley's pro-Republican *New York Tribune* denounced attempts by "the slave Democracy" to connect the Republican party "with Old Brown's mad outbreak." It also called Brown's Raid "the work of a madman" but added ominously that "what seems madness to others doubtless wore a different aspect to him." Harpers Ferry, the *Tribune* insisted, resulted from the violence and injustice of "Bleeding Kansas": The real responsibility belonged to those who "sustained the Border Ruffian Pro-Slavery war against Free labor in Kansas." Even William Lloyd Garrison's abolitionist newspaper,

The Liberator, called Brown's raid on Harpers Ferry "misguided, wild, and apparently insane." The raid was severely condemned as well in Kansas, birthplace of Brown's notoriety. The *Topeka Tribune* termed it "the wild scheme of a bad man who, seeking for personal distinction (not fame) and perhaps plunder, was ready to endanger the lives of thousands," while the *Atchison City Freedom's Champion* thought it "an insane effort to accomplish what none but a madman would attempt."[18]

It was tempting for both Democrats and Republicans to use the affair for partisan advantage, and few Democrats or Republicans resisted the temptation. Some Democrats found in the crisis an especially convenient opportunity to smear their Republican rivals, portraying the raid as part of some dark Republican plot. Others professed outrage that Republicans failed to show sufficient indignation over the raid. James Gordon Bennett's anti-abolitionist *New York Herald* asserted that Brown had been "rendered daring, reckless, and an abolition monomaniac by the scenes of violence through which he had passed." Old Brown deserved his fate, the *Herald* asserted, "but his death and the punishment of his criminal associates will be as a feather in the balance against the mischievous consequences which will probably follow from the rekindling of the slavery excitement in the South." According to Northern Democrats, talk of "the higher law" and of "the irrepressible conflict" would inevitably lead to violence. Brown may have been a "madman," but irresponsible orators were no less than "traitors."[19]

But there were Northern radicals equally eager to express their approval of Brown's efforts. One of the first prominent Northerners to speak out in behalf of John Brown was Concord's Henry David Thoreau. Within two weeks of the Harpers Ferry raid, the man who had eschewed the company of his neighbors for a winter at Walden Pond called a public meeting to plead the prisoner's cause. Thoreau polished his prose by careful rewriting, tailoring it to his audience. He began as though recounting informal memories of a close friend but became increasingly poetic as he depicted John Brown as "an angel of light." Poets, painters, and historians, he predicted, would one day compare Brown's action on behalf of the slaves to the signing of the Declaration of Independence or to the Pilgrims landing at Plymouth Rock.[20]

Thoreau's friend and sometime mentor, Ralph Waldo Emerson, took longer to formulate his position. Shortly after the raid he wrote to his brother that Brown had "lost his head" at Harpers Ferry. Nevertheless, he confided a few days later, he hoped for Brown's escape "to the last moment." By November 8, however, all of Emerson's doubts had been dispelled. In a Boston address he referred to Brown as "the Saint whose martyrdom, if it shall be perfected, will make the gallows as glorious as the cross."

He wished, he said, that men had "health enough to know virtue" when they saw it and "not cry with the fools, 'madman,' when a hero passes."[21]

In this historical moment individual instability and social instability increasingly came together. And they did so in such dramatic fashion that, under the sway of the root paradigm, the two dramas became increasingly coordinated in tragic counterpoint.

Act II: The Crisis

The initial breach of social relations was followed by a menacing phase in which the breach widened into a major cleavage. The increasingly threatening crisis took its place in the public forum, daring the custodians of order to deal with it. No longer was it possible to pretend that nothing was wrong; no longer could the crisis be ignored or wished away. At such a critical impasse some grasp at straws. John Brown seized roots. The root paradigm of martyrdom now claimed his attention and directed his actions. "Christ the great Captain of *liberty*," he wrote to a supporter, "saw fit to take from me a sword of steel after I had carried it for a time but he has put another in my hand: 'The sword of the Spirit.'" Writing his wife following the failure of his insurrection, Brown declared: "I have been *whip[p]ed* as the saying *is,* but am sure I can recover all the lost capital occasioned by that disaster by only hanging a few moments by the neck; & I feel quite determined to make the utmost possible out of a defeat." Brown's personal crisis marked a turning point, a threshold between stable phases.[22]

As slaveholders and abolitionists alike now began to realize the terrible implications of the social drama into which they had been thrust, they confirmed that thrust by their very realization. Thus the *Boston Journal,* for example, assured its readers that Brown's actions had "loosened the roots of the slave system." But as the crisis deepened, attitudes hardened. Those not previously activated by the issues more and more took sides; neutrality seemed less and less viable. Some in the North tried to draw fine distinctions between Brown's motives and Brown's means, between what he tried to do and how he tried to do it. But in the critical phase of the social drama motives and means were no longer easily separable. Now one either condemned slavery or tacitly supported it. Now those who detested slavery demonized slaveholders, for unless one wished to be seen as standing shoulder-to-shoulder with slaveholders, one was now constrained to support John Brown. Horace Greeley spoke for many when he wrote in the *New York Tribune* that he would not "by one reproachful word disturb the bloody shrouds wherein John Brown and his compatriots lie sleeping. They dared and died for what they felt to be right." Greeley left little doubt that he sympathized with "what they felt to be right" or that he regarded Brown as a hero for having the courage to do what lesser men wanted to see done but were afraid to do themselves. "Let their epitaphs remain unwritten," he wrote, "until the not distant day when no slave shall clank his chains in the shades of Monticello or the graves of Mount Vernon." Greeley went on to praise John Brown for what he called the "disinterestedness and consistent devotion to the rights of human nature" that had impelled his "desperate undertaking."[23]

As might be expected, the Harpers Ferry foray stirred Southern sensibilities even more deeply than Northern ones. The Brown crisis seemed to touch something dark, something archetypal, in the Southern psyche. Physical invasion and servile insurrection were not, of course, matters to be taken lightly under any circumstances. But under attack men who had once called slavery a necessary evil now defended it as a positive good. It was a dubious measure of abolitionist effectiveness that slaveholders became more defensive than ever in the late 1850s. Widespread agitation to reopen the African slave trade led to a bill to that effect actually being introduced in the South Carolina legislature in 1859, although it was eventually tabled after bitter debate. But the autumn of 1859 clearly polarized proslavery and antislavery positions, as the most ardent agitators on both sides spoke out with increased confidence. How long could they be kept from each other's throats?[24]

In the ritualized rhetoric of the social drama, the Philippic—a style of rhetoric abounding in acrimony—became the discourse of choice on each side. The Philippic is not a form of rhetoric intended to convert the skeptics. Rather, its purpose is to rally the faithful, to intensify the feelings of those already persuaded. The inevitable effect was further to polarize the estranged sections. As Southern opinion solidified, a salvo of invective blasted forth from editors and politicians below the Mason-Dixon line. In Georgia the *Savannah Republican* joined in the blood chorus. "Like the neighboring population," it said, "we go in for a summary vengeance. A terrible example should be made." Secessionist sentiment was growing as well. "The Harpers Ferry tragedy," the *Mobile Daily Register* declared, "is like a meteor disclosing in its lurid flash the width and depth of that abyss which rends asunder two nations, apparently one." The *Richmond Enquirer* asserted that "the Harpers Ferry invasion has advanced the cause of disunion more than any other event," noting ominously that "the people of the North sustain the outrage!" After all, who was behind the insurrection? Who gave Brown the money to buy guns and ammunition? The fact that only a handful in the North had actually voiced approval of Brown and his actions made little difference: precision was sacrificed to polemic. Earlier references to the "hairbrained" character of the undertaking "by a pack of crazy fanatics and poor deluded slaves" and "the impregnable safety of the

South" in no way lessened the symbolic significance of John Brown's Raid. John Brown had become the overarching symbol of sectional conflict.[25]

The widespread Southern fear of physical invasion and servile insurrection was not limited to fire-eaters. In Salisbury, North Carolina, J. J. Bruner, an old-line Whig and a persistent Unionist, was both owner and editor of the *Carolina Watchman*. In the inflamed and apprehensive autumn of 1859, however, Bruner praised the rapid deployment of Virginia and Maryland troops in the Harpers Ferry crisis. They had, he said, "reported themselves ready to march in the almost inconceivable space of one hour." Their readiness was evidence of "the temper of the people who will be called upon, some day, to defend their institutions, their homes, and their families." He further acknowledged that John Brown's raid gave the secessionists new propaganda with which to foster their cause. "Ah! Should it come, there will have been few such in the history of the world," he wrote, "for nothing short of extermination of millions of brave spirits would end a strife urged forward by madness on the one side and outraged rights on the other." He did not, however, say which side was which.[26]

Virginia's decision to prosecute John Brown for treason prompted South Carolina's elegant conservative William Henry Trescot toward constitutional speculation. Trescot had long maintained that the only real question was, "Can the Union and slavery exist together?" Despite his doubts that they could, he hoped that some kind of guarantee might grow out of this crisis that could hold the Union together, at least for a while longer. "Do you not think that it would have been better to have given the prisoner[s] to the United States?" he wrote to James Henry Hammond. "As it is, Virginia, if I understand correctly, will try them for not just murder. What I wanted was a decision *that the attempt to execute a servile insurrection is high treason against the United States and [is] to be punished with death by the Federal Government*."[27]

As the antagonists fell more and more under the sway of the root paradigm, then, the passion of John Brown was no longer individual but generic. And as the social drama unfolded, the ritualized nature of its discourse was more and more striking.

Act III: The Trial

In the third phase of a social drama representative members of the disturbed social system make an effort to limit the spread of crisis by some attempt at redress or reconciliation. Among other possibilities, the attempt may entail the performance of a public ritual in a formal juridical setting, as in the trial of John Brown. This attempt at redress is the critical phase of the social drama. Are the means of redress adequate? Are they capable, for example, of restoring the status quo ante? Are they even capable of restoring relative calm among the contending parties? If so, how? If not, why not? Clearly, the trial of John Brown failed to restore the previous status quo—and just as clearly that restoration would have been unsatisfactory to either side. As he reflected on his own impotence in the face of the power wielded by the slaveholding states, such considerations must surely have passed through John Brown's mind.[28]

Brown's contemporaries declared him "sane" or "mad" as it suited their mood or their purpose. Brown's court-appointed attorney accordingly questioned the prisoner's ability to stand trial: "Insanity is hereditary in that family. His mother and sister died with it, and a daughter of that sister has been two years in the Lunatic Asylum. A son and daughter of his mother's brother have also been confined," he told the court, "and another son of that brother is now insane and under close restraint." Brown, for his part, rejected a plea of insanity on his behalf. "I look upon it," he said, "as a miserable artifice and pretext of those who ought to take a different course in regard to me." Governor Wise likewise declared Brown sane. "He is a man of clear head, of courage, fortitude, and simple ingenuousness," the governor said. "He is cool, collected, and indomitable." (At the same time, Brown declared Wise to be mad.) But "insanity" is a concept much more clearly defined in legal statutes than in actual human life. The issue demands a more sophisticated formulation. John Brown became a powerful symbol not because he was "sane" or "insane" but because he represented a coincidence of opposites, expressing a tension between opposite poles of meaning, at once proud and meek, lion and lamb. While formally he suffered the fate of the lamb, in the social drama he played the role of the lion. Shrewd yet bold, humble yet angry, Brown's character may have seemed contradictory, but it was curiously consistent.[29]

Like a neophyte in an initiation ritual, John Brown went through an ordeal at the hands of the court. He was made to experience a ritual humiliation, a loss of honor, a form of "social death" not unlike that of the slaves on whose behalf he had attempted to act. He was isolated from secular society in his jail cell, in what some anthropologists have called a "liminal interlude." But in this interlude Brown was also able to stand aside from social conventions, to review past patterns of thought and action, to reconsider all previous standards and models, to interpret experience in fresh ways, and to formulate new courses of action. When he returned to society for his date with the hangman, he underwent what anthropologists call "a ritual of reaggregation," publicly confirming his new status as an initiated champion of freedom. This ritual of reaggregation was a necessary prelude to the rites of apotheosis that followed his execution.[30]

Northern response to the trial was mixed. Most Northern papers castigated Virginia for moving with such unseemly haste to bring Brown to trial. But it was impossible to conceal the unhappy choice faced by those Northerners who sympathized with Brown's antislavery ends but shrank from his bloody means. As Brown himself increasingly became a unified symbol, as sympathy for his ends consequently seemed less and less compatible with disdain for his means, men and women found themselves forced to choose between neither or both. It was an agonizing dilemma, from which many found their escape in the very root paradigm chosen by John Brown—in the symbolic image of a martyr for freedom, slain by the savage slaveholders. Writing from Rome, Theodore Parker defended Brown's actions on logical cum philosophical grounds. Since slavery itself depended on the use of force and terror against the slaves, Parker reasoned, the use of force and terror was justified to achieve freedom. If Brown had succeeded at Harpers Ferry, he contended, "the majority of men in New England would have rejoiced, not only in the end, but also in the means." As long as slavery endured, Parker predicted, insurrections would not only continue but would become more frequent and more powerful.[31]

Such pronouncements only further inflamed anxieties of the slave South, causing some Southern editors to become increasingly vociferous in calling for Brown's execution. But others in the slaveholding states warned of the consequences of creating a martyr. "If old John Brown is executed," Kentucky's *Frankfort Yeoman* noted, "there will be thousands to dip their handkerchiefs in his blood; relics of the martyr will be paraded throughout the North." Virginia's Governor Henry A. Wise, however, disdained such fears. Hanging, he contended, "would be no more martyrdom than to incarcerate the fanatic. The sympathy would have asked on and on for liberation and to nurse and soothe him while life lasted, in prison." Retrospect has not been kind to the governor's reasoning. Doubtless groups of diehards would have continued to agitate for the prisoner's release, but nothing solidified Northern opinion so powerfully as the image of John Brown on the gallows. Nothing inspired soldiers in blue so strongly as the mighty hymn by which John Brown's soul marched on with them into battle.[32]

Revelations that prominent Northerners had financed Brown's forays proved especially incendiary in the South. Until Harpers Ferry, most slaveholders had regarded the pronouncements of what Georgia's *Daily Enquirer* called "the raving of Northern fanatics" as no more than "pecuniary speculation." But now they learned that John Brown had not confined his fanaticism to rhetoric. Now they learned that the so-called "Secret Six"—Thomas Wentworth Higginson, Samuel Gridley Howe, Theodore Parker, Franklin B. Sanborn, Gerrit Smith, and George Luther Stearns—had been hiring thugs to stir up slave revolts in the South. How could Southern rights possibly be secure if the Republicans came to power? The *Charleston Daily Courier* had made up its mind that the continued existence of Southern security was impossible within the Union. To those who shared that conviction, the Harpers Ferry foray made plain "the destiny which awaits them in the Union, under the control of a sectional anti-slavery party in the free states." It was the Union itself "by which domestic disquietude is created and the mightiest dangers impend over the South," the *Charleston Mercury* contended. "Our connection with the North is a standing instigation of insurrection in the South." The conflict, as the *Mercury* saw it, was irrepressible and so must be waged to its bitter end.[33]

Unionist response in the South was only slightly milder than that of the disunionists. Charlotte's *North Carolina Whig* and other newspapers gave significant space to the Brown story under such headlines as "A NUT to be CRACKED," and "HARPERS FERRY AFFAIR." According to the *Whig*, Brown's attack on Harpers Ferry was more than an attack on the state of Virginia; it was an attack on the entire South. "The affair at Harpers Ferry was a deeply laid scheme by some of the abolitionists," the *Whig* argued, designed "to aid in murdering the people of the South by causing an insurrection of the Negroes." The movements and actions of abolitionists commanded front-page attention as well in Salisbury's *Carolina Watchman*, its banner headline proclaiming, "ABOLITIONISTS RUN MAD." The once moderately unionist *Lancaster Ledger* now took a giant step toward disunion: "Let us endeavor to move in concert, set our houses in order, looking to the grand event which has been mooted for years and which circumstances now indicate as affording the only haven of security, *viz.*, a dissolution of the Union."[34]

In the frontier southwest, where the Harpers Ferry raid seemed distant and Brown's threat far away, the *Arkansas Gazette* might believe that "too much importance has been attached to this matter." But across most of the South the reaction of the North inflamed opinion as much as the raid itself. The *Charleston Mercury* regarded the affair at Harpers Ferry as no more and no less than "a sign of the times and of the temper and intentions of the northern majority." The more extreme Northern opinions were the most widely quoted, on the grounds that for every Yankee who voiced such views there were thousands who applauded or gave silent assent. Governor Wise's *Richmond Enquirer* warned that the large throngs who gathered to cheer Wendell Phillips and other abolitionist orators were "fanning the flame of civil discord, which, in an unlooked for hour, will burst forth into a consuming conflagration." But the *Enquirer* was more inclined to help spread the fire than to extinguish it. "We shall feed the now smouldering embers with every particle of fuel furnished by the Northern fanatics," it proclaimed. "As long as conservatism sits silent, and listens coward-like to such treason, we shall inform our readers of public sentiment in the North, and if the information *inflames,* why let the consequence fall upon the authors and abettors." Conservatives in the South, it said, could expect no help from their Northern counterparts, who "are cowed and ,trampled under foot by the impudent, blatant Abolitionism."[35]

There is no greater illustration of the, critical significance of the redress stage than its impact on James Henry Hammond, a leading Southern politician. One admirer likened Hammond's election to the United States Senate two years earlier to an event in ancient Rome, when "Cincinnatus was called from his Farm to the head of the nation." Hammond took his seat on January 6, 1858, but did not deliver a speech on the Senate floor for nearly two months. When he finally spoke on March 4, however, he created a sensation with his ringing philosophical defense of slavery. "In all social systems there must be a class to do the menial duties, to perform the drudgeries of life," he argued, "a class requiring but a low order of intellect and but little skill." Such a class he described as "the very mud-sill of society." Without it, he said, there could not be "the other class which leads progress, civilization, and refinement." The strength of the South's social system, he further asserted, was matched by the strength of its economy. "You dare not make war on cotton," he warned the North. "No power on earth dares make war on it. Cotton is king."[36]

Hammond nevertheless shrank from disunion. He maintained that. Southern strength would guarantee the protection of Southern rights within the Union. Given his radical background—for more than two decades he had been an ardent disunionist—James Henry Hammond made an unlikely spokesman for conditional unionism. But in a speech on Beech Island in the summer of 1858, his lack of enthusiasm for secession was unmistakable. He told his fellow slaveholders that he desired not disunion, but for "the South to *rule* the Union." In a speech in Barnwell in October he elaborated on his doctrine of Southern dominance, declaring that the South was made up of "the most powerful people who now flourish on the globe." It was "not yet" time for secession; "no measure has yet been strong enough to stand against the South when united." A united South, he insisted, could look forward to "a magnificent future" within the Union. His old fire-eating comrades-in-arms were incensed: they felt he had betrayed them. For his part, Hammond seemed hurt and genuinely bewildered by the hostility his speech aroused in South Carolina.[37]

Perhaps Hammond's nouveau unionism was just political posturing, designed to gain time to unify the South in preparation for the inevitable separation. After all, he did not always voice such optimistic unionism in private letters. "How can any sane man have any hope of saving ourselves from the fate of Jamaica," he had written the implacable disunionist Edmund Ruffin, "but by cutting ourselves loose . . . as speedily as possible?"

But after the heady social whirl of Washington, Hammond seems seriously to have entertained the idea that he might become president, thus ensuring both protection of Southern rights and preservation of the Union. The response to his Barnwell speech north of the Mason-Dixon line had clearly fueled his fantasies. "This speech of mine produced an immense sensation throughout the Country," he exulted in his diary. "It was published in every leading paper North and South. It was read publicly in the streets of the great Northern Cities to immense crowds." What excited him even more, though, was that "I was nominated at once for the Presidency by an hundred newspapers on all sides." He wrote William Gilmore Simms that he had now attained a reputation in the North as an "honest, disinterested, & fearless" statesman "not without a fair share of talent." He was certain that "the thinking & patriotic men want just such a man for the next Presidency."[38]

Whatever hopes there might have been in the autumn of 1859 for Hammond's ambitions both to secure Southern rights and to save the Union by becoming president of the United States—indeed, whatever hopes remained for *any* peaceful resolution of the sectional conflict within the Union—they were fatally undercut by John Brown's raid and its aftermath. James Henry Hammond's individual instability became implicated in the general social instability. As John Brown's story had become generic, an overarching summation of the sectional conflict, so James Henry Hammond saw his story now taken away from him, saw it translated into another motif of the John Brown social drama. The failure of the redress phase here was especially critical. Unfortunately, whenever Hammond was faced with great opportunities or great challenges—such as the present test of his unionist convictions—he came down with real or imagined ailments that prevented his rising to the occasion. "Any great and severe mental labor," he had already confided to his diary, "prostrates me for months and months with my feeble health." He was certain his health would "not permit my assuming such a toil, and I gave a cold shoulder to it and political intrigue." He wrote to Simms that he was "ready to throw up my hands and retire." But supporters insisted that in this crisis he was needed more than ever. "This Harpers Ferry affair will bring up the slavery question in all its importance to the great interests of the South," wrote George P. Elliott. "The South needs her ablest men in council and South Carolina has a right to claim the talent of her every son. Your post of duty for the present is in the Senate."[39]

If James Henry Hammond wished to withdraw from the crisis he had spent most of his adult life trying to foment, another son of South Carolina could hardly wait to enter the fray. Francis W. Pickens had been appointed minister to Russia by President James Buchanan. Although fears that Russia might enter the Franco-Austrian war kept him at his post until August of 1860, Pickens correctly perceived in the social drama of John Brown a crisis of the Union. Hammond remained sullenly in his Senate seat until the presidential election of 1860, refusing after John Brown's raid to offer any leadership. But Pickens was impatient to return home and "take responsibility in the great events and in whatever may occur," although he disclaimed any plans to seek public office. A moderate by South Carolina standards, Francis Pickens had been radicalized by recent events. He believed the political response to this crisis would determine the fate of the nation. As their state stumbled toward secession, Pickens became more and more a leader, while the social drama increasingly cast Hammond in the role of bystander.[40]

The failure of reconciliation brought a deepening of the crisis. Since no verdict in the John Brown trial could have satisfied both sides, Northerners and Southerners resumed their elaborately choreographed pas de deux. Rumors of an attempt to rescue Brown spread rapidly. "Last night," a supporter wrote Hammond, "startling information was rec'd by Gov. [William Henry] Gist [of South Carolina]—from Gov. Wise advising South Carolina to *arm*." According to the *North Carolina Whig,* Gist offered Wise "any amount of military aid" he felt he needed to repel an attempt to free Brown. On the eve of the alleged rescue attempt a Colonel Elliott was reported to have told the troops guarding Brown that they "might have to undergo arduous and perilous duty," as the *Carolina Watchman* put it, but "if the venerable Commonwealth should be invaded . . . they would effectively wipe out the stain."[41]

An anonymous letter circulated through the South, warning of dire consequences if John Brown were harmed. The letter was also said to have been sent to Governor Henry A. Wise of Virginia. "You had better caution your authorities to be careful about what you do with Ossawatamie Brown," it read. "So sure as you hurt one hair of his head, mark my word—the following day, you will see every city, town, and village south of the Mason-Dixon line in flames." However prophetic of times to come, the threat contained in the letter was almost certainly a bluff. All the same, the *North Carolina Whig* was only one of many Southern newspapers to fan the flames by publishing the letter, nor did the *Whig* let the threat go unanswered. "If any of the abolitionists desire to liberate Brown and his accomplices," it responded in an editorial, "let them come and they will be met—force with force." In a similar vein the editor of the *Lancaster Ledger,* a South Carolina paper, wrote, "A few of our most zealous statesmen warned us time and again of the probability of such a condition of affairs being experienced in the South at some time in the future, if the tide of abolition fury was not checked. Many of us hooted at the idea and thought that the danger existed in the imagination of some of our fire-eating politicians; but the prophecy does not now seem so absurd." Battle lines were beginning to form.[42]

The essence of the doomed reconciliation stage was, however, perhaps best expressed in the pious optimism of President James Buchanan. Indeed, the president played his ritually prescribed role in the social drama to perfection. He correctly estimated both the impact of John Brown's raid and the reason for the extreme Southern reaction. "In the already excited condition of public feeling throughout the South," he noted, "this raid of John Brown's made a deeper impression on the Southern mind against the Union than all former events." Although he thought "it would have had no lasting effect" had it been "considered merely as the isolated act of a desperate fanatic," what spread apprehension and alarm across the South, he surmised, was "the enthusiastic and permanent approbation of the expedition by the abolitionists of the North." But if Buchanan had some insight into the cause of the crisis, he lacked the vision to imagine a solution. Like Pontius Pilate, he washed his hands of responsibility, as though no solution were necessary. "The events at Harpers Ferry, by causing the people to pause and reflect upon the possible peril to their cherished institutions, will be the means, under Providence, of allaying the existing excitement," he wrote optimistically, and "will resolve that the Constitution and the Union shall not be endangered." His optimism was, alas, misplaced.[43]

As the crisis deepened, the proslavery press in fact focused much of its outrage on the luckless head of James Buchanan, editors depicting the president embraced in the arms of "his abolitionist friends." The *Carolina Watchman* put the total blame for the crisis on the president "and his wishy-washy men he had around him." In Alabama the *Selma Watchman and Democrat* accused him of refusing to heed "the warning and advice" allegedly given him by "Government officers at Harpers Ferry." By doing so, it was claimed, Buchanan assisted Brown's raiders in "murdering innocent women and children and peaceable citizens and destroying their property." He had, the *Watchman* charged, turned "a deaf ear to their warnings and allowed the Rebels to carry out their hellish plans."[44]

In the opinion of the *North Carolina Whig,* since John Brown had threatened one of the institutions of the South, all Southern institutions (and thus a way of life) were at risk. According to the *Mississippi Free Trader,* if Brown's slave insurrection had succeeded, "out of the ashes of our fair Republic would have risen another Saint Domingo." Virginia's "soil would have reeked with human gore," the *Free Trader* declared melodramatically, "and the torch applied" across "the entire South." The *Whig* called on its readers "to organize a Volunteer Company at, or in the vicinity of, Pineland, North Carolina, that we may be better able to defend our homes and firesides from the incendiary and murderous attacks of Northern Abolitionists." Around the South military companies were forming in response to the raid. But civilians responded with equal vigor, forming "voluntary associations throughout the South" that pledged "not to eat, or use, or wear, any articles from the North."[45]

In South Carolina the period following the failure of redress was marked by formerly moderate newspapers embracing disunion. In the town of Pickens the editor of the *Keowee Courier* declared that if "the cut throats at Harpers Ferry are to be sustained, then the sooner we get out of the Union the better." Support for the upcoming Democratic national convention in Charleston was accordingly weakened by Brown's raid and rising disunion sentiment. As the editor of Spartanburg's *Carolina Spartan* boasted, "We do not care a fig about the Convention or election of another President, as we are convinced the safety of the South lies only outside the present Union— and this we believe to be the judgment of a large majority of our people." A moderate position, even by South Carolina standards, was becoming increasingly difficult to maintain.[46]

The major actors in the social drama were few, but each symbolized many persons, many relationships, many aims, many interests. Not surprisingly, then, there were many constraints on them to ponder carefully their courses of action, to weigh their words carefully, perhaps even to prefer judicious silence to well-chosen words. Is it not all the more remarkable, then, how melodramatic the social drama of John Brown became? Such intemperance in the face of such constraints merely underscores the ritual quality that a naked confrontation of this sort can acquire when it lacks any adequate means of mediation.[47]

Act IV: The Outcome

The fourth phase of a social drama, Turner suggests, provides an opportunity for the actors to take stock, to compare the situation that preceded the breach with the situation following the attempt at redress.[48] In the case of John Brown the immediate outcome was the creation of a hero; but there was also an intermediate outcome in the election of Lincoln and a long-range outcome in war and emancipation. In the long run the structure of the whole society was changed, and with it the nature and intensity of relations between its parts. Old power relations changed, for example, as former authority was diluted or replaced and a new party system replaced an older one.

The passion of John Brown was not a drama of one man's martyrdom; it was not a soliloquy but a drama of social relations. And every sacrifice in social drama requires a sacrificer as well as a victim. In the case of John Brown the sacrificer was Henry Wise, governor of Virginia. There was in fact a curious complicity between Brown and Wise, in which the governor at crucial moments virtually dared the prisoner to commit himself to the way of the cross. Wise apparently realized, at least subliminally, that Brown was archetypally controlled by the root paradigm of martyrdom. But Wise does not appear to have realized that he could only hang John Brown and give him the martyr's crown he sought at the expense of strengthening the antislavery cause. Thus, the hour of Brown's execution was the hour of Brown's triumph. In the ultimate act of what Brown and other Christian Yankees would denote as *conscience* he forced the South to become his hangman, forced the South to inflict the ultimate act of *shaming* upon him. In doing so he also forced the South to degrade itself, at least in the eyes of outside observers. Ultimately, by shifting the South so decisively toward secession, John Brown made slavery rather than himself the lost cause.[49]

As the day of John Brown's execution approached, the actors continued to perform their roles with ritual precision. On December 2, 1859, supporters in various Northern cities held meetings of sympathy. In Concord, Massachusetts, Louisa May Alcott described the gathering there in her journal. "The execution of Saint John the Just took place on the second," she wrote. "A meeting at the hall, and all Concord was there. Emerson, Thoreau, Father [Bronson Alcott] and [Franklin B.] Sanborn spoke, and all were full of reverence and admiration for the martyr." Her father even composed a sonnet for the occasion:

> Bold Saint, thou firm believer in the Cross,
> Again made glorious by self-sacrifice,—
> Love's free atonement given without love's loss,—
> That martyrdom to thee was lighter pain,
> Since thus a race its liberties should gain;
>
> . . . .
>
> O Patriot true! O Christian meek and brave!
> Throned in the martyrs' seat henceforth shalt sit;
> Prophet of God! Messiah of the Slave!

The transfiguration of John Brown, as portrayed by Bronson Alcott, was little short of miraculous. Given the centrality of the crucifixion in Western iconography, one might suppose that Brown had carried his own gallows up the hill at Charleston, where he was hanged between two thieves, while cadets from the Virginia Military Institute threw dice for his garments. Brown's embrace of the root paradigm had not been in vain.[50]

The final step in the process of deification occurred with the translation of Brown's death into the miracle of Christ's resurrection. In Boston's Tremont Temple William Lloyd Garrison addressed a large gathering assembled under the auspices of the American Anti-Slavery Society. They had come, he told them, to witness John Brown's resurrection. "As a peace man—an 'ultra' peace man—I am prepared to say: 'Success to every slave insurrection at the South,' " he declared. On the following day the *New York Daily Tribune* asserted that Americans ought to be "reverently grateful for the privilege of living in a world rendered noble by the daring of heroes, the suffering of martyrs,—among whom let none doubt that History will accord an honored niche to Old John Brown."[51]

In Philadelphia friends of John Brown staged a public prayer meeting at the hour of Brown's execution. The large hall was crowded with his supporters, both black and white, who were interrupted frequently by heckling from a group of Southern medical students enrolled at the University of Pennsylvania. The principal address was delivered by Theodore Tilton, managing editor of the *New York Independent.* "Today the nation puts to death its noblest citizen!" Tilton declared. "What was his crime? Guilty of what? Guilty of loving his fellow men too well." Cheers and jeers mingled as he commended the soul of John Brown "to that impartial history which vindicates the martyrs and turns their martyrdom into glory," going on to predict that "the deed of this day will not die! It will live in history as long as there shall be a history for heroes." Antiphonal choirs of applauders and hissers accompanied Tilton's closing prayer that "at this solemn and awful moment of death, this nation may be struck down upon its knees, by the sudden glory of God bursting out of heaven—and that it may be humbled in the dust until it shall rise repentant, and the scales shall fall from its eyes, and the whole nation shall stand at last in the light and liberty of the sons of God."[52]

In Cincinnati the Reverend Moncure Daniel Conway, a Virginia-born Unitarian, delivered a guest sermon the following Sunday at the First Congregational Church. Depicting John Brown as "a man dying for a religious principle," Conway urged the parishioners to "set aside the question of the abstract rectitude of the method. The stature of the hero dwarfs such considerations." John Brown, he preached, "summed up a century's work" and "sealed with his blood the death warrant of slavery." As the organ intoned the invitational hymn, Conway delivered a sacred charge to the assembled congregation: "Out of the ashes of our martyr a Revolution must come." It *would* come, he assured them, "and it will rise up to brood over this land, until the progeny of Freemen arise to crown America's destiny." He urged them all to be "baptized afresh to the cause of LIBERTY, HUMANITY, and GOD!"[53]

Like others in the grip of the root paradigm, the Grimké sisters of South Carolina regarded Brown's execution as the martyrdom of a man of profound and noble convictions. Although daughters of a prominent slaveholder, Sarah and Angelina Grimké had left their native state to become abolitionist activists as early as the 1830s. On the eve of Brown's hanging, Sarah wrote that she had gone "in spirit to the martyr. It was my privilege to enter into sympathy with him; to go down, according to my measure, into the depths where he has travailed and feel his past exercises, his present sublime position." She regarded Brown as "the John Huss of the United States" and wrote that he now stood ready "to seal his testimony with his life's blood." Devout Quakers and ardent abolitionists, the Grimké sisters were deeply moved by the passion of John Brown.[54]

Virginia's trial and execution of John Brown also convinced Abraham Lincoln's law partner, William H. Herndon, that disunion and war were inevitable, an opinion he expressed in almost equally passionate terms. "I am thoroughly convinced," he wrote to Charles Sumner, "that two such civilizations as the North and the South cannot co-exist on the same soil and be co-equal in the Federal brotherhood. To expect otherwise would be to expect the Absolute to sleep with and tolerate 'hell.' . . . Let this natural war—let this inevitable struggle proceed—go on, till slavery is *dead—dead— dead!*"[55]

By no means, however, was all Northern response sympathetic to the condemned man. On the day John Brown was hanged, Abraham Lincoln told an audience in Troy, Kansas: "We cannot object, even though he agreed with us in thinking slavery wrong. That cannot excuse violence, bloodshed, and treason." The racist *New York Weekly Day Book* went a good deal further. It openly praised Brown's execution and expressed distaste for "Negro equality," claiming that Brown and his followers made up only a small segment of the population and that "the great masses, the laboring class, are as uncorrupted with Negro equality doctrines as ever!" Moreover, the *Day Book* added, the South could be certain that the "North will rejoice when the old wretch gets his due."[56]

Other Northern Democrats, seriously alarmed at the widening sectional rift, held a series of "Union Meetings" throughout the region. On December 8 a large gathering of Democrats filled Faneuil Hall in Boston to pass resolutions condemning John Brown and his admirers. The venerable Levi Lincoln came out of retirement to preside. George Peabody, former President Franklin Pierce, and several former governors of Massachusetts sent letters of greetings that were read aloud. Among the speakers were former United States Attorney General Caleb Cushing and the noted orator Edward Everett.[57]

The assembled Democrats listened attentively as Everett proclaimed his conviction that the nation was "on the very verge of a convulsion, which will shake the Union to its foundation." He feared that continuation of violent speech and action would "bring us to the catastrophe," and he called on patriots to forego political issues for the time being. Everett then asked his New England audience to try to see John Brown's Raid and its aftermath through Southern eyes. He asked them to imagine that "a party of desperate, misguided men, under a resolved and fearless leader, had been organized in Virginia, to come and establish themselves by stealth in Springfield in this state, intending there, after possessing themselves, at the unguarded hour of midnight, of the National Armory, to take advantage of some local cause of disaffection, say the feud between Protestants and Catholics—which led to a very deplorable occurrence in this vicinity a few years ago—to stir up a social revolution." Everett next asked those present to suppose that "pikes and rifles to arm 2500 men had been procured by funds raised by extensive subscriptions throughout the South." Then, what if "at the dead of a Sunday night, the work of destruction had begun, by shooting down an unarmed man, who had refused to join the invading force; that citizens of the first standing were seized and imprisoned—three or four others killed."

But, Everett continued, the conspiracy failed, and its leader, having received a fair trial, had been convicted and executed. Everett then asked his New England audience to imagine how they would feel if "throughout Virginia, which sent him forth on his fatal errand, and the South generally, funeral bells should be tolled, meetings of sympathy held, as at the death of some great public benefactor." Imagine how they would feel if "the person who had plotted to put a pike or a rifle in the hands of 2500 men, to be used against their fellows, inhabitants of the same town, inmates of the same houses, with an ulterior intention and purpose of wrapping a whole community in a civil war of the deadliest and bloodiest type, in which a man's foe should be those of his own household," a man who had actually "taken the lives of several fellow-beings, should be extolled, canonized, placed on a level with the great heroes of humanity, nay, assimilated to the Saviour of mankind; and all this not the effect of a solitary individual impulse, but the ripe fruit of a systematic agitation pursued in the South, unrebuked, for years!" What, he asked his audience, did they believe they might "feel, think, say, under such a state of things?"[58]

In his address Caleb Cushing bitterly attacked the abolitionist supporters of John Brown. "By constant brooding upon one single idea—that idea, if you please, a right one abstractedly," he said, the abolitionists had "come to be monomaniacs of that idea, and so have become utterly lost to the moral relations of right and wrong." Cushing asked his audience of New England Democrats to repudiate those whom he called a "band of drunken mutineers" who were about to drive the ship of state onto the shoals. Cushing had expressed similar views in a letter to the chairman of the Massachusetts Democratic party. There were two sets of Northern sympathizers for "this traitor and murderer," he charged, "one set who say that his plans and arts were so stupidly criminal, and so criminally stupid, that he must have been crazy, and should therefore go unpunished—and another set who, moved by their own crazy false estimation of the moral quality of his acts, proceed to proclaim and honor him as a hero, a saint, and a god."[59]

Cushing further charged that the abolitionists were conducting what he called "a systematic *war in disguise*" against the South. The federal government, in his opinion, should give Virginia "at least as much security from invasion by Ohio or any other state of the Union as she has from invasion by England or France." Without such protection, Cushing declared it to be the right, "nay it is the duty, of the Southern States to separate from the Northern States and to form a confederation of their own." By Christmas of 1859 Cushing had come to the conclusion that a separation of some kind was inevitable. Of course John Brown's nineteen-man "invasion" of Virginia had been quickly crushed, not by Virginia but by the federal government, and yet the federal government had made no effort to interfere with Virginia's conduct of Brown's trial. But Cushing believed that the nation's problems had already passed beyond the nation's ability to handle them, and he feared that separation might now be the only solution to the sectional controversy. "The late murderous foray of Northern abolitionists into Virginia," he wrote, "and the endorsement, the canonization, the heroization, the apotheosis, of their head murderer, by so many of both clergy and laity at the North, have at length brought all these questions to a practice issue. The Southern States cannot meekly lie down to be trodden upon by the Northern." No fire-eater could have said it better.[60]

Thus did Northerners and Southerners increasingly play parts ritually prescribed by the root paradigm: ritual adulation of the martyr prompted a ritual backlash. Complexity and ambiguity became less and less tenable. The social drama accordingly seemed to unite much of the white South behind a common cause, in which loyalty to "the South" came to be defined in terms of loyalty to a single institution. In an address to the Virginia state legislature, Governor Wise charged that "the motive of the North is to see whether we will face a danger now sealed in blood," a danger he believed was now inevitable. "We must face it, and have a settlement at once," Wise declared, "the sooner the better."[61]

Fear manifested itself to the point of direct violence against anyone who dared to say a harsh word against slavery or a kind word in favor of John Brown. In North Carolina a man was arrested and held simply for "having uttered abolition and incendiary sentiments." In South Carolina another man dared to "utter antislavery sentiments and sympathy with old John Brown . . . upon the Capitol building at Columbia." After being warned to leave he was taken "to the depot, where [his abductors] first gave him thirty-nine lashes and then tarred and feathered him [before] placing him on a train."[62] In Georgia a Savannah vigilance committee undertook to tar and feather "a resident Yankee" who had "made himself obnoxious by distributing incendiary pamphlets among the negroes who can read, and *reading* them to those who cannot." The alleged agitator was "carried beyond the city limits, stripped to the buff—tarred and feathered and cotton overlaid." Five or six other individuals were given a deadline to leave the city. A correspondent reported Savannah to be "somewhat excited and the women are particularly scared—where will all this end!"[63]

In Louisiana the *New Orleans Daily Picayune* declared that "the action of Brown and his men was nothing compared with the fanaticism of hatred against slavery which the event had shown to exist throughout the North." The Northern response constituted what the *Picayune* called "Brown's treason without his courage, his frenzy without his nerve, with even greater malice, because safe from the penalties he was daring enough to brave in his own person—for we have no statutes against moral treason, the treason of disloyalty in the heart, to the peace and union of the confederacy." Word of the execution spread quickly through the slave quarters on hundreds of plantations, passed on by slaves who had learned to read. Just one day after the *Picayune*'s report, seventy-five miles up the Mississippi River from New Orleans a slave who worked in the sugarhouse on a large plantation told a free mulatto Creole all about the hanging of John Brown. His master had given him a newspaper to wipe the machinery with. He had read the newspaper and then spread the news of Brown's execution to the whole slave community.[64]

A train from Philadelphia arrived in Richmond just before Christmas, carrying more than two hundred medical students who had withdrawn from schools in Philadelphia in protest over the Northern response to John Brown's execution. "Let Virginia call home her children!" Governor Wise declared to the large crowd that gathered to welcome them. Indeed, many Southerners had come to feel that the North's true motives were finally unmasked by the response to John Brown. "The South wants and has a constitutional right to demand that slaves not be stolen," the *Carolina Watchman* declared, adding that Southerners also had "a right to demand that all interferences with the institution of the South by the North" such as "Brown's invitation" ought to be "put down by the North." The *Watchman* implied that such acts as the Harpers Ferry raid were backed and promoted by "the North" rather than by certain Northerners in particular. "Is this the Government of two people," the *Mississippi Free Trader* wanted to know, "as different in our sentiments of right and wrong as we are in our institutions?" In Salisbury, North Carolina, citizens were urged to "enroll once more your names, enter the school of the soldier, and handle the old Kentucky rifle." Tarheels not only encouraged military preparedness so that

Southerners could defend themselves from outside threats but also preparedness "to maintain [their] rank among the nations and to defend [to] the utmost the institution transmitted to us by our ancestors."[65]

The tempo of events increased, and, as the social drama gained momentum, even longtime South Carolina unionists dutifully embraced their miscast secessionist roles. Christopher G. Memminger, whose unionist credentials dated back to the nullification controversy, was outraged by what he considered Northern deification of John Brown. "Every [Yankee] village bell which tolled its solemn note at the execution of Brown," he wrote, "proclaims to the South the approbation of that village of insurrection and servile war." Memminger and other former unionists now embraced disunion as the only solution. In the South Carolina legislature "a rank Union man" was overheard to say that although he had "never expected to live to see the day when he would come to regard the Union as a nuisance . . . he was ready for Disunion now." Benjamin F. Perry, perhaps South Carolina's leading unionist, presented a resolution threatening secession, while Memminger wrote to a friend that "all of us are persuaded that in the Union there is no security—and either there must be new terms established or a Southern Confederacy is our only hope of safety."[66]

South Carolina's most ardent voice of secession, the *Charleston Mercury,* exulted that "the staunchest Union men, heretofore, are becoming the sternest in the vindication of the rights of the South." The *Edgefield Advertiser* seemed to have moved from conditional unionism to a kind of conditional Southern nationalism. "Neither justice nor patriotism requires that she [the South] forbear longer," the *Advertiser* declared, "unless a change of Northern sentiment and policy be shown by the Presidential election of the coming year." Likewise, Governor William Henry Gist, in his message to the South Carolina legislature on the eve of John Brown's execution, said: "It is unbecoming a free people to stake their liberties upon the successful jugglery of party politicians and interested office seekers, rather than a bold and determined resolution to maintain them at every hazard."[67] Privately, Gist had confided to William Porcher Miles, the secessionist congressman from Charleston District, his preference that South Carolina move in concert with other Southern states rather than undertaking any unilateral disunion. "I have not the least doubt," he wrote, "that South Carolina would sustain her [Congressional] members in almost anything they might do in concerted action with the Southern members, or any considerable portion of them." A resolution was accordingly introduced into the South Carolina Senate "that South Carolina, still deferring to her Southern sisters, nevertheless respectfully announce to them that, in her judgment, the safety and honor of the slaveholding states imperatively demand a speedy separation from other states of the Confederacy, and earnestly invite the slaveholding states to inaugurate the movement of Southern separation, in which she pledge herself promptly to unite." The resolution passed by an extremely close vote of twenty-two to nineteen. A stronger resolution for unilateral action was then introduced in the House, to the effect that "the Constitution of the United States, ordained and established to 'insure domestic tranquility,' has proven a failure, and the union of these States, so far as the fraternal relations are concerned, is dissolved; and, whereas, the highest intents of the slaveholding states demand that this dissolution shall in form be consummated, which consummation will probably involve the necessity of a resort to arms." This motion, however, was tabled by a vote of sixty-six to forty-four: not even the hotspur state was ready yet to face the possibility of war with the United States. W. S. Mullins of Marion District next introduced a less bellicose resolution "that the State of South Carolina is now ready to act with the slaveholding States of this Confederacy, or with such of them as desire present action in the formation of a Southern Confederacy." An effort to table the Mullins resolution on December 15 failed by a vote of fifty-one to sixty-one, but Mullins withdrew his resolution in deference to Christopher Memminger's resolution, which became part of the resolution finally adopted.[68]

The John Brown affair gave the fire-eaters hope that they could revive the secessionist spirit that had swept the state during the nullification crisis of 1833 and the secession crisis of 1850. South Carolina responded to the excitement of the John Brown affair by appropriating $100,000 for military preparedness; by sending invitations to other Southern states for a conference "to concert measures for united action" in order to obtain new terms as the price of remaining in the Union; and by dispatching Christopher G. Memminger as a special commissioner to Virginia "to express to the authorities of that state, the cordial sympathy of the people of South Carolina with the people of Virginia, and their earnest desire to unite with them in measures of common defence." W. W. Boyce wrote to Memminger proposing that he entice the Virginians into disunion while "letting them suppose that they are leading." Memminger should castigate the Harpers Ferry raid as an "outrage," an attack not only on Virginia but on South Carolina as well. He should assure the Virginians that "we stand with Virginia in this fray and all its consequences." The fire-eaters clearly found Virginia's lack of enthusiasm for disunion disheartening. Even so, by a "conservative estimate" almost half of South Carolina's House and more than half of its Senate were ready to secede in 1859. Not quite ready to go it alone, the state nevertheless took a decisive step toward disunion.[69]

There were still a few voices of moderation in the Palmetto state. "John Brown was only a symptom not more alarming . . . than many others," William Henry Trescot wrote to Senator James Henry Hammond. "I don't relish the idea of being frightened from our propriety by such a vagabond." Hammond began to draft a Constitutional Amendment, which he hoped to offer as a means by which slavery might be preserved within the context of the Union:

> All the rights to and of property of any kind which existed under the Constitution or laws or customs of each or any State, before the adoption of this and which were not surrendered by it, shall be fully recognized by this government in all its branches: shall be in no wise impaired by any act of any Department of it: shall be thoroughly protected in each and all of the Public Territories until a Territory by being admitted into this Union as a Sovereign State, shall become authorized and enabled to protect whatever is [illegible].

Surely he must have known, however, that such an amendment had no chance of passing in the polarized political atmosphere following the John Brown episode. How many in the North would support an amendment to guarantee slavery? And how many in the South believed that there was any longer a place for the South in the Union? Hammond's longtime friend Isaac Hayne wrote him that "the masses of this State would, you may be assured, rejoice in any movement tending to disunion, either on the part of Virginia or Georgia, and would be glad to move *pari passo* with either, and run the hazard of any further cooperation." Dispirited, Hammond confessed to William Gilmore Simms that he returned to Washington "more reluctantly than John Brown did to the gallows." The self-centered Hammond could never have comprehended Brown's embrace of self-sacrifice; he could only understand that Brown's actions had put additional burdens on his own shoulders. "But for Brown's raid I should have resigned certainly. I had my letter written and was holding for the meeting of the legislature."[70]

More and more South Carolina "moderates" were wavering. Writing to a friend about the fate of the Union, James McCarty concluded that "the only chance of saving it is to bring about some collision, which will show us the strength of the conservative element in the North. This element I have always considered as large enough to keep the Democratic Party in power with the aid of the South. If I am mistaken in this, my hope is gone." But "moderate" wavering was not enough for the fire-eaters. "So long as the Democratic party is a 'National' organization," Robert Barnwell Rhett, editor of the fire-eating *Charleston Mercury,* declared, "and so long as our public men trim their sails with an eye to either its favor or enmity, just so long need we hope for no Southern action."[71]

All the same, the new year brought renewed attacks on slavery in the name of John Brown. Ralph Waldo Emerson told a Salem audience in January that abolitionism was simply an inevitable response to slavery. "Who makes the abolitionist? The slaveholder. The sentiment of mercy is the natural recoil which the laws of the universe provide to protect mankind from destruction by savage passions." It was impossible, the transcendentalist maintained, not to sympathize with John Brown's "courage, and disinterestedness, and the love that casts out fear." Those who failed to sympathize with the martyr were lacking in "sensibility and self-respect." To those of "savage passions," however, Emerson's deification of John Brown as the "disinterested" champion of "mercy" transcended both evidence and common sense.[72]

In June Charles Sumner, the senator from Massachusetts, returned to the Senate to deliver an address castigating slavery. In 1856, after his "Crime against Kansas" speech had "insulted" South Carolina Senator Andrew Pickens Butler, Sumner had been brutally beaten in the Senate chamber by Butler's cousin, South Carolina Congressman Preston S. Brooks. Having selected a gutta-percha cane as his weapon, Brooks had approached the seated Sumner from behind and struck him repeatedly over the head. Trying in vain to stand, Sumner had wrenched his bolted desk from the floor while other senators grabbed the enraged Brooks. It was three years before Sumner again occupied his Senate seat, but Massachusetts reelected him, keeping his seat vacant until his return as a silent symbol of his "martyrdom." Now Sumner stood in the Senate chamber to declare that "American Slavery, as defined by existing law, stands forth as the greatest organized Barbarism on which the sun now looks."[73]

On Independence Day Henry David Thoreau spoke at Brown's burial place. "The North, I mean the LIVING North, was suddenly all transcendental," he noted. "It went beyond the human law, it went behind the apparent failure, and recognized eternal justice and glory." Thoreau echoed Emerson's disparagement of those who failed to see Brown's nobility. "When a noble deed is done, who is likely to appreciate it? Those who are noble themselves," he declared. "How can a man behold the light who has no inward light?" Thoreau asked. Brown's detractors, he charged, could not even *recite* poetry, let alone write it. "Show me a man who feels bitterly towards John Brown, and let me hear what noble verse he can repeat. He'll be as dumb as if his lips were stone."[74]

The renewed Northern approbation of John Brown really rankled Southern honor. The Southern press voiced complaints against what they considered the North's "pharisaical boast of 'holier than thou,' which they are constantly uttering as a reproach to the South." John Brown in fact became a major issue in North Carolina's 1860 gubernatorial election. In an address to the Democratic State Convention in Raleigh, incumbent Governor John W. Ellis attacked what he called the "unlawful acts" of the North. "How can the South expect protection to property from those who aid and

abet the assassin and murder as this party did in the case of John Brown?"
he asked. "We had two parties, Democrats and Whigs, but now democracy
is surrounded by antagonists known as Black Republicans." Ellis's speech
dramatized both the climate of fear resulting from Brown's raid and the
general identification of abolitionism with the Republican party in the
South.[75]

Republicans opposed slavery; therefore, reasoned myopic slaveholders,
Republicans endorsed John Brown, treason, insurrection, and murder. Such
subtlety as distinguishing between ends and means was viewed as mere
caviling. In an effort to combat such thinking, Abraham Lincoln rejected
any basis for identifying the Republican party with John Brown. "You
charge that we stir up insurrections among your slaves. We deny it," he
declared in February. "And what is your proof? Harpers Ferry? John Brown?
John Brown was no Republican, and you have failed to implicate a single
Republican in his Harpers Ferry enterprise." But slaveholders continued to
fear a Republican victory in November. The Republicans would not be satisfied merely with such acts as those John Brown had committed; they would
"aid and abet" the complete destruction of the South.[76]

When the Democratic National Convention met in April in Charleston,
the presence of John Brown was as palpable as that of Banquo's ghost. Delegates from South Carolina were instructed "to require of that body the
adoption of a platform of principles which will fully and clearly recognize
the rights of slaveholders to their persons and property in slaves, not in the
states [alone] but also in the common Territories of the United States." If
such a platform failed to carry the convention, the South Carolina delegates
were instructed "to withdraw from such convention." In a relatively close
vote, the convention rejected such a platform in favor of Stephen A. Douglas's "popular sovereignty" position. Forty-nine delegates from eight Southern states walked out. After fifty-seven ballots failed to yield any agreement
on a candidate, the remaining Democrats adjourned. Six weeks later the
Northern Democrats nominated Douglas as their candidate. The Southern
Democrats, meeting separately, nominated Vice-President John C. Breckinridge as their candidate.[77]

The Republicans held their national convention in May in Chicago.
There they not only nominated Abraham Lincoln as their presidential candidate but also passed a resolution declaring "that the maintenance invio-
late of the rights of the States, and especially the right of each State to order
and control its own domestic institutions according to its own judgment
exclusively, is essential to that balance of powers on which the perfection
and endurance of our political fabric depends." That sounded like the kind
of commitment Southern moderates had been looking for. But the Republicans went further. They made their repudiation of John Brown explicit in a

resolution denouncing "the lawless invasion by armed force of the soil of any state or territory, no matter under what pretext, as among the gravest of crimes." The resolution passed unanimously.[78]

But slaveholders and their spokesmen persisted in listening only to their own myths. In the months following John Brown's raid fire-eaters used the event as an excuse to heap more fuel on their secessionist bonfires. William Gilmore Simms "wondered how the North could countenance the actions of John Brown and other zealots who would not rest until slavery had been abolished." Warning that "the irrepressible conflict must come," Simms called on his state to defend slavery by force of arms.[79]

As the John Brown social drama unfolded during the presidential campaign of 1860, a curious series of events began to occur in North Carolina, almost as though the moderates finally saw the abyss of disunion ahead and were trying desperately to revive the unionism of the Old North State. Until May 15 Salisbury's *Carolina Watchman* used the North Carolina state seal, bearing the words "Constitution and Law," as its emblem. After May 22, however, the paper adopted a new emblem, an eagle clutching in his claws a ribbon upon which the words "Pluribus Unum" were imprinted. In the background was an American flag. This is but one of a series of symbolic changes that helped build a unionist movement in North Carolina in 1860. What is most significant about the *Carolina Watchman,* however, is that a newspaper with considerable influence in Rowan and surrounding counties switched the focus of its attention from state and local problems to matters of national interest, in which it showed an overwhelming concern for preserving the Union. Democratic threats of resistance in the event of a Republican victory were met with editorials urging, "Wake Up! Union men of Rowan."[80]

In the presidential campaign the *Watchman* endorsed the Constitutional Union Party's candidate, the "Hon. John Bell of Tennessee." Bell had considerable strength throughout North Carolina, due in part to a hastily organized effort by Whigs after John Brown's raid to elect congressmen and other public officials who were friendly to the Union. Bell supporters launched vigorous attacks against Breckinridge, warning that "treason is abroad in North Carolina." The *Watchman* reported that "one of Breckinridge's electors in this state came out on the stump and distinctly declared that in the event of Lincoln's election he would vote for resistance at once and before Lincoln was installed in office." There was a genuine movement for disunion in North Carolina, but it was a small one, pushed by a few fire-eaters and propagandists. There was little love for Lincoln in the Old North State, but most Tarheels believed that if he were elected he could be checked by the Congress. "Let all good men in every section do all in their power to defeat Lincoln," the *Watchman* urged, "but if he is elected let us show him that we have a Senate that detests his abominable heretics and that we will compel him to fill the important part of the government with good conservative men." But after John Brown's raid, not even North Carolina, a state once overwhelmingly unionist, was able to reunite Union forces. After the election, even North Carolina disintegrated into the final, fatal secession.[81]

The slaveholding South was outraged at the Republican electoral victory, depicting it as a victory for the spirit of John Brown. "They have invaded our States and killed our citizens," thundered the *New Orleans Daily Crescent*, "and finally they have capped the mighty pyramid of unfraternal enormities by electing Abraham Lincoln to the Chief Magistracy." In Charleston, Mary Boykin Chesnut overheard someone exclaim, upon hearing of Lincoln's election, "Now that the black radical Republicans have the power I suppose they will Brown us all." As she noted what she had heard in her journal, Chesnut added, "No doubt of it."[82] Amidst this crisis, the *Richmond Enquirer* declared, "the public mind" of the South was tossed "like the storm-whipped billows of an enraged sea." After Lincoln's victory, it was fatally easy for many Southerners to believe the entire North had become abolitionist. Since no Northern intellectuals had sympathized with the South after John Brown's raid, declared William Gilmore Simms, the South had no choice but secession.[83]

Lincoln's election completed the radicalization of Francis W. Pickens that the social drama following the raid had initiated. On November 30 the former moderate addressed the South Carolina General Assembly: "I would be willing to appeal to the God of battles," he declared defiantly, "if need be, cover the state with ruin, conflagration, and blood rather than submit." On December 12 the legislature elected him governor, and on December 20 South Carolina seceded from the Union, once again invoking John Brown when they declared that the free states "have encouraged and assisted thousands of our slaves to leave their homes; and those who remain, have been incited by emissaries, books, and pictures, to servile insurrection." Before it was over, South Carolina would indeed be covered with ruin, conflagration, and blood. But in the end the state would submit anyway.[84]

The passion of John Brown resonates with the stylized character of an initiation ceremony, an initiation into the status of martyr. In this rite of passage Brown was propelled by the root paradigm of martyrdom, embossed upon the actual events of history by a social drama governed partly by judicial edict and partly by its own inner logic. It brought before Brown's consciousness a crown to be won not so much by a meritorious life as by a painful death. Ritual seems often to achieve genuinely cathartic effects in societies, seems to bring about real transformations of individual character and of social relationships. One of the functions of ritual is to induce people to want to do what has to be done, to transform the necessary into the desirable. There is thus a sense in which the symbolic actions of ritual actually create society. It is in this sense that John Brown's martyrdom made the election of 1860 into a referendum on the future of slavery. And it certainly made the Civil War a war against slavery, regardless of Lincoln's initial position that it was only a war to save the Union, nothing more.[85]

The root paradigm of martyrdom—with its rich symbolism of blood and paradise—fortified John Brown for the final trial of will. "I am yet too young to understand that God is any respector of persons," he declared at his trial. "I believe that to have interfered as I have done—as I have always freely admitted that I have done—in behalf of His despised poor, was not wrong, but right. Now, if it is deemed necessary that I should forfeit my life for the furtherance of the ends of justice, and mingle my blood further with the blood of my children and with the blood of millions in this slave country whose rights are disregarded by wicked, cruel, and unjust enactments,—I submit; so let it be done!" John Brown had come to perceive that if he would be a winner then he must first become a loser. Once he understood that, once he understood he would have to die to set slaves free, he achieved a serenity of mind that never failed him, not even upon the scaffold. Under the control of the root paradigm, convinced that his death could accomplish what his life could not, Brown declined aid or escape. The shadow of death merely confirmed him all the more in his purpose.[86]

Such nearly inexplicable behavior provokes in some cultures the notion of fate or destiny to account for it. In Greek tragedy, which John Brown's passion closely parallels, the hero appears both freely to choose his behavior and at the same time to be helpless before the Fates, before the drama ultimately resolves through a catharsis inspired by pity and terror. In the case of John Brown, "the Fates" lay at the intersection of history and social drama. Sophocles could have written the plot.

Notes

I am grateful to Bertram Wyatt-Brown, Rhys Isaac, Roger D. Abrahams, William W. Freehling, David Hackett Fischer, Hannah Joyner, Shane White, Paul Finkelman, William McFeely, and Dan T. Carter for perceptive comments and criticisms: each of them has made suggestions that have stimulated my thinking and improved the study. I am also indebted to Avery O. Craven for his critique of a much earlier version of this essay. Indeed, this study had its origins more than thirty years ago in his seminar on the coming of the Civil War. I shall always be grateful for Professor Craven's rare combination of penetrating criticism and warm encouragement.

1. *Baltimore American,* reprinted in the *Richmond Enquirer,* Dec. 6, 1859; affidavit of John Avis, Apr. 25, 1882, quoted in Villard, *Biography,* pp. 670–71; Mary Ann Jackson, *Life and Letters of General Thomas J. Jackson* (New York, 1892), p. 130; Porte

Crayon [David Hunter Strother], quoted in Boyd P. Stutler, "An Eyewitness Describes the Hanging of John Brown," *American Heritage* 6 (Feb. 1955): 7–8. Journalist Strother's account was turned down by *Harper's Weekly*. A Virginia unionist and a relative of Brown's prosecutor, Strother became a Brevet Brigadier General in the Union Army and saw action in some thirty battles.

2. *Baltimore American,* reprinted in the *Richmond Enquirer,* Dec. 6, 1859; affidavit of John Avis, Apr. 25, 1882, quoted in Villard, *Biography,* pp. 670–71.

3. *Baltimore American,* reprinted in the *Richmond Enquirer,* Dec. 6, 1859; Porte Crayon [David Hunter Strother], *Harper's Weekly,* Nov. 12, 1859; Jackson, *Life and Letters,* pp. 390–91; Annie Brown Adams, quoted in Villard, *Biography,* p. 419; Israel Green, "The Capture of John Brown," *North American Review* 141 (Dec. 1885): 564–69; "Memoirs of Richard J. Hinton," in Richard Realf, *Poems of Richard Realf* (New York, 1898), xlii.

4. *Baltimore American,* reprinted in the *Richmond Enquirer,* Dec. 6, 1859.

5. Ibid.; affidavit of John Avis, Apr. 25, 1882, quoted in Villard, *Biography,* p. 671; Crayon [Strother], quoted in Stutler, "An Eyewitness Describes the Hanging of John Brown," pp. 8–9; Jackson, *Life and Letters,* pp. 131–32; John Brown's last note, Dec. 2, 1859, quoted in Franklin B. Sanborn, *Memoirs of John Brown* (Concord, Mass., 1878), p. 94. The original is owned by the Chicago Historical Society.

6. *Baltimore American,* reprinted in the *Richmond Enquirer,* Dec. 6, 1859; Crayon [Strother], quoted in Stutler, "An Eyewitness Describes the Hanging of John Brown," pp. 8–9; Jackson, *Life and Letters,* pp. 131–32.

7. Wendell Phillips, *Speeches and Lectures* (Boston, 1863), pp. 289–93; see also Thomas Drew, *The John Brown Invasion* (Boston, 1860), pp. 73–79.

8. Thomas Wentworth Higginson, one of Brown's close supporters, contends that Brown, had "studied military strategy" for the express purpose of organizing a slave insurrection, "even making designs (which I have seen) for a new style of forest fortification, simple and ingenious, to be used by parties of fugitive slaves when brought to bay": see Higginson, *Contemporaries* (Boston, 1899), pp. 219–43.

9. Henry Ward Beecher, address, Brooklyn, New York, Oct. 30, 1859, quoted in Redpath, *Echoes,* pp. 257–79.

10. See Victor Turner, *Dramas, Fields, and Metaphors: Symbolic Action in Human Society* (Ithaca, 1974), pp. 43 and 61–71.

11. Ibid., pp. 14, 36–40, and 78–79.

12. Ibid., pp. 35–36, 66–67, 96, and 55.

13. Ibid., pp. 45–46 and 60–61.

14. Ibid., pp. 37 and 63–68. Turner links the root paradigm with the concept of "communitas," which he describes as "an 'essential we' . . . which is at the same time a generic human bond underlying or transcending all particular cultural definitions and normative orderings of social ties" (p. 68).

15. Turner's social drama approach grows out of his studies of social structure, the phenomenon of communitas, and the concept of liminality. In his usage, structure is what separates people and constrains their actions, whereas communitas (or anti-structure) is what unites people above and beyond customary, formal social bonds. The bonds of communitas are antistructural, in that they are "undifferentiated, equalitarian, direct, nonrational (though not irrational), I-thou or Essential We relations, in Martin Buber's sense" (p. 47). "Liminality" is the state of being "betwixt and between" successive positions or clearly demarcated modes of participation in the social structure. The condition of being outside of or on the periphery of everyday life is thus considered "liminal," and a liminal phase is an essential component of the ritual process. Entire societies can be in liminal transition between different

social structures, as the United States was in December of 1859, and may thus be in a fundamentally sacred condition. See Victor Turner, *The Ritual Process: Structure and Anti-Structure* (Chicago, 1969).

16. See Turner, *Dramas, Fields, and Metaphors,* pp. 37 and 79. On Brown's lack of contact with or support from African Americans, see Oates, *Purge,* pp. 247–48 and 282–83; Potter, *Sectional,* pp. 201–18; Benjamin Quarles, *Blacks on John Brown* (Urbana, Ill., 1972), pp. 29–30; Quarles, *Allies,* pp. 43–51; and Merton Dillon, *Slavery Attacked: Southern Slaves and Their Allies, 1619–1865* (Baton Rouge, 1990), 235.

17. *Charleston Daily Courier,* Oct. 20, 1859; *Edgefield (S.C.) Advertiser,* Oct. 26, 1859. The *Advertiser* proudly published its prophetic motto beneath the paper's masthead: "We will cling to the pillars of the temple of our liberties, and if it must fall we will perish amid the ruins."

18. *New York Daily Tribune,* Oct. 19–22, 26, and 31, and Nov. 12, 1859; *The Liberator,* quoted in the *Boston Journal,* Oct. 29, 1859; *Topeka Tribune* and *Atchison City (Kans.) Freedom's Champion,* both quoted in Villard, *Biography,* p. 473.

19. *New York Herald,* Oct. 19, 1859; see also the *Washington Star,* Oct. 17, 18, and 20, 1859.

20. Robert C. Albrecht, "Thoreau and His Audience: 'A Plea for Capt. John Brown,'" *American Literature* 32 (1961): 395–99; James Ford Rhodes, *History of the United States from the Compromise of 1850,* 7 vols. (New York, 1893–1906), 3:383–416; Avery Craven, *The Coming of the Civil War,* 2d ed., rev. (Chicago, 1957), p. 408.

21. Robert A. Rusk, *The Life of Ralph Waldo Emerson* (New York, 1949), p. 402.

22. John Brown to H. L. Vaill, Nov. 16, 1859, in Ruchames, ed., *Revolutionary,* p. 143; John Brown to Mary Ann Day Brown, Nov. 10, 1859, quoted in Villard, *Biography,* pp. 540–41. See also Turner, *Dramas, Fields, and Metaphors,* pp. 37–38.

23. *Boston Journal* (supplement), Oct. 29, 1859; *New York Daily Tribune,* Oct. 19 and 31, 1859.

24. *South Carolina House Journal,* 1859, p. 32; *South Carolina Senate Journal,* 1859, pp. 5 and 75; *Charleston Mercury,* Oct. 19, 1859. See also Wyatt-Brown, "Antinomian"; Harold S. Schultz, *Nationalism and Sectionalism in Carolina, 1852–1860: A Study of the Movement for Southern Independence* (Durham, N.C., 1950), pp. 183–89; Jack Kenny Williams, "The Southern Movement to Reopen the African Slave Trade, 1854–1860: A Factor in Secession," *Proceedings of the South Carolina Historical Association,* 1960, pp. 23–31; Percy L. Rainwater, "Economic Benefits of Secession: Opinions in Mississippi in the 1830s," *JSH* 6 (Nov. 1935): 459–74.

25. *Savannah Republican,* quoted in Villard, *Biography,* p. 500; *Mobile (Ala.) Daily Register,* Oct. 25, 1859; *Richmond Enquirer,* Oct. 25, 1859.

26. *Salisbury (N.C.) Carolina Watchman,* Oct. 26, 1859. Bruner opposed secession, but once North Carolina seceded he quickly and completely supported the new Confederacy.

27. William Henry Trescot to William Porcher Miles, Feb. 8, 1859, in William Porcher Miles Papers, Southern Historical Collection, University of North Carolina (hereafter Miles Papers, UNC); William Henry Trescot to James Henry Hammond, Oct. 25, 1859, James Henry Hammond Papers, Library of Congress (hereafter Hammond Papers). In the meantime Hammond was urging his friend William Gilmore Simms to avoid a current literary feud. Would not "Harpers Ferry, and all that suffice, but South Carolina must have her bowels rent by these [illegible] unaccustomed feuds?" Hammond thought Simms had "a disposition to disparage his literary rivals," a disposition he ascribed to "a defect of his early education." Although Hammond described the writer as a "particular friend," he privately considered Simms to be lacking in "the delicacy of a thorough bred man." See James Henry Hammond to William Gilmore Simms, Oct. 24, 1859, in Hammond Papers; Carol

Bleser, ed., *Secret and Sacred: The Diaries of James Henry Hammond, a Southern Slave-holder* (New York, 1988), p. 49.

28. See Turner, *Dramas, Fields, and Metaphors*, pp. 38–41. The dilemma is at least partly inherent in the long controversy over slavery itself. Are there some questions that simply cannot be handled by democratic processes? If not, why did the contending parties resort to arms by 1861? If so, what are the implications for democracy today and tomorrow? See Charles Joyner, "From Civil War to Civil Rights," *Australasian Journal of American Studies* 10 (1991): 26–39. All that can be said with certainty is that neither the trial and execution of John Brown, nor congressional action, nor the electoral process in 1860, nor a combination of these, was successful in bringing this particular social drama to a peaceful conclusion.

29. Lawson Botts, quoted in the *National Intelligencer,* Oct. 29, 1859; John Brown, quoted in ibid.; Henry A. Wise, speech in Richmond, Va., Oct. 21, 1859, printed in the *Richmond Enquirer,* Oct. 25, 1859. See also Turner, *Dramas, Fields, and Metaphors,* pp. 88–89. For the best discussion of Brown's mental health, see Wyatt-Brown, "Antinomian," pp. 97–127. See also Potter, *Sectional,* esp. pp. 211–15; and Woodward, "Private War," pp. 41–68.

30. See Turner, *Dramas, Fields, and Metaphors,* pp. 13–15, 53, and 87. On loss of honor and social death, see Bertram Wyatt-Brown, *Southern Honor: Ethics and Behavior in the Old South* (New York, 1982); and Orlando Patterson, *Slavery and Social Death: A Comparative Study* (Cambridge, Mass., 1982).

31. See, for example, the *New York Herald,* Nov. 6, 13, and 27, 1859; and the *Pittsburgh Gazette,* Dec. 1, 1859; Theodore Parker to Francis Jackson, Nov. 24, 1859, in Francis Power Cobbe, ed., *Collected Works of Theodore Parker* (London, 1862), pp. 164–77.

32. *Frankfort Yeoman,* n.d., quoted in Villard, *Biography,* p. 502. Death is, of course, an essential prerequisite for martyrdom. Thus, despite his efforts to portray himself as a martyr to the antislavery cause, blue-clad soldiers chanted no marching song about Charles Sumner.

33. *Columbus (Ga.) Daily Enquirer,* Oct. 21 and 25, and Nov. 2, 5, 11, and 30, 1859; *Charleston Daily Courier,* Oct. 20, 1859; *Charleston Mercury,* Oct. 31, Nov. 1, 2, 5, and 26, and Dec. 10, 1859.

34. *Charlotte North Carolina Whig,* Nov. 1 and 8, 1859; *Salisbury Carolina Watchman,* Nov. 13, 1859; *Lancaster (S.C.) Ledger,* Nov. 2, 1859.

35. *Little Rock Arkansas Gazette,* Nov. 12, 1859; *Charleston Mercury,* Nov. 14, 1859; *Richmond Enquirer,* Nov. 5, 1859; *Raleigh Standard,* Oct. 26, 1859, and Nov. 12, 1859.

36. Beaufort T. Watts to James Henry Hammond, [November] 1857, in Beaufort T. Watts Papers, South Caroliniana Library, University of South Carolina; *Congressional Globe,* 35th Cong., 1st Sess., appendix, pp. 69–71. See also Drew Gilpin Faust, *James Henry Hammond and the Old South: A Design for Mastery* (Baton Rouge, 1982), pp. 350–55.

37. *Charleston Evening News,* July 29, 1858; James Henry Hammond, *Speech of James H. Hammond Delivered at Barnwell C[ourt] H[ouse], October 29th, 1858* (Charleston, 1858).

38. James Henry Hammond to Edmund Ruffin, Feb. 8, 1859, Edmund Ruffin Papers, Southern Historical Collection, University of North Carolina; James Henry Hammond to William Gilmore Simms, Jan. 1, 1859, in Hammond Papers; Bleser, ed. *Secret and Sacred,* p. 275.

39. Bleser, ed. *Secret and Sacred,* pp. 273–75; James Henry Hammond to William Gilmore Simms, July 30, 1859, in Hammond Papers; George P. Elliott to James Henry Hammond, Nov. 5, 1859, in ibid. For a sophisticated analysis of Hammond's mental

and physical health, see Faust, *James Henry Hammond and the Old South*, pp. 181–84 and 375–78.

40. Francis W. Pickens to Milledge Luke Bonham, Apr. 14, 1860, Milledge Luke Bonham Papers, South Caroliniana Library, University of South Carolina; John B. Edmunds, Jr., *Francis W. Pickens and the Politics of Destruction* (Chapel Hill, 1986), pp. 143–49.

41. Beaufort T. Watts to James Henry Hammond, Nov. 24, 1859, in Hammond Papers; *Charlotte North Carolina Whig*, Nov. 29, 1859; *Salisbury Carolina Watchman*, Nov. 29, 1859.

42. *Charlotte North Carolina Whig*, Nov. 15, 1859; *Lancaster Ledger*, Nov. 21, 1859. See also Turner, *Dramas, Fields, and Metaphors*, p. 41.

43. James Buchanan, quoted in Varina Howell Davis, *Jefferson Davis: A Memoir by His Wife* (New York, 1890), p. 646.

44. *Salisbury Carolina Watchman*, Nov. 22, 1859; *Salisbury Carolina Watchman*, Nov. 22, 1859, in which the *Selma (Ala.) Reporter and Democrat*, n.d., is reprinted.

45. *Charlotte North Carolina Whig*, Nov. 29, 1859; *Natchez Mississippi Free Trader*, Dec. 1, 1859; *Richmond Whig*, reprinted in *Charlotte North Carolina Whig*, Nov. 29, 1859.

46. *Pickens (S.C.) Keowee Courier*, Oct. 29, Nov. 5, and Dec. 10, 1859; *Spartanburg (S.C.) Carolina Spartan*, Nov. 24, 1859.

47. See Turner, *Dramas, Fields, and Metaphors*, p. 71.

48. Ibid., pp. 41–46.

49. Henry A. Wise, speech in Richmond, Va., Oct. 21, 1859, printed in the *Richmond Enquirer*, Oct. 25, 1859; John Brown, quoted in the *National Intelligencer*, Oct. 29, 1859. See also Turner, *Dramas, Fields, and Metaphors*, pp. 69 and 92.

50. Louisa May Alcott, quoted in Rusk, *Life of Ralph Waldo Emerson*, p. 402; A. Bronson Alcott, "Sonnet XXIV," addressed to John Brown, Harpers Ferry, in his *Sonnets and Canzonets* (Boston, 1882), p. 141. See also Emerson's speech on Brown delivered a month later in Salem, Massachusetts, Jan. 6, 1860, in Redpath, *Echoes*, pp. 118–22.

51. William Lloyd Garrison, quoted in Villard, *Biography*, p. 560; *New York Daily Tribune*, Dec. 3, 1859.

52. John Knox McLean Papers, South Caroliniana Library, University of South Carolina; Theodore Tilton, quoted in Ruchames, ed., *Reader*, pp. 272–75.

53. Moncure Daniel Conway, quoted in Ruchames, ed., *Reader*, pp. 278–80.

54. Sarah Grimké, quoted in William Birney, *James G. Birney and His Times* (New York, 1890), pp. 282–83. For a remarkable study of the Grimké sisters' abolitionist career, see Gerda Lerner, *The Grimké Sisters from South Carolina: Rebels against Slavery* (Boston, 1967).

55. William H. Herndon to Charles Sumner, Dec. 10, 1860, in Charles Sumner Papers, Harvard University.

56. Abraham Lincoln, speech in Troy, Kansas, Dec. 2, 1859, quoted in Villard, *Biography*, p. 564; *New York Weekly Day Book*, quoted in the *Salisbury Carolina Watchman*, Dec. 6, 1859. On racism among Northern workers, see Eric Foner, *Free Soil, Free Labor, Free Men: The Ideology of the Republican Party before the Civil War* (New York, 1970).

57. Claude M. Fuess, *Life of Caleb Cushing* (New York, 1923), pp. 235–37.

58. Edward Everett, speech in Boston, Massachusetts, Dec. 8, 1859, printed in the *Richmond Enquirer*, Dec. 16, 1859.

59. Caleb Cushing, speech in Boston, Massachusetts, Dec. 8, 1859, printed in the *National Intelligencer*, Dec. 17, 1859; Cushing to Chairman, Democratic Party of Massachusetts, quoted in Fuess, *Life of Caleb Cushing*, pp. 241–42.

60. Caleb Cushing to Chairman, Democratic Party of Massachusetts, quoted in Fuess, *Life of Caleb Cushing*, pp. 241–42.

61. Wise, quoted in the *Charlotte North Carolina Whig,* Dec. 13, 1859.

62. *Raleigh Standard,* quoted in the *Charlotte North Carolina Whig,* Jan. 23, 1860; *Petersburg (Va.) Express,* Dec. 17, 1859, quoted in the *Salisbury Carolina Watchman,* Jan. 3, 1860.

63. W. Duncan to James Henry Hammond, Dec. 2, 1859, in Hammond Papers.

64. *New Orleans Daily Picayune,* Dec. 2, 1859; James McKaye, *Mastership and Its Fruits: The Emancipated Slave Face to Face with His Old Master* (New York, 1864), p. 7, quoted in Janet Duitsman Cornelius, *When I Can Read My Title Clear: Literacy, Slavery, and Religion in the Antebellum South* (Columbia, S.C., 1991), pp. 3 and 84.

65. *Richmond Enquirer,* Dec. 23, 1859; *Salisbury Carolina Watchman,* Dec. 20, 1859; *Mississippi Free Trader,* Dec. 24, 1859; *Salisbury Carolina Watchman,* Dec. 12, 1859.

66. Christopher G. Memminger to William Porcher Miles, Jan. 3, 1860, in Miles Papers, UNC; D. H. Hamilton to William Porcher Miles, Dec. 9, 1859, in William Porcher Miles Papers, South Caroliniana Library, University of South Carolina (hereafter Miles Papers, USC); *South Carolina House Journal,* 1859, pp. 72–73; Christopher G. Memminger to William Porcher Miles, Dec. 27, 1859, in Miles Papers, USC.

67. *Charleston Mercury,* Dec. 5, 1859; *Edgefield Advertiser,* Dec. 14, 1859; message of Governor William Henry Gist of South Carolina to Legislature, Nov. 29, 1859.

68. *South Carolina House Journal,* 1859, pp. 12–24; *South Carolina Senate Journal,* 1859, pp. 11–23; William Henry Gist to William Porcher Miles, Dec. 20, 1859, in Miles Papers, USC; *South Carolina House Journal,* 1859, p. 263; *South Carolina Senate Journal,* 1859, p. 135; *South Carolina House Journal,* 1859, pp. 174–75, 176, and 191.

69. *South Carolina House Journal,* 1859, pp. 196–97, 199, 201, 202, 204, 263, 268, 274, and 276; *Reports and Resolutions of the General Assembly of the State of South Carolina, Passed at the Annual Session of 1859* (Columbia, 1859), p. 579; W. W. Boyce to Christopher G. Memminger, Jan. 14, 1860, Christopher G. Memminger Papers, Southern Historical Collection, University of North Carolina; Christopher G. Memminger to William Porcher Miles, Dec. 27, 1859, Jan. 3, 16, 24, and 30, and Feb. 4, 1860, in Miles Papers, UNC. On the nullification controversy, see William W. Freehling, *Prelude to Civil War: The Nullification Controversy in South Carolina, 1816–1836* (New York, 1966). On the secession crisis of 1850, see John Barnwell, *Love of Order: South Carolina's First Secession Crisis* (Chapel Hill, 1982). On Memminger's mission to Virginia, see Steven Channing, *Crisis of Fear: Secession in South Carolina* (New York, 1974), pp. 112–30; and Ollinger Crenshaw, "Christopher G. Memminger's Mission to Virginia," *JSH* 8 (Nov. 1942): 334–49.

70. William Henry Trescot to James Henry Hammond, Dec. 30, 1859; James Henry Hammond, draft of proposed Constitutional Amendment, marked CONFIDENTIAL, Dec. 1859; I[saac] W. Hayne to James Henry Hammond, Jan. 5, 1860; and James Henry Hammond to William Gilmore Simms, Dec. 19, 1859; all in Hammond Papers.

71. James McCarty to William Porcher Miles, Jan. 16, 1860, in Miles Papers, USC; Robert Barnwell Rhett to William Porcher Miles, Jan. 29, 1860, in Miles Papers, UNC.

72. Ralph Waldo Emerson, address in Salem, Mass., Jan. 6, 1860, in *Emerson's Complete Works,* ed. James Elliot Cabot, 12 vols. (Boston, 1883), 11:257–63.

73. Charles Sumner, speech before U.S. Senate, June 4, 1860, entitled "The Barbarism of Slavery," in *The Works of Charles Sumner,* 15 vols. (Boston, 1874–83), 5:17–26 (quote on p. 26). On Brooks's caning of Sumner, see David Herbert Donald, *Charles Sumner and the Coming of the Civil War* (New York, 1960).

74. Henry David Thoreau, address at North Elba, New York, July 4, 1860, in *The Writings of Henry David Thoreau,* ed. Bradford Torrey and Franklin B. Sanborn, 20 vols. (orig. publ. 1894–95 in 7 vols.; repr. Boston, 1906), 10:237–48.

75. *New Orleans Daily Crescent,* Jan. 21, 1860; *Salisbury Carolina Watchman,* Mar. 27, 1860.

76. Abraham Lincoln, speech at Cooper Union, New York City, Feb. 27, 1860, in Basler, ed., *Works of Lincoln,* 3:522–50.

77. Papers of the South Carolina Democratic Party, 1860, South Caroliniana Library, University of South Carolina.

78. Charles W. Johnson, ed., *Proceedings of the First Three Republican Conventions* (Minneapolis, 1893), pp. 131–33.

79. *Charleston Mercury,* May 23, 1860.

80. *Salisbury Carolina Watchman,* May 22, 1860; Sept. 11, 1860.

81. *Salisbury Carolina Watchman,* Sept. 11 and 18, 1860, and Oct. 9, 1860.

82. *New Orleans Daily Crescent,* Nov. 13, 1860; Mary Boykin Chesnut, entry for Nov. 8, 1860, *A Diary from Dixie,* ed. Isabella D. Martin and Myrta Lockett Avary (New York, 1905), p. 1. Chesnut's comment does not, however, appear in either the Ben Ames Williams edition of *A Diary from Dixie* (Boston, 1949) or in C. Vann Woodward's *Mary Chesnut's Civil War* (New Haven, 1981). For more of Chesnut's comments on John Brown, see C. Vann Woodward, *Mary Chesnut's Civil War,* pp. 114, 148, 245, 269, 409, 413, 428, 440, and 466.

83. *Richmond Enquirer,* Jan. 21, 1860; for Simms's remarks, see the *Charleston Mercury,* Jan. 17, 1861.

84. *Charleston Courier,* Dec. 3, 1860, *Charleston Mercury,* Dec. 4, 1860; South Carolina's "Declaration of the Causes of Secession," Dec. 20, 1860, in Frank Moore, ed., *The Rebellion Record,* 12 vols. (New York, 1861–68), 1:3–4.

85. See Turner, *Dramas, Fields, and Metaphors,* pp. 56 and 72.

86. John Brown's speech to the Virginia Court, Nov. 2, 1859, in Sanborn, ed., *Life,* p. 585; see also Turner, *Dramas, Fields, and Metaphors,* pp. 85–89, and *Schism and Continuity in an African Society* (Manchester, Eng., 1957), p. 94.

Contributors

James O. Breeden is Professor of History at Southern Methodist University. He was educated at the University of Virginia and at Tulane University. His research specialty is Civil War medicine, and he is the author of *Joseph Jones, M.D.: Scientist of the Old South* (1975).

Seymour Drescher is University Professor of History at the University of Pittsburgh. The author of a number of studies of Alexis de Tocqueville, his more recent research has focused on comparative approaches to slavery and abolition. His publications in this field include *Econocide: British Slavery in the Era of Abolition* (1977); *Capitalism and Antislavery: British Mobilization in Comparative Perspective* (1986); *The Abolition of Slavery and the Aftermath of Emancipation in Brazil*, with Rebecca Scott et al. (1988); "British Way, French Way: Opinion Building and Revolution in the Second French Slave Emancipation," *American Historical Review* 96 (1991); and "The Long Goodbye: Dutch Capitalism and Antislavery in Comparative Perspective," *American Historical Review* 99 (1994). He is also coeditor of *The Meaning of Freedom: Economics, Politics, and Culture after Slavery* (1992).

Paul Finkelman is Associate Professor of History at Virginia Polytechnic Institute and State University. His books include *An Imperfect Union: Slavery, Federalism, and Comity* (1981); *Slavery in the Courtroom* (1985), which received the Joseph L. Andrews Award of the American Association of Law Libraries; *The Law of Freedom and Bondage: A Casebook* (1986); *American Legal History: Cases and Materials*, with Kermit L. Hall and William M. Wiecek (1991); and, with Stephen Gottlieb, *Toward a Usable Past: Liberty under State Constitutions* (1991).

Charles Joyner is Burroughs Distinguished Professor of History at Coastal Carolina University and the author of *Down by the Riverside: A South Carolina Slave Community* (1984), which won the National University Press Book Award and has been called "the finest work ever written on American slavery." He is also the author of *Remember Me: Slave Life in Coastal Georgia* (1989) and the coauthor of *Before Freedom Came: African-American Life and Labor in the Antebellum South* (1991). He has taught at the University of California at Berkeley, the University of Mississippi, and the University of Alabama, and as well as in Australia, at the University of Sydney, and has held fellowships from the National Endowment for the Humanities and the Social Science Research Council.

Peter Knupfer is Associate Professor of History at Kansas State University. He is the author of *The Union as It Is: Constitutional Unionism and Sectional Compro-*

mise, 1787–1861 (1991), and "Henry Clay's Constitutional Unionism," *Register of the Kentucky Historical Society* 89 (1991), which won the society's Richard H. Collins Award for best article of 1991. He received his M.A. and Ph.D. degrees from the University of Wisconsin—Madison and is currently a fellow of the Institute for Social and Behavioral Research at Kansas State University.

Daniel Littlefield is Professor of History at the University of Illinois—Urbana-Champaign. He is the author of *Rice and Slaves: Ethnicity and the Slave Trade in Colonial South Carolina* (1981; repr. 1991). He was a fellow at the National Humanities Center in 1988–89, and in 1990 he was awarded a prize for the best article in the *South Carolina Historical Magazine,* for "The Slave Trade to Colonial South Carolina: A Profile."

Robert E. McGlone is Assistant Professor of History at the University of Hawaii at Manoa. He is the author of articles on John Brown that have appeared in the *Journal of American History* and *Civil War History* and is currently completing a book, *Apocalyptic Visions: John Brown's Witness against Slavery.* He received his B.A. and Ph.D. degrees from the University of California at Los Angeles, where he was an NDEA fellow.

Wendy Hamand Venet is Associate Professor of History at Eastern Illinois University. The author of *Neither Ballots nor Bullets: Women Abolitionists and the Civil War* (1991), she has also published articles in *Civil War History* and the *New England Quarterly.*

Peter Wallenstein is Associate Professor of History at Virginia Polytechnic Institute and State University. His publications include *From Slave South to New South: Public Policy in Nineteenth-Century Georgia* (1987) and two prizewinning essays: " 'More Unequally Taxed Than Any People in the Civilized World': The Origins of Georgia's Ad Valorem Tax System," *Georgia Historical Quarterly* (1985), and "Which Side Are You On? The Social Origins of White Union Troops from Civil War Tennessee," *Journal of East Tennessee History* (1991).

Bertram Wyatt-Brown is Richard J. Milbauer Professor of History at the University of Florida, Gainesville. His works include *Lewis Tappan and the Evangelical War against Slavery* (1969); *Southern Honor: Ethics and Behavior in the Old South* (1982), which was a finalist for both the Pulitzer Prize and the National Book Award in 1983; and *Yankee Saints and Southern Sinners* (1985). He was awarded the ABC/Clio Award in 1989 and has held fellowships granted by the John Simon Guggenheim Foundation, the Shelby Cullom Davis Center at Princeton University, the National Endowment for the Humanities, the National Humanities Center, and the Earhart Foundation. He is also a contributing editor of the *Wilson Quarterly.*

Index

Brown, Mary Day (wife), 4, 18, 20, 28, 30, 47–48, 53–57, 63n.35, 65n.72, 100, 107, 177, 265

Brown, Martha Brewster (daughter-in-law), 231

Brown, Oliver (son), 7–8, 21, 27

Brown, Owen (father), 15–18, 36n.40

Brown, Owen (son), 7–8, 60, 65

Brown, Ruth (daughter), *see* Thompson

Brown, Salmon (son), 7, 65n.65

Brown, Thomas (abolitionist), 62n.16

Brown, Watson (son), 7–8, 27, 231

Bruner, J. J. (Whig, Unionist), 306

Bryant, William Cullen, 108

Buber, Martin, 329n.15

Buchanan, James (U.S. president), 8, 125, 131–32, 143n.6, 249n.57, 261, 272, 311, 313

Buffalo, N.Y., 71, 92n.19

Buffman, Arnold (abolitionist), 104

Bullard, Edward (abolitionist), 114n.15

Bunker Hill, Mass., 48

Burns, Anthony (fugitive slave), 88, 89

Butler, Andrew Pickens (senator), 324

Byrd, Dr. Harvey L. (dean, Oglethorpe Medical College), 176, 200–201, 202

Cain and Abel, 258

Cambridge, Mass., 46–47, 48

Campbell, E. D., gov. of Wisconsin, 215

Campbell, James (sheriff), 297–98

Canada, 6, 8, 62n.18, 70, 78, 83, 94n.44, 99, 162, 267, 276, 277

Caribbean slavery, 260, 263, 270

Carlyle, Thomas (historian), 264, 265, 284

Carmichael, Stokely, 95n.69

Carolina Spartan, 314

Carolina Watchman, 306, 309, 312–13, 320, 326

Cartwright, Samuel A. (Southern medical propagandist), 175

Catholics, 318

Central America, 125, 259, 267

Central Southern Rights Association, 185

Chambersburg, Pa., 83

Chandler, Zachariah, 135

Channing, William Ellery (abolitionist), 22–23, 99, 108

Chapman, Maria Weston, 110

Charleston, S.C., 87, 96n.76, 121, 137, 180, 188, 189, 302, 314–15, 325, 327

Charleston Daily Courier, 302, 309

Charleston Mercury, 309, 321, 323

Charlestown, Va., 3–4, 50, 109, 219, 255, 285

Charlotte, N.C., 309

Chatham, Ont., and Chatham Convention, 78–80, 86, 94n.45

Chestnut, Mary Boykin, 327

Chicago, 46, 113, 129, 325

Chicago Medical Journal, 197

Chicago Press and Tribune, 189–91, 194

Child, David Lee, 14

Child, Lydia Maria, 47, 51–58, 61n.3, 64n.57, 98, 100, 102–4, 106–10, 114n.15

    Correspondence between Lydia Maria Child, Gov. Wise and Mrs. Mason, of Virginia, 58, 109

    The Duty and Disobedience to the Fugitive Slave Act: An Appeal to the Legislators of Massachusetts, 110

    letters to Margaretta Mason, 54, 58, 107–9

    letters to Wise, 54, 58, 106–9

    The Patriarchal Institution as Described by Members of Its Own Family, 111, 115n.43

    plans to write Brown biography, 55–56

    The Right Way the Safe Way, 111

Chisolm, Shirley, 77

Chivalry, 266

Christianity, 69–70, 76, 78–79, 83, 85–86, 88, 101, 266, 274–77, 290n.35

Cincinnati, 316

Cincinnati Lancet and Observer, 197, 198, 199

Cincinnati Medical and Surgical News, 198

Cincinnatus, 310

Civilization, 255, 257–58

Civil War, 14, 56, 59, 61, 74, 79, 152, 168, 170, 255, 279–83, 285, 291n.42, 292n.49, 293n.53, 295n.83, 300, 328

    black regiments in, 102

    causes, 10, 33

    draft riots during, 99

Clark, Daniel (U.S. senator, N.H.), 159–
60
Clark, John C., 178
Clay, Henry, 120, 128, 129, 135, 138,
146n.64
Cleaver, Eldridge, 95n.69
Cleveland, 6, 45, 67
Cleveland Leader, 302
Clingman, Thomas L. (U.S. senator,
N.C.), 152
Cobden, Richard, 280
Cocke, Thomas, 15
Colored Convention of 1843 (Buffalo),
71
Communitas, 329n.15
Compromise of 1850, 128–29, 300
Concord, Mass., 315
Confessions of Nat Turner, 95n.68
Congressional Black Caucus, 77
Congressional debate over and inves-
tigation of raid, 159–65, 236, 238
Congressional elections, 1858, 134
Connecticut, 6–8, 15, 49, 67, 230
conservatism, 119, 120, 122, 123, 126,
139
Republicans, 119, 145n.46, 147n.67
Constitution, *see* United States Consti-
tution
Constitutional Convention, 300
Constitutional unionism, 120–22, 124–
28, 130–32, 136–38, 142, 144n.22
Constitutional Union party, 4, 122, 127,
129, 130, 136, 144n.29, 148n.72,
326
Conway, Moncure Daniel, 316
Cook, John E. (raid participant), 6,
62n.18, 64n.54, 229, 230, 249n.58,
249n.59
Coolie labor, 270
Cooper Union, 46, 135, 136
Copeland, John Anthony (raid partici-
pant), 7, 24, 27, 49–50, 63n.39, 83–
84, 231, 249–50n.63
Coppoc, Barclay (raid participant), 7–8,
62n.18
Coppoc, Edwin (raid participant),
62n.18, 230–31
Corinthian Hall (Rochester, N.Y.), 101,
113
Cornish, Samuel (black abolitionist),
72–73, 92n.24
Corwin, Thomas, 133–34, 145n.49

Cotton, 310
Crisis of the 1850s, 139
Crittenden, John J., 121, 128, 134,
143n.8
Crofts, Daniel, 128
Cromwell, Oliver, 58, 60, 69, 264, 280
Crucifixion, 315
Cuba, 125, 130, 260, 267
Cultural anthropology (*see also* Turner,
Victor), 300
Currier & Ives lithograph of John
Brown, 51
Curtis, George W. (abolitionist), 177,
178, 195
Cushing, Caleb (U.S. attorney general),
130, 143n.5, 145n.36, 317–19

Daily Enquirer, 308
Daily National Intelligencer, 129
Dana, Richard Henry, Jr., 18
Danbury, Conn., 49
Davis, David (Republican politician), 41
Davis, Jefferson, 14, 15, 26, 123
Davis, Nathan S., 197
Davis, Samuel, 15
De Bow, J. D. B. (propagandist), 175,
200
Declaration of Independence, 303
Deification, 315; *see also* Martyrdom
Delany, Martin (black abolitionist), 79,
80, 85, 86, 94n.45, 287n.14
Democratic National Convention, 314,
325
South Carolina demand for slavery
platform at, 325
Democratic party, 4, 58, 119–25, 128–
33, 136–38, 141, 143n.8, 323
Democratic State Conventions,
145n.35, 324
Democrats, 120–28, 303, 317, 325, 326
Denman, Lord, 294n.66
Denmark, 259
Depression, mental, 12–14, 18, 29, 30,
217
Dessalines, Jean Jacques (Haitian gen-
eral), 263, 281
Dickens, Charles, 272–73
Dillon, Merton (historian), 68
District of Columbia, 73
Disunion or disunionists, 309, 314, 321,
326; *see also* Secession
Dix, Dorothea, 129

Luckett, Dr. Francis E. (*cont.*)
    defended against tampering charges,
        195, 202–3
Lusk, Milton, 18

Macaulay, Thomas Babington (historian), 273, 284
McCarty, James, 323
McCaw, Dr. James B., 187
McGlone, Robert E. (historian), 12, 30, 32, 34n.7, 37n.67
McGuire, Dr. Hugh Holmes, 181
McGuire, Hunter H., 180, 181, 182, 184, 187, 201
    accused of inducing Southern medical students to secede, 181, 193
    defended against tampering charges, 195, 202–3
McKim, J. Miller (abolitionist, Pa.), 47–49, 51–52, 55, 57, 62n.18
M'Naghten test of insanity, 217, 221
Madisonian constitutional tradition, 122, 138
Madness and historical causation, 242–43
Mahler, Gustav, 13
Maine, 151
Malcolm X, 88, 95–96n.69
Mallory, Stephen R. (U.S. senator, Florida), 160
Manayunk (Pa.) Reports, 191
Manic-depressive illness (bipolar disorder), 217
Manliness and masculinity, 54–56, 60, 66n.85, 68–69, 76, 265, 266
Manly, Charles, 156
Martin, J. Sella, 70, 75, 79, 80
Martineau, Harriet (author), 274
Martyrdom, 42–46, 52, 58–61, 67, 89, 112, 253, 265–66, 268, 282, 304, 307, 314–19, 323–24, 327–28
    see also Abolitionists; Brown, John
Marx, Karl (revolutionary), 268, 270, 291n.42
Maryland, 7, 78, 79, 133, 306
Masculinity, *see* Manliness
Mason, James M. (U.S. senator, Va.), 54, 107, 159, 160, 229, 233, 236
Mason, Margaretta J. (Chew), 54, 106–11
Mason committee, 236, 238
Mason-Dixon line, 305, 311, 312

Massachusetts, 5–7, 73, 77, 110, 132, 272, 317, 324
Massachusetts Anti-Slavery Society, 68
Massachusetts 54th Regiment, 102
Mathews, D. A., 188–89
May, Rev. Samuel J. (abolitionist, N.Y.), 49
Mazzini, Giuseppi, 280, 281
Mechanics Hall (Worcester, Mass.), 101
Medical and Surgical Reporter (Philadelphia), 197, 199
Medical College of Georgia, 188–89
Medical College of the State of South Carolina, 180, 189
Medical College of Virginia, 184, 185, 186, 201
    agrees to admit seceding Southern medical students, 179
    enrollment of seceding Southern medical students, 188
    reception for seceding Southern medical students at, 187
Melodian Hall (Cleveland), 67
Melville, Herman, 213
Memminger, Christopher G., 321, 322
Memorabilia, 44
    see also Iconography
Memory of Brown, 44, 54, 55, 58, 284, 294n.78
Memphis, 151
Mental illness, 41–42, 214, 217
    and "logic" of politics of insanity, 214
Meriam, Francis Jackson (raid participant), 7, 8
Mexico, 125, 126, 280
Michelangelo, 13
Miles, William Porcher, 321
Militia, 156
Mill, John Stuart (philosopher), 280
Misérables, Les, 255
Mississippi, voters in, 153
    social structure, 153–54
    appropriates funds for military, 157
Mississippi Free Trader, 313, 320
Mississippi River, 320
Missouri, 5, 6, 121, 154, 162
Missouri Compromise, 21, 121, 129, 300
Mobile Daily Register, 305
Monomania, 216, 218, 220–21
Monthly Anglo-African, 95n.66
Monticello, 134, 305